FROM LITERACY TO LITERATURE

Christopher Cannon was educated at Harvard, and has taught at UCLA, Oxford, Cambridge, and NYU. He is now Bloomberg Distinguished Professor of English and Classics at Johns Hopkins University. He has written books on the traditional nature of Chaucer's language, early Middle English and literary form, as well as a cultural history of Middle English, and has held fellowships from the UK's Arts and Humanities Research Council, a Guggenheim Memorial Foundation Fellowship, and won the William Riley Parker Prize from the MLA. He collaborated with James Simpson on an edition of the complete works of Chaucer for OUP.

T0346676

From Literacy to Literature

England, 1300–1400

CHRISTOPHER CANNON

OXFORD

UNIVERSITY PRESS

OXFORD
UNIVERSITY PRESS

Great Clarendon Street, Oxford, OX2 6DP,
United Kingdom

Oxford University Press is a department of the University of Oxford.
It furthers the University's objective of excellence in research, scholarship,
and education by publishing worldwide. Oxford is a registered trade mark of
Oxford University Press in the UK and in certain other countries

First published 2016
First published in paperback 2021

Published in the United States of America by Oxford University Press
198 Madison Avenue, New York, NY 10016, United States of America

British Library Cataloguing in Publication Data
Data available

Library of Congress Cataloging in Publication Data
Data available

ISBN 978–0–19–877943–8 (Hbk.)
ISBN 978–0–19–285635–7 (Pbk.)

Acknowledgments

This book had its beginnings in a graduate class on medieval school texts Jill Mann used to teach in the Cambridge English Faculty: I owe her a great debt for opening my eyes to the importance of this subject and for the peerless scholarship and always-attentive readings that guided me as I explored it. I benefited greatly from the papers of every speaker and the thoughtful questions of the participants at the conference on "The Schoolroom and the Literary Arts" that Nicolette Zeeman, Rita Copeland, and I organized at King's College, Cambridge and the Cambridge Centre for Research in the Arts, Social Sciences and Humanities in 2008. Conversations with Rita and Nicky about this topic in more recent years have been as valuable as they were enjoyable. Along the way I have also benefited from conversations with Mary Carruthers, Pat Crain, Carolyn Dinshaw, Simon Gaunt, John Guillory, Sarah Kay, Kathryn Kerby-Fulton, Michael Lapidge, Traugott Lawler, Deidre Lynch, Paula McDowell, James Simpson, David Thomson, Diane Vincent, Michael Warner, Andrew Webber, Deanne Williams, Jocelyn Wogan-Browne, and Marjorie Curry Woods. Audience members for papers I gave in Cambridge, at NYU, the Medieval Club of New York, Columbia, Harvard, Northwestern, and Yale all asked questions that proved decisive in the shaping of the arguments of individual chapters. An invitation to the English Institute in 2011 made me understand the importance of re-reading to this topic (and incisive questions from the audience there helped me refine that understanding). Cynthia Bland-Biggar kindly gave me her meticulous transcription of part of the *Speculum grammaticale* so that I could check my own. Martin Camargo offered helpful readings of parts of my manuscript and Vincent Gillespie and Paul Strohm read every word in its penultimate form, offering many improving suggestions. Jacqueline Norton has been as kind as she has been careful and expeditious in guiding this manuscript into print. Joanna North copy-edited my manuscript with great care and tact.

Parts of the introduction appeared in *PMLA* as "From Literacy to Literature: Elementary Learning and the Middle English Poet" 129 (2014): 349–64. Parts of Chapter 2 appeared in an earlier version as "The Middle English Writer's Schoolroom: Fourteenth-Century English Schoolbooks and their Contents," *New Medieval Literatures* 11 (2009): 19–38 in a special issue containing proceedings from the Cambridge conference on grammar in 2008. Parts of Chapter 4 appeared in an earlier version as "Langland's *Ars Grammatica*" in *The Yearbook of Langland Studies* 22 (2008): 1–25. Some of the material and the general view of proverbs I advance in Chapter 6 appeared as "Proverbs and the Wisdom of Literature: *The Proverbs of Alfred* and Chaucer's Tale of Melibee," *Textual Practice* 23 (2010): 407–34. An earlier version of Chapter 7 appeared in *ELH* 80 (2013): 401–25 and I have also borrowed a key example for the revised version of this argument from "Reading Knowledge," *PMLA* 130 (2015): 711–17. A grant from The Abraham and Rebecca Stein Faculty Publication Fund defrayed the cost of reproducing the images for the book and the fees for permission to print them.

My partner, Matthew Hamill, knows more about this book and its journey to print than he really ought to, but, then, it is impossible not to rely on someone so wise and capable and strong.

These pages were first researched and written as my son, Raymond, passed through primary school and were finished as my daughter, Josephine, was just learning to read and write. I swore I would never burden my children by dedicating a book to them (lest they feel compelled to read it), and I have never been able to see a connection in my interest in elementary learning and my devotion to them. And yet, for almost a decade these passions have been completely entwined, almost every day, in the happy round from school drop off, to my desk, to school pick up. And so it also seems exactly right to say: Ray and Josie (with apologies and love) this book is for you.

Contents

List of Illustrations

List of Abbreviations

EETS o.s.   Early English Text Society, Original Series
EETS e.s.   Early English Text Society, Extra Series
MED   *The Middle English Dictionary*, ed. Hans Kurath et al. (Ann Arbor, MI: University of Michigan, 1954–)
OED   *The Oxford English Dictionary*, 2nd edition, 20 vols., ed. J. A. Simpson and E. S. C. Weiner (Oxford: Clarendon Press, 1989; 1st edition 1888–1933)
VCH   Victoria County History

Note on Texts

I have generally provided full references for every text in the bibliography as well as in the first citation in each chapter. For schoolroom texts, Middle English texts, and Scripture, however, I provide full references, orienting information about titles and translations, and the method of citation I will use throughout in the following lists.

Unless otherwise noted translations throughout are my own.

MEDIEVAL SCHOOL TEXTS

Alain of Lille, *Liber parabolarum* (sometimes called the *Parabolae*)
Liber Parabolarum, ed. Oronzo Limone (Galatina: Congedo, 1993) and pp. 149–75 in *An English Translation of* Auctores Octo*: A Medieval Reader*, trans. Ronald E. Pepin (Lewiston, NY: Edwin Mellen Press, 1999). Citations are by line number from this edition and page number from this translation.

Avianus, *Fables*
pp. 669–749 in *Minor Latin Poets*, ed. and trans. J. Wight Duff and Arnold M. Duff (Cambridge, MA: Harvard University Press, 1961; first published 1934). Citations are by the number of the fable (in roman numerals) and line number.

Claudian, *On the Rape of Proserpina*
2: 293–377 in *Claudian*, ed. and trans. Maurice Platnauer, 2 vols. (London: William Heinemann, 1963). Citations are by book and line number.

The Distichs of Cato
(as *Dicta Catonis*), pp. 585–639 in *Minor Latin Poets*, ed. and trans. Duff and Duff. Citations are by book and distich (rather than line) number. I have generally altered this rhyming translation for accuracy.

Facetus (beginning "cum [or est] nihil utilius")
edited as *Der deutsche Facetus*, ed. Carl Schroeder (Berlin: Mayer and Müller, 1911); and pp. 41–54 in *An English Translation of* Auctores Octo, trans. Pepin (Pepin takes his text from a 1538 edition of the *Auctores Octo* [see his translation p. 3] and therefore presents the maxims in a different sequence than Schroeder's edition, sometimes

also omitting maxims Schroeder includes). Citations to the Facetus throughout this book are to this version of the text (rather than the *Facetus* beginning "moribus et vita" mentioned in the following item; I give references to that text as well because it is also common in schoolbooks, including a number of texts discussed in Chapter 2). Citations to this *Facetus* (beginning "cum [or est] nichil utilius") are by maxim number in Schroeder's edition and page number in the translation (where the translation is running).

Facetus (beginning "moribus et vita")
    edited and translated in Alison Godard Elliott, "The *Facetus*: or, The Art of Courtly Living," *Allegorica* 2 (1977): 26–51.

Liber cartule (sometimes called *Chartula* or *Cartula* after its incipit)
    attributed to Bernard of Clairvaux as *Carmen Paraeneticum ad Rainaldum* in *Patrologiae cursus completus, series latina*, ed. J.-P. Migne, 221 vols. (Paris, 1844–64), 184: cols. 1307–14, and translated as "On Contempt for the World" in *An English Translation of* Auctores Octo, trans. Pepin, 55–77 (Pepin takes his text from a 1538 edition of the *Auctores Octo* [see his edition p. 3] where it has acquired a lengthy continuation [translated by Pepin on pp. 66–77]). Citations are by column number in this edition and page number in the translation. I have occasionally altered Pepin's translation for clarity.

Liber penitencialis (sometimes known as *Peniteas cito* after its incipit)
    edited as attributed to William of Montibus in *William de Montibus (c.1140–1213): The Schools and the Literature of Pastoral Care*, ed. Joseph Goering (Toronto: Pontifical Institute of Mediaeval Studies, 1992), 107–28. Citations are by line number and page number.

Matthew of Vendôme, *Tobias*
    Matthei Vindocinensis, *Opera*, 3 vols., ed. Franco Munari (Rome: Edizioni di storia e letteratura, 1977–88), 2: 161–255 and pp. 79–148 in *An English Translation of* Auctores Octo, trans. Pepin. Citations are by line number in this edition and page number in this translation.

Maximian, *Elegies*
    The Elegies of Maximianus, ed. Richard Webster (Princeton, NJ: Princeton University Press, 1900) and pp. 319–36 in *Gabriele Zerbi, Gerontocomia: On the Care of the Aged and Maximianus, Elegies on Old Age and Love*, trans. L. R. Lind (Philadelphia, PA: American Philosophical Society, 1988). Citations are by elegy and line number (which are identical in edition and translation).

Stans puer ad mensam
> edited in Servus Gieben, "Robert Grosseteste and Medieval Courtesy Books," *Vivarium* 5 (1967): 56–62; there is a loose verse translation in *The Babees Book*, ed. F. J. Furnivall (London: Chatto & Windus, 1908).

Statius, *Achilleid*
> pp. 508–95 in *Statius*, ed. and trans. J. H. Mozley, 2 vols. (New York, NY: G. P. Putnam, 1928), citations by book and line number.

Theodulus, *Eclogue*
> pp. 26–36 and 111–49 (notes) in *Seven Versions of Carolingian Pastoral*, ed. R. P. H. Green (Reading: University of Reading, 1980) and *The Eclogue of Theodulus*, 25–40 in *An English Translation* of Auctores Octo, trans. Pepin.

MIDDLE ENGLISH

Unless otherwise noted all quotations from Chaucer are taken from *The Riverside Chaucer*, ed. Larry D. Benson, 3rd edn. (Boston: Houghton Mifflin, 1987). *The Canterbury Tales* is cited from this edition by fragment number (in roman numerals) and line number. All quotations from *Piers Plowman* are from the B-text unless otherwise noted and taken from William Langland, *The Vision of Piers Plowman: A Complete Edition of the B-text*, ed. A. V. C. Schmidt. 2nd edn. (London: J. M. Dent, 1995) cited by passus number and line number. All quotations from John Gower's *Confessio Amantis* are taken from *Confessio Amantis*, ed. Russell A. Peck, 3 vols. (Kalamazoo, MI: Medieval Institute Publications, Western Michigan University, 2006–13) and are cited by book number and line number.

SCRIPTURE

I quote throughout from the *Biblia Sacra Iuxta Vulgatam Versionem*, 5th edn., ed. Roger Gryson first edited by Robert Weber with B. Fischer, I. Gribomont, H. F. D. Sparks, and W. Thiele (Stuttgart: Deutsche Bibelgesellschaft, 2007; first edn. published 1969) and take my translations from *The Holy Bible: Douay Version* (London: Catholic Truth Society, 1956).

Introduction

Abcd,
efg,
hijk,
lmnop,
qrs,
tuv,
wxyz.

"The hand should not grasp the pen too quickly" [non manus ad calamum praeceps . . . sit], Geoffrey of Vinsauf instructed medieval poets, because the "art of poetry" [poesis] is acquired only through careful study.[1] We might not look to an art of poetry these days when describing how a poet received such instruction, and yet we still tend to see poetry as difficult enough to require some learning before it can be fully understood, let alone written. So how is it that in both British and American culture the alphabet is already a poem, recited by most boys and girls before formal schooling even begins, as if it scans in trochaic rhythm ("a b c d/e f g . . . "), rhyming first as a couplet (". . d . .g"), then as a quatrain ("p . . v"), then as a couplet again ("v . . . z")?[2] The practice is certainly of long standing, since Greek schoolboys seem to have learned their letters as if they formed a poem.[3] In the Middle Ages,

---

[1] Geoffrey of Vinsauf, *Poetria Nova*, 194–262 in *Les Arts Poétiques du XIIe et du XIIIe Siècle*, ed. Edmond Faral (Paris: Champion, 1962), lines 48 ("poesis") and 50 ("non manus").

[2] In UK English the last letter of the alphabet is referred to as "zed" (a habit that is attested from the fourteenth century on), but the resulting slant rhyme (or absence of rhyme) seems to be easily absorbed to the general pattern of rhymes in recitation. See *OED*, s.v. "zed n."

[3] The verse, in iambic trimeters, is preserved by Athanaeus and is in full: "The letter *alpha, beta, gamma, delta, ei* (which belongs to god), / *zeta, eta, theta, iota, kappa, labda, mu,* / *nu, xei,* the letter *ou, pei, rho,* the letter *sigma, tau,* the letter *u,* / also the letters *phei* and *chei,* followed by the letter *psei,* and ending in the letter *o*," *Athenaeus: The Learned Banqueters,* 8 vols. (Cambridge, MA: Harvard University Press, 2009), 5: 170–1. H. I. Marrou says this verse was used in the schoolroom but it is not clear what his evidence is since Athanaeus is quoting from the preface to a play by Callias (*A History of Education in Antiquity,* trans. George Lamb [Madison, WI: University of Wisconsin Press, 1982; first published in

since primers regularly placed a red cross before the row of letters and the word "amen" just after them, the alphabet functioned first and foremost as a prayer.[4] But a number of surviving poems make clear that this prayer was a poem too, begun with a propitiatory couplet ("Christes crosse be my speede / In all vertue to proceede") followed by the chanting of letters "in roughly stressed or metrical lines."[5] An alphabet learned in this way was not just an "abece," as it was sometimes called, but a poetic form routinely described as the "Christ-cross-row" or "Christ-cross."[6] Just as lawyers versified laws and monks versified library catalogues, it seems that the most basic tool of literacy training has always tended toward poetry the better to be remembered.[7] But familiarity has also concealed the under-lying paradox: if poetry is usually the culmination of literacy training, it is almost always that training's first step.

It has been difficult to notice this hysteron proteron because it recurs in the very categories we might use to analyze the disorder. "Grammar" or *grammatica* is the term we traditionally apply to the most basic training in letters, the "ground of al" (B 15.372) as Anima puts it firmly in *Piers Plowman*, but this term is also used to describe the first of

English, 1956], 151). This report may therefore constitute earlier evidence of the subtle process I am trying to detail in the body of this book: the durable effects of basic literacy training in the making of literature.

   4   Helen Phillips, "Chaucer and Deguileville: The 'ABC' in Context," *Medium Aevum* 62 (1993): 8. See also Nicholas Orme, *Medieval Children* (New Haven, CT: Yale University Press, 2001), 246–54; W. J. Frank Davies, *Teaching Reading in Early England* (London: Pitman House, 1973), 132; and the example in George A. Plimpton, *The Education of Chaucer: Illustrated from the Schoolbooks in Use in his Time* (London and New York, NY: Oxford University Press, 1935), 18.

   5   Orme, *Medieval Children*, 260. See also Martha Dana Rust, *Imaginary Worlds in Medieval Books: Exploring the Manuscript Matrix* (New York, NY: Palgrave Macmillan, 2007), 41. The couplet I quote is taken from a song by Thomas Morley (1597), but a great number of texts that include similar phrases survive from the later Middle Ages (see Orme *Medieval Children*, 253 and 260). Such verse was already current in the fourteenth century too, as is proved by the phrasing of the poem John of Trevisa wrote as preface to his translation of Bartholomeus Anglicus's *De Proprietatibus rerum*: "Croys was maad al of reed / In þe bigynnynge of my book / That is clepid God me spede / In þe firste lessoun þat I took / Thanne I lerned *a* and *be*. And oþir lettres by here names" (Rust, *Imaginary Worlds*, 41 citing *On the Properties of Things: John of Trevisa's Translation of Bartholomaeus Anglicus* De Proprietatibus Rerum: *A Critical Text*, ed. M. C. Seymour. 3 vols. [Oxford: Oxford University Press, 1975–88], 1: 40).

   6   *OED*, s.vv. "ABC n1.," "Christ-cross, criss-cross n." See also Katherine Breen, *Imagining an English Reading Public, 1150–1400* (Cambridge: Cambridge University Press, 2010), 93–4; Orme, *Medieval Children*, 251; and Patricia Crain, *The Story of A: The Alphabetization of America from The New England Primer to The Scarlet Letter* (Stanford, CA: Stanford University Press, 2000), 24.

   7   On versified laws and catalogues see Mary Carruthers, *The Book of Memory: A Study of Memory in Medieval Culture*, 2nd edition (Cambridge: Cambridge University Press, 2008), 99; on alphabet poems as mnemonic see Rust, *Imaginary Worlds*, 43.

the "seven liberal arts," the founding discipline of the *trivium* in university education.[8] Not only was the primary school teacher in early Greek education called the "grammatist" [γραμματιστής] but the secondary school teacher was called the "grammarian" [γραμματιχός].[9] By the first century AD, Quintilian was defining grammar not only as "the study of correct speech" [recte loquendi scientia] but as the "explication of the poets" [poetarum enarratio].[10] In the Middle Ages, grammar could be defined as knowledge of "how to fit case to case, number to number, gender to gender" [reddere casum casui, numerum numero, genus generi], but it was also the "science of interpretation" [scientia interpretandi].[11] Medieval *grammatica* tended to absorb many of the topics of rhetoric, the more sophisticated discipline that followed it in both elementary and

---

[8] On "grammar" as part of the *trivium* see Jeffrey F. Huntsman, "Grammar," 58–95 in *The Seven Liberal Arts in the Middle Ages*, ed. David L. Wagner (Bloomington, IN: Indiana University Press, 1983), esp. 62–4; Martin Irvine with David Thomson, "*Grammatica* and Literary Theory," 15–41 in *The Cambridge History of Literary Criticism*, vol. 2, ed. Alastair Minnis and Ian Johnson (Cambridge: Cambridge University Press, 2005), 21–2; and Damien Riehl Leader, "Grammar in Late-Medieval Oxford and Cambridge," *History of Education* 12 (1983): 9–14.

For the long history of the meaning of the term "grammar" see Ian Michael, *English Grammatical Categories and the Tradition to 1800* (London: Cambridge University Press, 1970), 24–30. Modern definitions have tended to emphasize the term's ambiguity, since "it can be used to refer to languages (in whole or in part) or, alternatively, to descriptions of languages," John Lyons, "Grammar and Meaning," 221–54 in *Grammar and Meaning*, ed. F. R. Palmer (Cambridge: Cambridge University Press, 1995), 223. On the other hand, modern definitions also converge on the proposition that "grammar ... gives rules for combining words to form sentences," John Lyons, *Introduction to Theoretical Linguistics* (London: Cambridge University Press, 1968), 133. For definitions of *grammatica* based on the structures of medieval grammars see Vivien Law, *Grammar and Grammarians in the Early Middle Ages* (London: Longman, 1997), 261–2.

[9] Marrou, *History of Education in Antiquity*, 160. As David L. Wagner notes, too, grammar first emerged as a subject "in the context of rhetoric" in the Hellenistic period (from the death of Alexander in 323 BCE, through the second century of the Roman Empire), "The Seven Liberal Arts and Classical Scholarship," 1–31 in *The Seven Liberal Arts in the Middle Ages*, ed. David L. Wagner (Bloomington, IN: Indiana University Press, 1986), 9.

[10] Quintilian, *The Orator's Education*, ed. and trans. Donald A. Russell, 5 vols. (Cambridge, MA: Harvard University Press, 2001), 1.4.1 (1: 102–3). No definition of grammar is cited with greater frequency. For a representative set of examples see James J. Murphy, "Roman Writing Instruction as Described by Quintilian," 36–76 in *A Short History of Writing Instruction: From Ancient Greece to Contemporary America*, ed. James J. Murphy, 3rd edition (New York, NY: Routledge, 2012), 53; Douglas Kelly, "The Scope of the Treatment of Composition in the Twelfth- and Thirteenth-Century Arts of Poetry," *Speculum* 41 (1966): 270; John Guillory, *Cultural Capital: The Problem of Literary Canon Formation* (Chicago, IL: University of Chicago Press, 1993), 62.

[11] The first phrase comes from a commentary on Priscian quoted in R. W. Hunt, "Studies on Priscian in the Eleventh and Twelfth Centuries," *Medieval and Renaissance Studies* 1 (1943): 211. The second is from Rabanus Maurus, *De Clericorum Institutione*, III.18 (*Patrologia Latina*, ed. Migne, 107, col. 395b): "Grammatica est scientia interpretandi poetas atque historicos, et recte scribendi loquendique ratio."

university curricula. The basic grammars that were every medieval school-boy's starting point provided a detailed account of tropes and figures.[12] *Grammatica* had such wide reference as a term that "medieval people themselves did not always distinguish clearly between one level of instruction and another," and, as a result, modern scholars regularly use evidence drawn from the university even when they claim that they are describing "grammar schools."[13]

This, however, is a book about those schools, the *grammatica* of the most basic literacy training, and that training's lasting and significant effects.[14] My title is a variation on Michael Clanchy's *From Memory to Written Record*, first published in 1979, just as Clanchy's was a variation on H. J. Chaytor's *From Script to Print*, first published in 1945.[15] This book is also an attempt to fill the gap between these two studies, describing changes in literate culture in England after the explosion of literacy that Clanchy documented (from 1066 to 1307) but before the arrival of movable-type printing in 1485 that Chaytor described, detailing the long moment during which a profusion of writing in Latin slowly mutated into a profusion of writing in English. This is also, then, an account of events between two different technological changes, the spread of literacy that allowed William the Conqueror to transform record-keeping into an instrument of royal power, and the dawning of the age of

[12] For details of these figures in the basic grammars see Chapter 2, pp. 70–1. For discussion of the general absorption of rhetorical subjects by grammar see Rita Copeland, *Rhetoric, Hermeneutics, and Translation in the Middle Ages: Academic Traditions and Vernacular Texts* (Cambridge: Cambridge University Press, 1991), esp. 57–8.

[13] Jo Ann Hoeppner Moran, *The Growth of English Schooling, 1340–1548* (Princeton, NJ: Princeton University Press, 1985), 21 ("medieval people"). A representative example of the confusion in modern scholarship is William J. Courtenay's description of "grammar schools": "this secondary level of education was concerned with Latin grammar, and it was almost exclusively linguistic and literary. Lasting anywhere from six to ten years, the course included correct spelling, syntax, inflections and standard constructions, reading and writing at an advanced level, speaking and comprehension, and the student might even be introduced to the rudiments of logic and speculative grammar," *Schools and Scholars in Fourteenth-Century England* (Princeton, NJ: Princeton University Press, 1987), 17.

The substitution of the sophisticated for the elementary is so common that even where scholarship has attempted to make a careful distinction between "pedagogical" and "scholarly" grammar, as Jeffrey Huntsman does, basic linguistic training is still thought to have striven for the "rhetorically effective" and to involve study of "elaborate commentaries" on the most advanced grammatical texts ("Grammar," 62–3).

[14] In this sense this book is an attempt to fill the gap Tony Hunt identified some decades ago: "Regrettably little has been done to investigate the links between the characteristics of literary production in the Middle Ages and the nature of the reading and exposition which were taking place in the schools," *Teaching and Learning Latin in Thirteenth Century England*, 3 vols. (Woodbridge: D. S. Brewer, 1991), 1: 59.

[15] On the echo, see M. T. Clanchy, *From Memory to Written Record: England, 1066–1307*, 2nd edition (Malden, MA: Blackwell, 1993; first published 1979), 3.

mechanical reproduction. It could also be seen as an effort to describe the passage from the dominance of one textual kind to another, from the "business documents and legal records" on which Clanchy focused to the "vernacular and literary works" that were Chaytor's chief concern.[16] Most of all, however, this book describes how the texts used to teach schoolboys their grammar also prepared them to make the kind of writing subsequently called "literature."

"Literacy" is not a stable category of course. As Clanchy has noted, modern methods of measuring competence in letters are inevitably inaccurate for the Middle Ages when the manipulation of ink and a quill was a sophisticated skill and men and women might be able to read well enough even though they could not write a letter.[17] As recent decades have shown, such competencies are so easily politicized that their very description constitutes a critique. Richard Hoggart's account of the "uses" to which literacy was put in post-war Britain is in fact an account of its modern abuses; E. D. Hirsch defined "cultural literacy" in a way that sought to transform the phrase into an imperative.[18] The category remains so volatile because skill in reading and writing is always a means of social distinction: as John Guillory has so well shown, literacy is not only a set of linguistic skills but a set of privileges conferred by the access those skills give to a canon of lionized texts.[19] The term will be used in these pages in this last sense, since training in letters in the fourteenth century was firmly bound to a particular set of texts and the facility necessary to read them. But it is also the aim of this book to show that even though medieval literacy was sometimes a narrower category than it is now (so often

---

[16] Clanchy, *From Memory to Written Record*, 3.

[17] Clanchy, *From Memory to Written Record*, 183–4.

[18] Richard Hoggart, *The Uses of Literacy: Aspects of Working Class Life* (London: Chatto & Windus, 1957); E. D. Hirsch, Jr., *Cultural Literacy: What Every American Needs to Know* (Boston, MA: Houghton Mifflin, 1987). On the "politics of literacy" generally see Stanley Aronowitz and Henry A. Giroux, *Postmodern Education: Politics, Culture and Social Criticism* (Minneapolis, MN: University of Minnesota Press, 1991), 24–56.

[19] As Guillory puts the point: "The literary canon has always functioned in the schools as a pedagogic device for producing an effect of linguistic distinction, of 'literacy.' The production of this effect does not depend upon the biasing of judgment—the educational system works better with better works—nor is it a question of insuring the ideological orthodoxy of texts by extraordinary procedures of exclusion and censorship (these measures have for the most part been imposed from above, by church or state). Literary curricula, historically, the substance of most educational programs, are capable of assimilating the otherwise dangerous heterodoxies expressed in some works by means of homogenizing methods of textual appropriation exercised within institutional structures of symbolic violence. The ideological effect rides on the back of the effect of sociolinguistic differentiation produced by access to the literary language, which is therefore its vector," *Cultural Capital*, 62–3.

excluding writing of any kind) it was often much broader, particularly insofar as what the fourteenth-century poet might have called "reading" shaded into the acts of perception and thought that we would be inclined to call "experience" or "knowing."

The aspect of medieval literacy that has attracted most recent comment from scholars is not its definition, however, but the violence that so often attended its teaching. In its most subtle form this was the sort of affective friction common to any movement from ignorance to knowledge (we get upset when we are confused; we feel fear when a new idea is hard to grasp). A model for English-to-Latin translation preserved in a fifteenth-century schoolbook, Oxford, Lincoln College, MS Latin 129, vividly describes such feelings:

> A hard laytn to make, my face wexyth blakke.
> Difficilem latinitatem composituri, facies mea nigrescit.
>
> [My face grows black when I have a hard Latin (sentence) to compose.][20]

But other models for translation in this same schoolbook make clear that learning in medieval classrooms was sometimes much more painful:

> Hyt befallyth þe mayster to bete roberd and me ȝyf we fayle wan we beþ aposyd yn a lyȝt matyr.
> Interest a magistro vapulare m[e] et robert[um] si deficiamus cum in materia facili nobis apponatur.
>
> [It is the master's responsibility to beat Robert and me if we err when examined in a simple matter.]
>
> My felow y-bete with a byrch ȝerd, y ham to be bete with a whyppe.
> Socio vapulante cum virga lentiscina, ego sum vapulaturus cum scutica.
>
> [My peer was beaten with a birch rod, and I am to be beaten with a whip.][21]

It is appropriate that attention should be focused on the human costs of such discipline and the way it may shape the knowledge it inculcates. As Bruce Holsinger has observed, beatings of this kind were so common

---

[20] Nicholas Orme, "A Grammatical Miscellany from Bristol and Wiltshire," 86–111 in his *Education and Society in Medieval and Renaissance England* (London: Hambledon Press, 1989), 104. The exercise is reprinted in Nicholas Orme, *English School Exercises, 1420–1530* (Toronto: Pontifical Institute of Medieval Studies, 2013), 57. Orme notes in the introduction to this volume that "discipline is a frequent topic of exercises" and describes a number of representative examples (32). His index catalogues a large number under "beating and punishment" (428).

[21] Orme, "A Grammatical Miscellany from Bristol," 101–2; Orme, *English School Exercises*, 53–4.

in medieval teaching that it produced a "pedagogical body" for which elementary learning was equivalent to pain.[22] The standard curriculum of reading texts also insisted that young boys read narratives in which sexual violence against women was made to seem a normal part of a boy's maturation.[23] Much in that curriculum was also allied to the discourse of self-punishment or penance.[24] I do not explore this territory further in the following pages, in part because it has been so well explored already, but also because I think the consequences of such violence are easier to discern than the effects of basic literacy training on literary technique and form. This relationship is so subtle, and its nuance so fine, that it will take several chapters of this book to identify the salient pedagogical structures.

But a helpfully simple and suggestive instance of the sorts of relationships such identifications will then make it possible to describe can be found in the poem usually called Chaucer's *ABC* (because each of its twenty-three stanzas begins with a letter of the Latin alphabet).[25] Careful scholarship has placed this poem in the literary tradition of the *abecedarium* that extends back at least as far as Psalms 118 and 119.[26] Since it translates the lyric embedded in Guillaume Deguilleville's *La pélerinage de la vie humaine* so closely it is usually seen as one of Chaucer's "most derivative" productions.[27] Because Chaucer "began his career" with this poem, these

---

[22] Bruce Holsinger, *Music, Body and Desire in Medieval Culture: Hildegard of Bingen to Chaucer* (Stanford, CA: Stanford University Press, 2001), 271.

[23] Marjorie Curry Woods, "Rape and the Pedagogical Rhetoric of Sexual Violence," 36–86 in *Criticism and Dissent in the Middle Ages*, ed. Rita Copeland (Cambridge: Cambridge University Press, 1996), esp. 60–5. Woods also suggests that narratives of rape allowed schoolboys to "explor[e] the role of the powerless victim" (73).

[24] See Marjorie Curry Woods and Rita Copeland, "Classroom and Confession," 376–406 in *The Cambridge History of Medieval English Literature*, ed. David Wallace (Cambridge: Cambridge University Press, 1999). On the relationship of punishment to learning in other periods see, in particular, Rebecca W. Bushnell, *A Culture of Teaching: Early Modern Humanism in Theory and Practice* (Ithaca, NY: Cornell University Press, 1996), 10–72; Richard Halpern, *The Poetics of Primitive Accumulation: English Renaissance Culture and the Genealogy of Capitalism* (Ithaca, NY: Cornell University Press, 1991), 26; Walter Ong, "Latin Language Study as a Renaissance Puberty Rite," *Studies in Philology* 56 (1959): 103–24; and of course Michel Foucault on the "means of correct training" in *Discipline and Punish: The Birth of the Prison* (New York, NY: Vintage Books, 1995), 170–94.

[25] This is "the only independent Chaucerian lyric seriously shaped as a prayer," Georgia Ronan Crampton, "Chaucer's Singular Prayer," *Medium Aevum* 59 (1990): 191.

[26] Crampton, "Chaucer's Singular Prayer," 193.

[27] *The Riverside Chaucer*, ed. Benson, 1076. Skeat prints the Deguilleville poem alongside Chaucer's *ABC* in *The Complete Works of Geoffrey Chaucer*, ed. W. W. Skeat, 6 vols. (Oxford: Clarendon Press, 1899), 1: 261–71. Although his translation is often exact, Chaucer also changes the words that form the alphabetical shape of the work (where Deguilleville has "a" Chaucer has "almighty," for "bien" he has "bountee," for "contre" "comfort," for "dame" "dowte," and so on).

perceived limitations are customarily attributed to his general "want of skill."[28] Those who have noticed that the *ABC* is a hymn to the Virgin and therefore Chaucer's "only completely devotional work" have thought more highly of it, judging it to have "the same relation to Marian penitential lyrics as *Troilus and Criseyde* does to medieval romance."[29] But, if this was one of Chaucer's first poems, it finds him deftly reversing the founding paradox of literacy training: if that training always began in the Middle Ages with an alphabet-as-poem, Chaucer marks his poetic beginnings with a poem-as-alphabet. This structural fact shows in itself how deeply the first steps of elementary education could inform literary production, just as it makes clear how much Chaucer's *ABC* is about the intimate connection between letters and devotion, an extension, elaboration, and enrichment, by means of a source, of the way the alphabet or "Christ-cross row," functioned as a prayer in the medieval imagination. These relationships equipped Chaucer to insist with ceremony—as *grammatica* equipped the Ricardian poet to show generally—that what he first learned in school shaped his writing ever afterwards.

ELEMENTARY LEARNING AND THE MIDDLE ENGLISH POET

This book details this persistence in the literature written in England in the latter part of the fourteenth century. There is, on its face, a certain perversity in picking this particular time and place for such an account, since, little as we know about how most medieval children were taught to read and write, the flood of evidence about elementary education in England (schoolbooks, descriptions of schoolroom activity, syllabi) only begins in the first decades of the fifteenth century. Historians of education have generally made much of the resulting evidence without really noticing or accounting for this change, usually offering descriptions of the "medieval schools of England" while relying chiefly on fifteenth-century materials.[30] But the timing of the flood itself suggests that there

---

[28] Crampton, "Chaucer's Singular Prayer," 192 ("began"); *Complete Works of Geoffrey Chaucer*, ed. Skeat, .1: xlvii.

[29] *The Riverside Chaucer*, ed. Benson, 1076. See also Crampton, "Chaucer's Singular Prayer," 193.

[30] Nicholas Orme acknowledges this problem in *Medieval Schools: From Roman Britain to Medieval England* (New Haven, CT: Yale University Press, 2006), 128, although his study still relies very largely on fifteenth-century evidence for its own generalizations. The problem can also be discerned in the date range specified in two other important studies of elementary learning in the period: Michael Van Cleave, *The Growth of English Education,*

were significant changes in the degree or quality of literacy training just prior to 1400 well worth examining. And then there are the "Ricardian" poets, all of whom begin to produce poetry in quantity just prior to this watershed.[31] Whether the efflorescence of English literature by Gower, Chaucer, and Langland is unprecedented depends, of course, on the criteria by which we measure textual production (and whether we agree that there is a kind of writing worth calling "literature"), but for generations of readers just after the fourteenth century, as well as generations of scholars in more recent centuries, the quality of the work of these writers seems to mark a significant cultural change.[32] There is, also, John of Trevisa's famous observation that "all the grammar schools" in England suddenly began to teach in English rather than French in the late 1340s.[33] The dearth of fourteenth-century evidence makes difficult investigation of these phenomena and the relationships between them but it does not wholly disable inquiry. Moreover, as I will try to demonstrate in Chapter 1, a careful sifting of the evidence we do have suggests that it has appeared more unhelpful than it actually is because we have tended to interrogate it with the wrong questions.

There is, to be sure, an even greater perversity in trying to reconstruct the elementary education of Chaucer, Langland, and Gower of all the figures we might name in the fourteenth century, since our ignorance about their schooling is almost complete. But I think that ignorance is also a function of the kind of attention we have been willing to pay, since scholars has often skated right by the issue of elementary learning in order to focus on the relationships that might be construed between Ricardian writing and university learning: even when attempting to "stay in primary school," studies of Chaucer have moved smartly to an examination of "fourteenth-century academic discourse," and Langland has been seen to have an "ongoing encounter...with higher education" in which his knowledge of grammar is best understood as a function of the "study of

---

1348–1648: A Social and Cultural History (University Park, PA: Pennsylvania State University Press, 1990) and Moran, *Growth of English Schooling, 1340–1548*.

[31] The category of "Ricardian poetry" was convened as a "literary period" by John Burrow in *Ricardian Poetry: Chaucer, Gower, Langland and the "Gawain" Poet* (London: Routledge & Kegan Paul, 1971).

[32] The obvious omission from this list is the *Gawain*-poet, although his work had much smaller immediate effects than the writings of Chaucer, Gower, and Langland because it survives in a single codex, London, British Library, Cotton Nero A. x and was largely unknown and unread until the last century. But the *Gawain*-poet's work also had an unusual relationship to *grammatica* as I suggest at the conclusion of Chapter 5 (see pp. 196–8).

[33] Trevisa's claims are quoted and their relationship to other evidence is analyzed in some depth in Chapter 1, pp. 17–24.

language in English university curricula."[34] It is equally true that attempts to investigate the earliest stages of literacy training for these poets have routinely drawn a blank. Chaucer may have been educated in court since he was "born in the atmosphere of the royal household," or he may have attended what has become St Paul's School because the original foundation "was near his father's house in Thames Street," but "no direct evidence as to Chaucer's schooling has come to light."[35] Of Gower's "formal education we know nothing positive" and we know almost nothing about Langland's *life* (we probably do not even call him by the name he used) let alone how he learned to read and write.[36] A strong case has been made for the importance of "extra-grammatical" literacy in the Middle Ages, a familiarity with, and knowledge of, texts through their repetition in liturgical performance that further confounds the distinctions we are accustomed to make between those who can recognize letters and those who cannot.[37] And yet, it makes methodological sense to focus on individuals, even in a broad history of education, since literacy training is

---

[34] Peter Travis, "The Nun's Priest's Tale as Grammar School Primer," *SAC, Proceedings* 1 (1985): 88 ("stay" and "academic discourse"); Andrew Galloway, "*Piers Plowman* and the Schools," *Yearbook of Langland Studies* 6 (1992): 89 ("realm"); Anne Middleton, "Two Infinites: Grammatical Metaphor in *Piers Plowman*," [*ELH*] 39 (1972): 174 ("study of language"). John Alford documents a general "trend" toward crediting Langland with a certain scholasticism in "Langland's Learning," *YLS* 9 (1995): 2. Ralph Hanna offers a similar diagnosis in "Langland's Ymaginatif: Images and the Limits of Poetry," 81–94 in *Images, Idolatry and Iconoclasm in Late Medieval England: Textuality and the Visual Image*, ed. Jeremy Dimmick, James Simpson, and Nicolette Zeeman (Oxford: Oxford University Press, 2002), 94.

[35] Thomas F. Tout, "Literature and Learning in the English Civil Service in the Fourteenth Century," *Speculum* 4 (1929): 382 ("born"); Edith Rickert, "Chaucer at School," *Modern Philology* 39 (1932): 257 ("was near"); *Chaucer Life-Records*, ed. Martin M. Crow and Clair C. Olson (Austin, TX: University of Texas Press, 1966), 12 ("no direct evidence"). On Chaucer and St Paul's School see also Plimpton, *Education of Chaucer*, 18; Donald Howard, *Chaucer: His Life, His Works, His World* (New York, NY: Dutton, 1987), 25; and Derek Pearsall, *The Life of Geoffrey Chaucer* (Oxford: Blackwell, 1992), 30–1.

[36] *The Major Latin Works of John Gower: The Voice of One Crying and the Tripartite Chronicle*, trans. Eric W. Stockton (Seattle, WA: University of Washington Press, 1962), 5. On Langland as a cleric in minor orders see E. Talbot Donaldson, *Piers Plowman: The C-Text and Its Poet* (New Haven, CT: Yale University Press, 1966; first published 1949), 202–26. Moran comments on the more concrete evidence of Langland's schooling: "Thus, when William Langland, in *Piers Plowman*, tells us how his father and friends 'fonde me to scole' till he could understand the Latin of the Bible, he could conceivably be referring to a reading school education, although it is clear elsewhere that he was quite familiar with fourteenth-century grammar and grammar schools. His description of the tools from which he derived his living, his '*pater-noster* and my prymer, *placebo* and / *dirige*, and my sauter some tyme and my sevene psalms', can also serve to describe a reading school curriculum" (*Growth of English Schooling*, 48–9). On how little is known about Langland's early life generally see Ralph Hanna, *William Langland* (Brookfield, VT: Ashgate, 1993), 4.

[37] Katherine Zieman, *Singing the New Song: Literacy and Liturgy in Late Medieval England* (Philadelphia, PA: University of Pennsylvania Press, 2008), esp. 117 and 179–90.

inevitably local, a process of making general rules about language meaningful in the particular.[38] Since it is the quantity and quality of the writing Chaucer, Langland, and Gower produced that marks them out for our attention as historical figures, it also seems worth knowing what we can about how these men in particular learned to write. They are, by the measure of their own achievements in letters, three of the best grammar-school students of their century.

Trevisa's claim that English was first used in all grammar schools in exactly the decade during which these three poets would have been learning their abc's makes it tempting to say that Chaucer, Langland, and Gower became English poets because they were the first generation of schoolboys to have been taught in English.[39] But I will claim just the opposite, in part because the decision to write in English was clearly made on different grounds for each one of these poets. Since Gower could and did write in both French and Latin, his English poetry was but one aspect of a carefully managed trilingual career. Langland might have been surprised to learn that he *had* decided to write in English, since roughly 1,200 lines of *Piers Plowman* are in Latin.[40] Chaucer's close attachments to a deeply Francophone court make his "decision to write in English, and subsequently exclusively in English . . . extraordinary," a truly revolutionary rejection of cultural norms and expectations.[41] The evidence I will examine in Chapter 1 suggests that Trevisa has confused rather than explained the language choices any Middle English poet would have made because they

---

[38] In his study of elementary schooling in trecento Florence Paul F. Gehl helpfully described this particularity: "Our understanding of elementary education in the Middle Ages has also been handicapped by an almost obsessive search by scholars for order and standardization. It is hard to understand why this is so. Surely we have long since learned that there were many Middle Ages, and that no five-hundred or even two-hundred-year period can be very uniform in cultural terms. In education particularly, the talents and preferences of individual teachers have always resulted in wide variations of practice within even the most rigidly standardized curricula. So, although we may badly want to generalize, we need to realize the limits of any such attempt. Medieval education, and especially grammar, was an essentially conservative field, but its conservatism functioned first on a social and ethical level, secondarily on the level of technique and preference for individual texts, and only in a very weak and inconsistent way in the matter of systematic curricula," *A Moral Art: Grammar, Society and Culture in Trecento Florence* (Ithaca, NY: Cornell University Press, 1993), 11.

[39] Cynthia Bland has suggested that Chaucer chose to write in English instead of French because he "was taught his Latin grammar by way of English," "John of Cornwall's Innovations and Their Possible Effects on Chaucer," 213–35 in *The Uses of Manuscripts in Literary Studies: Essays in Memory of Judson Boyce Allen*, ed. Charlotte Cook Morse, Penelope Reed Doob, and Marjorie Curry Woods (Kalamazoo, MI: Western Michigan University, Medieval Institute Publications, 1992), 225.

[40] John A. Alford, *Piers Plowman: A Guide to the Quotations* (Binghamton, NY: Center for Medieval and Early Renaissance Studies, 1992), 1.

[41] Pearsall, *Life of Geoffrey Chaucer*, 73 (on the general issue see this volume 68–73).

were not in fact taught grammar in English. Moreover, whatever the language commonly used by schoolmasters, the grammar Gower, Chaucer, Langland, and every fourteenth-century schoolboy learned was *Latin* grammar, and so the shaping fact of their literacy training was that they were taught to read and write in a second language, and therefore had to repurpose every element of the grammar they learned when they decided to write in the English or French they had learned first.[42] The Ricardian poets may have little in common if we focus on the grounds for their commitment to English, in other words, but they share the experience of having chosen to make literature in a language other than the one they were taught in school.

To put this last point in more historical terms, the Ricardian poets were the *last* generation of medieval English schoolboys to learn their grammar in Latin but simultaneously the *first* generation of writers in England to make a significant and steady commitment to English in the writing they produced. The most important and widespread consequence of these overlapping phenomena was what I will call "grammaticalization," the varied but constant recognition that English *had* a grammar.[43] One manifestation of this process is that English literature of the fourteenth century elevated grammar into something like a literary technique, often using grammatical concepts and terminology as the shaping material of allegory, metaphor, and image. The literature the Ricardian poets made was also grammaticalized insofar as it hewed so closely to schoolroom practice that its forms were often identical to the forms used to teach reading and writing. Insofar as such forms often mobilized aspects of a basic literacy training that had been common since antiquity, it is also the

---

[42] "Moreover, it is crucial to realise that the alphabet the *puer* learns is not the alphabet of the mother-tongue—French or English—but the alphabet of Latin. In other words, even at its very earliest stages, learning to read means learning to read a foreign language," Suzanne Reynolds, *Medieval Reading: Grammar, Rhetoric and the Classical Text* (Cambridge: Cambridge University Press, 1996), 8.
[43] Linguists use the verb "grammaticalize" to mean "express by means of the grammatical structure; to adopt as a grammatical requirement (*OED* s.v. "grammaticalize v."), and the term might refer, say, to a particular convention assuming an obligatory status (a correctness) in subsequent usage. Sarah Kay uses the term to describe the ways that Occitan grammars made the language of troubadour poetry "more like Latin" by systematizing its forms (*Parrots and Nightingales: Troubadour Quotations and the Development of European Poetry* [Philadelphia, PA: University of Pennsylvania Press, 2013], 28; see also 59, 160). My use of the term describes the ways in which the Ricardian poets came to understand English as similar to Latin by noticing that English too had a grammar. Gehl has noted a similar process in trecento Florence where "the *volgare* was widely assumed to have no rules of its own, so language-by-the-rules was already what we would call a second-language skill," *A Moral Art*, 84. Elsewhere Kay has also said that grammaticalization in the Occitan grammars "contributed a layer of reflexivity to a process of standardization that seems to have been operative from the time of the very earliest troubadours" ("Occitan Grammar as a Science of Endings," *New Medieval Literatures* 11 [2009]: 45).

case that what has often appeared the most innovative in Ricardian poetry is in fact the most conservative. As I will suggest in Chapter 2, elementary learning in the fourteenth century gave even the youngest schoolboy the strong sense that the rules of language, so far from requiring blind adherence, licensed experimentation and exploration, since knowledge of grammar was most fully proved when a student could deploy it to make phrases or sentences that were wholly new.

THE ERA OF GRAMMATICALIZATION

Framed in the broadest terms, this book describes how a fourteenth-century English "culture of teaching" produced a period style.[44] It joins a variety of recent studies that construe similar relationships for elementary learning in later periods.[45] It also responds to Mark McGurl's observation that the kind of training students have received in creative writing programs in the latter half of the twentieth century make it worth designating those decades in American fiction "The Program Era."[46] McGurl is focused on secondary education rather than basic literacy training, but his powerful argument puts before us the prospect of a new kind of literary history periodized, not by particular writers or the movements their writing shaped, but by the form of the pedagogy that trained them. Were such periods to be named according to the institutions in which that pedagogy occurred, McGurl's nomenclature would not get us very far in describing the fourteenth century, since it would simply be one part of a Grammar-School Era that stretched from antiquity until (at least in the UK) the present day. If the era can be named by a defining effect, however—by the characteristics it produced in the writing itself—then the fourteenth century in England, and the subject of this book, could be described as "The Era of Grammaticalization."

If my first two chapters describe this era's formative conditions, the three chapters after them explore the implications of these conditions for literature. As I will argue in Chapter 3, one outcome of fourteenth-century

---

[44] The phrase is Rebecca Bushnell's (see n. 24 in this chapter).

[45] On this relationship from 1875–1930 in Great Britain, and 1870–1950 in the United States see Catherine Robson, *Heart Beats: Everyday Life and the Memorized Poem* (Princeton, NJ: Princeton University Press, 2012). For recent studies of Renaissance schooling and its effects see Halpern, *Poetics of Primitive Accumulation*, 19–100; Jeff Dolven, *Scenes of Instruction in Renaissance Romance* (Chicago, IL: University of Chicago Press, 2007); and Lynn Enterline, *Shakespeare's Schoolroom: Rhetoric, Discipline, Emotion* (Philadelphia, PA: University of Pennsylvania Press, 2012).

[46] Mark McGurl, *The Program Era: Postwar Fiction and the Rise of Creative Writing* (Cambridge, MA: Harvard University Press, 2009), esp. 287.

English literature's absorption of the period's methods of grammatical training is what I will call a grammar-school style, particularly visible in the writing of Chaucer and the techniques he developed for positioning subjects in narrative. In Chapter 4 I will explore the way that Langland parlayed the most basic exercises of literacy training into the largest formal elements of *Piers Plowman*. Chapter 5 will then reverse this emphasis and look at the basic texts used in literacy training *as* literature, for, if grammar was first taught as a set of rules and exercises, those rules were reinforced and honed by early exposure to a great variety of poetry that was often memorized. Modern histories of education have usually understood this syllabus to provide training in ethics, but closer scrutiny makes clear that it was also a primer in literary possibility, a collection of forms and techniques that contained and conveyed an idea of what literature was and could be.

The book concludes with two long codas exploring the larger effects and implications of that idea. As I will suggest in Chapter 6, the narrowness of the syllabus, and the astonishing familiarity it bred with a particular set of texts, ensured that the "literary" was often defined afterwards as so many acts of recognition, in and as the comfort given by the confirmation that the long-held truth remained true. Often the very point of a Middle English poem—the point of arrival for its largest structural arc—was just such a realization. As I will explore in Chapter 7, so frequent was this effect, and so deeply were some schoolroom texts absorbed by those who learned them early and by heart, that they affected the shape of knowledge itself. The grown medieval schoolboy often perceived the world *through* these texts, changing and deepening what he understood them to mean, while also experiencing the phenomenal world as if he were reading it.

It is probably worth acknowledging from the start that there is never any reason to be sure that a schoolboy learned anything, even from a schoolbook we can be absolutely certain he held in his hands. As Bourdieu and Passeron have observed, there is often such a high degree of "wastage" in the process of pedagogy that, at times, "the quantity of information transmitted tends to zero."[47] Viewed in these terms, pedagogy is always governed by an "epistemological problem" and even the most basic schoolroom activity is designed to ask the student, on behalf of the teacher, "How do I know you understand?"[48] Classroom activities are therefore

[47] Pierre Bourdieu and Jean Claude Passeron, *Reproduction in Education, Society and Culture* (London: Sage in association with Theory, Culture & Society, Dept. of Administrative and Social Studies, Teesside Polytechnic, 1990), 107–8. See also Stanley Aronowitz and Henry A. Giroux, *Postmodern Education: Politics, Culture and Social Criticism* (Minneapolis, MN: University of Minnesota Press, 1991), 8–9. For another version of this model see Guillory, *Cultural Capital*, 38.
[48] Dolven, *Scenes of Instruction in Renaissance Romance*, 15 ("How") and 18 ("epistemological").

sometimes best understood as a means for satisfying a teacher's anxieties, designed, above all, to "produce representations" that provide "signs" that the student has learned something.[49] Particularly when it is absorbed to literature, such a procedure may consist of a series of "misrecognitions," the failures of knowing that constitute the processes we still insist on describing as "understanding."[50] Where such difficulties are assumed to be the norm, scholarship's method must be to trace the homologies between those misrecognitions and similar scenes of instruction in literature, as Jeff Dolven has done so well for the Renaissance, or to characterize what appear to be the poet's "resistance" to what he was taught, as Lynn Enterline has done with particular care in the case of Shakespeare.[51]

The claim of the chapters that follow, however, is that there is a remarkably straight line from the schoolbooks that survive from fourteenth-century English schoolrooms, through the agile understandings of Chaucer, Gower, and Langland, to the techniques that made the literature these three writers produced distinctive. If grammatical tools are designed, as Vivien Law observed, "for a specific cultural context," then my assumption here is that we may read that context straight out of those tools.[52] What is discovered in the reconstruction is not any hidden sophistication or overlooked literary training but, rather, a set of simple forms and activities that were shrewdly repurposed *as* sophistication. In the century-long moment after 1300 the acquisition of the basic skills of literacy was strenuous for the English poet not only because beating was such an important component of pedagogy, but because he always had to move every element of his grammatical knowledge from one language into another. This friction alone—what we would now rightly call "stress"—meant that those movements left particularly visible traces, preserving the elements of a certain sort of teaching, by dint of repetition and elaboration, as a particular kind of English literature.

---

[49] Dolven, *Scenes of Instruction*, 27. These may include (but are doubtless not limited to) repetition ("exercises where the student is asked to give back what he is given" [30]), catechism ("which provides particular questions as cues for particular answers" [32]), drills ("routines of declining and conjugating" [35]), analysis ("understand[ing] something simply by breaking it apart" [38]), epitome ("deriving from a text a shorter formulation" [40]), translation ("providing word by word equivalents" [42]), composition ("synthesis of . . . training in grammar, logic and rhetoric" [45]), and disputation ("where understanding equals winning" [49]).

[50] Dolven, *Scenes of Instruction*, 27.

[51] Enterline, *Shakespeare's Schoolroom*, 14.

[52] Law, *Grammar and Grammarians*, 55. For a survey of the various kinds of things that the study of grammars may teach us, see Law's second chapter ("The Historiography of Grammar in the Early Middle Ages," 4–27).

1

The Language of Learning

Histories of education have long assumed that French was the language used to teach children in England how to read and write until the middle of the fourteenth century. The assumption is both fair and obvious since contemporary accounts tell us that this was the case. The first of these is Ranulph Higden's (1280–1364) who describes the languages traditionally spoken on the island of Britain ("Concerning the Language of the Inhabitants" [De incolarum linguis]) in his *Polychronicon*.[1] According to Higden, "after the arrival of the Normans, children in schools were compelled to leave their own vernacular, and to construe in French, against the customs of other nations" [pueri in scholis contra morem caeterarum nationum a primo Normannorum adventu, derelicto proprio vulgari, construere Gallice compelluntur] (158). When John of Trevisa translated the *Polychronicon* in 1385–7 he confirms Higden's view ("gentil men children beeþ i-tauȝt to speke Frensche from þe tyme þat þey beeþ i-rokked in here cradel"), but he also extends it by observing that teaching practice in England changed drastically after "the first death" (usually understood to refer to the severe plague of 1348) as a result of the new methods of an Oxford grammar-school master:[2]

> Iohn Cornwaile, a maister of grammer, chaunged þe lore in gramer scole and construccioun of Frensche in to Englische; and Richard Pencriche lerned þe manere technynge of hym and oþere men of Pencrich; so þat now, þe ȝere of oure Lorde a þowsand þre hundred and foure score and fyue, and of þe secounde kyng Richard after þe conquest nyne, in alle þe gramere scoles of

---

[1] *Polychronicon Ranulphi Higden monachi Cestrensis*, vol. 2, ed. Churchill Babington, Rolls Series 41 (London: Kraus Reprint, 1964; first published 1869): 156–62. Citations hereafter are by page number in the text.

[2] On Trevisa and his translation see David C. Fowler, *The Life and Times of John Trevisa, Medieval Scholar* (Seattle, WA: University of Washington Press, 1995), esp. 119 and 177. For discussion of this passage the date of this change see Nicholas Orme, *Medieval Schools: From Roman Britain to Medieval England* (New Haven, CT: Yale University Press, 2006), 106 and Douglas A. Kibbee, *For To Speke Frenche Trewely: The French Language in England, 1000–1600: Its Status, Description and Instruction* (Amsterdam: John Benjamins, 1991), 55–6.

Engelond, children leueþ Frensche and construeþ and lerneþ an Englische.
(160–1)

[*lore*: teaching; *leueþ*: leave; *an Englische*: in English]

Historical account could hardly be more helpful, and there is also corrob-
orating material evidence. A variety of local records make clear that there
was a grammar master in Oxford by the name of John of Cornwall in the
first part of the fourteenth century, one of these records locates his school
very precisely to Catte Street, and surviving extracts from his will are dated
June 8, 1349.[3] We also have a treatise which concludes by calling itself the
Speculum grammaticale, declares that it was written by "John Brian of
Cornwall," and dates itself to 1346.[4] The treatise draws on speculative
grammar for what R. W. Hunt characterized as its "armory of arguments"
(it begins, for example, with a discussion of the relationship between the
syntactic order of words and the structure of understanding), and it represents itself as a commentary rather than a grammar per se (its colophon
declares that it is a "tractatus super donatum" or a commentary on Donatus,
presumably referring to his basic grammar, the *Ars minor*).[5] But the treatise
also unfolds as a very basic account of the parts of speech and their
construction in Latin.[6] When the treatise arrives at the conjugation of
verbs it also illustrates exactly the sort of teaching Trevisa attributed to
John of Cornwall, offering its examples in English as well as Latin:

---

[3] For a summary of these records see Cynthia Renée Bland, *The Teaching of Grammar in
Late Medieval England: An Edition, with Commentary, of Oxford, Lincoln College MS Lat.
130* (East Lansing, MI: Colleagues Press, 1991), 89–91 and Cynthia Renée Bland, "John of
Cornwall's Innovations and Their Possible Effects on Chaucer," 213–35 in *The Uses of
Manuscripts in Literary Studies: Essays in Memory of Judson Boyce Allen*, ed. Charlotte Cook
Morse, Penelope Reed Doob, and Marjorie Curry Woods (Kalamazoo, MI: Medieval
Institute Publications, 1992), 213–14.

[4] "Et sic finitur tractatus super donatum de congruetatibus gramatice qui intitulatur
speculum grammaticale editus a magistro Johanne Brian dicto de Cornubia: Anno domini
MoCCCoXLovjo et cetera quod J. B.," Oxford, Bodleian Library, MS Auctarium F.3.9,
p. 180. This manuscript is in two columns, but paginated rather than foliated throughout;
hereafter I will cite it by these page numbers in my text and notes.

[5] "Ad primum dico quod constructio siue oratio constructa est congrua dictionum
ordinacio congruum intellectum in animo auditoris faciens" [an appropriate ordering of
words creating an appropriate understanding in the mind of the hearer], MS Auctarium
F.3.9, p. 1. For the colophon see note 4. See also R. W. Hunt, "Oxford Grammar Masters
in the Middle Ages," 167–97 in his *The History of Grammar in the Middle Ages: Collected
Papers*, ed. G. L. Burshill-Hall (Amsterdam: John Benjamins, 1980), 182.

[6] The main sections in the first pages of the treatise treat the most basic aspects of Latin
morphology and syntax: "constructio" (p. 1), "locutio transitiva et intransitiva" (p. 2), "quot
accidentium conformitas requirit—inter nomina et verba" (p. 4), "a quo vel ex qua vi
regitur nominis casus" (p. 5), "De declinatione" (p. 6), "De nominibus que dicuntur dubii
generis" (p. 8), "coniugaciones verborum" (p. 10).

Item querendum est quot sunt persone in verbo, dicendum quod tres sunt: prima seconda et tertia. Vnde prima persona est que significat rem de se loquentem ut lego *y rede*, legimus *we rede*, legis *þu redis*, legitis *ȝe redin* vel *ȝe redith*, iste legit *þis redith*, isti legunt *þei redyn*. (Oxford, Bodleian Library, MS Auctarium F.3.9, p. 9)

[Likewise, if it should be asked how many persons in the verb there are, it ought to be said that there are three: first, second, and third, whereof the first person refers to someone speaking about itself as *lego* "y rede," *legimus* "we rede," *legis* "þu redis," *legitis* "ȝe redin" or "ȝe redith," *iste legit* "þis redith" (this one reads), *isti legunt* "þei redyn."]

At the conclusion of these explanations (and this page of the manuscript also gives English examples for the conjugations of "amo" and "doceo"), this treatise also insists that this is the "method" [modus] that "ought to be used for teaching boys all the conjugations" [Iste est modus informandi pueros per omnes conjugationes] (p. 9).

Not everyone has been convinced by this evidence and these accounts, however, not least because it seems unlikely that they could attest to practice in "all the gramere schools of England."[7] To be sure, a certain amount of other evidence substantiates Higden's and Trevisa's insistence on the wide-spread use of French. There are, for example, many French glosses in books that contain the most basic Latin teaching texts. The most copious of these survive in three thirteenth-century manuscripts containing two popular versified grammars Alexander of Villa-Dei's *Doctrinale* (*c*.1200) and Evrard of Béthune's *Graecismus* (*c*.1212).[8] There are also French glosses in seven different surviving volumes containing the Latin texts commonly used in basic literacy training, usually described as the *libri Catoniani*.[9] There is

---

[7] For dissent see Ardis Butterfield, *The Familiar Enemy: Chaucer, Language and Nation in the Hundred Years War* (Oxford: Oxford University Press, 2009), 325; Tim William Machan, *English in the Middle Ages* (Oxford: Oxford University Press, 2003), 84; Andrew Galloway, "Latin England," 41–95 in *Imagining a Medieval English Nation*, ed. Kathy Lavezzo (Minneapolis, MN: University of Minnesota Press, 2004), 47.

[8] The manuscripts are London, British Library, MS Arundel 394 (*c*.1200–50), Durham, Cathedral Chapter Library, MS C.VI.26 (*c*.1250–1300), and Dublin, Trinity College, MS 270 (about twelfth/fourteenth century). There are also substantial glosses in the copy of the *Doctrinale* in Cambridge, University Library, MS Oo.6.110 (*c*.1250–1300). For these manuscripts, their glossing, and these dates see Tony Hunt, *Teaching and Learning Latin in Thirteenth Century England*, 3 vols. (Cambridge: D. S. Brewer, 1991), 1: 83–98. For transcriptions of the glosses see these volumes, 2: 15–34. On these two texts as basic grammars see John M. Miner, *The Grammar Schools of Medieval England: A. F. Leach in Historiographical Perspective* (Montreal and Kingston: McGill-Queen's University Press, 1990), 225. See also Chapter 3 in the present volume, pp. 94–6.

[9] On the *libri Catoniani* see, especially, Chapter 2 in this volume, pp. 40–4 and 63–4. Hunt transcribes the glosses for Lincoln, Cathedral Chapter Library, MS 132 (*c*.1250–1300), London, British Library, MS Additional 16380 (*c*.1250–1300), Cambridge, Peterhouse College, MS 207 (thirteenth and fourteenth centuries) and MS 215 (*c*.1250–1300), London,

even more copious French glossing in what are sometimes called *nominalia* or "wordbooks": of the thirteen surviving copies of Adam of Petit Pont's *De Utensilibus*, a treatise that "deals with common objects of everyday life as well as warning against love of material objects," for example, five thirteenth-century manuscripts are heavily glossed.[10] Of the thirty manuscripts that survive of Alexander Neckam's *De nominibus utensilium*, designed, as the *accessus* that commonly accompanies it indicates, to teach the names of kitchen tools ("de utensilibus que pertinent ad coquinam"), five thirteenth-century manuscripts are heavily glossed.[11] And, of the thirty manuscripts of John of Garland's *Dictionarius*, four thirteenth-century manuscripts are heavily glossed.[12] But the very copiousness of these French glosses disguise their concentration, and it is also true that the most heavily glossed copies of all these *nominalia* are to be found in the same three books (Cambridge, Gonville & Caius College, MS 136, Dublin, Trinity College, MS 270, and Lincoln Cathedral, Chapter Library, MS 132).[13] Although the glosses in the grammars and workbooks are extensive at times, the glosses on many of the reading texts are meager. On the sixteen sides of the, roughly, 300 hexameter lines of the *Distichs of Cato* in Lincoln MS 132, for example, there are only five glossed words ("*semotum*: aloiniez, *discere*: aprendre, *loquatur*: parler, *demissos*: abessez, *vita*: achuez").[14]

If Latin was widely taught in French in England until 1340, and then in English, as John of Trevisa suggests, there are also two very odd silences in the record. First, there is not a single surviving Latin grammar *in French* in any of the surviving schoolbooks from the eleventh, twelfth, thirteenth, or even fourteenth centuries—that is, in any part of the period in which French could be described as a vernacular in England. There is, in other words, nothing in French to compare with the abundance of ad hoc grammatical treatises in Latin that can be found in the schoolbooks

British Library, MS Harley 4967 (*c*.1200–50), and Oxford, Bodleian Library, MS Auctarium F.5.6 (late thirteenth century) in *Teaching and Learning Latin*, 2: 3–12. All but MS Additional 16380 are discussed in Hunt 1: 74–9. Hunt also transcribes glosses on the basic schoolroom texts in London, British Library, Royal 15 A XXXI (*c*.1250–1300) at 2: 74.

[10] Hunt, *Teaching and Learning*, 1: 165. For a discussion of these manuscripts and the manner of their glossing see 1: 166–76. For the glosses see 2: 37–62.

[11] Hunt, *Teaching and Learning Latin*, 1: 178 (for the *accessus*). For these glosses see 2: 65–108.

[12] For the number of manuscripts of John of Garland's *Dictionarius*, see G. L. Bursill-Hall, "Johannes de Garlandia—Forgotten Grammarian and the Manuscript Tradition," *Historiographia Linguistica* 3 (1976): 162–3. For the glosses, see Hunt, *Teaching and Learning Latin*, 2: 125–53.

[13] For this overlap see Hunt, *Teaching and Learning Latin*, 1: 166, 178, and 192.

[14] Hunt, *Teaching and Learning Latin*, 2: 3.

surviving in England from these centuries. If any quantity of such French texts ever existed, nothing is now left but the "grammatical notes . . . and explanations in French" in Cambridge, Trinity College, MS R.3.56.[15] Second, while there are many English treatises for the teaching of Latin from the second decade of the fifteenth century onward, no *English* texts for the teaching of Latin survive from before 1400.[16] If French was taught in English prior to 1340, where are the texts used in that teaching? If John of Cornwall "chaunged þe lore in gramer scole" in 1346, substituting English for French in his grammatical teaching, where are the texts other than the *Speculum grammaticale* itself that would have enabled or reflected this change? This is probably the appropriate place to note too that, while the explicit at the end of the unique copy of John of Cornwall's *Speculum grammaticale* in MS Auctarium F.3.9 says that this text was completed in 1346, this unique copy of the text was copied over 100 years later, sometime in the middle of the fifteenth century.

Historians of education have probably been wrong, then, to believe John of Trevisa's account of the language of schoolroom learning in his day and earlier in the fourteenth century. But how could Trevisa have made such a monumental error? Like John Brian of Cornwall, Trevisa was an Oxford man as well as Cornish, and, while these commonalities might not in themselves produce a distorting bias they suggest that Trevisa may have moved in circles sufficiently close to John Brian's for him to over-estimate the influence and significance of John's writings or his grammar-school teaching.[17] A statute surviving from the latter part of the fourteenth century suggests that Trevisa was right about the importance of French to the teaching in Oxford grammar schools, for it enjoins grammar masters to have their students "construe" in either English or French.[18] French is to be used, the statute specifies, "lest the French language completely die out" [ne illa lingua Gallica penitus sit omissa]. The anxiety also corroborates Trevisa's claim that French was on the wane in Oxford grammar schools

[15] M. R. James, *The Western Manuscripts in the Library of Trinity College, Cambridge: A Descriptive Catalogue*, 4 vols. (Cambridge: Cambridge University Press, 1900–4), 2: 123–5. For the ad hoc treatises in Latin see the present volume, Chapter 2, pp. 67–9.

[16] David Thomson collects and prints all of the Middle English grammatical texts in *An Edition of the Middle English Grammatical Texts* (New York, NY: Garland, 1984), where he also discusses their emergence (p. xii). A more thorough discussion of manuscripts and probable dates is given in David Thomson, *A Descriptive Catalogue of Middle English Grammatical Texts* (New York, NY: Garland, 1979), 4–22.

[17] On Trevisa's relationship to Cornwall see Fowler, *Life and Times*, 3.

[18] *Statuta Antiqua Universitatis Oxoniensis*, ed. Strickland Gibson (Oxford: Clarendon Press, 1931). 171. On the statute see William Henry Stevenson, "The Introduction of English as the Vehicle of Instruction in English Schools," 421–9 in *An English Miscellany Presented to F. J. Furnivall*, ed. William P. Ker, Arthur S. Napier, and Walter W. Skeat (Oxford: Clarendon Press, 1901), 421 n. 1 and Kibbee, *For to Speke Frenche Trewely*, 56–7.

by this point; on the other hand, if John of Cornwall really had brought about the shift to English that Trevisa credits him with, why was it necessary for this statute to enjoin grammar masters to use English as well? What seems most probable is that Trevisa's general view was affected by the linguistic politics operating in his narrow circle. The contours of those politics are already visible in the way Higden bridles against what came to be called the Norman Yoke, and they clearly persisted for Trevisa, who also cites "a comyn prouerbe" which holds that "Jack wold be a gentilman if he coude speke frensshe" and therefore "uplondyssh [rustic] men will counterfete and likene hem self to gentilmen and arn [are] besy to speake frensshe, for to be more sette by [esteemed]" (159). Such an attitude makes any claim that French had been expunged from elementary education in England triumphalist. It parlays a general Francophobia into the image of schoolboys freed from the grip of social pressures to emulate the Francophone aristocrats who were literate in what would also come to be called the "native tongue."

In order to uncover the practices that such convictions caused Trevisa to overlook, we must bracket off these politics and look much more carefully at the schoolroom. As Ardis Butterfield has noted, these determinations are still hard to make objectively because a disciplinary politics has replaced fourteenth-century pressures pitting literary scholars against linguists in making the crucial estimations.[19] The view that French was a "true vernacular" in England was not only foundational in the field that became Anglo-Norman studies, but also has great currency in recent literary scholarship.[20] Linguists, on the other hand, have long been convinced that, even in the thirteenth century (and therefore no later) the "role of French...was not at all that of a vernacular."[21] If numbers

---

[19] "It remains difficult, nonetheless, to assess the evidence, and this is partly because methodological approaches are caught between history, linguistics, and literature, as well as between Anglo-American and continental perspectives; Anglo-French and French philological approaches; English, Anglo-French, and French literary partialities," Butterfield, *Familiar Enemy*, 56.

[20] Helen Sugget, "The Use of French in England in the Later Middle Ages," *Transactions of the Royal Historical Society* 28 (1946): 79. In Johan Vising's foundational view there was a "complete dominance of the Anglo-Norman language during the second half of the twelfth and most of the thirteenth century" as well as a "penetration even into the lower strata of society" (*Anglo-Norman Language and Literature* [London: Oxford University Press, 1923], 18). For the recent view that "English vernacularity" in some way "includ[ed] French" and we must therefore regard French as "England's other vernacular" see Butterfield, *Familiar Enemy*, 317.

[21] William Rothwell, "The Role of French in Thirteenth-Century England," *Bulletin of the John Rylands University Library of Manchester* 58 (1976): 455. See also Sarah Grey Thomason and Terence Kaufman, *Language Contact, Creolization, and Genetic Linguistics* (Berkeley, CA: University of California Press, 1988), 308 and Ian Short, "On Bilingualism in Anglo-Norman England," *Romance Philology* 33 (1980): 478.

matter, then the salient fact is that French was always "the language of a minority" in medieval England, and French was therefore always "hier-archizing."[22] But both extremes can be accounted for by a third view which notes that those who spoke and wrote French were "numerically small" but, because of their social position and the quantity or writing they produced, also hugely "significant... culturally."[23]

Even more distracting than his claims about French and English in the end may be Trevisa's general assumption that Latin must be learned with help from *some* vernacular. Certainly medieval grammars suggest that the language a schoolboy knew when he first entered the classroom played some role in how he was taught to read and write. The proem to Alexander of Villa-Dei's *Doctrinale* advises the grammar master to use the school-boy's first language in teaching Latin whenever the subject matter was particularly difficult:

> Si pueri primo nequeant attendere plene
> Hic tamen attendet, qui doctoris vice fungens,
> Atque legens pueris laica lingua reserabit;
> Et pueris etiam pars maxima plana patebit.

> [If, at first, the boys are unable to pay attention fully, he should, nevertheless, pay attention, who, fulfilling the role of teacher and reading to the boys, will expound (it) to them in lay language, and the greatest part of it will then be clear to the boys.][24]

Although Alexander uses the phrase "lay language" [lingua laica] to refer to what the schoolboy already knows, this is not to make the common medieval distinction between the secular and the priestly—"laicus" as against "clericus"—but, rather, to point more broadly to the language that preceded literacy.[25] It is equivalent, in this case, to what Thomas

[22] Rolf Berndt, "French and English in Thirteenth-Century England: An Investigation into the Linguistic Situation after the Loss of the Duchy of Normandy and Other continental Dominions," *Sitzungsberichte der Akademie der Wissenschaften der DDR, Gesellschaftswissenschaften* 1G: 371 ("language"); Susan Crane, "Social Aspects of Bilingualism in the Thirteenth Century," 103–15 in *Thirteenth Century England*, VI, ed. Michael Prestwich (Woodbridge: Boydell & Brewer, 1997), 104–5 ("hierarchizing").
[23] Jocelyn Wogan-Browne, *Saints' Lives and Women's Literary Culture c.1150–c.1300* (Oxford: Oxford University Press, 2001), 151. On this demographic scaling and the claim that French competence was simply too limited to play the large role in literate practice sometimes claimed for it see my "Class Distinction and the French of England," 48–59 in *A Modern Medievalist: Traditions and Innovations in the Study of Medieval Literature*, ed. Charlotte Brewer and Barry Windeatt (Woodbridge: Boydell & Brewer, 2012).
[24] Alexander of Villa-Dei, *Doctrinale*, ed. Theodore Reichling (Berlin: A. Hofmann, 1893), proemium, 7–10.
[25] On the "antithesis *clericus: laicus*" see M. T. Clanchy, *From Memory to Written Record: England, 1066–1307* (Cambridge, MA: Harvard University Press, 1979), 177–81.

Usk would be the first to refer to in English as his "dames tongue," what we now quite commonly call a "mother tongue," "first" or "birth language."[26] But if it seems unlikely that French or English were used in the fourteenth-century schoolroom then what "lay language" did the grammar master use for clarification? The evidence I have so far provided suggest that Alexander of Villa-Dei was not describing a widespread practice either, and historians of education have, for a long time, been asking exactly the wrong question: it is not *which* language was used in the classroom to teach Latin but *whether*—despite the contemporaneous views to the contrary—the vernacular was used in basic literacy training at all.

"SAYING EVERYTHING IN LATIN"

Much about classroom practice is revealed in the schoolroom grammars that survive, but the grammars that reveal most about the language in which Latin was taught are, interestingly enough, the very grammars cropping up in this period for the teaching of French. The oldest of these dates from the very beginning of the thirteenth century and, while it is only thirty-four lines long, that is long enough to tell us a great deal, since these lines are in neither English nor French, but in Latin:

> Preteritum perfectum modi indicativi verb activi duobus modis construitur, verbi gracia, amavi: *jo amai* et *jo ai amé*.
>
> [The preterit perfect of the indicative mode of the verb is construed in two ways, for example, I loved: *jo amai*, (I loved) and *jo ai amé* (I loved).][27]

As a text that uses "known Latin verb forms to teach French verbal morphology" it also makes clear that Latin literacy could precede even the need to know French.[28] There is also a thirteenth-century volume of vocabularies in Glasgow, University Library, MS U.6.10 which gives the "French equivalent" for "groups of words in Latin, parts of the house, parts of the body, tools and utensils, names of animals and birds," and, while also clearly intended for someone who wanted to learn French, the

[26] See Thomas Usk, *The Testament of Love*, ed. R. A. Shoaf (Kalamazoo, MI: Medieval Institute Publications, 1998), Pro. 27. See also *OED*, s.v. "mother tongue, n. and adj."
[27] Östen Södergård, "Le plus ancien traité grammatical français," *Studia neophilologica* 27 (1955): 193.
[28] William Rothwell, "The Teaching and Learning of French in Later Medieval England," *Zeitschrift für französische Sprache und Literatur* 111 (2001): 2. Rothwell criticizes Kibbee for suggesting that the treatise "describes the different French translations possible for each Latin tense," but he thereby locates it even more firmly in schoolroom practice, as a set of "school translation exercises." For Kibbee's views see *For To Speke Frenche Trewely*, 26.

"starting-point" here too is Latin.[29] In about 1300 we find another work
that uses Latin to teach French, usually described in manuscripts as the
Tractatus orthographiae and said to have been the work of "T. H. Parisii
Studentis."[30] This treatise is also short, but it works its way through the
alphabet explaining how the various letters ought to be sounded and
written:

> Et sciendum est quod *a* aliquando debet sonari fere sicut *e* litteram, verbi
> gracia: *Sauez vous faire un chauncoun. Sauez vous traire del ark. Sauez vous
> raire la barbe*, et sic de similibus.

> [And it ought to be understood that *a* at times ought to be sounded almost as
> if it were the letter *e*, for example: *Sauez vous faire un chauncoun* (Do you
> know how to compose a song), *Sauez vous traire del ark* (Do you know how
> to draw a bow), *Sauez vous raire la barbe* (Do you know how to shave a
> beard), and thus in similar cases.][31]

There is also a fourth text, usually described as the *Orthographia gallica*,
which survives in manuscripts from the thirteenth to the early fifteenth
centuries and also presents its rules (with the exception of one fourteenth-
century manuscript) "entirely in Latin."[32] As we move later in the fourteenth
century, the presumption of Latin competence in such a wide range of
teaching is finally made explicit: a guide to Latin verb forms in Cambridge,
University Library, MS Ee.4.20 says outright that it is providing "conjugations...in French with their explanations in Latin" [coniugaciones...in
Gallicis cum expositione earumdem in Latinis].[33] All of these treatises led
Douglas Kibbee to ask the obvious question: "if Latin w[as] used to teach
French, then what language was used to teach Latin?"[34] When looking at all
these treatises together the answer to that question seems equally obvious:
Latin is the only language a reader of these basic, grammatical texts is ever
assumed to know.

It is not entirely right, then, that "Latin was a completely foreign
language...for students in England," since there is not only evidence

[29] Rothwell, "Role of French in Thirteenth-Century England," 460. For an edition of
this text and discussion of the manuscript in which it survives see A. Ewert, "The Glasgow
Latin–French Glossary," *Medium Aevum* 25 (1956): 154–63.
[30] For this text see Mildred Pope, "The Tractatus Orthographie of T. H. Parisii
Studentis," *Modern Language Review* 5 (1910): 185–92. For other discussion of this text
see Kibbee, *For To Speke Frenche Trewely*, 47–8.
[31] Pope, "Tractatus Orthographie," 189.
[32] Kibbee, *For to Speke Frenche Trewely*, 52. For a description of this text see Kibbee,
pp. 47–52. For the text itself see *Orthographia gallica*, ed. R. C. Johnston (London: Anglo-
Norman Text Society, 1987).
[33] For the text see Hunt, *Teaching and Learning Latin*, 1: 114–16. See 1: 99–100 for the
text's history. On this text see also Rothwell, "Teaching and Learning of French," 11.
[34] Kibbee, *For to Speke Frenche Trewely*, 56.

that Latin competence was immediately assumed in the schoolroom, but, also, that Latin was regularly *spoken* there.[35] Although the record comes from the century after the one that concerns me most, it is still revealing that statutes for the choristers of Wells Cathedral from 1459 insist that if "at dinner or supper time, they shall want something on the table they shall ask for anything they want in Latin, not in English."[36] The same presumption governs an account from Southwell Minster grammar school in 1484 that notes with disapproval that its pupils "do not speak Latin in school but English" [non locuntur latinum in scola sed anglicum].[37] In a collection of "passages for translation into Latin," also from the fifteenth century, a schoolboy was taught to say that "wis men saye that nothyng may be more profitable to them that lurns grammer than to speke latyn."[38] Another fifteenth-century schoolbook, London, British Library, Additional MS 37075, contains a selection of Latin exercises (paired versions of the same idea, "the second of which improves on the first and is probably the master's version") which includes the following observation:[39]

Si puerorum mentes tantam proprie reperirent moles[tiam] in Anglicana loquela quantam habent dummodo oppo[sitio] magistralis illos detinet in difficilibus, nulla foret occa[sio] praepediendi quin omnes sermones profer- endi haberentur in latinis.

[If boyish minds found just as much trouble in the English language as they have when the master's questioning entangles them in difficulties, there would be no reason to prevent them from saying everything in Latin.] (fol. 195r)[40]

[35] Martin Camargo and Marjorie Curry Woods, "Writing Instruction in Late Medieval Europe," 114–47 in *A Short History of Writing Instruction: From Ancient Greece to Contemporary America*, ed. James J. Murphy, 3rd edn. (New York, NY: Routledge, 2012), 118.
[36] *Dean Cosyn and Wells Cathedral Miscellanea*, ed. Aelred Watkin, Somerset Record Society 56 (1941), 106. Watkin does not provide the Latin for this phrase. Cited in Orme, *Medieval Schools*, 148 and Jo Ann Hoeppner Moran, *The Growth of English Schooling, 1340–1548* (Princeton, NJ: Princeton University Press, 1985), 36.
[37] *Visitations and Memorials of Southwell Minster*, ed. A. F. Leach, Camden Society, n.s., no. 48 (London, 1891): 49. Cited in Moran, *Growth of English Schooling*, 36.
[38] *A Fifteenth-Century School Book: from a Manuscript in the British Museum (MS Arundel 249)*, ed. William Nelson (Oxford: Clarendon Press, 1956), 22. Nicholas Orme prints the shorter passages from this schoolbook that Nelson excludes in *English School Exercises, 1420–1530* (Toronto: Pontifical Institute of Mediaeval Studies, 2013), 346–59. The manuscript is described in Thomson, *Descriptive Catalogue*, 233–8.
[39] Thomson, *Descriptive Catalogue*, 226.
[40] See Miner, *Grammar Schools of Medieval England*, 160 (for translation) and 281 (for text). I have emended Minder's readings after consultation with the manuscript and the transcription and translation Orme provides in *English School Exercises* (197), adapting my own translation accordingly.

Although this is a counterfactual which takes as its premise that English was much easier than Latin for schoolboys and therefore that every word in the classroom ("omnes sermones") was *not* "in Latin" [in latinis], this point is made in Latin nonetheless and it is also clear that "saying everything in Latin" was this teacher's goal. Jacques Rancière has written powerfully about Joseph Jacotot, who, when exiled from France to Louvain in 1815, successfully taught French to Flemish-speaking students when there "was no language in which he could teach them," since he himself knew no Flemish.[41] Rancière and Jacotot understand this as emancipatory, what they called "universal teaching" (demonstrating that "all men have equal intelligence"), but it is also a universal teaching because it is so common.[42] Even though spoken Latin has had no practical use for most students in the West for a very long time, classrooms still sometimes immerse a student in the language from the very beginning of his or her training. There was, for example, a very influential program of what was called "Direct Method" teaching at the Perse School in Cambridge in which all the teacher's questions were posed in Latin and students were forbidden to speak English during lessons.[43] Since 1955 in Europe, and in a variety of settings in the United States today, a method called "Active Latin" emphasizes oral proficiency while also using Latin as the language of instruction.[44]

The glosses on school texts I have already mentioned also provide clear evidence that immersion was a common method for grammar schools in thirteenth- and fourteenth-century England. These words and phrases have almost always been understood as attempts to use a more familiar language "to help . . . pupils construe the Latin of their textbooks," and, as I have already noted, the bulk of this glossing is in French.[45] But it is not at all clear what sorts of students such glossing was actually meant to help, since it is not only in French, but in English and sometimes in French and English simultaneously, and, in a large number of cases the French or English of these glosses is identified *as* French or English as if the student they were designed for would not himself have recognized this fact. Here, for example, are the glosses provided for a representative passage from

---

[41] Jacques Rancière, *The Ignorant Schoolmaster: Five Lesson in the Intellectual Emancipation*, trans. Kristin Ross (Stanford, CA: Stanford University Press, 1991; French text first published 1987), 1.

[42] Rancière, *The Ignorant Schoolmaster*, 18.

[43] Christopher Stray, "Success and Failure: W. H. D. Rouse and Direct-Method Classics Teaching in Edwardian England," *The Journal of Classics Teaching* 22 (2011): 5–7.

[44] Neil Coffee, "Active Latin: Quo Tendimus," *Classical World* 105 (2012): 255–69.

[45] Hunt, *Teaching and Learning Latin*, 1: vii.

Alexander Neckam's *De Nominibus Utensilium* in Cambridge, Gonville &
Caius College, MS 136 (mid-thirteenth century):

> *disponere*: ordiner [arrange]/ *in supellectilibus*: granz uteylem[en]s [large
> furniture]/ *uncus*: croc [hook]/ cacabus: *caudroun* [cooking pot]/ *exenterari*:
> eystreir [to disembowel]/ *fuscina*: anglice algere [in English, trident]/ *hamite*:
> hamet [fishing pole]/ *nassa*: gallice bewet [in French, basket], anglice bellep
> [in English, basket][46]

Where these glosses are said to be "in French" (gallice), as in the penultimate term above, or "in English," as in the last gloss, the *gloss* is
effectively glossed. Moreover, as in the glosses on a copy of Alexander of
Villa-Dei's *Doctrinale* in Durham Cathedral Chapter Library, MS C.
VI.26 (mid-thirteenth century), by far the most common of these secondary glosses identify the term or terms they accompany as "in French":

> *verubus*: gallice spitis [in French, spit]/ *carbasus*: gallice sigle [in French,
> canvas]/ *arbutus*: gallice cireneres, anglice sirne-tre [in French, briar; in
> English, briar]/ *porrum*: gallice porré [in French, leek]/ *suparus*: gallice rochet
> [in French, smock]/ *colus*: conil, anglice roke [distaff, in English distaff]/
> *lupinus*: gallice vesce [in French, lupine]/ *appello*: gallice ariver [in French, to
> land]/ *exta* gallice bueus [in French, entrails]/ *nuptias*: gallice esposalies [in
> French, marriage]/ *sospes*: gallice estu [in French, preserver][47]

As his title very firmly insists, Hunt understood all of the glosses in his
monumental edition to be instruments in the "teaching and learning of
Latin," designed "to explicate Latin texts to students whose mother tongue
was French or English."[48] But, in the particular cases of "glossaries and
glossed vocabularies," Hunt follows Rothwell and suggests that some of
the French glosses may have been "intended for the clerkly class who
would learn French as a second language after Latin."[49] The example
I have just given from the *Doctrinale* makes clear that any of these French
glosses could have been used for this purpose. The student using these
books is not told in some general rubric that these glosses are "in French,"
moreover, but told so again and again, as if even having learned that this
is a Latin text with French glosses, he needs to be reminded of this fact
word by word.

The terms used to identify these glosses as "French" or "English" are not
French or English either but invariably in Latin (i.e. "gallice," "anglice").

---

[46] Hunt, *Teaching and Learning Latin*, 2: 65. On the manuscript see 1: 178.
[47] Hunt, *Teaching and Learning Latin*, 2: 15. On the manuscript see 1: 86.
[48] Hunt, *Teaching and Learning Latin*, 1: vii.
[49] Rothwell, "Role of French in Thirteenth-Century England," 460; Hunt, *Teaching
and Learning Latin*, 1: 13.

Were these glosses really designed to help Francophone schoolboys we would expect French and English words to be identified as "en françois" or "en anglais"; were they designed to help students who knew only English we would expect these terms to be identified as "in Frenche" and "in Englische." The linguistic competence these *glosses* assume is not French or English, then, but Latin.[50] That assumption is even clearer in a few longer glosses in another thirteenth-century copy of the *Doctrinale*, Cambridge, University Library, MS Oo.6.110. Although most of these glosses are in French and accordingly, marked "gallice," the word "vagio" is not only glossed in French ("waynter gallice" [to sheathe, in French]) but defined in Latin ("flere vel in vagina apponere" [to weep or to place in a scabbard]).[51] The term "iapix" is also defined at some length in Latin ("ventus qui dicitur nothus" [the wind which is called Nothus]), as are a whole variety of other Latin terms:

> *edilis*: est maior ville: gallice mere [is the mayor of a town: in French, mayor] / ... *ambesus*, ab an, quod est circum et esus, -sa, -sum: gallice mangé [from "an," which is "around" and "eaten": in French, eaten] *stiga*, stigo, -gas. i: lacessito, -tas gallice entarier [provoke: in French, challenge]/ ... *obex*: . i. obstaculum [obstacle] stake anglice [stake, in English] vel repagulum [or bolt], barre [bar]/ ... *amasum*: (corr. omasum) parvus mons vel amasum [small hill or tripe] tripe de berbis [tripe of sheep]/ ... *acumen*: est granum uve quod ponitur in vino, quod dicitur "raspe," vel granum quod remanet in uva vini, hoc *acumeni*: gallice drasche [is the grape-seed which is put in wine, which is called "raspe," or the seed which remains in the grape of wine, this *acumen*: in French "residue"].[52]

If it can be said that the glosses Hunt collects in the manuscripts he studies are "consistently in French" it can also be said that the apparatus of those glosses is consistently in Latin. Even if they are vastly outnumbered by the French terms they explain, or whose language they identify, the Latin words and phrases in these glosses alter the function of every one of those French terms, teaching the French competence they do not assume by means of the Latin competence they do.

[50] The primacy of Latin is proved even more emphatically by the way glossators sometimes confuse English and French and vice versa (e.g. "*orphanus* gallice *stepchil*" or "*exploratores* anglice *espiurs*"), as if Latin is the one language they know well. For this point see Ian Short, "*Tam Angli Quam Franci*: Self-Definition in Anglo-Norman England," 153–75 in *Anglo-Norman Studies* 18, Proceedings of the Battle Conference 1995, ed. Christopher Harper-Bill (Woodbridge: Boydell & Brewer, 1996), 158. Short finds similar examples in Tony Hunt, "The Vernacular Entries in the 'Glossae Sidionium' (MS Oxford Digby 172," *Zeitschrift für französische Sprache und Literatur* 89 (1979): 130–50 (see pp. 131–3).

[51] Hunt, *Teaching and Learning Latin*, 2: 21.

[52] Hunt, *Teaching and Learning Latin*, 2: 21–3.

These facts make it possible to notice another form of evidence for school-room practice so obvious and so general that it is almost never understood to be evidence at all: every one of the standard grammars that a grammar-school teacher would have had to hand to teach the most basic skills of literacy—from Donatus's *Ars minor* to the *Doctrinale*—are entirely in Latin too. In addition, the host of ad hoc grammars that survive in fourteenth-century English schoolbooks, the wordbooks or early "dictionaries" that accompany them, and every single one of the basic reading texts, in all their own complex repetition and variety, are also exclusively in Latin. The only language a grammar-school teacher *could* have used, in other words, was Latin because that was the only language used in the teaching tools he had to work with.

"FIANT LATINA!"

The strongest support for the claim that Latin was the language of learning in the thirteenth- and fourteenth-century English schoolroom can be found—again, paradoxically given the role it the text has routinely played in histories of education—in John of Cornwall's *Speculum grammaticale*. Although Trevisa's description of the text has stood in for its content for so long that those who have never read it could be forgiven for assuming that it is replete with English—and it has rarely been opened since it has never been transcribed or edited—it contains very little English, and however startling that English may be in each case, it plays a very minor role in John of Cornwall's pedagogy. As the passages I quoted at the beginning of the chapter may have already made clear, the *Speculum* never employs a purely English example, but, rather, glosses certain Latin forms with their English equivalent. There is even one passage in the *Speculum* that appears to contradict everything that is said about John of Cornwall and the change he made to grammar-school instruction since it glosses the various forms of the verb *venire* in French:

> Mei venientis, vel qui veni, et tui venientis, vel qui venisti, adventus sit bene veniens, vel qui venit. Gallice. *Moy venu, toy venu bensoyt le venu.*

> [Of me coming, or who have come, and of you coming or you who have come, let the one who has arrived (or who comes) be welcome! *In French: of me having come, of you having come, may the one having come be welcome!*] (MS Auctarium F.3.9, p. 141)[53]

---

[53] R. W. Hunt quotes this passage and says that "there seems to be no system" in the "extent to which English is used" in the *Speculum grammaticale*. He also says that this is the only instance of French in the text ("Oxford Grammar Masters," 180 and 180 n. 1).

This might be one of those few exceptions that actually proves a rule, however, because these French forms are identified as French in Latin ("gallice"), just as in the glosses I examined previously, as if Latin literacy were, again (or still), the only competence it was safe for the *Speculum grammaticale* to assume. But, for any reader whose first language was either English or French, what would matter most about the language of this text is that almost all of its Latin is *un*glossed Latin—and it is extremely long. Moreover, the whole of the single copy in which the *Speculum grammaticale* survives is heavily abbreviated, and can therefore only really be read in this form by someone who knows Latin very well. As in the case of the other ad hoc Latin grammars, such a reader was almost certainly a schoolmaster. But for that reason too the English and French glosses must be guides to pedagogy, examples of how to teach a particular point of Latin grammar, not direct aids for a student's learning. They provide a vivid impression of how the vernacular might have been employed in classrooms, but not as a starting point or gateway, nor as a means of deciphering what would otherwise be an unintelligible lesson, but as an occasional, illustrative supplement or enhancement, parallel to, but too infrequent to substitute for, the explanations that were themselves almost certainly in Latin.

In fact, most of the examples in the *Speculum grammaticale* are themselves in Latin, and they often take the form of the kind of sentences a student might employ, as if part of their purpose was to create a classroom in which teacher and student alike were saying everything in Latin. For example, when concluding a section describing what are presented as the three different forms of a comparison ("comparaciones gradus quot sunt tres" [there are three kinds of comparison]), the "positive," "comparative," and "superlative" ("positivis, comparativis, et superlativis") the student is offered a sequence of illustrative sentences that begin like this:

Sum doctus, tu es doctior sapiencie, frater meus est doctissimus sapiencie.

[I am learned, you are more learned in wisdom, my brother is the most learned in wisdom.]

Interest sororis mee digne, vel digni honoris vel honore amare quemdam hominem cuius frater reputatur dignissimus honoris, vel honore.

[It is important to my sister to love a man worthily, or of worthy honor, or with honor, whose brother is reputed to be most worthy of honor or in honor.]

Sum doccior sorore mea, margareta veteriore me, stante coram domino et domina mea, hominibus amandis a me suo filio.

[I am more learned than my sister Margaret, who is older than I, standing before my lord and lady, people who ought to be loved by me, their son.]
(MS Auctarium F.3.9, p. 70)

R. W. Hunt says that the use of such sentences "in a grammatical work in England" was "new" with John of Cornwall, although he also notes that there are similar illustrations in Thomas de Hanney's *Memoriale iuniorum* (*c*.1313) as well as one of the surviving ad hoc grammatical texts (in this case, an anonymous thirteenth-century treatise in Worcester, Cathedral Library, MS Q.50).[54] It is a little hard to see why Hunt singles out the *Speculum grammaticale* in this way, however, since Alexander of Villa-Dei's *Doctrinale* (*c*.1200) and Everard of Béthune's *Graecismus* (*c*.1212) are filled with illustrative, Latin sentences, many of them drawn from other schoolroom texts (the *Thebaid* in particular, and Theodulus) as well as Virgil and Ovid.[55] These works may not have been written in England but, as will become clear in the subsequent chapters, they were routinely used in medieval English schoolrooms. Hunt also confusingly calls the sentences in the *Speculum grammaticale* "Latins" or *latinitates*, since this term is used most commonly by historians of education to describe a Latin sentence that has been translated from an English prompt (just as "vulgars," or *vulgares*, are the English sentences translated from Latin prompts).[56] But John of Cornwall's Latin sentences clearly played no part in translation exercises because they are invariably introduced by the command, "Fiant Latina." The grammar of this phrase is not easy to parse, since "Latinum" is not a common Latin noun (and "Latina" cannot therefore be the direct object of the verb "fiant"), and the verb *fieri* normally means "become" or "happen." On the other hand, it is clear that the meaning of this common phrase would have been obvious in John of Cornwall's classroom. He often uses *fieri* as the equivalent of *esse* (so, for example, the phrase "Aliud exemplum fiat" means "Another example might be"), and "Latina" can be understood either as an adjective modifying the omitted, plural, neuter noun, "exempla," or as the plural of a new word, "latinum," coined in order to describe the unique sorts of "Latins" [latina] John of Cornwall used in his teaching.[57] The phrase is best translated,

---

[54] Hunt, "Oxford Grammar Masters," 179.

[55] For examples of such sentences and their sources in the *Doctrinale*, see Rita Copeland and Ineke Sluiter, *Medieval Grammar and Rhetoric: Language Arts and Literary Theory, AD 300–1475* (Oxford: Oxford University Press, 2009), 576–83. For a tabulation of its sources see Evrard of Béthune, *Graecismus*, ed. Johannes Wrobel (Hildesheim; G. Olm, 1987; first published 1887), 250–1.

[56] Hunt, "Oxford Grammar Masters," 179 and 179 n. 3. On *latinites* see Chapter 2 in the present volume, pp. 71–83.

[57] I take this example from MS Auctarium F.3.9, p. 23. The example is quoted in full in the present chapter, p. 39. I am grateful to Jill Mann, Michael Lapidge, and Traugott Lawler for their help in puzzling out this oddly ungrammatical phrase.

then, as "Let there be Latin [examples]" or, more simply, "Let there be Latin!"[58] Either way, the command that begins the phrase makes abundantly clear that such "Latins" were not meant to be translated but, rather, demanded still more Latin.

There are analogs for such active Latin use in other grammatical treatises surviving from medieval England, the closest of which is probably the anonymous work that survives in the fifteenth-century manuscript, London, British Library, MS Harley 1002.[59] John Miner thought that this grammar was of an "advanced nature" because it is "entirely in Latin" but, as should by now be clear, that criterion is meaningless since grammatical training at the elementary level also had to occur in Latin. This grammar teaches the most basic elements of Latin morphology and syntax, but it also parses exemplary sentences in Latin. For example, after a representative sentence like "Jesus Christus filius beate Marie iuvet et expediat Laurencium de Londoniis" [May Jesus Christ, son of the blessed Mary help and save Lawrence of London], it poses a set of questions about the sentence's form and syntax as well as the appropriate responses to those questions:[60]

Cuius casus beate Marie in latinitate premissa? Genitivi et regitur de ly filius ex vi possessoris vel possessionis. Quare? Quia omnis diccio significans possessorem vel possessionem potest regere genitivum causm ex vi possessoris vel possessionis, ut rex Anglie, equus regis.

[Of what case is *beate Marie* (blessed Mary) in the preceding Latin? In the genitive, and it is governed by *filius* (son) through the power of the possessor or of possession. Why? Because every word signifying a possessor or possession can govern the genitive case by the power of the possessor or possession, such as *rex Anglie* (king of England), *equus regis* (the horse of the king).]

---

[58] This is Nicholas Orme's assumption in *English School Exercises*, 10.

[59] Miner dates the manuscript to the "late fourteenth or early fifteenth century" (*Grammar Schools of Medieval England*, 137), but Thomson dates it to the middle of the fifteenth century or later (*Descriptive Catalogue*, 239). Thomson notes that his grammar is not only found on ff. 13r–29v in this manuscript but, also, in Aberystwyth, National Library, MS Peniarth 356b, ff. 116r–131r (*Descriptive Catalogue*, 126). For another grammar that provides Latin sentences "illustrating points of grammar, syntax and word order" see Lincoln Cathedral, Chapter Library, MS 88, ff. 66v–67v (Thomson, *Descriptive Catalogue*, 188).

[60] Here and in the following I quote from the helpful passage of this treatise that Miner has printed, *Grammar Schools of Medieval England*, 280. For discussion of this treatise (which Miner calls "Iesus Christus, filius beate Marie" after its incipit) see Miner pp. 142 and 157–8. See also Miner (publishing under the name Brother Bonaventure) in the appendix to his "The Teaching of Latin in Later Medieval England," *Medieval Studies* 23 (1961): 18–19.

These explanations are then followed by several lines of mnemonic verse that Miner suggests were designed for "recapitulating the lesson and assisting its retention in the memory":[61]

> Versus:
>> Possessor vel possessum substans quoque nomen
>> Post se constructum semper poscit genitivum
>> Sum dominus ville sed equus regis fuit ille.

[Verses: The substantive noun, [of the] possessor or possession always requires the genitive construction to follow it: "I am lord of the town but he was the horse of the king."][62]

Such exercises model Latin immersion by showing how Latin might be used, not only to pose questions, but also to answer them. They also call attention to the way such pedagogy is actually implied from the very first words of the most common of the basic of the Latin grammars, Donatus's *Ars minor*:

> Partes orationis quot sunt? Octo. Quae? Nomen, pronomen, verbum, adverbium, participium, coniunctio, praepositio, interiectio.[63]
>
> [How many parts of speech are there? Eight. Which are? Noun, pronoun, verb, adverb, participle, conjunction, preposition, interjection.]

Although the *Ars minor* is usually described as a "textbook" from which the student acquired "definitions," the form in which those definitions are supplied is a script whereby both teacher and student may say everything in Latin.[64] It is worth noting too that, on some occasions, the *Speculum grammaticale* uses its own sequences of Latin questions and answers:

> Nomen: quid est?
> Pars oracionis.
> Construe "Nomen: quid est?"
> O magister, "quid": *what þing*
> "nomen": *a noun,*
> "est": *is.*
>
> [The noun: what is it?

---

[61] Miner, *Grammar Schools of Medieval England*, 157.

[62] Implicit here I think is that this unmarked order differs from English where it would be "the town's lord" and "the king's horse."

[63] Donatus, *Ars Minor*, 585–612 in Louis Holtz, *Donat et la tradition de l'enseignement grammatical* (Paris: Centre National de la Recherche Scientifique, 1981), 585.

[64] For Donatus's *Ars minor* as a "textbook" see Clanchy, *From Memory to Written Record*, 217 and Katherine Breen, *Imagining an English Reading Public, 1150–1400* (Cambridge: Cambridge University Press, 2010), 100–1. For the book as a source of "definitions" see Miner, *Grammar Schools of Medieval England*, 225.

A part of speech
Construe: "*Nomen: quid est?*"
O teacher, "*quid*," what thing
"*nomen*": a noun,
"*est*": is. (MS Auctarium F.3.9, p. 13)

If David Thomson is right that such a passage "preserves a fragment of classroom dialogue," then, a much more important aspect of the exchange modeled here than the English in the student's responses is the unglossed Latin of the teacher's questions.[65] What the *Speculum grammaticale* strongly implies here, in other words, is a classroom that produced Latin competence by presuming it.

The phrase "fiant Latina" is also used in the *Speculum grammaticale* to pose questions, thereby insisting that those questions be answered in Latin. For example, after a long explanation of noun declensions and verb forms, the phrase introduces the following passage:

Fiant Latina: Quot homines sunt hic intus duo vel tres etc. Quot mulieres sunt hic intus due vel tres etc. Quot mancipia sunt nobis deserviencia duo vel tria. Quot scolarium interest audire informacionem magistri nostri duorum vel trium etc. Quot mulierum interest deservire scolaribus magistri nostri duarum vel trium etc.

[Let there be some Latin (examples): How many men are there in here, two or three, etc.? How many women are there in here, two or three? How many servants are in service with us, two or three? Of how many students is it the business to hear the teaching of our teacher, two or three? Of how many women is it the business to serve the students of our teacher, two or three?] (MS Auctarium F.3.9, pp. 12–13)

The instruction that follows such a script is clearly meant to occur in Latin, as it clearly is when these questions are interrupted with a brief reminder about the plural forms of *duo*:

Unde nota quod *duo* in genitivo facit duorum duarum -orum vel duum.

[So take note that *duo* in the genitive makes *duorum, duarum -orum*, or *duum*.] (MS Auctarium F.3.9, p. 13)

After this reminder there are more Latin questions interspersed with more explanations:

Quot scolaribus servietur a magistro nostro, uni duobus vel tribus? Unde nota quod ista nomina *unus, ullus, totus, solus* etc. secundum antiquos declinabantur prout patet per Priscianum in *Maiori* in genitivis et

---

[65] Thomson, *Descriptive Catalogue*, 40.

dativis singularibus tam secundum primam quam secundum secundam
declinacionem ut *unus, -a, -um* genitivo: *uni -e -i; alius, alia aliud,* genitivo:
alii -e -i etc. Quot scolares oportet magistrum nostrum docere gramaticam
unum, duos, vel tres etc. A quot scolaribus promouebitur magister noster vel
recipiet promocionem uno, duobus, vel tribus et.

[How many scholars are served by our teacher, one, two, or three? Note here
that those nouns *unus, ullus, totus, solus* etc. are declined among the
ancients—just as it is clear according to Priscian in the [*Ars*] *Maior*—in
the genitive and dative singular, according to both the first and the second
declension, such as *unus, -a, -um,* in the genitive, *uni, -e, -i, alius, alia, aliud,*
in the genitive, *alii, -e, -i* etc. How many students is it necessary for our
teacher to teach grammar, one, two, or three? From how many students will
our teacher be promoted or receive promotion, one, two, or three, etc.?] (MS
Auctarium F.3.9, p. 13)[66]

So frequently and fully are classroom circumstances reflected in a sequence
like this that these exercises sometimes refer to that classroom. This self-
reference could be understood as a mode of ornament. Evrard of Béthune
favored this sort of wit, often providing examples that involved his own
name.[67] The *Speculum grammaticale* also points a set of Latin questions on
the subject of pronouns at its author by means of such a signature:

Fiant Latina de pronominibus: Ego Johannes qui sedeo sum obviaturus tibi
qui es iturus romam caput mundi. ego tu et ille coram domino nostro hic
staturi ibimus ad campum herbas collectum vel collecturi. Tu et ille qui tota
die estis hic sedentes carebitis vna re qua e iure non interesset vestra vel
vestrum carere.

[Let us have some Latin (examples) of pronouns: I, John, who sit before you,
am about to meet you, who are about to go to Rome, the head of the world.
I, you, and he, about to stand here before our lord will go to the field having
collected grass, or about to collect [it]. You and he who are sitting here all day
will lack one thing which by right it was not in your interest to lack.]
(MS Auctarium F.3.9, p. 90b)

But the self-reference that makes a text by "John of Cornwall" about the
activities of someone called "John" also invites a student to provide
answers that are in some measure about himself. Where a teacher's
sentences refer to the environment in which they are uttered ("Ego
Johannes qui sedeo" [I, John, who sit before you]) the student's Latin
might describe his classroom too.

---

[66] For this point on "special *-ius* adjectives" see Frederic M. Wheelock, *Wheelock's Latin*,
rev. Ricard A. LaFleur, 6th edn. (New York, NY: HarperCollins, 2000), 57–8.
[67] "Vocor Ebrardus" (XXVII.19) provides an example of the use of the nominative and
"liber Ebrardi" (XXVV.25) of the genitive, Evrard of Béthune, *Graecismus*, ed. Wrobel.

Even where the *Speculum grammaticale* makes English examples central to its explanations, a close look at the contours of that use make clear that such English was part of a fundamentally Latin pedagogy. Here, for example, the text shows how certain impersonal uses of the verb "fieri" are equivalent to passive constructions in English:

> Unde nota quod quandocumque aliqua locucio passivalis per unum illorum facienda proferatur, fieri debet per e[am] impersonal[is]: *I am wel imett*, mihi bene obuiatur id est mihi bene obuiacio sit, Item *3if I go to the carfocus of misdoars I mai be mett* Si vadam ad quadriuium a malefactoribus, potest mihi obuiari, id est, obuiacio mihi potest fieri. Secundum quemdam tractatum dicitur id est obviacionem fieri, unde sciendum quod potest ibi fiat personaliter et habet pro suo supposito infinitum subsequentem, et sic per ipsum infinitum subsequentem constructio est incipienda. Si dicatur anglice, *I am wel served of a man todai of þe whiche I was 3isterdai wel y ansuerid*, sic fiat latinum, Mihi bene seruitur hodie ab uno homine a quo mihi heri bene respondebatur, id est responsum fiebat.

> [Note then that whenever some passive locution is to be construed through one of these it ought to be construed thereby in the impersonal: "I am wel imett," *mihi bene obuiatur* that is *mihi bene obuiacum sit*. Also, "3if I go to the cross-roads of misdoars I mai be mett," *Si vadam ad quadriuium a malefactoribus, possit mihi obuiari*, that is, *obuiacio mihi potest fieri*. According to a certain treatise it is said in this way *obviacionem fieri*. Whence it ought to be understood that it may be made personally and has as its subject the subsequent infinitive and so the construction ought to begin with the subsequent infinitive. Thus in English it would be said, "I am wel served of a man todai of þe whiche I was 3isterdai wel y-ansuerid," the Latin is constructed thus: *Mihi bene seruitur hodie ab uno homine a quo mihi heri bene respondebatur*, that is *responsum fiebat*]. (MS Auctarium F.3.9, p. 10)[68]

Although what a student knows of English was almost certainly helpful here (so that passive constructions in English are seen as parallel to impersonal constructions in Latin), and he is being taught how Latin should be translated into English, Latin is the language that carries him from English example to English example (not "that is," but "id est," not "next" but "item"). As in the case of the French and English glosses in the manuscripts discussed above, Latin is also the language in which the English example is identified as such ("sic dicatur anglice"). It is helpful to explain the method for such translation because these students know English better than Latin, but the explanation does not itself substitute the

---

[68] This example is important enough to have been transcribed, in print, once before. See Bland, "John of Cornwall's Innovations," 220.

familiar for the foreign, but, rather, makes English part of the substance of this teaching. Such a pedagogical technique is also self-referential at root, drawing the circumstances of the student it is addressing into the text insofar as he is assumed to have English as his "dames tongue," but for this same reason English competence is not essential, a resource pedagogy makes use of but does not require for its basic work, equivalent to the student's name, say, or his location or position (sitting or standing, say) in the classroom.

Another way to put this is that the English employed in the *Speculum grammaticale* is a species of realism, just one technique—even if a defining one—in a pedagogical method in which the site of instruction or the experiences the student brings into the room are regularly recruited to make a given grammatical fact clear and pertinent. Other aspects of this method, and the more extended uses to which it can be put will be described in greater detail in Chapter 3, but it is worth noticing at this point that the whole of this method teaches grammar by putting *grammar* to use; it is a species of realism achieved by the use of the very rules it is unfolding, a method for invoking or implying a teacher teaching and a student learning by a strategic use of the forms that position and represent subjects. Rather than say that the sentence "Ego diligo me" [I love myself] is transitive or intransitive, for example, the *Speculum grammaticale* begins by, in effect, moving into the position of a student who might encounter such a sentence and then ask his teacher about it:

> Item si queratur an ista locutio "ego diligo me" sit transitiva vel intransitiva . . .
>
> [If it should be asked whether the phrase "I love myself" is transitive or intransitive . . .] (MS Auctarium F.3.9, p. 3a)

The text then evokes the voice of the teacher to explain the various ways in which this phrase could be considered intransitive ("'ego' et 'me' eandem subiectam et personam significat ergo intransitiva" ['"I" and "me" signify the same subject and person therefore it is intransitive']) as well as the ways in which it might be considered transitive ("omnis illa constructio est transitiva ubi transit actus unius parte in alium" [every construction is transitive in which the action of one part occurs to another]). It then proceeds as if providing responses (from the imagined teacher) to questions (posed by the imagined student):

> Ad istud respondeo et dico quod ista locutio vel constructio potest dupliciter considerari aut quantum ad rem aut quantum ad modum, si quantum ad rem sic dico quod est intransitiva cum eadem substantia inportetur pro ly "ego" et pro ly "me." Si quantum ad modum sic dico quod est transitiva quod patet cum ibi sint diversi casus.
>
> [To this I respond and say that that phrase or construction can be considered in two ways either according to the thing or according to the mode, and if

according to the thing, I say thus, that it is intransitive since the same subject is referred to by the "*ego*" and the "*me.*" If it is according to the mode, I say that it is transitive, which is obvious since there are different cases.] (MS Auctarium F.3.9, p. 3a)

Teacher and student are not only implied by the contents here (a set of precepts described as a "response") but also by a grammar that absorbs the student's question to a condition ("si vero queratur" [if it should be asked]) and the teacher's answer to the precept that is that condition's consequence ("respondendum est" [it ought to be answered]). In this way, the statement of a set of rules proceeds by ventriloquizing the student's voice as well as the teacher's, as if, in other words—and again—what the *Speculum* provides is a record of, or a script for, an actual classroom exchange:

> Si vero queratur quando comparatiuus gradus habet construi cum genitiuo partitue, respondendum est quod quandocumque profertur aliqua locucio superlatiua in anglico vel in gallico, vel in alio ydiomate a latino, habens in se genitiuum minus signantem quam tria, tunc comparatiuus in latinis construeretur cum genitiuo et hoc partitiue, verbi gracia. Ego sum doccior nostrum duorum, anglice, *I am [th]e wiseste of us too.* Aliud exemplum fiat Doctior nostrum duorum est senior seniore vestrum duorum, anglice, *[Th]e wiseste of us too is eldere [th]an [th]e eldest of [y]ou too.*

> [If indeed it should be asked when the comparative is constructed with the partitive genitive it ought to be answered that whenever some superlative construction is employed in English or French or any idiom other than Latin, with a genitive referring to fewer than three items, then the comparative in Latin should be constructed with the partitive genitive, for example: I am more learned of the two of us, in English: *I am the wisest of us two.* Another example might be: The more learned of the two of us is older than the older of you two, In English: *The wisest of us two is older than the eldest of you two.*] (MS Auctarium F.3.9, p. 23)

Here, too, English enters the script as an aspect of realism, transforming grammatical precepts into an implied conversation, although not to explain how to translate Latin into English, but how to translate English into Latin. So far from using English to explain Latin, the references to other languages here orient this explanation within the student's understanding of language as such. The English sentence is, again, a technique for developing a point made in Latin rather than a substitute for Latin pedagogy.

As I have already suggested, the modeling of classroom behavior in grammatical instruction has roots as deep as the most basic classroom grammar, the *Ars minor* of Donatus, although there is an extraordinary

richness in the elaboration of these techniques and the resulting pedagogical realism that finally characterizes the *Speculum grammaticale*.
Although it crosses a linguistic boundary that has come to seem determinate in histories of education, the English of the *Speculum* is no more
than an extension of principles of language learning that were usually
confined to Latin—and were, insofar as this English was not an essential
requirement for learning, *still* confined to Latin. The example with which
I began this chapter in which Latin conjugations were followed by their
English versions might now be re-seen in this light as a typical response to
the most basic of grammatical question ("If it should be asked how many
persons of verb there are..." [Item querendum est quot sunt persone in
verbo]) in which that response is not rendered intelligible but simply made
clear—vivid and immediate—by the English glosses that refer the Latin
grammar to the grammar of the student's mother tongue ("it ought to be
said that there are three [dicendum quod tres sunt]: lego *y rede* legimus *we
rede* legis *þu redis* legitis *ʒe redin* vel *ʒe redith* iste legit *þis redith* isti legunt
þei redyn"). Such English, like all the English in the *Speculum grammaticale*, is of historical importance, not because it "changed the lore" in
England, as Trevisa claimed, but because it elaborated and enriched a
pedagogy in which the language of learning had long been, and remained,
Latin.

2

The Ad Hoc School

"Medieval education," it has long been thought, "was highly standardized," and the texts used for basic literacy training have also long seemed the stable center of a grammar-school program as homogeneous as it was unchanging.[1] For generations of scholars these reading texts have constituted, not just a "school curriculum," but a "reader" so invariable that, even in a manuscript culture in which each book was an individual and *sui generis* production, there was a grammar-school "textbook."[2] That "book" has long been described as the *"Liber Catonianus"* [Cato Book] after the first text it usually contained (the *Distichs of Cato*).[3] It is sometimes also called the *"Sex Auctores"* after the number of texts regularly grouped in such manuscripts (the *Distichs*, Avianus's *Fables*, Theodulus's *Eclogue*, Claudian's *On the Rape of Proserpina*, Statius's *Achilleid*, and Maximian's *Elegies*).[4] This normative course of study has often seemed to have been entrenched by the twelfth century, so that, when the schoolmaster Alexander Neckam (1157–1217) gives what has been described as a

[1] Percival R. Cole, *A History of Educational Thought* (London: Oxford University Press, 1931; reprinted Westport, CT: Greenwood Press, 1972), 141.

[2] Nicholas Orme, *Medieval Schools: From Roman Britain to Medieval England* (New Haven, CT: Yale University Press, 2006), 98 ("curriculum"); Marjorie Curry Woods and Rita Copeland, "Classroom and Confession," 376–406 in *The Cambridge History of Medieval English Literature*, ed. David Wallace (Cambridge: Cambridge University Press, 1999), 380 ("reader"); Paul Clogan, "Literary Genres in a Medieval Textbook," *Medievalia et Humanistica* n.s. 11 (1982): 199–209 ("textbook").

[3] For the original formulation of this grouping of texts see M. Boas, "De Librorum Catonianorum Historia atque Compositione," *Mnemosyne* n.s. 42 (1914): 2–46. For detailed discussion of these texts and what is known about their date and origin see Jill Mann, " 'He Knew Nat Catoun': Medieval School-Texts and Middle English Literature," 41–74 in *The Text in the Community: Essays on Medieval Works, Manuscripts, Authors and Readers*, ed. Jill Mann and Maura Nolan (Notre Dame, IN: University of Notre Dame Press, 2006), see esp. 44–8 and 67–9 nn. 2 and 15–20.

[4] The phrase *"Sex Auctores"* is widespread in modern histories of education, but never (so far as I know) with explicit license from medieval use; see, for example, Woods and Copeland, "Classroom and Confession," 380; Orme, *Medieval Schools*, 98; and Jan Ziolkowski, "Latin Learning and Latin Literature," 229–44 in *The Cambridge History of the Book in Britain*, vol. 2: *1100–400*, ed. Nigel Morgan and Rodney M. Thomson (Cambridge: Cambridge University Press, 2008), 235. For a summary of editions and translations of these texts see "Note on Texts" (pp. xiii–xv) in the present volume.

"list of textbooks" for schoolboys in his *Sacerdos ad Altare*, he lists many of these texts:

> After he has learned the alphabet and has been imbued in other fundamentals suitable for childhood, let him learn Donatus, and that useful moral compendium of morality which common opinion attributes to Cato, and let him move on from the *Ecloga* of Theodulus to the eclogues of the *Bucolics* . . . From the delightful *Thebaid*, let him pass to the divine *Aeneid*, but let him not neglect the poet born in Cordova [Lucan]. . . . Let him read the *Satires* and *Epistles* of Horace, and the *Ars poetica* and the *Odes* and the book of *Epodes*. Let him hear the *Elegies* of Naso and the *Metamorphoses* of Ovid, but let him be especially familiar with the *Remedia Amoris* . . . Also, Statius's *Achilleid* is approved by men of great reverence.[5]

The classical texts listed here alongside the *Distichs of Cato*, the *Fables* of Avianus, and the *Eclogue* of Theodulus have also been thought to be standard school texts since they can be found in many schoolbooks.[6] It is also usually assumed that there was a great deal of stability in this course of study over time. When we next have a good glimpse of the curriculum from a teacher's perspective, in the record of weekly teaching sent by the schoolmasters at Winchester and Eton to a schoolmaster in Saffron Walden, *c*.1530, we could say that not much has changed:

> The seconde fforme
> . . . throwh the weke hath a verbe sett up over nyght, and makith vulgaris on it, and dothe like at laten as the thrid forme. Ther rulys, Parvula of Stanbridge, and ij. verses of his vocables. There constructyones Esopes fabuls throwh all the weke, save that on the saterday in the Mornyng they

---

[5] "Postquam alphabetum didicerit et ceteris puerilibus rudimentis imbutus fuerit, Donatum et illud utile moralitatis compendium quod Catonis esse vulgus opinatur addiscat et ab Egloga Theodoli transeat ad egglogas Bucolicorum . . . A Thebaide iocunda transeat ad divinam Eneida, nec neggligat vatem quem Corduba genuit . . . Sermones Oratii et Epistolas legat et Poetriam et Odas cum libro Epodon. Elegias Nasonis et Ovidium Metamorfoseos audiat, sed et precipue libellum De remedio amoris familiarem habeat . . . Statius Achilleidos etiam a viris multe gravitatis probatur," *Sacerdos ad Altare* as edited in Tony Hunt, *Teaching and Learning Latin in Thirteenth Century England*, 3 vols. (Woodbridge: D. S. Brewer, 1991), 1: 269–70. On this text see also Suzanne Reynolds, *Medieval Reading: Grammar, Rhetoric and the Classical* (Cambridge: Cambridge University Press, 1996), 7–12. On other such lists in the Middle Ages see Mann, "'He Knew Nat Catoun,'" 49–50.

[6] For volumes containing texts of the "*Liber Catonianus*" and these classical authors see Eva Matthews Sanford, "Classical Authors in the *Libri Manuales*," *Transactions and Proceedings of the American Philological Association* 55 (1924): 224 (#211), 226 (#239, #244), 230 (#290, #296), 235 (#360, #361), 237 (#378, #385), 238 (#389, #391), 239 (#399, #400, #404, #405), 240 (#412, #413). On the use of Horace's *Ars Poetica* see Rita Copeland, "Horace's *Ars Poetica* in the Medieval Classroom and Beyond," 15–33 in *Answerable Style: The Idea of the Literary in Medieval England*, ed. Frank Grady and Andrew Galloway (Columbus, OH: Ohio State University Press, 2013).

have iiij. verses of Cato to be renderid withowte boke, with the examynat-
yon of the same.

The Fyrst forme.

In the mornyng a part of stanbridge accidens, and a verbe of the same
accidens to be said withowte booke, and then a Latin to be said at the
after noon; after that repetycyon of rules. The Friday there Comparisons
with the verbe sum. *es. fui.* to be said; At the after none repetytyon of there
rules. At Saterday repetytyon of there Cato. The Sonday a fabull of Aesope.[7]

The "reptytyon" so basic to the classroom practices described here seems
to have ensured that for at least four centuries children began to read Latin
with the "verses of Cato."

But the stable items in this curriculum could also be said to distract
from a fundamental fluidity that surrounds every fixed point. Even
Alexander misses out three of the texts normally thought to be part of
the standard "textbook," and we could also say that by 1545, when the
masters at Eton and Winchester are writing, most of the texts constituting
the normative medieval reader have fallen by the wayside. Although recent
scholars write regularly of a "Cato *Book*" [*Liber Catonianus*] as if it could
be reached right off the shelf, Boas, the scholar who introduced this
terminology, only ever referred to the "Cato *Books*" [*libri Catoniani*] in
order to acknowledge variability in the very manuscripts he was using to
define this group.[8] He was himself immediately criticized for overlooking
many exceptions.[9] And the *libri Catoniani* are most properly understood
as "a theme upon which endless variations are played" in the manuscript
tradition, neither a book nor even a curriculum in the current sense of that
word, but something very like a literary canon: a group of texts constituting a horizon of possibilities but never fully present in any single
instance.[10] However sure we have now become that a collection like the
one found in New Haven, Connecticut, Beineke Library, Yale MS 513

---

[7] *Educational Charters and Documents, 598 to 1909*, ed. Arthur F. Leach (Cambridge:
Cambridge University Press, 1911), 449–50. See also Thomas Wright, "Rules of the Free
School at Saffron Walden," *Archaeologia* 34 (1852): 41. On earlier curricula (from 1528)
from Eton College that pay slightly less attention to reading texts see Nicholas Orme,
English School Exercises: 1420–1530 (Toronto: Pontifical Institute of Mediaeval Studies,
2013), 11. These documents are described in Nicholas Carlisle, *A Concise Description of the
Endowed Grammar Schools in England and Wales* (London: Baldwin, Cradock and Joy,
1818), 2: 594–7 and A. F Leach, "Schools," 397–440 in *Victoria History of the County of
Sussex*, ed. William Page (London: Constable and Co., 1907), 2: 416–21 and 417–19.
[8] Boas, "De Librorum Catonianorum Historia."
[9] Rino Avesani, "Il primo ritmo per la morte del grammatico Ambrogio e il cosidetto
'Liber Catonianus'," *Studi medievali* ser. 3, 6 (1965): 455–88. Cited and summarized in
Mann, "'He Knew Nat Catoun,'" 48 and 69 n. 21.
[10] Mann, "'He Knew Nat Catoun,'" 48.

(*c.*1300) is a "standardized textbook," it is very different in its contents than the readings Alexander Neckam recommends even though it was compiled just after Alexander wrote:[11]

ff. 1–10v   Theodulus, *Eclogue* (complete)
ff. 11r–21v   Avianus, *Fables* (complete)
ff. 21v–31r   Maximian, *Elegies* (end of the fifth elegy missing)[12]

This "small volume … of thirty-one vellum leaves, worn from hard usage, and darkened from thumbing, particularly the earlier folios," contains only texts associated with the *libri Catoniani* but also only half their "standard" number, even omitting what otherwise seems to be the fixed center of this grouping of texts, the *Distichs of Cato* themselves.[13]

This is a relationship that ought to be familiar enough to literary scholars, since it is also foundational for the category of "literature," another "imaginary totality," created from "a list of texts (syllabus, curriculum) [that are] continuously changing in response to the frictional relations between institutional and social reproduction."[14] In the modern case, the stable terms in the list are misrecognized as the whole of the literary past. In the medieval case, six texts that recur frequently in surviving schoolbooks conjure up the "*Liber Catonianus*," and any medieval book that contains only three of them (such as Beinecke Library, 513) or any medieval list that does not name all of them (such as Alexander Neckham's) is partial.[15] We can also say, however, that the *Liber Catonianus must* be imagined because the schoolbooks that survive are so various. So far from tracing a fixed course, in other words, the typical medieval schoolbook is a wide-ranging improvisation around a very meager set of common terms.

---

[11] Cora E. Lutz, "A Medieval Textbook," *Yale University Library Gazette* 49 (1974): 215.

[12] Beinecke Library, Medieval and Renaissance Manuscripts <http://brbl-net.library.yale.edu/pre1600ms/docs/pre1600.ms513.htm>, based on *Catalogue of Medieval and Renaissance Manuscripts in the Beinecke Rare Book and Manuscript Library, Yale University*, ed. Barbara Shailor et al. Medieval and Renaissance Texts and Studies 34, 48, 100, 176 (Binghamton, NY: Center for Medieval and Renaissance Studies, 1984–).

[13] Lutz, "A Medieval Textbook," 213. The power of the idea of the "*Liber Catonianus*" to configure expectation leads Lutz to suggest that "the omission of the *Disticha Catonis*, normally found at the beginning, may indicate that it had been bound separately, as a kind of first reader" (p. 213).

[14] John Guillory, *Cultural Capital: The Problem of Literary Canon Formation* (Chicago, IL: University of Chicago Press, 1993), 31 ("imaginary") and 59 ("a list of texts").

[15] For the assumption that Alexander Neckham is talking about the "*Liber catonianus*" see Copeland and Sluiter, *Medieval Grammar and Rhetoric*, 535. For the presumption that the Beinecke book should include all six of these texts see Lutz, "A Medieval Textbook," 212–13.

The physical structure of the medieval English school was similarly improvisatory. The earliest "purpose-built" schoolroom that survives in England—a simple rectangle, 45 feet 6 inches long and 28 feet 10 inches wide—was not built until the late fourteenth century for what would become Winchester College.[16] When Jocelin of Brakelond (d. 1121) describes how the hero of his *Chronicle* of Bury St Edmunds, started a school, he says that Abbot Samson "bought a stone house [domos lapideas] in the town" and he then "gave it to the schoolmaster" [eas scolarum regimini assignavit].[17] Most records of actual teaching in the Middle Ages suggest neither a uniform nor a dedicated space, nor anything like a school building or room. As a sixteenth-century record from Durham (1593) shows with particular clarity, the space for basic literacy training was often carved out of structures normally devoted to other purposes:

> There was in þe Centorie garth in under þe south end of þe church...
> betwixt two pillers adioyning to þe ix alter Dour, a song schoole buylded, for
> to teach vj children for to learne to singe...wch said schoole was buylded
> many yers since wthout memorie of man...and þe said schoole was verie
> fynely bourded wth in Rownd about a mannes hight about þe waules and a
> long deske did reache from one end of þe scooole to thother to laie there
> bookes upon, and all the floure Bourded in under foote for warmenes and
> long formes sett fast in the ground for the Children to sitt on. And þe place
> where þe mr did sitt & teach was all close bordede both behinde and of either
> syde for warmnes.[18]

[*Centorie*: sanctuary; *garth in*: enclosed; *dour*: door; *wth in*: within; *formes*: benches; *mr*: master]

Although this description is late, elementary teaching in Durham Cathedral dates back to the twelfth century, and other records show that churches often hosted schools throughout the Middle Ages.[19] Later evidence

---

[16] A. F. Leach, *A History of Winchester College* (London: Duckworth, 1899), 123–6 and Malcolm Seaborne, *The English School: Its Architecture and Organization* (London: Routledge & Kegan Paul, 1971–7), 3 as cited in Orme, *Medieval Schools*, 138.

[17] Jocelin of Brakelond, *Chronica Jocelini de Brakelonda* (London: Camden Society, 1840), 33. Jocelin of Brakelond, *Chronicle of the Abbey of Bury St Edmunds*, trans. Diana Greenway and Jane Sayers (Oxford: Oxford University Press, 1989), 41. Cited in A. F. Leach and E. P. Steele Hutton, "Schools," 301–56 in *The Victoria History of the County of Suffolk*, ed. William Page (London: Archibald Constable, 1907), 2: 306.

[18] *The Rites of Durham (1593)*, ed. J. T. Fowler (Durham: Andrews & Co, 1903): 62. Cited in Jo Ann Hoeppner Moran, *The Growth of English Schooling, 1340–1548* (Princeton, NJ: Princeton University Press, 1985), 86.

[19] On earlier teaching in Durham see Reginald of Durham, *Libellus de Vita et Miraculis S. Godrici, Heremitae de Finchale* (London: J. B. Nichols and Sons, 1847), 59–60; and *Reginaldi Monachi Dunelmensis Libellus de Admirandis Beati Cuthberti* (London: J. B. Nichols and Sons, 1835), 149–50; both cited in Orme, *Medieval Schools*, 136. See also A. F. Leach, *Schools of Medieval England* (London: Methuen, 1915), 142.

suggests that there was often no designated schoolroom space even in the church, and a priest might simply teach his pupils just inside the church door near the font.[20] In 1373, for example, the bishop of Norwich prohibited teaching in churches because the noises made by pupils when they were beaten disrupted the divine office.[21] In this sense, medieval schooling neatly illustrates the modern claim that a school, "reduced to its barest recognizable elements," need never be more than "a single place of meeting, a teacher, a means of instruction, a means of inscription, an organized form of seating (usually arranged in lines) a shared purpose and . . . children."[22] Since it is clear enough that many instances of medieval schooling did not involve writing (since it was "a skill distinct from reading because the use of parchment and quills made it difficult"), schools in this period were probably simpler than even this schema.[23] As Jo Ann Hoeppner Moran has very precisely put it, schooling in the Middle Ages "did not necessarily imply 'schools.'"[24]

It is important to begin a description of such schooling by emphasizing the variety in its spaces and basic teaching texts because there has been such a long-standing "bias toward institutionalized history," as Moran also observes.[25] This bias has ensured that the relationship between elementary learning and literary production has seemed to scholars a matter, above all, of divining and then fixing institutional affiliations. Edith Rickert's influential claim that Chaucer was "most likely to have attended" St Paul's School since it "was near his father's house in Thames Street" is a case in point.[26] Here, St Paul's School in the present-day City of London exerts a retrospective pressure that transforms what was clearly—and at most—an "almoner's school" in

---

[20] In depositions of 1496–7 one witness describes his schooling "within the space of five feet of the font" of the parish church in Kirkham, Lancashire. See Janet Burton, "Priory and Parish: Kirkham and its Parishioners 1496–7," 329–47 in *Monasteries and Society in Medieval Britain, Proceedings of the 1994 Harlaxton Symposium*, ed. Benjamin Thompson (Stamford: Paul Watkins, 1999), 338; cited in Orme, *Medieval Schools*, 136.

[21] John Raymond Shinners and William J. Dohar, *Pastors and the Care of Souls in Medieval England* (Notre Dame, IN: University of Notre Dame Press, 1998), 106; cited in Orme, *Medieval Schools*, 136.

[22] Catherine Burke and Ian Grosvenor, *School* (London: Reaktion Books, 2008), 13.

[23] M. T. Clanchy, *From Memory to Written Record: England, 1066–1307* (Cambridge, MA: Harvard University Press, 1979), 183.

[24] Moran, *Growth of English Schooling*, 14. Moran is here citing Joan Simon, *Education and Society in Tudor England* (Cambridge: Cambridge University Press, 1966), 14.

[25] Moran, *Growth of English Schooling*, 8. Moran is here speaking particularly of the work of A. F. Leach.

[26] Edith Rickert, "Chaucer at School," *Modern Philology* 39 (1932): 257. It was also George Plimpton's view that "Chaucer was born not far from St Paul's Cathedral" and, so, "it is likely that he attended the school attached to that church," *The Education of Chaucer: Illustrated from the Schoolbooks in Use in his Time* (London: Oxford University Press, 1935), 18.

the fourteenth century (a charitable foundation designed to train poor boys as clerics) into something it has seemed right to call "the old cathedral grammar school."[27] Rickert's main evidence was the geographic relationship of the modern institution to the place where Chaucer lived 600 years earlier, although she also had a "list of books" left to the school by William Ravenstone in 1358 which she took as "confirmation" of Chaucer's attendance since that "list of books parallels to an extraordinary degree the hypothetical list of those which Chaucer, from internal evidence, seems to have read in his youth."[28] The argument is not very convincing: because the list represents the texts that were known in St Paul's almonry school in the fourteenth century, and Chaucer knew these texts, he must have attended this school. But the real problem is that Rickert's investment in these deductions ensured that she never consulted the most detailed evidence we have of fourteenth-century schooling in England—which she herself discovered.

We might suppose that a great deal of medieval schooling occurred outside institutions because, as Lynn Thorndike observed, any parent who had the means might well "pay local schoolmasters fees to instruct their children."[29] Such "schooling" would be hard to trace, however, because its governing organization could have consisted of no more than money passing from hand to hand—and yet Rickert found evidence of exactly such exchanges in the one place in which they do leave a durable trace: an account book. London, Public Record Office, E 101 509/19 e, records a series of transactions in 1390–5 for Gilbert Maghfeld, a London merchant. This book was of interest to Rickert because it contains the names of "thirty or forty persons . . . who are in some other way unmistakably associated with Chaucer" and therefore furnished "material for a better understanding of London life."[30] The book shows Chaucer incurring, and then repaying, a small a debt to Maghfeld in July of 1392, a close association that caused Rickert to wonder if Maghfeld might have been "the original of the Merchant" in the *Canterbury Tales*.[31] A series of transactions recorded in this book also outlines the arrangements Maghfeld made for the "schooling" [scoleyement] of his son, William,

---

[27] See A. F. Leach, "St Paul's School before Colet," *Archaeologia* 62 (1910): 195–9 (on the almonry school) and 204 (on the "grammar school").

[28] Rickert, "Chaucer at School," 257.

[29] Lynn Thorndike, "Elementary and Secondary Education in the Middle Ages," *Speculum* 15 (1940): 402–3.

[30] Edith Rickert, "Extracts from a Fourteenth-Century Account Book," *Modern Philology* 24 (1926), 112 ("material") and 118 ("thirty").

[31] Rickert, "Extracts from a Fourteenth-Century Account Book," 256.

along with John Frogenhale (who seems to have been Gilbert's ward), both of whom he "sent" [envoyes] to a "master" [mestre], or "scolemestre" as he is also called, in Croydon, when they were boys ("enfantz"):

Anno xvijo mensis Maij

Johan Frogenhale & William Maghfeld fuerent enuoyes a Croydon al	
escole le veille de seint Dunstan paiant par symaigne	ij s.
Item paie en le veille de seint Michel anno xviijo pour xix symaigne	xxxviij s.
Item done al mestre pour lour scoleyement	iij s. iiij d.
...	
Item deliuere a Noell une liuere appelle este qe coste	vij s.
Item done al mestre pour lour scoleyement	iij s. iiij d.
Item pour ij payre chaux pour le deux	xvj d.
Item done al vycare de Croydon le viij iour de Feb [sic] anno xviijo vn	
Cade haryng pris vj s. * j petit freyel Fygus	xvj d.[32]

[In the 17th year, in the month of May	
John Frogenhall and William Maghfeld were sent to Croydon on	
St Dunstan's Day, paid weekly	ii. s
Also paid on the vigil of St Michael in the 18th year for 19 weeks	xxxviii.s
Also given to the teacher for their schooling	iij s. iiij d.
...	
Also delivered at Christmas a book called "este"[?] that cost	vij s.
Also given to the master for their schooling	iij s. iiij d.
Also for two pairs of shoes for the two of them	xvj d.
Also given to the vicar of Croydon the 8th day of February in the 17th	
a cade of herring costing vj s. and a small basket of figs	xvj d.]

Rickert thought that the gift of the "cade of herring" and "small basket of figs" to the "vicar of Croydon" as well as the gifts recorded on this same page to the "servants in the vicar's dwelling" [seruantz deinz lostiell del vicare] suggested that the "school" was an arrangement for cohabitation and regular tuition in the vicar's home.[33] What Rickert never said, however, was that Gilbert Maghfeld was not just similar to Chaucer's Merchant but similar to the merchant who was Chaucer's father. She also failed to notice that Maghfeld's son was identical in social position and geographical circumstance to the young *Chaucer*, whose father would have had to arrange for his schooling with exactly the same resources available to Maghfeld when arranging schooling for William.[34] Rickert therefore never drew the obvious generalization that this particular book makes

---

[32] Rickert, "Extracts from a Fourteenth-Century Account Book," 251–2.

[33] Rickert, "Extracts from a Fourteenth-Century Account Book," 252.

[34] Rickert does note that there is one entry that clearly refers to a small loan of money from gilbert Maghfeld to the adult Chaucer, "Extracts from a Fourteenth-Century Account Book," 119.

possible, not only about Chaucer's schooling, but the sort of grammar-school education available in England in the fourteenth century to the large number of boys who resembled him: where there was ready cash (or surplus herring and figs) a "school" might have been assembled wherever there was a priest with enough time, the inclination, and some space in which to teach a boy or two for a fee.

Such schooling is best defined, not as a looser version of the institution we are now familiar with, but as the sort of practice Bourdieu described as a "set of durable dispositions," neither a building nor an organized body of people, but, rather a "logic" that reproduces itself in and as habit.[35] Any description of such "regulated improvisation"—what Bourdieu described in his most vivid image as "a train laying its own rails"—could never begin with a set of fixed buildings or records, but would have to characterize the variations that only together imply a norm.[36] Describing this variety, as I will now try to do, should constitute further proof of the arguments advanced in the previous chapter, that, however ad hoc particular pedagogical arrangements may have been, their common term was always Latin (it was a priest's skill in reading and writing Latin that qualified him to teach grammar even though this might have been his *only* such qualification). As I will also try to show in the following pages, nested subtly but firmly within such an improvisational logic was, of necessity, a set of lessons *about* improvisation. Although the repetition of word forms and rules of syntax were always the basic tool for training a boy to read and write, he was also shown how to take those forms beyond the paradigms and exercise in which they were first taught. In order to *be* literate, in other words, the schoolboy had to know how to take the grammatical knowledge that had been drilled into him and adapt it to a sequence of new demands and circumstances. In this fundamental sense, the departure from Latin teaching constituted by the decision to write in Middle English in each Ricardian poet's life—the sudden leap each of these poets made when they decided to write in their mother tongue rather the language in which they'd been trained to read and write—was no more than a lesson well learned, an almost-inevitable consequence of the improvisatory form in which the grammar they had learned was taught.

---

[35] Pierre Bourdieu, *The Logic of Practice* (Stanford, CA: Stanford University Press, 1990), 58.
[36] Bourdieu, *Logic of Practice*, 57.

THE INFORMAL SCHOOLROOM

A wide range of social processes might be described as "elementary education." When writing about the Middle Ages, it is necessary to include in this category, not only literacy training, but also instruction in manners and mores in the home, the vocational training often of a lettered sort that occurred in the sprawling bureaucracy of the courts and large aristocratic households, as well as the craft skills acquired in daily activities on the farmyard and in the trades in cities and towns.[37] There was also a wide range of teaching in what has been called the "extragrammatical literacy" of prayer and liturgical performance in the church, activities that might not involve understanding at the level of the word or syntactic unit but which still involved an ability to put language to use.[38] Since Christianity is, fundamentally, a religion of the book, and the terms *clericus* and *litteratus* were synonyms as a result, it is safe to say that most boys in the Middle Ages were taught to read and write by priests.[39] Although A. F. Leach famously dedicated his pioneering scholarship on medieval schooling in England to establishing its "secular" origins—the extent to which the modern independent schools of England were not church sponsored—even Leach recognized that "the school was an adjunct of the church, and the schoolmaster was an ecclesiastical officer."[40] This was very much the view of the non-ecclesiastical arms of authority too, and so a case concerning the rights of Llanthony priory over teaching at the "Grammer Schole de Gloucester" was dismissed from the court of common pleas on the grounds that "the teaching of children is a spiritual matter" [que enformacion des enfantes est chose espirituel].[41]

---

[37] See Joan Simon, *The Social Origins of English Education* (London: Routledge & Kegan Paul, 1970), 50–1 and Simon, *Education and Society*, 3–4. On education in the household see Orme, *Medieval Schools*, 251; Nicholas Orme, *From Childhood to Chivalry: The Education of the English Kings and Aristocracy, 1066–1530* (London: Methuen, 1984), 18–28; and Moran, *Growth of English Schooling*, 82–3.

[38] See Katherine Zieman, *Singing the New Song: Literacy and Liturgy in Late Medieval England* (Philadelphia, PA: University of Pennsylvania Press, 2008), esp. 117–18.

[39] Of 150 schoolmasters alive in the period 1200–1548 in the west of England, the majority (83) were priests, 15 were clerks in minor orders, and the rest were probably clerics of some sort but can not be verified to be. For this data see Nicholas Orme, *Education in the West of England, 1066–1548: Cornwall, Devon, Dorset, Gloucestershire, Somerset, Wiltshire* (Exeter: University of Exeter Press, 1976), 19.

[40] John M. Miner, *The Grammar Schools of Medieval England: A. F. Leach in Historiographical Perspective* (Montreal & Kingston: McGill-Queen's University Press, 1990), 24 citing Leach, *Schools of Medieval England*, 235.

[41] *Les Reports del cases en ley . . . En le temps de . . . Les roys Henry le IV. Et Henry le V. H* [Yearbooks 1413–22] (London, 1679; reprinted: Abingdon: Professional Books, 1981), 11,

The institutional church also asserted its authority over elementary education at the highest level. A decretal issuing from the Fourth Lateran Council (of 1215) insisted that "every cathedral or other church of sufficient means" shall provide a "grammarian."[42] A papal statute of 1335 insists that "all monastic cathedral churches, priories or other conventual and solemn places of sufficient means" of the Benedictine order shall have a master of the "elementary sciences, viz. grammar, logic and philosophy."[43]

A direct consequence of the general dependency of elementary schooling on the clerisy in medieval England is that "it is difficult to find any educational institutions," even where founded or endowed by the laity, "that did not retain some ecclesiastical characteristics."[44] It is customary, as a result, to divide the medieval schools we know of into the following typologies according to the arm of the church that fostered and funded them:

1. cathedral and ancient collegiate churches

2. chantry colleges

3. monastic origin

4. hospitals and almshouses

5. friaries

6. guild schools[45]

Such a typology provides evidence of a certain variation, for, despite the similarities it would have ensured between schools separated by great distance, it also describes a variety of relationships between schools and the church, with basic literacy training emanating from all sorts of ecclesiastical lives (secular, communal, fraternal) and many different functions within those lives (the provision of alms or the apprenticing new members, for example). Even within the regimenting institution of the church

Henry IV (p. 47). Orme also cites this record but slightly misrepresents it (*Medieval Schools*, 201).

[42] *Educational Charters and Documents*, ed. Leach, 143.

[43] *Educational Charters and Documents*, ed. Leach, 291.

[44] Moran, *Growth of English Schooling*, 182. For a similar point, see Nicholas Orme, "Lay Literacy in England, 1100–1300," 35–56 in *England and Germany in the High Middle Ages*, ed. Alfred Haverkamp and Hanna Vollraith (Oxford: Oxford University Press, 1996), 51.

[45] Moran, *Growth of English Schooling*, 82–3. Moran also gives a list of exemplary schools (in Yorkshire, of each kind). Percival Cole also saw six distinct "types of medieval schools" but his types ("monastic or cloistral schools," "cathedral schools," "collegiate schools," "chantry schools," "guild and municipal schools," and "elementary schools") differed from Moran's. See *History of Educational Thought*, 133–8.

there was, in other words, a "rich miscellaneity."[46] In ways that I will detail in what follows, there were also various gray areas and loose affiliations within these large categories as well as between them, and, however commonly education was the business of clerks, there were also some schools it is best to think of as "independent" precisely because they were "not closely associated with ecclesiastical foundations."[47]

The strong sense that histories of education often have that "the medieval school" was itself an institution is in part the substantial legacy of Leach's attempt to insist that the "true models and sources of the schools of England" were not church schools but "the schools of... Athens, and Alexandria."[48] In order to make this difficult case, Leach had to develop shibboleths, and chief among these was the "almonry school" which Leach thought evolved out of the almoner's duty to distribute charity as it was extended to the maintenance of the "choir-boys, who learnt singing at the choir school."[49] There were, in fact, as many as seventy schools that were called "almonry schools" in medieval England, but they were a late development (with the earliest known instance recorded in Norwich some time between 1272 and 1289).[50] These schools were also not exclusively ecclesiastical since they were generally "open" to "external fee-payers" who often outnumbered those students who were destined for a religious life.[51] The connection of such schools to the "almonry" or the monastery was often loose too, a consequence of the general habit of making the almoner the monastic official in charge of education. In a record of 1338, for example, we find that the "almoner" [elemosinarium] of St Alban's was a teacher and his young students were understood as the "poor scholars in the Almonry" [pauperum scolarium in eleemosynaria], but the school itself had nothing obvious to do with the monastery since it was located in the "grammar school house" [domus scolarum grammaticalium] in the town ("in villa Sancti Albani").[52] Eight other "almonry schools" of which we know were clearly located outside a monastery.[53] And, in a very revealing deed, dateable to the beginning of the twelfth century (*c.*1111–28), the "almonry school" of St Paul's in London—as I have already noted,

---

[46] Roger Bowers, "The Almonry Schools of the English Monasteries, 1265–1540," 177–222 in *Monasteries and Society in Medieval Britain*, ed. Thompson, 177.

[47] Moran, *Growth of English Schooling*, 83.

[48] Leach, *Schools of Medieval England*, 13.

[49] Leach, *Schools of Medieval England*, 214. For Leach's history of such schools see 213–34.

[50] Bowers, "Almonry Schools," 182.   [51] Bowers, "Almonry Schools," 203.

[52] *Educational Charters and Documents*, ed. Leach, 296–7.

[53] See Bowers, "Almonry Schools," 221–2.

frequently seen as the foundation for the modern independent school—had the most improvisatory form of all, consisting of no more than a "schoolmaster" [magistrum scolarum], some books, and a "place" [statio] allotted for teaching "in the angle of the tower" [in angulo turris].[54]

Leach's insistence that the almonry school trained choristers also led to the idea that there was something it is right to call a "song school," but both the phrase and the institution it posits are chimerical too. Although there were clearly schools devoted to training singers to perform the canonical offices at the very beginning of the Middle Ages in England—a survival of the ancient *scola cantorum*—such training was quickly absorbed to the broader scheme of elementary education.[55] The tendency of historians of education to insist that there were "either song or grammar . . . schools," or that, within the typology of ecclesiastical affiliations, it was also possible to distinguish between "song," "writing," and "reading" schools, extrapolates whole institutions and traditions from the various different tasks a single school tended to perform.[56] As Katherine Zieman has shown in some detail, "reading" and "singing" were constantly joined in the phrase "scientia legendi et cantandi" [knowledge of reading and singing] which described the aggregation of skills that constituted basic literacy training.[57] By the fourteenth century, if there ever had been English "song schools," they were a "residual institution," absorbed to grammar schools by a stratification in which instruction in singing was often just one step among many in literacy training as a general program.[58] Thus, when the "master of the grammar school" [magister scolarum gramaticalium] of Warwick Cathedral complains, in 1319, of the "undue encroachment" [indebite usurpaciones] on the teaching of the "Donatists" [donatistis] by the "music schoolmaster" [magistrum scolarum musice], the boundary dispute is resolved by putting the music schoolmaster in charge of the most basic stages of literacy ("those learning their first letters, the psalter, music, and song" [primas litteras addiscentes

---

[54] *Educational Charters and Documents*, ed. Leach, 80–1. See also Leach, "St Paul's School Before Colet," 193.

[55] On the ancient *scola cantorum* see Christopher Page, *The Christian West and its Singers* (New Haven, CT: Yale University Press, 2010), 245–59. On the evolving use of the related term *scola cantus*, see Zieman, *Singing the New Song*, 11–18.

[56] Miner, *Grammar Schools of Medieval England*, 203 ("either") and Moran, *Growth of English Schooling*, 39–64 (on "reading," "writing," and "song" schools). Although Orme notes the disappearance of any evidence of the song school from the record (*Medieval Schools*, 64), he tends to write as if such schools were constant and separable institutions (see, especially, his "list of schools," 346–71).

[57] Zieman, *Singing the New Song*, 30–9.   [58] Zieman, *Singing the New Song*, 18.

psalterium, musicam, et cantum]), with the grammar master of the same
school in charge of the rest.[59]

Even where basic literacy training was provided directly by the institutional church, it really had no fixed form, and church "schools" were
very often sets of improvised activities rather than fixed institutions. The
schools arrayed around Lincoln Cathedral provide a richly documented
set of cases in point here. The earliest statutes in the chapter act books of
the Cathedral mention a "song school" and a "grammar school."[60] But it
is clear from a Chapter Act of 1406–7 that the song school had developed into something of a grammar school for "commoners" as well as
"relations of the canons and vicars of the church" and that there was also,
therefore, in the gift of the cathedral, a separate "grammar school of the
city."[61] The cathedral also maintained a chantry with five priests, created
by a bequest of Sir Bartholomew of Burghershe in 1345, which ran a
sufficient surplus (£10 per year) for money to be diverted by "an
ordinance of children" to the creation of a boarding house for six boys
who were to be taught grammar.[62] The cathedral also maintained, in
parallel to these institutions, what the *Victoria County History of Lincolnshire* very accurately calls a "galaxy" of grammar schools sited in
towns and villages.[63] There is a record surviving from 1329, for example,
in which the dean and chapter appoint schoolmasters to the Grammar
School of Barton ("scolas gramaticales de Barton"), the school of Partney
("scolas de Partenay"), the school of Grimsby ("scolas de Grimesby"),
the school of Horncastle ("scolas de Horncastre"), the school of
St Botolph, or Boston ("scolas de Sancto Botulpho"), and the school
of Grantham ("scolas de Grantham").[64] There is also a separate record of
a school at Louth which shows that, from 1276, it too was under the
jurisdiction of the prebendary of Lincoln Cathedral.[65] There also seem
to have been a variety of even looser pedagogical arrangements alongside
this galaxy. In 1359, for example, the bishop of Lincoln granted license
to the rector of Barnack in Northamptonshire to choose a "lettered
[litteratus] and fit master in the parish to teach the boys and others
going to him . . . reading, song, and grammar, to the increase of divine

---

[59] *Educational Charters and Documents*, ed. Leach, 273–5.
[60] A. F. Leach, "Schools," 421–92 in *The Victoria History of the County of Lincoln* [*VCH Lincs*], ed. William Page (London: Archibald Constable, 1906), 2: 421–2.
[61] Leach, "Schools," in *VCH Lincs*, 2: 426.
[62] Leach, "Schools," in *VCH Lincs*, 2: 427.
[63] Leach, "Schools," in *VCH Lincs*, 2: 479.
[64] *Educational Charters and Documents*, ed. Leach, 280–1.
[65] Leach, "Schools," in *VCH Lincs*, 2: 460.

learning."[66] There is also a demand in the court records from the lord of Long Bennington, Lincolnshire in 1378 for the names of those tenant farmers who had failed to pay a license to send their sons to school, as well as the "blank refusal" with which this was greeted on the grounds that "by ancient custom" tenants "had a right to send their sons to school without permission" from any lord.[67] The document that reveals most about the variety of schooling available in Lincolnshire is a letter dated February 7, 1311 from the bishop of Lincoln to his chancellor which directs him to "put down rival grammar schools" that had been set up "outside of prebends" [extra loca prebendalia]—that is, schools that lay outside even the complicated network of ecclesiastical governance—on pain of canonical censure.[68] A document from 1305 suggests, moreover, that such unlicensed schools were probably as much the rule as the exception in Lincolnshire in this period, for it shows "all the clerks of the parish churches of the city who were teaching boys in their churches song or music" without license being summoned before the chapter, and, although these clerks deny that they are teaching without license at present "they could not deny that at some time they had done so."[69]

The prominence and frequency of references to these "adulterine" or unlicensed schools in the record make clear just how fully elementary schooling slipped the reins of the church even where clerics were doing the teaching. In an entry from 1367 in his register, for example, Archbishop Thoresby decries the elementary instruction occurring "in parish churches, homes and other places" [ecclesiis parochialibus, domibus, et aliis locis].[70] In Bury, in about 1279, there is a generic document (protecting the jurisdiction of "Sir C") designed to stop (on pain of excommunication) "pedagogues" who "keep adulterine schools within the liberty of Saint Edmund . . . meeting indiscriminately and publicly" [infra libertatem Sancti Edmundi regant adulterinas . . . pupplice congregatos indistincte].[71] In the twelfth century the bishop of Lincoln writes to the Archdeacon of Huntingdon to impose "silence" [silencium inponatis] on the school set up

---

[66] A. F. Leach, "Schools," 201–88 in *The Victoria History of the County of Northampton* [*VCH Northants*], ed. R. M. Serjeantson and W. Ryland D. Adkins (London: Archibald Constable, 1906), 2: 280.

[67] Sylvia Thrupp, "The Problem of Replacement-Rates in Late Medieval English Population," *Economic History Review* n.s. 18 (1965): 113.

[68] Leach, "Schools," in *VCH Lincs*, 2: 422.

[69] Leach, "Schools," in *VCH Lincs*, 2: 423.

[70] For the text see A. F. Leach, *Early Yorkshire Schools*, vol. 1: *York, Beverley, Ripon* (Leeds: Yorkshire Archaeological Society, 1899), 22–3. Cited in Zieman, *Singing the New Song*, 17.

[71] Leach and Steele Hutton, "Schools," in *The Victoria History of the County of Suffolk*, ed. Page, 2: 309.

in the local church "contrary to the Pope's granting of privileges to the canons of Huntingdon" [contra tenorem domini pape privilegii et nostrum confirmacionem in preiudicium scolarum de Huntingdon] to maintain the grammar school of the town; in so doing what he registers most clearly is that a school has simply sprung up—without any institutional impetus— in a parish church.[72] Such informal schooling was almost certainly even more prevalent than the record discloses, since there is an inevitable bias toward the church in a record it was largely responsible for keeping. There are only "scanty indications of schooling" at Abingdon Abbey, for example, but because its "earliest chartulary" (*c.*1100) mentions a "boys' school" [scola puerorum] and a "precentor" [cantor] responsible for them, it is seems certain that some looser arrangements preceded the almonry school that this school had become by the fourteenth century.[73] Sometimes when we have specific references to elementary learning in the abbey's fourteenth-century accounts there is no mention of a school at all, but, just as in Gilbert Maghfeld's account book, there is still a sequence of payments to clerics who clearly taught (to a "scol mayster" for the "public grammar school of the town" in 1375–6, for example, and to a "teacher of the youths" [instructor juvenum] in 1383–4).[74]

Elementary schooling may also have occurred in unsanctioned and fugitive forms in nunneries since this seems to explain best why so many children were fostered there. In 1359, for example, Bishop Gynewell writes to the nunnery in Elstow to forbid all boarders, except girls under ten and boys under six.[75] There is another complaint lodged in 1440 against a nun in Catesby who has "six or seven young folk of both sexes, that do lie in the dorter."[76] Although nuns clearly boarded such children as a simple fee-earning proposition, a record from the late twelfth century in which Bishop Hugh of Lincoln sends Robert of Noyon "when he seemed to be about five years old, or a little older" [annorum vero quinque videbatur esse, aut paululum majoris aetatum] to Elstow nunnery "to be taught his letters" [literis informandum] suggests that such boarding often enabled, or was undertaken for the purpose of, literacy training, not least because almost all of these boarders were of

---

[72] Mary Bateson, "The Huntingdon Song School and the School of St. Gregory's, Canterbury," *English Historical Review* 72 (1903): 713.

[73] A. F. Leach, "Schools," 244–85 in *The Victoria History of the County of Berkshire* [*VCH Berks*], ed. P. H. Ditchfield and William Page (London: Archibald Constable, 1907), 2: 260.

[74] Leach, "Schools," in *VCH Berks*, 2: 261.

[75] Eileen Power, *Medieval English Nunneries c.1275–1535* (Cambridge: Cambridge University Press, 1922), 262–3.

[76] Power, *Medieval English Nunneries*, 272.

school age.[77] A statute of 1256–7 forbidding the education of boys in Cistercian nunneries helps to confirm such a supposition.[78] And there are still other documents forbidding the education of boys at Wherwell convent in 1284, at Romsey convent in 1311, and at Heynings convent in 1359.[79] Although nuns were illiterate as a rule, some religious women knew enough to teach, as Aelred of Rievaulx indicates when he writes to his sister, who has become an anchorite:

> Pueris et puellis nullum ad te concedes accessum. Sunt quaedam inclusae quae docendis puellis occupantur, et cellam suam uertunt in scholam. Illa sedet ad fenestram istae in portico resident.
>
> [Allow neither boys nor girls to have access to you. There are certain women anchorites, who are busied in teaching girls and turn their anchorhold into a school. The anchorite sits at her window, and girls sit in the porch.][80]

A similar prohibition can be found in *Ancrene Wisse* (*c*.1215–24) a guide for women anchorites written in English:

> Ancre ne schal nawt forwurthe scol-meistre, ne turnen ancre-hus to childrene scole. Hire meiden mei learen sum other meiden thet were pliht of to leornin among wepmen other bimong gromes.
>
> [An anchorite should not reduce herself to a school-teacher, nor turn her anchor-house into a school for children. Her maiden may teach some other little girl for whom it would be a danger to learn among men or boys.][81]

The last of these examples shows, again, that the essential structure for elementary learning in medieval England was often no more than the opportunity for contact between the literate and illiterate and a "school," therefore, no more than the circumstances that created that opportunity.

Medieval elementary schools in this sense had no definable shape other than the activity of teaching itself. They were what Bourdieu called, in another helpful formulation, "structuring structures," arrangements and activities of people that only become a "school" after much repetition, and

---

[77] Adam of Eynsham, *Magna Vita S. Hugonis Episcopi Lincolniensis*, ed. James F. Dimock (London: Longman, Green, Longman, Roberts, and Green, 1864), III.iv (p. 146).

[78] *Cistercian Statutes, A.D. 1256–7*, ed. J. T. Fowler (London: Bradbury, Agnew, 1890), 105.

[79] Power, *Medieval English Nunneries*, 263.

[80] Aelred of Rievaulx, *De institutione inclusarum*, 635–82 in Aelred of Rievaulx, *Opera Omnia*, ed. A. Hoste and C. H. Talbot, Corpus Christianorum, Continuatio Mediaevalis 1 (Turnhout: Brepols, 1971), §4 (p. 640). On the limited literacy of nuns in this period see Sally Thompson, *Women Religious: The Founding of English Nunneries After the Conquest* (Oxford: Clarendon Press, 1991), 13–15 and Power, *Medieval English Nunneries*, 244–55.

[81] *Ancrene Wisse*, ed. Robert Hasenfratz, (Kalamazoo, MI: Medieval Institute Publications, 2000), VIII: 162–4.

therefore always retrospectively.[82] A deed of 1384 from Lady Katherine of Berkeley to two chaplains, Walter Burnet and William Pendock, that Leach sees as the "foundation of Wotton-under-Edge Free Grammar School" offers a detailed example of this process. On the one hand the deed has in mind the "foundation" [fundacio] of an undying institution:

> We, the said Katharine, closely and attentively considering that the purpose of many wishing to be taught grammar...caused the said Walter and William to acquire to them and their heirs in fee the lands and tenements underwritten, that they might newly build a school-house in Wotton-under-Edge, and may dispose of them for the habitation and foundation, and likewise for the maintenance of a master and two poor scholars of the art of grammar; which master and his successors shall govern and teach all scholars coming to the same house or school for instruction in such art.

> [Nos dicta Katerina considerantes propensius et attente propositum multorum in gramatica...certa terras et tenementa subscripta, dictos Walterum et Willelmum adquirere procurauimus, sibi et heredibus suis in feodo, ut ipsi quondam domum scolarum in Wotton under Egge de nouo construere et pro inhabitacione siue fundacione, et similiter pro sustentacione, unius magistri et duorum pauperum scolarium artis gramatice ea valeant disponere;qui quidem magister et successores sui gubernabunt et informabunt omnes scolares ad eandem domum siue scolam pro erudicione huiusmodi artis venientes.][83]

But, as the deed goes on to reveal, the institution imagined here is really nothing more than a house on two acres of land, and the school at the point of inception is nothing but a "dwelling" in which there is a literate person (the "master") and precisely enough students to constitute a class:

> And to the same master and scholars...we give and grant and by this our deed have confirmed the said place containing two acres of land with the appurtenances in Wootton-under-Edge to hold...for their dwelling and living in the same house forever to possess freely and wholly.

> [Eidemque magistro et scolaribus clericis...damus et concedimus ac presenti carta nostra confirmauimus dictam placeam continentem duas acras terre cum pertinenciis in Wotton under Egge tenendum...pro mora et inhabitacione suis in eadem domo imperpetuum possidendum libere integre.][84]

Identical in what its outlines imply, but less detailed in its description, is the kind of structuring structure established by a tenant in

---

[82] Pierre Bourdieu, *Outline of a Theory of Practice*, trans. Richard Nice (Cambridge: Cambridge University Press, 1977; first published 1972), 53.

[83] *Educational Charters and Documents*, ed. Leach, 330–1.

[84] *Educational Charters and Documents*, ed. Leach, 332–5.

Wilberton, Cambridgeshire, who allowed a clerk who was the cousin of his wife to live in a hut in their garden. This may have been no more than an arrangement for lodging but, as Sylvia Thrupp observed, "if such a man was doing anything at all, it is likely to have been a little teaching."[85] And there are many other indications that grammar-school teaching occurred as exactly this sort of sideline. A record from Dunham, Nottinghamshire, shows that the "master of the Grammar School" was not only called "Robert le Taillor" (a name suggesting that teaching was not his primary profession) but that he was a landholder, since he offers a quitclaim in the rights in some of his land from one person in the town to another.[86] In 1391 the roll of the borough courts of Higham Ferrers record a quitclaim of property to "Master Henry Bartone, Scholemayster" who seems also to have been the mayor of the town.[87] These last two figures are not said to be clerks, although they may have had literacy training of the very kind they seem to have provided (informal, local, and improvised) and records from Preston, Lancashire, from *c*.1230 suggest how this amalgamation of property and school teaching could have occurred. In that case we find William of Kirkham, "magister" [master] receiving a number of parcels of land in the town fields "with the common assent of the town" [communi concensu et assensu tocius villae de Preston], likely as a mode of payment or maintenance for his duties as master of their school.[88]

Although the paucity of detail in the records makes it very difficult to assess the issue over long periods of time or in a large variety of locales, elementary education in the Middle Ages seems to have been, on the whole, ad hoc.[89] Whenever a medieval person had occasion to write about how he learned to read and write, in fact, he almost always described a local tutelary relationship rather than an institution. Orderic Vitalis

---

[85] Thrupp, "Problem of Replacement-Rates in Late Medieval English Population," 112–13.

[86] A. F. Leach, "Schools," 179–251 in *The Victoria History of the County of Nottingham*, ed. William Page (London: Constable and Company, 1910), 2: 179.

[87] *Educational Charters and Documents*, ed. Leach, 348–9 (see also a document in this volume recording the appointment of the school's master by the king, 372–5); see also, Leach, "Schools," in *VCH Northants*, 2: 217–18.

[88] *The Chartulary of Cockersand Abbey of the Premonstratensian Order*, 3 vols. in 7, ed. William Farrer (Manchester: Chetham Society, 1898–1909), 1, pt. 2: 220 (for a variety of other land grants that seem to be part of this transaction see 1, pt. 2: 217–19). These transactions are mentioned in A. F. Leach and H. J. Chaytor, "Schools," 561–624 in *The Victoria History of the County of Lancaster*, ed. William Farrer and J. Brownbill (London: Archibald Constable, 1908), 2: 569–70.

[89] This was clearly also true in antiquity as Robert Kaster notes in his account of elementary learning in the period: "It seems that most *grammatici* were likely to be sole practitioners in their towns; as such they would have been free from competition but at the same time isolated, large fish in small ponds," *Guardians of Language: The Grammarian and Society in Late Antiquity* (Berkeley, CA: University of California Press, 1988), 107.

(1075–*c*.1142), for example, says that when he was five years old his he was "put to school in Shrewsbury" [apud urbem Scrobesburiam scoliae traditus sum] but that schooling seems to have consisted of five years of one-on-one instruction in "letters" with the priest, Siward [illic Siguardus insignis presbiter per quinque annos . . . litteras docuit me].[90] A century later, John of Salisbury in the *Policraticus* says that, as a boy, he was "sent to a priest in order to be taught the psalms" [dum enim puer ut psalmos addiscerem sacerdoti traditus essem].[91] A similar picture emerges when we look behind the charter of 1138 that grants three schools, St Mary-le-Bow, St Martin-le-Grand, and St Paul's School, a monopoly on elementary education in London.[92] In a deed of 1298 the "school" of St Martin-le-Grand consists of no more than a payment of £8 from another London merchant, John the Cap-Maker of Fleet Street, to a single schoolmaster ("magistro scolarum"), Master Hugh of Wytington.[93] This is not a small amount of money and suggests that Hugh did a significant amount of teaching in return, but in form—as a logic or structuring structure—such schooling is identical to the local arrangements made by Gilbert Maghfeld with which I began this chapter, a payment that implies neither schools nor classrooms of students but, rather, literacy training at its zero degree: one literate man training at least one illiterate boy how to read and write.

SCHOOLBOOK VARIATIONS

Even where a school was no more than a nook in a church and the schoolmaster was no more than a priest prepared to offer tuition for money, the defining condition for all literacy training was writing itself: some sort of book containing the abc's, or a grammar, or basic texts to read. A number of the books that provided this foundation survive from the fourteenth century and the decades before and after, and their contents provide another sort of window onto the ad hoc practices of elementary learning in the period. The dating of these books as well as their contents is inevitably imprecise, not least because most of them consisted of layers, often as fascicles from different periods were brought together into a single codex, but, also, as a primary text was later glossed. If careful attention is

[90] *The Ecclesiastical History of Ordericus Vitalis*, 6 vols., ed. and trans. Marjorie Chibnall (Oxford: Clarendon Press, 1969–78), 6: 552.

[91] John of Salisbury, *Policraticus*, ed. K. S. B. Keats-Rohan, Corpus Christianorum, Continuatio Mediaevalis 118 (Turnhout: Brepols, 1993–), II: ch. 28.

[92] For the granting of the monopoly by the chancellor see *Educational Charters and Documents*, ed. Leach, 90.

[93] Leach, *Schools of Medieval England*, 142.

paid to the composition of such layers, however, as well as ancillary information about dating often embedded in them, and if a range of manuscripts from before and after the fourteenth century are included as a kind of baseline for the particularities of this pivotal century, these books also offer another account of the improvisatory nature of basic literacy training in the period from this most material of perspectives.

Although there are doubtless more in existence, I have discovered thirty-one volumes from either the fourteenth century or roughly fifty years on either side of it whose contents suggest that they were elementary schoolbooks, and whose provenance seems most likely to have been England.[94] These English schoolbooks fall into three distinct categories. First there are two "notebooks" containing exercises, responses to exercises, as well as some unsystematic notes on grammar (Oxford, Bodleian Library, MS Rawlinson D 328 and London, Public Record Office MS C 47/34/13). Second, there are five collections of Latin grammars (Dublin, Trinity College MS 270; Worcester, Cathedral Library MS F 61; Cambridge, Gonville & Caius, MS 383; Lincoln Cathedral, Chapter Library, MS 88; and Oxford, Bodleian Library MS Auctarium F.3.9). Third, there are twenty-four basic readers on the model of Yale MS 513 which I mentioned in the introduction to this chapter. They contain versions of—really variations on—the usual set of reading texts which other evidence makes clear was common in basic literacy training. The list of all thirty-one of these books is in rough chronological order, giving approximate dates as well as any explicit indications of provenance in the manuscripts themselves.

Surviving schoolbooks from late medieval England

Oxford, Bodleian Library, MS Auctarium, F.5.6 (thirteenth century)
Cambridge, Peterhouse College, MS 215 (thirteenth century)
London, British Library Royal, MS 15.A.VII (thirteenth century)

---

[94] Some of these schoolbooks have been discussed before. See, for example, the landmark article by Brother Bonaventure [also known as John M. Miner], "The Teaching of Latin in Later Medieval England," *Medieval Studies* 23 (1961): 1–20. Bonaventure does not examine all the manuscripts dealt with here, and he discusses a large number of later fifteenth-century books that I ignore. There is also an analysis of "grammatical manuscripts relevant to the curriculum of the grammar schools" in Miner, *Grammar Schools of Medieval England*, 136–51. In his account of the thirteenth-century use of the "liber Catonianus" (59–79) Tony Hunt offers detailed comments about a number of the schoolbooks I describe, including Cambridge, Trinity College, MS 0.5.4 (*Teaching and Learning Latin*, 1: 70 and 1: 75–6), Lincoln Cathedral, Chapter Library, MS 132 (1: 71), Cambridge, Peterhouse College, MS 2.1.0 (1: 172, identified here as MS 215), and Oxford, Bodleian Library, MS Rawlinson G.60 (1: 76–7) in *Teaching and Learning Latin in Thirteenth-Century England*. A number of thirteenth-century schoolbooks are described in Clogan, "Literary Genres," 199–209.

London, British Library Royal, MS 15.A.XXXI (thirteenth century)
Nottingham, University Library, Mi(ddleton) LM 2 (thirteenth century)
Dublin, Trinity College, MS 270 (thirteenth to fourteeenth century)
Cambridge, Peterhouse College, MS 2.1.0 (thirteenth and fourteenth centuries)
Lincoln Cathedral, Chapter Library, MS 132 (thirteenth century)
Worcester, Cathedral Library, MS F 147 (thirteenth century)
New Haven, Connecticut, Beineke Library, Yale MS 513 (*c.*1300)
Worcester, Cathedral Library, MS F 123 (fourteenth century; English writings added in fifteenth century)
Worcester, Cathedral Library, MS F 61 (fourteenth century)
London, British Library, Additional MS 10090 (fourteenth century)
London, British Library, Additional MS 10093 (fourteenth century)
Oxford, Bodleian Library, MS Digby 26 (fourteenth and fifteenth centuries)
Cambridge, Gonville & Caius College, MS 203/109 (later fourteenth century)
Cambridge, Gonville & Caius College, MS 383 (fourteenth and fifteenth centuries)
London, British Library, MS Harley 4967 (fourteenth and fifteenth centuries)
Oxford, Bodleian Library, MS Digby 100 (fourteenth and fifteenth centuries)
Oxford, Bodleian Library, MS Hatton 58 (fourteenth and fifteenth centuries)
Oxford, Bodleian Library, MS Rawlinson D 328 (fourteenth and fifteenth centuries)
Cambridge, Trinity College, MS O.5.4 (*c.*1410)
Lincoln Cathedral, Chapter Library, MS 88 (Oxford, *c.*1414)
London, Public Record Office, MS C 47/34/13 (*c.*1416)
Cambridge, St John's College, MS 147 (fifteenth century)
Oxford, Lincoln College, MS Lat. 129 (1427–8)
Cambridge, St John's College, MS 163 (1438 and after)
Cambridge, Trinity College, MS R.3.56 (fifteenth century and early thirteenth century)
Oxford, Bodleian Library, MS Bodley 837 (fifteenth century)
Cambridge, University Library, Additional MS 2830 (1434/5)
Oxford, Bodleian Library, MS Auctarium F.3.9 (1400–50)

Most of these books contain only Latin writings, but Gonville & Caius, MS 383 also contains some material in French and five of them contain a significant amount of writing in English (Worcester Cathedral, MS F123, Rawlinson MS D 328, Hatton MS 58, Trinity College, MS 0.5.4, and Lincoln Cathedral, MS 88).[95]

---

[95] The contents and composition of all of these books is carefully analyzed in David Thomson, *A Descriptive Catalogue of Middle English Grammatical Texts* (New York: Garland, 1979), 158–68 (Trinity College, MS 0.5.4), 185–92 (Lincoln Cathedral, MS 88), 285–9 (Hatton MS 58), 290–315 (Rawlinson MS D 328), 316–22 (Worcester, Cathedral Library, MS F 123). I have excluded from my survey any of the books Thomson analyzes with putative dates after 1450. Ralph Hanna describes the Nottingham volume

The twenty-four of these schoolbooks that contain literary texts rather than only grammars or other works of instruction seem, at first, to confirm the traditional, scholarly grouping of the "libri Catoniani" since the paradigmatic collection of these six texts (the *Distichs of Cato*, Theodulus, *Eclogue*, Avianus, *Fables*, Maximian, *Elegies*, Statius, *Achilleid*, Claudian, *On the Rape of Proserpina*) can be found in six thirteenth-century books (Nottingham, University Library, Mi LM 2, Peterhouse College, MS 215 and MS 2.1.0, Royal MS 15.A.VII, Lincoln MS 132, and Worcester Cathedral F.147).[96] Taking these books as a base line it is possible to construct a narrative of decline in this tradition, with Royal 15.A.XXXI, in the thirteenth century, containing only three of the formerly "standard" texts (the *Distichs of Cato*, Theodulus, *Eclogue*, Avianus, *Fables*), and Yale 513, copied at the very beginning of the fourteenth century, containing a slightly different three (Theodulus, Avianus, and Maximianus). That narrative could be traced through a more severe winnowing later in the period, so that, in the fourteenth century, British Library, London Additional MS 10090 contains only Avianus and Statius and, by the turn of the fifteenth century, MS Digby 100 and Trinity College, MS O.5.4 contain only the *Distichs* and Theodulus. The standard syllabus is then worn down to the barest stump of a single *liber*, the *Distichs of Cato* (in MS Digby 26, Additional MS 10093, MS Hatton 58, Rawlinson MS D 328, or St John's College, MS 147), or Avianus (in MS Harley 4967), or Theodulus (in Trinity College, MS R.3.56). And yet, if we go back to other books in the thirteenth century it is clear that any such a progressive narrative is undermined from the start, not least because MS Auctarium F.5.6, one of the earliest of the schoolbooks listed previously, includes only three of the *libri Catoniani* (Maximian, Statius, and Claudian). Taken together these schoolbooks clearly demonstrate a normative sense among their compilers of the range of texts suitable for basic literacy training, but they do not finally converge on the same six texts in the way histories of education suggest that they should. It is truer to say that each schoolbook is "individualistic," as Moran has put it well, a set of selections constrained

---

(Mi LM 2) as a "fairly typical schoolbook" with the "traditional set of texts taught in medieval grammar schools . . . in the traditional order," "Literacy, Schooling, Universities," 172–94 in *The Cambridge Companion to Medieval English Culture*, ed. Andrew Galloway (Cambridge: Cambridge University Press, 2011), 177.

[96] Part of Peterhouse, MS 2.1.0 was copied in the fourteenth century, but the book is "two volumes in one," and the *libri Catoniani* are in the first volume which was copied in the thirteenth century. See M. R. James, *A Descriptive Catalogue of the Manuscripts of the Library in Peterhouse* (Cambridge: Cambridge University Press, 1899), 247–9. For editions and translations of these texts see "Note on Texts" (pp. xiii–xv) in the present volume.

by a normative sense of possibilities but more generally characterized by the variety of their contents.[97]

In that variety these twenty-four books could also be seen to narrate a different sort of progress toward the newer canon of schoolroom texts that replaced the *libri Catoniani* with less pagan and more penitential content over time, "finally stabiliz[ing] as a group... in the early part of the fourteenth century."[98] These texts include *Stans puer ad mensam* (sometimes known as *De civilitate morum* and habitually attributed to Robert Grosseteste because it begins with a short poem he wrote), the *Liber cartule* (sometimes simply called "*Chartula*"), the *Liber penitencialis* (often identified by its incipit, "Peniteas cito"), the *Facetus* beginning "Cum (or 'Est') nihil utilius," the *Facetus* beginning "Moribus et vita," Matthew of Vendôme's *Tobias*, and Alan of Lille's *Liber parabolarum*.[99] MS Auctarium F.5.6 fits this narrative, since it puts the *Liber cartule*, the *Liber penitencialis*, and *Tobias* alongside Maximian, Statius, and Claudian, as if the new syllabus is slowly edging out the old.[100] But this story is also frustrated by the contents of these books, since to lay them out chronologically is not to see the growing dominance and then stability of this "new" group but, rather, more and different variations. Many of these books only contain one text from this new "group": MS Royal 15.A.VII, Nottingham University Library, Mi LM 2, Peterhouse College, MS 2.1.0, MS Harley 4967, Additional MS 2830 contain only the *Liber penitencialis*, Worcester Cathedral, MS F 147 contains only the *Liber cartule*, MS Royal 15.A.XXXI contains only the *Liber parabolarum*, Trinity College, MS R.3.56 contains only the *Tobias*. Where books contain more than one of these texts, the combinations are also varied, with the *Liber cartule*, *Liber penitencialis*, and *Tobias* in one (MS Auctarium F.5.6, as I have noted), the *Liber cartule*, *Facetus* ("Moribus et vita"), and *Tobias* in another (MS Digby 26), and the *Liber cartule*, *Liber penitencialis*, *Facetus* ("Est nihil utilius"), and *Liber parabolarum* in yet another (Gonville &

---

[97] Moran, *Growth of English Schooling*, 26.

[98] Hunt, *Teaching and Learning Latin*, 1: 70. On the penitential emphasis of these later additions see Woods and Copeland, "Classroom and Confession," 384–9; Mann, "'He Knew Nat Catoun,'" 49–52.

[99] For editions and translations of these texts see "Note on Texts" in the present volume. On the Middle English translations of *Stans puer ad mensam* see *A Manual of the Writings in Middle English*, 11 vols., ed. J. B. Severs, (vols. 1–2), Albert E. Hartung (vols. 3–10), Peter G. Beidler (vol. 11) (New Haven, CT: Connecticut Academy of Arts and Sciences, 1967–), 9: 3004.

[100] This progressive history can be found in Nicholas Orme, "Schools and Society," 1–21 in his *Education and Society in Medieval and Renaissance England* (London: Hambledon Press, 1989), 29; Orme, *Medieval Schools*, 100–4; Woods and Copeland, "Classroom and Confession," 384–5.

Caius College, MS 203/109). As this summary should also make clear, these groupings do not function as an alternative to the *libri Catoniani*—they in no way replace it—since they are also regularly accompanied by those texts. Indeed, as the next list shows in summary, fourteen of the English schoolbooks I have been describing mix elements of the *libri Catoniani* with this "newer" canon.

The schoolroom texts in English schoolbooks
(*libri Catoniani* in bold)

Oxford, Bodleian Library, MS Auctarium F.5.6 (thirteenth century)
Maximian, *Elegies*; Statius, *Achilleid*; Claudian, *On the Rape of Proserpina*; *Liber cartule*; *Liber penitencialis*; *Tobias*

Cambridge, Peterhouse College, MS 215 (thirteenth century)
Distichs of Cato*; Theodulus, *Eclogue*; Avianus, *Fables*; Maximian, *Elegies*; Claudian, *On the Rape of Proserpina*; Statius, *Achilleid

London, British Library, MS Royal 15.A.VII (thirteenth century)
***Distichs of Cato*; Theodulus, *Eclogue*; Avianus, *Fables*; Maximian, *Elegies*; Claudian, *On the Rape of Proserpina*; Statius, *Achilleid*;** *Liber penitencialis*

London, British Library, MS Royal 15.A.XXXI (thirteenth century)
***Distichs of Cato*; Theodulus, Eclogue; Avianus, *Fables*;** *Liber parabolarum*

Nottingham, University Library, Mi(ddleton) LM 2 (thirteenth century)
***Distichs of Cato*; Theodulus, *Eclogue*; Avianus, *Fables*; Maximian, *Elegies*; Claudian, *On the Rape of Proserpina*; Statius, *Achilleid*;** *Liber penitencialis*

Cambridge, Peterhouse College, MS 2.1.0 (thirteenth and fourteenth centuries)
***Distichs of Cato*; Theodulus, *Eclogue*; Avianus, *Fables*; Maximian, *Elegies*; Claudian, *On the Rape of Proserpina*; Statius, *Achilleid*;** *Liber penitencialis*

Lincoln Cathedral, Chapter Library, MS 132 (thirteenth century)
Distichs of Cato*; Theodulus, *Eclogue*; Avianus, *Fables*; Maximian, *Elegies*; Claudian, *On the Rape of Proserpina*; Statius, *Achilleid

Worcester, Cathedral Library, MS F. 147 (thirteenth century)
***Distichs of Cato*; Theodulus, *Eclogue*; Avianus, *Fables*; Maximian, *Elegies*; Claudian, *On the Rape of Proserpina*; Statius, *Achilleid*;** *Liber cartule*

New Haven, Connecticut, Beineke Library, Yale MS 513 (*c*.1300)
Theodulus, *Eclogue*; Avianus, *Fables*; Maximian, *Elegies*

London, British Library, Additional MS 10090 (fourteenth century)
Avianus, *Fables*; Statius, *Achilleid*

London, British Library, Additional MS 10093 (fourteenth century)
Distichs of Cato

Oxford, Bodleian Library, MS Digby 26 (fourteenth and fifteenth centuries)
  Distichs of Cato; *Liber cartule*; *Facetus* (beginning "Moribus et vita"); *Tobias*

Cambridge, Gonville & Caius College, MS 203/109 (later fourteenth century)
  Liber cartule; *Liber penitencialis*; *Facetus* ("Cum [Est] nihil utilius"); *Liber parabolarum*

British Library, MS Harley 4967 (fourteenth and fifteenth centuries)
  Avianus, Fables; *Liber penitencialis*

Oxford, Bodleian Library, MS Digby 100 (fourteenth and fifteenth centuries)
  Distichs of Cato; **Theodulus, Eclogue**; *Tobias*; *Facetus* ("Cum [Est] nihil utilius"); *Liber penitencialis*

Oxford, Bodleian Library, MS Hatton 58 (fourteenth and fifteenth centuries)
  Distichs of Cato; *Liber parabolarum*; *Liber cartule*

Oxford, Bodleian Library, Rawlinson MS D 328 (fourteenth and fifteenth centuries; notebook)
  Distichs of Cato; *Liber penitencialis* [fragment]

Cambridge, Trinity College, MS O.5.4 (*c.*1409)
  Distichs of Cato; **Theodulus, Eclogue**; *Stans puer ad mensam*, *Liber cartule*; *Facetus* ("Cum [Est] nihil utilius"); *Liber parabolarum*

Cambridge, St John's College, MS 147 (fifteenth century)
  Distichs of Cato; *Liber cartule*; *Facetus* ("Cum [Est] nihil utilius") ("Est") nihil utilius"; *Liber penitencialis*; *Liber parabolarum*

Cambridge, Trinity College, MS R.3.56 (fifteenth century and early thirteenth century)
  Theodulus, Eclogue; *Tobias*

Oxford, Bodleian Library, MS Bodley 837 (fifteenth century)
  Stans puer ad mensam

Cambridge, Additional MS 2830 (1434/5)
  Liber penitencialis

Such varied collections of texts could also be described as ad hoc insofar as none is like any of the others. But the truly improvisatory quality of such schoolbooks is best demonstrated by the large number of them that include a text or texts that appear in no other book. In many cases these are fragments of the kind of classical texts that have also been shown to be a consistent part of elementary learning.[101] Ovid's *Remedia Amoris* can

---

[101] On the classical texts that were a staple of schoolbooks see Sanford, "Classical Authors in the *Libri Manuales*"; Hunt, *Teaching and Learning Latin*, 1: 59–66; Suzanne Reynolds, *Medieval Reading: Grammar, Rhetoric and the Classical Text* (Cambridge: Cambridge University Press, 1996), esp. 7–16; Vincent Gillespie, "From the Twelfth

only be found in MS Auctarium F.5.6, for example, and Horace's *Carmina*, Juvenal's *Satires*, and Lucan's *De Bello Civili* only in Worcester, MS 147, the (psuedo-) Ovid, "De mirabilibus mundi" and Horace's *Epistolae* only in MS Digby 100, and Virgil's *Eclogues* only in MS Harley 4967. In other cases these isolated works are late antique works of philosophy (only Additional MS 10093 contains the first two books of Boethius's *Consolatio Philosophiae*) or wisdom (such as a collection of epigrams attributed to Augustine present only in Additional MS 10093).[102] Sometimes these unique items are treatises on rhetoric or poetics: Worcester, MS F 123, for example, is the only volume to contain Peter the Chanter's *De Tropis Loquendi*, John of Beauvais's *De Quantitate Vocalium*, and Bede's *De Schematibus et Tropis*, while MS Digby 100 is the only volume to contain Marbod of Rennes, *De Ornamentis Verborum*. In some books these unique texts are works of medieval literature (Worcester MS 147 is the only volume to contain Walter of Chatillon's *Alexandreis*), but in others they are works of devotion (only MS Digby 26 contains a copy of Hildebert's *Vita Beatae Mariae Egyptiacae*, and only Lincoln Cathedral, MS 88 contains the *Expositio Hymnorum*).

These thirty-one books illustrate their ad hoc nature best, however, in the unique grammars they collect. To be sure, it is easy to see that many of these volumes *are* schoolbooks because they contain the most commonly used grammars in the Middle Ages, Donatus's *Ars minor* (which appears in Peterhouse College, MS 215, MS Digby 26, MS Hatton 58, Worcester Cathedral, MS 61, Trinity College, MS 0.5.4, Lincoln Cathedral, MS 88, St John's College, MS 163, and MS Auctarium F.3.9), Alexander of Villa-Dei's *Doctrinale* (in Nottingham, University Library, Mi LM 2, Worcester Cathedral, MS F 147, MS Digby 26, Rawlinson MS D 328, and Dublin, Trinity College, MS 270) and Evrard of Béthune's *Graecismus* (in Nottingham, University Library, Mi LM 2, Worcester Cathedral, MS F 147, and Dublin, Trinity College, MS 270).[103] But almost as common as such standard grammars in these books are grammars that occur in only one

---

Century to c. 1450," 145–235 in *The Cambridge History of Literary Criticism*, vol. 2: *The Middle Ages*, ed. Alastair Minnis and Ian Johnson (Cambridge: Cambridge University Press, 2005), 150–60.

[102] On the nature of "wisdom literature," and its importance to elementary learning, see Chapter 6 in the present volume.

[103] On these as the standard grammars see Orme, *Medieval Schools*, 88–93 and Copeland and Sluiter, *Medieval Grammar and Rhetoric*, 82–5 (on Donatus and the *Ars minor*), 573–6 (on Alexander of Villa-Dei's *Doctrinale*), and 584–6 (on Evrard of Béthune's *Graecismus*).

book, each presumably written by a particular grammar-school master to address a local set of pedagogical needs. As John Miner put this point, "there appear to be as many treatises as there are masters."[104] Some of these treatises are metrical, such as the various verses on verbs ending in "-do" and the mnemonics for Latin vocabulary in Gonville & Caius College, MS 383,[105] or the 3,500-line metrical grammar in MS Auctarium F.3.9.[106] But most of them are in prose and often short, addressing a very specific grammatical concept or issue. Two different fourteenth-century books, Worcester Cathedral, MS 61 and Worcester Cathedral, MS 123 suggest that some of these treatises circulated to a limited extent: these books share an elementary grammatical treatise, as well as treatises on the parts of speech, on the formation of tenses, and on the quantities of middle syllables, although none of these texts is found in any other book.[107] However, each of these books also contains grammatical treatises that the other—and no other surviving book—lacks: MS 61 includes a unique treatise on verbs and one on the quantities of first syllables,[108] and MS 123 contains unique treatises on the parts of speech and on syntax.[109] It is also the case that ten of the thirty-one schoolbooks I have been describing contain a grammatical treatise that occurs in no other surviving text (Nottingham, University Library, Mi LM 2, Gonville & Caius College, MS 203/109, Digby 100, Hatton 58, Rawlinson MS D 328, Trinity College, MS O.5.4, Lincoln Cathedral, MS 88, St John's College, MS 163, Bodley MS 837, Additional MS 2830).[110] In all this variety, the

[104] Miner, *Grammar Schools of Medieval England*, 147.

[105] M. R. James, *A Descriptive Catalogue of the Manuscripts in the Library of Gonville and Caius College*, 2 vols. (Cambridge: Cambridge University Press, 1907), 2: 435–7 (see items 2 and 4 in this MS).

[106] R. W. Hunt, *A Summary Catalogue of Western Manuscripts in the Bodleian Library at Oxford*, 7 vols. in 9 (Oxford: Clarendon Press, 1895–1953), 2, part 2: 689–90 (see item 3 in this MS).

[107] For the treatises these texts share see R. M. Thomson, *Descriptive Catalogue of the Medieval Manuscripts in Worcester Cathedral Library* (Woodbridge: Boydell & Brewer, 2001), 37–8 and 84–5 where the overlapping items are 17 in MS 61 and 27 in MS 123 (on tenses), 20 in MS 61 and 4 in MS 123 (on parts of speech), 21 in MS 61 and 16 in MS 123 (on quantities of medial syllables), and 22 in MS 61 and 3 in MS 123 (elementary treatise on grammar).

[108] See items 17 (on verbs) and 18 (on first syllables) in Thomson, *Descriptive Catalogue of the Medieval Manuscripts in Worcester Cathedral Library*, 38.

[109] See items 7 (on parts of speech) and 8 (on syntax) in Thomson, *Descriptive Catalogue of the Medieval Manuscripts in Worcester Cathedral Library*, 84.

[110] For these treatises see James, *Descriptive Catalogue of the Manuscripts in the Library of Gonville and Caius College*, 1: 232–4 (for item 1 in MS 203/109); W. D. Macray, R. W. Hunt, and A. G. Watson, *Digby Manuscripts*, 2 parts (Oxford: Bodleian Library, 1999), part 1: 114–15; part 2: 55–6 (for item 5 in Digby MS 100); Thomson, *Descriptive Catalogue of Middle English Grammatical Manuscripts*, 158–68 (for items 2, 22, 24, and 28 in Trinity MS O.5.4), 185–92 (for items 3g and 5 in Lincoln Cathedral, MS 88), 169–78

ad hoc grammatical treatise is not only a constant feature of these books but representative of the variation that characterizes all their contents in every textual kind.[111]

SCHOOLBOY IMPROVISATIONS

It was once assumed that medieval poets were trained in their craft from the many classical and medieval manuals designed to teach poetry as an art. Since John Manly first tried to describe the relationship between "Chaucer and the rhetoricians," there has been a general tendency to assume that "Chaucer and his contemporaries" must have learned their techniques from the Latin textbooks of the late twelfth and early thirteenth centuries, the *artes poetriae* of writers like Matthew of Vendôme, Geoffery of Vinsauf, and others.[112] But, as Robert Payne pointed out, while Chaucer names Geoffrey of Vinsauf in The Nun's Priest's Tale, and parodies Geoffrey's exemplary lamentation on the death of Richard I (repurposing it as the lament for a chicken seized by a fox), he only ever cites a "serious statement of general aesthetic principle...directly from the theorists" on one occasion.[113] Horace's *Ars Poetica* was present in some elementary schoolbooks, but it was in many ways ill-suited to elementary learning, since it "speaks to fellow poets rather than to students" and was most concerned with the "Roman assimilation of the Greek literary canon."[114] The *artes poetriae* were developed in the twelfth and thirteenth centuries to mediate Roman texts like Horace's to grammar-school students, and the

---

(for items 1, 2, and 5 in Additional 2830), 285–9 (for item 2 in Hatton MS 58), 293–313 (for items 5, 22, 30, and 32 in Rawlinson MS D 328); M. R. James, *A Descriptive Catalogue of the Manuscripts in the Library of St John's College* (Cambridge: Cambridge University Press, 1913), 195–7 (for items 4, 6, and 8–12 in St John's College, MS 163); Hunt, *Summary Catalogue of Western Manuscripts in the Bodleian Library*, 2, part 1: 427–8 (for item 1a in Bodley 837).

[111] This is a point also made by David Thomson, "The most notable thing about the specifically grammatical material found in the manuscripts is its variety," "A Study of the Middle English Treatises on Grammar," 3 vols., D.Phil. thesis, University of Oxford, 1977, 1: 107.

[112] Martin Camargo, "Chaucer and the Oxford Renaissance of Anglo-Latin Rhetoric," *Studies in the Age of Chaucer* 34 (2012): 173–20, esp. pp. 173–4. For Manly's seminal claim see J. M. Manly, "Chaucer and the Rhetoricians," *Proceedings of the British Academy* 12 (1926): 95–113.

[113] Robert O. Payne, *The Key of Remembrance: A Study of Chaucer's Poetics* (New Haven, CT: Yale University Press, 1963), 16.

[114] Copeland, "Horace's *Ars poetica*," 26.

medieval circulation of the *Poetria Nova*, which "penetrated into every level of teaching," was vast (it survives in over 200 manuscripts).[115] But as Martin Camargo has shown in a number of recent studies, the popularity of these technical manuals declined seriously at the end of the thirteenth century, and they were not widely read again until a "Renaissance" at the end of the fourteenth century. Chaucer would almost certainly not have encountered the *Poetria Nova* in school but "as an already-mature poet, in the 1380s."[116]

Schoolboys in the fourteenth century did not need to consult the *artes* to learn poetry's rules, however, since the basic grammars provided their own detailed accounts of poetic technique. The fourth part of Alexander of Villa-Dei's *Doctrinale* is devoted to "grammatical figures" [grammaticas figuras] and includes a discussion of accent, quantity, and meter, as well as a variety of "tropes" [tropus].[117] Evrard of Béthune begins the *Graecismus* with a chapter on the *figurae*, and then treats the "colors of rhetoric" [de coloribus rhetoricis] and the nature of "metrical feet" [de pedibus metrorum].[118] Even the most basic grammar of all, Donatus's *Ars minor*, includes poetic examples from the *Aeneid* in its discussion of the preposition.[119] Moreover, as careful attention to the rhetorical manuals has shown, what the reader with a mind to write poetry may take away from any list of figures and their description is not so much (or not only) the rules for employing particular figures in his poetry, but, rather, the attitude toward language and its potential for careful ordering that makes clear that "poetry is possible."[120] The ad hoc school was positioned better than any *ars poetriae* to teach such a lesson, moreover, because the ad hoc

---

[115] Copeland, "Horace's *Ars poetica*," 27. See also Marjorie Curry Woods, *Classroom Commentaries: Teaching the "Poetria Nova" across Medieval and Renaissance Europe* (Columbus, OH: Ohio State University Press, 2009).

[116] Camargo, "Chaucer and the Oxford Renaissance of Anglo-Latin Rhetoric," 176–7. See also Martin Camargo, "The Late-Fourteenth-Century Renaissance of Anglo-Latin Rhetoric," *Philosophy and Rhetoric* 45 (2012), 107–33.

[117] Alexander of Villa-Dei, *Doctrinale*, ed. Theodore Reichling (Berlin: A. Hofmann, 189), lines 23 ("grammaticas") and 2362 ("tropus"). For part four of the treatise see lines 2282–645.

[118] See Evrard of Béthune, *Graecismus*, ed. Johannes Wrobel (Hildesheim: G. Olm, 1987; first published 1887), cap. 1–4 and, more specifically cap. 3 ("de coloribus rhetoricis") and cap. 4 ("de pedibus metrorum").

[119] See Donatus, *Ars Minor*, 585–612 in Louis Holtz, *Donat et la tradition de l'enseignement grammatical* (Paris: Centre National de la Recherche Scientifique, 1981), 601. See also James J. Murphy, "Literary Implications of Instruction in the Verbal Arts in Fourteenth-Century England," *Leeds Studies in English* n.s. 1 (1967): 124.

[120] Payne, *Key of Remembrance*, 49.

grammars so many schoolmasters wrote and the exercises such school-masters invented modeled the process of verbal creation for each student daily. The grammar-school boy was *asked* to invent at precisely the moment his teacher's inventions ceased, when the repetition and memorization of rules and sentences yielded, in each lesson, to the stage at which he was asked to make sentences of his own.

Many of the ad hoc grammatical treatises that survive also take such training as their explicit purpose, as can be seen best in the text that has sometimes been called the "first English grammar" because it uses English so extensively in its explanations (rather than in its examples, as in the *Speculum grammaticale*). This treatise survives on fols. 5–8 of Cambridge, Trinity College, MS 0.5.4 (and so is hereafter described as the "Trinity Grammar") and it straddles the divide between Latin and English throughout, preserving in its own forms the liminal phase between the fourteenth-century norm in which Latin was the language of learning in the grammar school, and the change that must have occurred in the early decades of the fifteenth century, when Latin grammar began to be taught in English.[121] Since what a student often had to invent was the Latin to translate an English prompt, this text is uniquely helpful in equipping the schoolboy for the purpose since it models that alternation in its use of both Latin and English. The Trinity Grammar also makes clear that its purpose was to teach invention from its very first words which ask "In how many maners schalt thou by gynne to make Latyn" (98), where a "Latyn" is

[121] The text is described and edited in Sanford Brown Meech, "An Early Treatise in English Concerning Latin Grammar," in *Essays and Studies in English and Comparative Literature, University of Michigan Publications, Language and Literature* 13 (1935): 81–125. Hereafter I will cite this treatise in the text by page number from Meech's edition. Thomson edits the text in two pieces with what Meech calls part 3 as "Text D" of the *Accedence* and what Meech calls parts 1, 2, 4, and 5 as "Text EE." The twelve texts that Thomson groups together as "texts of the *Accedence*" are, nonetheless, highly variable in content, phrasing, subject matter, and length. See David Thomson, *An Edition of the Middle English Grammatical Texts* (New York, NY: Garland, 1984), 32–43 (*Accedence* Text D) and 178–85 ("Text EE").

The Trinity Grammar offers a survey of the various kinds of agreement (between noun and verb, adjective and noun, etc.), describes the eight parts of speech, and catalogues a few rhetorical figures. The movement between English and Latin throughout these descriptions could also be described as ad hoc since it sometimes provides them in Latin and explains them in English, but the discussion that follows a Latin example sometimes remains in Latin for some time (see, for example, description of the meaning and use of the relative pronoun *cuius* [109–10]. The interchangeability of English and Latin is particularly pronounced in the fifth of the Trinity Grammar's five parts, which Meech describes as "more in Latin than in English," but which often achieves this preponderance by absorbing both languages to a single syntax ("Ego is governed by *sum ex vi persone*" [*Ego* is governed by *sum* by the power of person] [121]).

clearly what later schoolroom texts call a *latinitas*, a sentence putting the
rules of grammar the schoolboy has learned into active use. It teaches a
student to "make" such sentences by first giving him the rule his "Latyn"
will employ (say, that there must be "acorde . . . by twene the adiectyf and
the substantyf," "in thre" different "maners," "case, gender, and noum-
ber"), then providing an "ensaumple" that will illustrate the use of that
rule, often in English first ("as thys good man yaf me a faire yyfte"), then
in Latin ("iste bonus homo dedit michi pulchrum donum") (99). It is a
necessary corollary to the invention such teaching produces that it will not
record the "Latyns" which are its proper outcome. But it is possible to see
what must have happened next in the kind of classrooms in which the
Trinity Grammar was used by looking at a similar lesson in the basic
grammar that was its effective successor. The *Informacio* (*c*.1415), the
earliest Middle English grammar we have, also begins by asking "In how
mony maner of wyse shall thu bygyn to mak Latten and to construe by
rughtwyse [correct] ordyr of construccion?"[122] It then teaches the student
that there are five such constructions, and works through these five
constructions with a series of questions which it answers, first with English
examples, and then, in each case, with an exemplary "Latten" that it
thereby shows the student how to "make":

> As William make fyre, *Willelme fac ignem.* How by a nominatif case and a
> verbe of certayn person? As "The mayster syttis yn the scole," *Magister sedet
> in scola.* How by sumwhat sett yn the stud of a nominatif case? As "To dyne
> betyme shall comfort monys hert," *Iantari tempestiue confortabit humanum
> cor.* How by an ablatif case absolute? As "The mayster techyng yn the scole
> (I am agayste)," *Magistro docente in scola, ego sum perteritus.* How by a verbe
> inpersonell? As "Me syttis yn the scole," *Sedetur in scola.* (82).

> [As "William make fire," *William make fire.* How would it be formed with a
> nominative case and a verb of a certain person? As "The master sits in the
> school," *The master sits in school.* How would it be formed by something put
> in place of the nominative case? As "To dine sometimes comforts a man's
> heart," *To dine at times will comfort the human heart.* How would it be
> formed with an ablative absolute? As "With the master teaching in the school
> (I am aghast)," *With the master teaching in school, I am frightened.* How would
> it be formed with an impersonal verb? As "I am seated in school," *He is seated
> in school.*]

---

[122] *Informacio* [Text T], 82–92 in Thomson, *Edition of the Middle English Grammatical
Texts*, 82. Hereafter citations to the *Informacio* will be to this text in this edition by page
number in the text. Thomson discusses the authorship and dating of this text thoroughly in
"Study of the Middle English Grammatical Treatises," 18–19.

Insofar as it insists that "making Latin" is both the means to, and proper outcome of, grammatical training, the *Informacio* is not really "in English" either but finally as macaronic as the Trinity Grammar. It also makes clear that a grammar-school teacher might have employed Latin in his teaching even if that teaching was largely in English. It shows most clearly, however, how grammars taught a practice as much as a body of knowledge, preparing a student by means of its rules for constantly varying and varied expressive needs—a training in fixed rules, in other words, that could be wielded in the making of something wholly new.

A few instances of such schoolboy invention or "making" do survive as "notes" or marginalia in schoolbooks. London, British Library, MS Harley 5751, a fifteenth-century volume "intended for the instruction of young clerks proceeding to holy orders" contains a variety of guides to confession and penance, but it also contains the following practice translations, as if a schoolboy was working out how to form sentences with impersonal verbs:

> I have no house to wonne in.
> Non est mihi domus manendi.
> [I have no house to live in.
> *There is no house remaining to me.*]
>
> I have no pen to wrytt my lattyng with.
> Deest mihi pena sermonem scribendum latinum.
> [I have no pen to write my Latin with.
> *There is no pen for me to write in the Latin language.*]
>
> I have no boke to say my mattyns on.
> Non est mihi liber dicendum matutinas.
> [I have no book to say my Matins with,
> *There is no book for saying my Matins.*]
>
> (MS Harley 5751, fol. 146)[123]

A late fifteenth-century schoolbook, London, British Library, Additional MS 37075, "evidently the school-book of a grammar-school boy in London" (not included in the earlier survey because of its late date) shows how such exercises might involve the making of Latin using an English proverb as a prompt:

> A gode be gynnyng makyth a gode endyng.
> Felix principium finem facit esse beatum.
>
> [A good beginning makes a good ending.
> *A happy start makes for a good end.*]

---

[123] Miner, *Grammar Schools of Medieval England*, 140 (for the description of the manuscript) and 159 (for a transcription of the sentences).

The nerer the cyrch the further fro God.
Quanto propinquior vir sit [ad] ecclesiam, tanto remorciorus a Deo.

[The nearer the church the further from God.
However far the man is from church, he is that much further from God.]

(MS Additional 37075, fol. 70)[124]

A similar sort of making survives in London, British Library MS Harley 1587, the "exercise book" of a fifteenth-century grammar-school student:

Better is a byrd in hond than iv owt.
Plus valet in dextera volucris quam quatuor extra.

[Better is a bird in hand than four out of it.
A bird is worth more in your right hand than four out of it.]

(MS Harley 1587, fol. 104)[125]

Such exercises were about lexis and syntax as much as anything, but the formal balance inherent in so many proverbs means that, as in this last example, where that balance nearly becomes rhyme ("dextera/extra"), such translation could also edge the student into the writing of verse.

An Oxford statute from 1344 makes clear that teaching a young student how to make Latins was often a way of teaching him to make poetry:

Item, tenentur singulis quindenis versus dare, et literas compositas verbis decentibus non ampullosis aut sesquipedalibus, et clausulis succinctis, decoris, metaphoris manifestis, et quantum possint, sententia refertis, quos versus et quas literas debent recipientes in proximo die feriato vel ante in pergameno scribere, et inde sequenti die, cum ad scholas venerint, Magistro suo corde tenus reddere et scripturam suam offere.

[Every fortnight they (i.e. the students) must present verses and compositions, put together with fitting words, not swollen or half a yard long, and with the *clausulae* concise and appropriate, displaying metaphors, and, as much as possible, replete with *sententiae*; which verses and compositions, those who are given the task should write on parchment on the next free day or before, and then on the following day when they return to school they must recite them by heart to the master, and hand in their writings.][126]

---

[124] For a description of this volume see also Thomson, *Descriptive Catalogue of Middle English Grammatical Texts*, 219–32. The text is transcribed in Miner, *Grammar Schools of Medieval England*, 159.

[125] Jonathan Nicholls, *The Matter of Courtesy: Medieval Courtesy Books and the Gawain-Poet* (Cambridge: D. S. Brewer, 1985), 68. For the transcription see Miner, *Grammar Schools of Medieval England*, 159.

[126] Henry Anstey, *Munimenta academica: or, Documents Illustrative of Academical Life and its Studies at Oxford*, 2 vols. (London: Longmans, Green, Reader, and Dyer, 1868), 2: 437–8, cited and translated in Murphy, "Literary Implications of Instruction in the Verbal Arts in Fourteenth-Century England," 126.

The Latin and English sentences that survive in two fifteenth-century proverb collections, Manchester, John Rylands, MS Latin 394 and Oxford, Bodleian Library, Douce 52, contain a number of Latins that take such a poetic form.[127] These two books are very similar in content, although there are a number of other surviving collections that also contain proverbs in both Latin and English just as these books do.[128] In the case of the John Rylands and Douce collections, however, the proverbs are arranged into alphabetical sections according to a Latin keyword, and English and Latin sentences are frequently grouped as "equivalents," even though the number of Latin lines in the book vastly outnumbers the number of English lines.[129] This weighting means that what were clearly models for translation also provide a variety of guides for invention, exploring several different grammatical forms for making what is in essence the same Latin sentence. For example, in the John Rylands manuscript the English proverb "he who loves the toad thinks it is the moon" (a more colorful version of the modern idea that "beauty is in the eye of the beholder") is followed by four different versions of this idea in Latin that work through synonyms for "bufo" ("rana") and "luna" ("diana and cynthia"), transform verbs from active ("amat") to deponent ("curetur") and then to passive ("fiet"), and replace independent clauses ("luna videtur") with dependent infinitives ("putat esse") or a relative clause ("quod sit"):[130]

Whoso loveth the toode he wenyth yt is the mone.
[He who loves the toad thinks he is the moon.]

---

[127] For descriptions of both manuscripts, much of the English in the John Rylands manuscript, and a comparison of their contents see W. A. Pantin, "A Medieval Collection of Latin and English Proverbs and Riddles, from the Rylands Latin MS. 394," *Bulletin of the John Rylands Library* 14 (1930): 81–113. For the contents of the Douce manuscript see Max Förster, "Die mittelenglische Sprichwörtersammlung in Douce 52," *Festschrift zum XII. Allgemeinen Deutschen Neuphilologentage in München, Pfingsten 1906*, ed. E. Stollreither (Erlangen: Fr. Junge, 1906), 40–60. Both manuscripts and their contents are discussed in Traugott Lawler, "Langland Versificator," *The Yearbook of Langland Studies* 25 (2011): 37–76 with a careful comparison of their contents in his Appendix 1 (69–70).

[128] For other such collections of proverbs see Thomson, "Study of the Middle English Treatises on Grammar," 113. For a careful analysis of the proverbs and their translations (both from English to Latin and vice versa) in another fifteenth-century schoolbook see Venetia Bridges and Joanna Bellis, " 'What Shalt Thou Do When Thou Hast an English to Make into Latin?': The Proverb Collection of Cambridge, St John's College F.26," *Studies in Philology* 112 (2015): 68–92.

[129] Pantin says that the proverbs are grouped "alphabetically by subject," "Medieval Latin and English Proverbs," 82. Lawler points out that a single "subject" is sometimes spread across a number of different words, and that some of the word groupings are adjectival ("beatus") and so do not precisely define subjects, "Langland Versificator," 21–2 n. 48.

[130] Douce 52 is not yet running for this sequence, since it is defective until the "C" section.

Bufonem cura fiet te iudice luna.
[Love the toad (and the toad) will become the moon in your opinion.]
Bufo curetur iam bufo luna videtur.
[If the toad is loved the toad immediately seems to be the moon.]
Siquis amat ranam ranam putat esse dianam.
[Anyone who loves the toad thinks the toad to be the moon]
Ranam siquis amat quod sit sibi Cinthia clamat.
[Whoever loves the toad proclaims that he is, for him, the moon.]
(Manchester, John Rylands, MS Latin 394, fol. 2r)

The extent of such invention is best illustrated by the equivalents given in both collections for an English proverb insisting that no gift is too small.[131] The English in the John Rylands manuscript is gnomic in this case ("He þat a lytul me yevyth, to me wyllyth longe lyffe" [He who gives me (even) a little wants me to have a long life]), but the version in Douce 52 makes clear that this collection of sentences generally means even the smallest gift is of value.[132] Very little changes between the different versions in the John Rylands collection: "life" is always referred to by the same noun ("vita") or verb ("vivere"); the gift's size is always indicated by some version of "modicum" or "parvum"; the action of giving is always some version of the active verb *do, dare*; and, really, only two sorts of constructions are used (a relative of characteristic, "qui . . . dat," and an impersonal clause). And yet, as Traugott Lawler has observed when describing this same sequence, the "abundance is remarkable," illustrating just how "variously one might vary," and even these subtle changes model eight different ways of making a single Latin:[133]

He that yeueth me a litel wol my life.
[He that gives me a little wishes me to live.]
Qui modicum michi dat michi vitam longius optat.
[He who gives me a little wishes me a longer life.]
Me vult vitalem qui dat michi rem modicalem.
[He wishes me alive who gives me a small thing.]
Qui michi dat parvum per villam sive per arvum
Vitam custodit; credo quod me [minus] odit.
[He who gives me a small thing by town or field looks after
my life; I believe that he does not hate me.]
Non michi vult funus qui parvum dat mihi munus.
[He does not wish me dead who gives me small rewards.]
Dans quicunque parum me vivere vult sibi carum.

---

[131] Lawler notes how rich the John Rylands MS is when compared to the Douce collection: "the comparison makes clear just how fertile the compiler of Rylands 394 was. Again and again Rylands simply offers more," "Langland Versificator," 42.
[132] Förster, "Die mittelenglische Sprichwörtersammlung in Douce 52," 44.
[133] Lawler, "Langland Versificator," 56.

[In giving whatever small thing to me he wants me to live
valued by him.]
Qui michi dat modicum me vivere vult ut amicum.
[He who gives me a small thing wishes me to live as his friend.]
Qui modicum michi dat semper me vivere captat.
[He who gives me a small thing wants me to live always.]
Qui parvas aptat michi res me vivere captat.
[He who furnishes small things to me wants me to live.]

(Manchester, John Rylands, MS Latin 394, fol. 5r)[134]

As remarkable as the grammatical variety of these lines, moreover, is their metrical precision, for each of the Latin variations above, and, in fact, *every* Latin line in both of these collections, as Pantin first pointed out, is versified, either as an unrhymed or leonine hexameter.[135] Since there are also Latin lines with no English equivalent, and since the book is also finely produced (not an exercise book, clearly, but a reference tool) it probably served as a *Gradus ad Parnassum*, "for a student versifier to learn quantities and look up a word he wants to use and see it used in an actual line."[136] On the other hand, the English versions of the proverbs in both collections could have nothing to do with helping a student learn the quantities or appropriate use of Latin words and so they were also clearly designed to offer instruction in making Latin verse from English.[137]

They also show how such versified Latins were sometimes made from English verse since much of the English in these two collections is also in verse, most frequently as a kind of calque of a Latin leonine line whereby an internal rhyme links the middle of the line with its end. This English verse is usually set out in long lines, but its pattern of rhyme ensures that it can also be construed in the rough couplets typical of popular Middle English lyric and romance:

> Seldom dyeth his oxe
> þat wepeth for a kok
>
> [He who weeps for his cock rarely loses his ox.]

(Manchester, John Rylands, MS Latin 394, fol. 2r)

In the case of such a Middle English couplet, the Latin sentences that follow are not only Latin equivalents, showing how the sense of the

---

[134] Lawler also prints these lines ("Langland Versificator," 55). "Minus" in line 2, is his emendation from Douce 52 for "munus" in John Rylands 394.

[135] Pantin, "Medieval Collection of Latin and English Proverbs and Riddles," 81.

[136] Lawler, "Langland Versificator," 58. Pantin makes the suggestion that Rylands MS functioned as a "*Gradus ad Parnassum*," 83.

[137] Bridges and Bellis offer a detailed analysis of some of the more artful translations of English proverbs into Latin found in Cambridge, St John's College MS F.26. See "'What Shalt Thou Do When Thou Hast an English to Make into Latin?,'" 75–82.

English may be remade, but models for how poetry in English may be made into poetry in Latin:

> Bos moritur rare qui gallo plorat amare.
> [The ox of him who weeps bitterly for a cock, rarely dies.]
> Bos obit huic rare qui gallum luget amare.
> [The ox of him who mourns bitterly for a cock, rarely dies.]
> (Manchester, John Rylands, MS Latin 394 fol. 2r)

That such modeling was common enough is indicated by yet another schoolbook, Oxford, Bodleian Library, Rawlinson MS D 328, which also contains English verse translated into equivalent Latin verse:[138]

> Hyt is mery in hall when berdys waggyth all
> Aula gaudescit cum barbula queque mouescit.
>
> [A good time is had in the hall when all the beards wag.
> *All rejoice in the hall when the little beards move.*] (120)

Sometimes the metrical prompt extends for so many lines it is as if an entire English lyric has been translated into Latin:

> Serue god herteli
> And the wer[ld]e be sely
> Ete the mete merely
> Thanke god hertely
> Yeffe thu leue porely;
> He may mende hys layse
> with-owte eny grese.
>
> Deo serv[i] potenter
> Mundoque diligenter.
> Cum gaudio cibum tuum comede.
> Si diu viuere queras
> Gratias sublime reddas
> Quam-vis tu inopem vitam ducas.[139]

---

[138] For the contents of this volume and a description see Sanford B. Meech, "A Collection of Proverbs in Rawlinson MS D 328," *Modern Philology* 38 (1940): 113–31. Hereafter citations from these exercises will be to this edition by page number in the text. As Meech notes and is evident from the texts I quote here there are "numerous obscurities occasioned by the bad writing and curious spelling of the collection." This manuscript, as well as its likely connection to Exeter High School, is discussed in Nicholas Orme, "An English Grammar School, ca. 1450: Latin Exercises from Exeter (Caius College MS 417/447, Folios 16v.–24v)," *Traditio* 50 (1995): esp. 262–3.

[139] The last two lines of the English are not the Latin, and the fifth line of the English is translated as the last line of the Latin. Although the last line reads "Quam-vis tu inopem vitam viuas ducas" it seems likely that "ducas" is a correction for "vivas" so I omit the former here. I thank Traugott Lawler for this suggestion.

[Serve God willingly;
If the world is holy;
Eat your food merrily,
And thank God eagerly,
even if you live meagerly;
He may mend his lathe(?)
Without any ointment.
Serve God strenuously,
And the world diligently;
Eat your food with joy,
If you wish to live for a long time
Give thanks to heaven
Although you lead a poor life.] (122–3)

These two schoolbooks suggest that such wholesale translation was common because they both contain a number of other translations of similar length:

Sore I syke and well I may
For thre thyngis, þat comyn ay.
þe fyrst is: I schall hen;
þe secunde: I not neuer when;
þe þrydde is most care:
I not nere, whidur I schall fare.

Sunt tria vere, que faciunt me sepe dolere.
Est primum durum, quia nosco me moriturum;
Atque sequens plango magis, quia nescio quando.
Inde magis flebo, quia nescio quo remanebo.

[I sigh deeply, and well I may
For three things that always come.
The first is: I must go hence;
The second: I do not know when;
The third is the most sad:
I do not know where I shall go.
There are three things that often make me grieve,
The first is hard, because I know that I will die;
And I lament more for the next, because I know not when.
So I wil weep more for the last because I do not know
where I will end up.][140]

In such extended exercises, schoolboys were not only using Middle English verse as a model for grammar-school exercises, they were learning English poetry as one step in the process of learning Latin.

[140] Pantin only prints the English part of this sequence from the John Rylands collection, so I quote here from Förster's transcription from Douce 52, "Die mittelenglische Sprichwörtersammlung," 51.

A curious but inevitable consequence of a pedagogy so fundamentally based on invention is that it can be difficult to differentiate a poem from an exercise. A number of texts now understood as Middle English poems clearly survive only because they were copied into schoolbooks to serve as prompts. The "earliest example... of a quotation from a poem on Robin Hood," for example, only survives in the schoolbook, Lincoln Cathedral, MS 132:[141]

> Robyn hod in scherewod stod
> hodud and hathud hosut and schod
> ffour And thuynti arowus he bar In hit hondus.

[Robin Hood stood in Sherwood, hooded and hatted, in hose and shoes, four and twenty arrows he bore in his hand.]

The Latin prose version of this verse immediately after it makes clear that these rhymes were jotted down in order to be so translated:[142]

> Robertus hod stetit in... de metore capiciatus et capellatus calligatus et cauciatus tenens quatuor et viginti sagittas in mane sua.

[Robert Hood... hooded and hatted as a reaper, in hoes and shoes, holding twenty-four arrows in his hand.]

The same process preserved the whole of the tail-rhyme poem copied on the recto side of the same leaf of this book:

> Wenest þu husch[er] wt þi coyntyse
> Yche day beten us [on] þ[is] wyse
> As þu wer lord of toun
> We had son[er] scole forsake
> & iliche of us an-oþer crafte take
> þen long to ben in þi baundoun
> But wolde God þt we myth ones
> Cache þe at þe mulne stones
> Or at þe crabbe tre
> We schuld leue in þe such a probeyt
> ffor þt þu hast us don & seyd
> þt alle þi kyn suld rwe þe

---

[141] George R. Morris, "A Ryme of Robyn Hode," *Modern Language Review* 43 (1948): 507–8. After consulting the manuscript I have slightly emended the lines from Morris's printing in line with some of his own speculations. On this poem more generally see also R. B. Dobson and John Taylor, *Rymes of Robyn Hood* (Pittsburgh, PA: University of Pittsburgh Press, 1976), 18 and n. 3.

[142] Morris also transcribes this Latin ("A Ryme of Robyn Hode," 507) but says no more about its purpose than that "the whole passage... follows the meaning of the Middle English that precedes it" ("A Ryme of Robyn Hode," 508).

& þow sir robert wt his cloke
wold þe helpe & be þi ppokke
   þe werre þu schust fare.
& for his prayer þe raþer we wold
ȝyuen hym stripes al [un]colde
   not for hym þe spare
ffor ofte sore we abye
þe twynkelingis of his hye
   þe mayster us to bete,
ffor he & [þu a]re oft at asent
þis day ȝyuen agagement
   To ȝyuen us strokes grete.

[Do you think, usher, with your cleverness, to beat us every day as if you were lord of the town? We would sooner leave school, and each of us take up another craft, than to remain for very long under your authority. If God wills that we should ever catch you at the mill stones or at the crab tree, we should leave such a proof because of what you have done and said, that all your relatives would pity you. And though sir Robert with his cloak were to help you and be your evil spirit, you would fare the worse. And despite his entreaty, we would rather give bitter beatings, nor spare you on his behalf. For we often pay for the twinklings in his eye, as the master beats us. For you and he assent, all day in agreement, to give us hard blows.]

This poem has long been treated as a freestanding "lyric," and anthologized as such, not least because it seems to paint such a vivid picture of the medieval schoolroom. But, as I suggested in Chapter 1, exercises often made themselves more comprehensible by referencing the schoolboy's circumstances, and the Latin prose equivalent just after it in this book makes clear that this poem was copied as a prompt for a translation exercise:

Credis tu osterie cum tua cautula qualibet die uerberare nos isto modo sicut esses dominus uille nos mallemus scolas relinquere & quilibet nostrum aliam artem apprehendere [quam] inesse in tua ... orum ut ... uellet.[143]

[Do you think, usher, with your caution, to beat us every day as if you were lord of the town? We would sooner leave school, and each of us take up another craft, than to remain for very long under your ...]

---

[143] There is a diplomatic transcription of this poem in Reginald Maxwell Woolley, *Catalogue of the Manuscripts of Lincoln Cathedral Library* (London: Oxford University Press, 1927), 93–4. Woolley also notes that following the truncated translation a different hand adds: "Corpus debilitat animas et corpora fedat / et carnem fligit cicius senescere cogit / ffamam tollit opes sensum furiosa libido." I quote the lyric here as sensibly (if silently) amended in *Secular Lyrics of the XIVth and XVth Centuries*, ed. Rossell Hope Robbins, 2nd edn. (Oxford: Clarendon Press, 1955), 105. It is also printed, with helpful glosses, in *Middle English Lyrics*, ed. Maxwell S. Luria and Richard L. Hoffman (New York: W. W. Norton, 1974), 130–1; and *The Oxford Book of Medieval English Verse*, ed. Celia and Kenneth Sisam (Oxford: Clarendon Press, 1970), 488–9.

Even if this poem was written with a view to being translated, it is still a
mode of literary production, and the evidence from other schoolbooks
suggests that many of the medieval poems we now value as literature were,
in fact, produced in this way. The schoolbook that survives as Aberystwyth, National Library of Wales Peniarth, MS 356b contains a poem that
absorbs the process of translation from Latin to English to its form
(because of the poem's length I print only the first two stanzas here):[144]

> The krycket & þe greshope wentyn here to fyȝght
> With helme and haburyone all redy dyȝght;
> The flee bare þe baner as a duȝty knyȝth,
> The cherubud trumpyt with all hys myȝth.

> Salamandraque cicada domitatum p[ererraverunt],
> Gal[e]aque cum lorica presto se parauerunt;
> Musca vexillum portabat vt miles egregius,
> Scarabius buccinauit totis suis viribus.[145]

> [The cricket and the grasshopper went out to fight here,
> With helm and habergeon all prepared,
> The fly bore the banner like a doughty knight,
> The beetle trumpeted with all his might.

> The grasshopper and the cricket went to fight,
> They prepared themselves with helmet and shield to hand,
> The fly carried the banner as a brave knight,
> The beetle trumpeted with all his strength.]

Robbins prints both the Latin and English of this text together as a single
lyric, but, since the English of this poem survives nowhere other than
this schoolbook, and so never without the Latin stanzas translating this
English, this is clearly not a poem written on the model of a translation
exercise, it *is* such an exercise.

Training in the making of Latins also allowed the grammar-school
master to provide the future Middle English poet with some models for
his later efforts since the same catachresis that now transforms grammar-
school exercises into anthologized poems made it possible to bring English

---

[144] The date of this book (*c*.1425–50) is contemporaneous with a number of the later
schoolbooks I have looked at, but I have not examined it in detail because the quantity of
English writing it includes makes clear that it belongs to another epoch in schoolroom
practice. It is, however, a schoolbook on the general model of those I have described in this
chapter. Alongside a collection of the earliest Middle English grammars (the *Informacio*, the
Comparacio, the *Accedence*) it also includes one of the basic Latin reading texts (Theodulus's
Eclogue). On this manuscript and for its contents see Thomson, *Descriptive Catalogue of
Middle English Grammatical Texts*, 114–31.
[145] *Secular Lyrics of the XIVth and XVth Centuries*, ed. Robbins, 104. Brackets indicate
my emendations.

poems produced earlier and elsewhere into the classroom as prompts for Latins. The overall paucity of evidence from medieval classrooms along with the difficulty of distinguishing purpose-built English prompts from freestanding lyrics makes it difficult to find evidence of such a practice, but Rawlinson MS D 328 offers one example proving conclusively that such methods were used:

> Whanne Adam dalfe & Eve spanne ho was tho a gentelman
> Cum vanga quadam tellurem foderat Ada[m]
> Ac Eva nens fuerat quis generosus erat.

> [When Adam dug and Eve spun who was then the gentleman.
> *When Adam dug the earth with a spade,*
> *And Eve was spinning, who was noble?*] (121)

Though we do not anthologize it for its lyric grace or importance to a prior or subsequent tradition, this couplet is familiar to students of English literature because it was so powerfully effective (and, we may well think, affecting) in the last decades of the fourteenth century. As the chronicler Thomas Walsingham tells us, John Ball took this verse as his text for the sermon on Black Heath that incited a mob in 1381 and led them to protest aristocratic privilege and interests by marching on London, burning considerable property, and beheading both the Archbishop of Canterbury and the king's treasurer.[146] We may well imagine that a schoolmaster included such verse to spice up a lesson, but, to that extent, his lesson was not just exploiting the power of this couplet to inspire action but providing, along with his Latin teaching, a kind of cultural history of the sorts of power literature can have. The student only needed to be good at the tasks of translation set him to see too that what this poem so powerfully advocated was freedom from rule. The lesson would have been local to the teaching circumstances in which Rawlinson MS D 328 was written and used, but it may still stand, in conclusion, for all the ways that the lessons of the fourteenth-century English grammar school encouraged such freedom. In a pedagogical circumstance that was informal in the most fundamental ways, where every schoolboy in fourteenth-century England was asked to make Latins in prose as well as verse, shown how to make that prose or verse from the example of English poetry, and urged in every way to shrug off restriction, the idea that he might write English verse of his own was almost impossible for such a schoolboy *not* to have.

---

[146] Thomas Walsingham, *Historia Anglicana*, ed. Henry Thomas Riley, 2 vols., Rolls Series 28 (London, 1863–4), 2: 32; *The Peasants' Revolt of 1381*, ed. R. B. Dobson, 2nd edn. (London: Macmillan Press, 1983; first edition published 1970), 374.

3

The Basic Grammars and the Grammar-School Style

Literacy training in the medieval English schoolroom encouraged the making of English poetry by inculcating an improvisatory attitude along with the rules of grammar, but beneath even these effects it trained students to imitate a particular set of movements. The most basic of these was the movement of knowledge from one person to another (that is, in the first instance, from the teacher who had mastered the rules of grammar to the student who needed to know them). Riding right alongside this was the movement from one language to another, first as the schoolboy left his mother tongue and encountered the Latin spoken and written by his teacher, and, second, as he was asked to move English prose and verse into Latin to demonstrate that he had learned the grammar he was being taught. Behind these two obvious movements was also a much more subtle feedback loop as the learning of Latin worked backward to the schoolboy's understanding of his own English: not only as he made Latins from English, but, also, as he had to move every rule and example he learned in Latin back into English in order to understand it, the fourteenth-century schoolboy was inevitably made to realize that English was grammatical too. As I will describe in the next chapter, such "grammaticalization" could expand to include the whole of a poem, and it was also the realization that English and Latin were on a par that led the schoolboy to move from the making of Latins to the making of wholly new English poetry. Before looking at those large-scale phenomena, however, I want to focus in this chapter on the more basic pedagogical movements I have just described. As will become clear, schoolroom techniques for moving knowledge from teacher to student proved an extraordinary resource for the ambitious Middle English poet. I also want to look at the rules of grammar that were the simplest elements in this knowledge-transfer and the extraordinary ways that even such rules, as Marjorie Curry Woods has observed, could be "turned to artistic use."[1]

---

[1] Marjorie Curry Woods, *Classroom Commentaries: Teaching the* Poetria Nova *Across Medieval and Renaissance Europe* (Columbus, OH: Ohio State University Press, 2010), 93.

Our most explicit description of the way knowledge of those rules affected writing in English in the fourteenth century comes from a passage in the "General Prologue" to what is usually described as the "Wycliffite Bible."[2] This volume is like any grammar as it moves knowledge from "clerkis" to what it calls "puples" [pupils], but, in so doing, it also offers a step-by-step account of how such a pupil would move particular grammatical structures "oute of Latyn into English."[3] The Prologue pays especially close attention to Latin's "ablative absolute," its present participle, and its relative pronouns:

> An ablatif case absolute may be resoluid into these thre wordis, with couenable verbe, *the while, for, if,* as gramariens seyn, as thus, *the maistir redinge, I stonde,* mai be resoluid thus, *while the maistir redith, I stonde,* either *if the maistir redith,* etc. either *for the maistir,* etc.; and sumtyme it wolde acorde wel with the sentence to be resoluid into *whanne,* either into *aftirward,* thus, *whanne the maistir red, I stood,* either *aftir the maistir red, I stood*; and sumtyme it mai wel be resoluid into a verbe of the same tens, as othere ben in the same resoun, and into this word *et,* that is, *and* in English, as thus, *arescentibus hominibus prae timore,* that is, *and men shulen wexe drie for drede.* Also a participle of a present tens, either preterit, of actif vois, either passif, mai be resoluid into a verbe of the same tens, and a coniunccioun copulatif, as thus, *dicens,* that is *seiynge,* mai be resoluid thus, *and seith,* either *that seith....* Also a relatif, which may be resoluid into his antecedent with a coniunccioun copulatif, as thus *which renneth, and he renneth* (1:57).

> [*resoluid into*: represented by; *couenable*: suitable; *wolde*: will; *tens*: tense; *in the same resoun*: on the same grounds]

This discussion comes many decades before the first surviving grammars in English and its precocity has everything to do with the urgency of its content, which has been translated in order to "saue" the "lewid puple" who "crieth aftir holi writ" (1: 57). By giving us such a detailed account of process, however, the General Prologue makes clear that grammaticalization not only involved the understanding that a schoolboy's "modir language" (1: 59) was subject to the same rules as Latin, nor even the simpler understanding that certain Latin forms were equivalent to certain English forms (knowing, that

---

[2] On the relationship of this translation of the Bible to Wycliff and the Wycliffites and of the "General Prologue" to these translations see Anne Hudson, *The Premature Reformation: Wycliffite Texts and Lollard History* (Oxford: Oxford University Press, 1988), 23–4, 238–47.

[3] *The Holy Bible,* ed. Josiah Forshall and Frederic Madden, 4 vols. (Oxford: Oxford University Press, 1850), 1: 56 ("clerkis," "pupels") and 57 ("oute"). Hereafter all subsequent quotations from this text will be by volume and page number in the text. The passage I quote here is also printed in Rita Copeland and Ineke Sluiter, *Medieval Grammar and Rhetoric: Language Arts and Literary Theory, AD 300–1475* (Oxford: Oxford University Press, 2009), 338.

is, that an "ablatif" in Latin can be rendered by a subordinate clause introduced by one of "thre wordis" in English), but also that the movement between English and Latin posed an extended chain of problems that only the resourceful and creative application of the knowledge of the grammar of both languages could "resolve."

When we look closely at the method and manner of the basic grammars what becomes even clearer is that such knowledge equipped the student to produce a certain vivacity—what literary criticism came to call "realism"— in language. As I suggested in Chapter 1 this often involved the recruitment of the student's classroom circumstances to the processes of pedagogy (and, as I also suggested, it is to this end that English was first used in basic literacy training in medieval England). A closer account of the basic grammars also shows that the material of grammar provided even deeper resources for such vivacity as it equipped the student to create subjects and then to orient them in space and time. As in the following example from the *Formula*, this often meant that grammatical teaching often posited that student *in* the text:[4]

> *Intendo ire oppositum scolaribus.* Þis word *oppositum* is þe frist suppyn, for when I have a Englich of a infinitif mode comyng after a verbe betokenyng to a place eny þyng to be don it schall be set in the first suppyn. *Venio lectu libros.* This word *lectu* is þe latin suppyn, for when I haue an Englich of infinitife comyng after a verbe betokenyng meuyng fro a place it schal be sett in þe later suppyn.[5]

> [*Intendo ire oppositum scolaribus*: I intend to go debate scholars; *suppyn*: supine; *Venio lectu libros*: I come to read books]

We could describe the procedure here as a mobilization of indexicals whereby the first person pronoun "indexes" a subject and thereby creates it ("I").[6] We could also say that a careful sequence of tenses positions the evoked subject and an implied set of activities in time ("whan I haue . . . it schal be sett"). But it is probably truest to the *Formula*'s purposes to say

---

[4] On this text and its relationship to the other early Middle English grammars see David Thomson, *A Descriptive Catalogue of Middle English Grammatical Texts* (New York, NY: Garland, 1979), 10.

[5] *Formula* ["Text Z"], 131–9 in David Thomson, *An Edition of the Middle English Grammatical Texts* (New York, NY: Garland, 1984), 136. Hereafter passages from this text will be taken from this edition and cited in the text.

[6] "If a sign is an index, it must stand for its object through some existential or physical fact," Albert Atkin, "Peirce on the Index and Indexical Reference," *Transactions of the Charles S. Peirce Society* 41 (2005): 163. In this article, Atkin also gives a helpful summary of the complex history of Pierce's account of the "index" (163–4 and 186–7 nn. 6–10). For the classic account of the term see Charles Peirce, *Collected Papers*, 6 vols., ed. Charles Hartshorne and Paul Weiss (Cambridge, MA: Harvard University Press, 1931–36), 2: 248.

that it creates a kind of classroom right in the text, the image of a student learning by way of a pedagogy that not only taught the rules of grammar but made those rules vivid.

We could also say that, rather than simply declare a simple rule ("when a verb in the infinitive mode comes after a verb referring to a place where something is done, use the supine") basic grammars like the *Formula* construct *narratives*, explaining grammatical relationships by creating subjects and putting them into action, assembling those actions so as to convene what Jeff Dolven has helpfully called a "scene of instruction."[7] Another example from the *Formula* will show both how variously, but also how invariably, grammatical precepts in these basic grammars adopted such a narrative form:

> When schal I have a gerundive in -*do* in comen spech? In ij maner of wys. On ys when þis Englich "in" cometh byfore the Englich of a partisipul of the presentens wtowt a substantife to hym, þan schal I have a gerundive in -*do* (wt thys preposicion *in*). Exemplum: *In dimicando multi homines sunt vulnerati* [many men were wounded in the fighting]. The secunde maner ys when þe Englich of a participul of þe presentens comyng after a substantif, þan I maye chese wheþer that I wolle have a participull of þe presentens or a gerundyve in -*do* (136).
>
> [*comen*: common; *partisipul*: participle; *wtowt*: without; *hym*: it; *wt*: with; *In dimicando multi homines sunt vulnerati*: many men were wounded in the fighting]

Here the procedure remains indexical as the "I" creates a subject but the temporal movement is even more carefully articulated as the adverb "when" ("whan schal I have?") is supplemented by "then" ("than schal I have . . . ") thereby creating a sequence that moves that subject through time. Because it repeatedly uses the same techniques of language to create the same set of effects, it is also right to say such teaching and its narratives constitutes an identifiable *style*.[8] This might be called a "pedagogical style" were it referred it to its purposes; it might be called a "grammatical style" were it referred only to the elements of its technique; but because the style was native to the grammar school and because its principal function was to absorb the practices of such schools to a text—because it always tended to reproduce the school in the text—I will characterize these techniques as a

---

[7] The phrase provides Dolven's title, but he spells out the mechanics of its generation most clearly in a discussion of the "poetics of pedagogy" in *Scenes of Instruction in Renaissance Romance* (Chicago, IL: University of Chicago Press, 2007), 27–52.

[8] As John Guillory has observed, "style is nothing other than a certain relation to grammar," *Cultural Capital: The Problem of Literary Canon Formation* (Chicago, IL: University of Chicago Press, 1993), 78.

"grammar-school style" here, a way of writing common to the basic grammars like the *Formula* that draws them together, not by the grammar they take as their subject, but by the grammar they employ.

If that style was born out of a set of pedagogical tasks and can be firmly associated with a particular sort of instruction, how did it become important in other sorts of writing? How did the "grammar-school" style become a literary style? One answer may be that there is a natural alliance between imaginative literature and teaching because, as Elaine Scarry has observed, the "vivacity" of literature depends upon "an instructional character" wherein a text uses various tutelary postures to replicate the "'givenness' of perception."[9] In this view, novels and poems are not unlike the basic grammars insofar as they consist of "a steady stream of erased imperatives," an implied set of demands for activity (in the case of novels and poems for image-creation) that succeed because, even as they seem to rely on images, they provide a reader with instructions in *how* to make those images.[10] A more mechanical explanation could be given using Jerome Bruner's distinction between "paradigmatic" and "narrative" modes of thought.[11] In this typology, the paradigmatic mode is what we normally take grammar to be, a "system of description and explanation" in which "basic statements" are "generated and tested against observables" whereas the narrative mode, "essentially temporal rather than timeless," concerning "action[s]" that are "lifelike," a method for the "constructing [of a] world," is what we normally take literature to be.[12] Using such terminology it could also be said that the *Formula* and its style, like the many basic grammars it resembles, renders paradigmatic thought (e.g. "This word *oppositum* is the frist suppyn") in the narrative mode ("for when I have a Englich of a infinitif mode comyng after a verbe betokenyng to a place . . . it schall be set in the first suppyn"), and therefore comprises a set of rules for creating the "lifelike" in language.

As the latter parts of this chapter will demonstrate, no Middle English poet put basic grammar to artistic use to quite the degree, or to quite such defining effect, as Geoffrey Chaucer. The grammar-school style

---

[9] Elaine Scarry, *Dreaming by the Book* (New York, NY: Farrar, Straus & Giroux, 1999), 38. This book's first chapter is called "On Vivacity" (3–9).

[10] Scarry, *Dreaming by the Book*, 35.

[11] Jerome Bruner, "Narrative and Paradigmatic Modes of Thought," *Yearbook of the National Society for the Study of Education* 84, Part 2: *Learning and Teaching: The Ways of Knowing* (1985): 97–115. For an account of elementary education using Bruner's terms see Dolven, *Scenes of Instruction in Renaissance Romance*, esp. pp. 58–9 although Dolven generally associates paradigmatic thought with schoolroom training and narrative thought with literary expression; rather than understanding both of them, as I do, as schoolroom modes.

[12] Bruner, "Narrative and Paradigmatic Thought," 98–9.

requires a chapter that focuses on this relationship if only because that effect is the realism that readers have so often identified as the singular achievement of Chaucer's style. It is impossible to say whether that style was more influenced by elementary learning because Chaucer too wrote an elementary work, *The Treatise on the Astrolabe*, or whether the strength of that influence is easier to trace because the *Treatise* provides the necessary genealogy. It is certainly true that, insofar as every element of the grammar-school style derives from the kind of learning every literate person had, its techniques are spread wide in English poetry and prose produced throughout the Era of Grammaticalization. But it is equally true that an account of the style of the *Astrolabe* makes clear just how important particular elements and techniques of this style were to Chaucer's other works, and grammars that rendered rules intelligible by making such strategic use of what we could also call a student's "reality" were bound to be invaluable to a poet so generally interested in representations of the contemporary, the demotic, and the quotidian.

The stylistic achievement at issue here is finally what has been *called* "realism" rather than what can more casually be assumed to be the representation of "reality," but the distinction is meaningless when referred to the genealogy of the reactions of readers so many of whom have subscribed to the view that a certain vivacity in language and narrative was Chaucer's signal achievement. Dryden was already singling out such vivacity when he felt that he could see the Canterbury pilgrims "as perfectly before" him as if he "supp'd with them at the Tabard in Southwark," as was George Crabbe when he wrote of the "naked and unveiled character" of all Chaucer's poetry, or Hazlitt when he said that "Chaucer attended chiefly to the real and natural," or Walter Savage Landor whose paean "To Chaucer" praised him for inventing "creatures like ourselves."[13] At the dawn of what could be understood as the modern age of Chaucer criticism, Kittredge also wrote of the "liveliness with which Chaucer conceived of his individual *dramatis personae*."[14] The convergence of so many reactions on this view could be seen a function of critical convention and, in particular, the embrace of "mimesis" as a meaningful category. But the reaction has also been sufficiently strong to persuade even the most scholarly of readers that the figures in Chaucer's poems were "real persons...with whom Chaucer can be shown to have had

[13] These moments in Chaucer criticism are all carefully documented in *Chaucer: The Critical Heritage*, ed. Derek S. Brewer, 2 vols. (London: Routledge, 1978), 1: 163 (Dryden), 1: 265 (Crabbe), 1: 273 (Hazlitt), 2: 124 (Landor).
[14] G. L. Kittredge, "Chaucer's Discussion of Marriage," *Modern Philology*, 9 (1912): 442.

definite personal contacts."[15] These phrases are John Manly's in 1926, but the tradition continues right up to the present day in the assumption that the scribe depicted in the lyric usually called "Adam Scriveyn" was a nameable person it is right for us to call "Chaucer's scribe."[16] Even where their observations remain firmly rooted in Chaucer's texts and what is therefore also called his "style," in other words, it is right to say that most Chaucerians still take as given Charles Muscatine's claim that Chaucer's poetry gives the "impression of dealing with life directly, with something of life's shape and vitality."[17]

The weight of this tradition need not compel us to share such reactions, but it makes it well worthwhile to specify the extent to which these reactions were produced by grammaticalization. To detail the techniques Chaucer deployed so strategically and with such defining effect as they can be found in the basic grammars, then the *Treatise on the Astrolabe*, and, finally, in some of the more memorable passages of *The House of Fame* and the *Canterbury Tales*, as I will do here, is also to reach behind, not only the effects so many readers have reported when reading Chaucer, but the stylistic traditions whose importance Charles Muscatine described with such care. One of the most important ramifications of this genealogy must be that, however right Muscatine was about the conventions he described, not all the techniques of Chaucerian realism originated in the "French tradition," since, as I established in Chapter 1, the grammar Chaucer knew, as well as the grammars in which he learned, were written, not in French, but in Latin.

---

[15] John Manly, *Some New Light on Chaucer* (Gloucester, MA: Peter Smith, 1926), 73. Manly begins this inquiry with these impressions: "The manner of their assembling, their looks and characters, their actions and words on the journey to Canterbury, have been set down for us with a vivid naturalism which has made many readers feel that Chaucer merely described an actual group of pilgrims of which he himself was a member and merely reported the incidents and tales of an actual pilgrimage" (70).

[16] Lynne Mooney, "Chaucer's Scribe," *Speculum* 81 (2006): 97–138. I am querying here, not Mooney's identification of Adam Pinkhurst as the scribe who copied Chaucer's *Canterbury Tales*, but the presumption, nested within it, that a poem by Chaucer is necessarily about a real person: "That Pinkhurst, scribe of the Hengwrt and Ellesmere manuscripts of *The Canterbury Tales*, has the given name Adam means that he was very probably the 'Adam scriveyn' whom Chaucer chastises (probably humorously) for his 'necglygence and rape' in his single-stanza poem, 'Chaucers Wordes unto Adam, His Owne Scriveyn'" (101).

[17] Charles Muscatine, *Chaucer and the French Tradition: A Study in Style and Meaning* (Berkeley, CA: University of California Press, 1957), 59. On Chaucer's realism see also Morton Bloomfield, "Authenticating Realism and the Realism of Chaucer," *Thought* 39 (1964): 335–58, substantially reprinted in *The Cambridge Companion to Chaucer*, ed. Jill Mann and Piero Boitani (Cambridge: Cambridge University Press, 1986), 179–93.

PEDAGOGIC POSITIONS

The forms of the basic grammars vary but all those in common use in fourteenth-century English grammar schools are what can be called *Schulgrammatik*, "systematic" accounts of Latin, "progressing through the parts of speech one by one . . . defin[ing] each part of speech and its properties (*accidentia*), and discuss[ing] each property in turn."[18] The account these texts give of basic grammatical forms is often incomplete. Donatus's *Ars minor*, for example, "traditionally . . . regarded as the beginners' textbook *par excellence*" provides only five paradigms for nouns and the conjugation of only a single verb, *legere* [to read].[19] Such grammars were not designed to provide a thorough knowledge of Latin, but, rather, terminological and conceptual starting points; they were tools for approaching Latin sentences and texts so that more complex forms could be learned through more detailed, ad hoc instruction.[20] In this sense, these grammars could be said to impart a pedagogical structure rather than a body of knowledge, a system by which pupils might learn rather than the whole substance of "grammar" and all its constitutive rules.

The pedagogical structure of the *Schulgrammatiken* can also be categorized by the techniques they use to evoke a scene of instruction and, in particular, by the various ways they unfold their paradigms so as to posit both a teacher and student in the text, in this way creating—as if by a method of image-creation all their own—what might be called pedagogic *positions*.[21] This is always a version of the procedure I have just described in the *Formula* whereby the system of description and explanation of the paradigmatic mode is converted into the lifelike world of the narrative mode. But such conversion even occurs when a rule is couched

---

[18] Vivien Law, *Grammar and Grammarians in the Early Middle Ages* (London: Longman, 1997), 54. In Law's typology *Schulgrammatiken* are opposed to *regulae* which "contain numerous paradigms (*regulae* or *kanónes*), and often lists of examples as well" (55).

[19] Law, *Grammar and Grammarians*, 72.

[20] On the function of medieval grammars more generally see Vivien Law, "Grammar," 288–95 in *Medieval Latin: An Introduction and Bibliographical Guide*, ed. F. A. C. Mantello and A. G. Rigg (Washington, DC: The Catholic University of America Press, 1996).

[21] Although it is not a grammar common in medieval England and I do not, therefore, discuss it here, Robert Kaster writes of the way the early grammarian Pompeius also "brings us directly into the grammarian's classroom" because "we hear in Pompeius's text a teacher's voice, speaking with some immediacy," *Guardians of Language: The Grammarian and Society in Late Antiquity* (Berkeley, CA: University of California Press, 1988), 158. As Richard Sharpe puts the general point, "As long as languages have been taught in schools, schoolmasters have provided for use as exercises texts that deal with objects and activities familiar to pupils," "Latin in Everyday Life," 315–41 in *Medieval* Latin, ed. Mantello and Rigg, 316.

in the simplest, declarative form. Take, for example, the explanation of how to decline a noun in the dative and ablative plural in the *Catholicon* (1286) by John of Genoa (sometimes known as Johan Balbus), a dictionary preceded by a simple and commonly-used grammar:[22]

> Dativus et ablativus pluralis quarte declinacionis fit a nominativo singulari, mutata *u* in *i* et interposita *bu* ut *haec manus, hiis* et *ab hiis manibus*.
>
> [The plural of the dative and ablative of the fourth declension is formed by changing *u* of the nominative singular to *i* and inserting *bu* thus: *haec manus, hiis* and *ab hiis manibus*.][23]

Plainness is the most beguiling of qualities—the hardest to notice *as* a style—but this simple statement produces immediate effects, gathering to itself all the authority of any unproved assertion and depositing it in the tutelary position the process of knowledge-transfer insists upon. To put this more simply, a statement of this kind adopts the form of a teacher's utterance:

> Prima autem persona pluralis formatur a tercia singulari remota *t* et addita *mus* ut *amat, amamus*, in omnes coniugationes.
>
> [The first person plural, then, is formed from the third person singular with the *t* removed and *mus* added, for example *amat, amamus*, in all the conjugations.] (*Catholicon*, 47r b)

Just as such a declarative creates a tutelary site for the authority insisted upon by the rule, it also implies a destination for the knowledge it proposes to transfer, someone in the position of needing or wanting to know how to construct "the plural of the dative and ablative of the fourth declension" or "the first person plural" of a verb. In other words, just as such an authoritative declaration creates the position of the teacher required to utter it, it also creates the position of the student that teacher must be addressing. Thus, even the most plainly stated grammatical rule will conjure up the activities of a grammar school simply because it is a rule, and it not only implies two actors, but also the circumstances (which

---

[22] The *Catholicon* divides its grammar into four parts, an "orthographia" [spelling], an "etymologia" [word history], a "diasyntactica" [syntax], and a "prosodia" [prosodic guide], but, as David Thomson notes "the work overrides this ostensible plan to treat etymologia and diasyntactica together," David Thomson, "A Study of the Middle English Treatises on Grammar," 3 vols. (D.Phil. thesis, University of Oxford, 1977), 1: 44. This grammar is often discussed in relation to grammar in medieval England even though it is not present in any of the schoolbooks examined in the previous chapter. It was almost certainly in wide circulation in fourteenth- and fifteenth-century England, not least because the Trinity Grammar refers to it and draws upon it heavily.

[23] Joannes Balbus, *Catholicon* (Mainz, 1460), 39v a. Hereafter citations to this grammar will be by folio number in the text.

is to say the scene of instruction) in which the imposing and obeying of rules about language would occur.

As they unfold these same grammatical rules the other basic grammars used in medieval England produce these very same positions by means of six further techniques (in addition to the declarative statements I have just described). First, as the *Doctrinale* of Alexander of Villa-Dei illustrates with particular clarity, precepts often index the position of the teacher because they are couched in the first person, as if they were being spoken in a classroom ("ut levius potero, te declinare docebo" [I will teach you how to decline, in as easy a way as I can]).[24] The position of the teacher is often produced, second, as it is absorbed to the rule itself, so that it is as if the *rule* is speaking, in this way, gently constructing an allegory in which the grammatical form—here providing the endings for nouns of the first declension—is the tutelary person (teaching us about itself):

> Rectis -*as* -*es* -*a* dat declinatio prima,
> atque per -*am* propria quaedam ponuntur Hebraea,
> dans ae diphthongon genetivis atque dativis.

[The first declension gives -*as*, -*es*, -*a* to the nominatives, and certain Hebrew proper names end in -*am*, giving the diphthong -*ae* for the genitives and the datives.] (*Doctrinale*, ch. 1, 29–31)[25]

These two techniques can be found together in another of the commonly-used grammars, Evrard of Béthune's *Graecismus*, where there is a first person in the orienting statements of its first lines ("in hoc opere volo doctrinare minores" [in this work I want to instruct the young]), and rules also sometimes declare themselves as if they are personifications ("Vult, si praeueniat uerbum, rectus tibi fiat / Regula" [the rule wishes that, where (the substantive) comes before the verb, you take it in the nominative]).[26] But rules in the *Graecismus* also employ a third technique, indexing the position of the teacher as well as the student in direct speech, using the second person to give the rule the form of a *spoken* statement addressing another person (here to make clear that a substantive in the nominative can follow a verb):

---

[24] Alexander of Villa-Dei, *Doctrinale*, ed. Theodore Reichling (Berlin: A. Hofmann, 1893), pro. 12. Hereafter this grammar will be cited from this edition by chapter and line number in the text. For this line see also Copeland and Sluiter, *Medieval Grammar and Rhetoric*, 577.

[25] See also Copeland and Sluiter, *Medieval Grammar and Rhetoric*, 578.

[26] Evrard of Béthune, *Graecismus*, ed. Johann Wrobel (Hildesheim; G. Olm, 1987; first published 1887), ch. 14, 4 (p. 143) ("in hoc opere"), ch. 27, 14–15 (p. 247) ("vult, si praeueniat"). Hereafter this grammar will be cited from this edition by chapter, line, and page number in the text. For the second of these passages see also Copeland and Sluiter, *Medieval Grammar and Rhetoric*, 592.

> Si sequitur uerbum, datur haec tibi regula: uerbum
> Omne vocativum substantiuumque uel altrum
> Istis consimile casus similes habet in se:
> Ut *uocor Ebrardus*, uel *sum bonus, ambulo rectus*.

[If it follows the verb, this is the rule given to you: every vocative word or substantive or any other one like these has matching cases within itself: e.g. "*vocor Ebrardus*" [I am called Eberhard], or "*sum bonus*" [I am good] "*ambulo rectus*" [I walk straight] (*Graecismus*, ch. 27, 17–20 [p. 247])[27]

As can be seen in the *Doctrinale*, direct address can also couple the second person with a future tense, extending the scope of the instruction, and the position of the student addressed, beyond the confines of the text:

> Quando mas fit in -*us*, in -*a* femineum sine neutro,
> femineis -*abus* sociabitur, ut *dominabus*,
> sexum discernens; istis *animas* superaddes.
> accusativis pluralibus -*as* sociabis.
> versibus his nota fit declinatio prima.

[When a masculine word ends in -*us* and the feminine in -*a* without there being a neuter, (the ending), -*abus* will be connected to the feminine forms, e.g. *dominabus* [ladies, dat. abl.], in order to distinguish the gender: you may add *animas* [souls, plur.] to this group. You will add -*as* to the plural accusatives. In these verses the first declension is made known.] (*Doctrinale*, ch. 1, 41–5)[28]

Precepts that use a sequence of tenses of this kind operate according to the same indexical principles as precepts in the first person, those that personify the rule, and those in the second person, but the progression also brings the *process* of literacy training into the rule, not only evoking the subject positions that create a scene of instruction (teacher and student) but putting those positions or the confected figures in motion, absorbing to the text not only the activity of instruction but the use of grammar outside the classroom that such instruction is designed to prepare.

Although these elements of the grammar-school style are beguiling in their simplicity, there is an even simpler method and style of pedagogy in these grammars that I have left until this point to describe because it is so hard to see it *as* an element of a style. The text that makes most use of this defining technique is the most basic and common of the medieval grammars, Donatus's *Ars minor*, and this is also doubtless why the technique was so much used in all the later English grammars, but yet

---

[27] Here, in the *Graecismus*, the teacher's position is also indexed by a self-reference that insists the text's author is actually propounding these rules ("I am called Eberhard"). For this passage see Copeland and Sluiter, *Medieval Grammar and Rhetoric*, 592.

[28] For this passage see also Copeland and Sluiter, *Medieval Grammar and Rhetoric*, 578.

another reason why it is hard to see as a technique rather than grammatical pedagogy as such. This fourth element is, in shape, the series of questions and answers that constitute most of the form of the *Ars minor*. I already quoted the first of these in Chapter 1 so I will quote the beginning of the next section here ("De Nomine" [On The Noun]) which continues as if it were a transcription of a schoolroom scene:

> Nomen quid est? Pars orationis cum casu corpus aut rem proprie commu-niterue significans. Nomini quot accidunt? Sex. Quae? Qualitas, conparatio, genus, numerus, figura, casus.[29]
>
> [What is a noun? A part of speech that names a person or thing in particular or in general. How many properties does it have? Six. Which are? Quality, comparison, gender, number, form, case.]

Because this text lacks an orienting proem of the kind that became standard in the more discursive grammars such as the *Doctrinale* and *Graecismus*, these questions instantly acquire a kind of verisimilitude, but the scene of instruction is also evoked here because these questions index the position of teacher and student by effectively splitting a precept into two, distributing the information a simple statement would dispose across both a query and its appropriate response. Thus, the first pairing is really a more vivacious version of the statement "Nomen est pars orationis cum casu corpus aut rem proprie communiterue significans" [A noun is a part of speech that names a person or thing in particular or in general]. Of course, without any kind of narrative frame, there is an inevitable ambiguity about which position is articulated by each half of the precept, not least since, in any classroom, a student might pose questions just as often as a teacher. But the questions of the *Ars minor* generally seem to be voiced by a tutelary figure particularly since they often give way to the fifth element of the grammar-school style, rules propounded in the imperative mood:

> Da declinationem uerbi actiui. *Lego* uerbum actiuum indicatiuo modo dictum temporis praesentis, numeri singularis, figurae simplicis, personae primae, coniugationis tertiae correptae, quod declinabitur sic:
> *Lego legis legit*, et pluraliter *legimus legitis legunt.*
>
> [Give the inflection of the active verb. *Lego,* an active verb, expressed in the indicative mode of the present tense, singular in number, in simple form, in the first person, and third short conjugation, which will be conjugated thus: *lego, legis, legit,* and plural, *legimus, legitis, legunt.*] (593)

---

[29] Donatus, *Ars Minor,* 585–612 in Louis Holtz, *Donat et la tradition de l'enseignement grammatical* (Paris: Centre National de la Recherche Scientifique, 1981), 585. Hereafter citations to the *Ars minor* will be from this edition and cited by page number in the text.

Such imperatives index the position of the teacher just as declaratives do, creating that position in the authority they assume, but they index the position of the student just as vividly for the command implies the subject meant to execute it. They also often introduce the last element of this style I want to detail, a sequence of examples like those that follow this command ("lego, legis, legit," etc.). There will be reason to explore this technique at much greater length in what follows, but here I hope it will be enough to say that such lists evoke both the teacher and the student—or, perhaps better, either of them—as they script how the teacher will exemplify the point he is making or the student will prove that he has learned the lesson he has just been taught.

There are other pedagogical methods in use in these grammars and many other grammatical structures used repeatedly in their teaching, but (1) simple declaratives, (2) rules in the first person, (3) rules as personifications, (4) rules in the second person (with or without a progression of tenses), (5) rules as queries and responses, (6) rules as commands, and (7) rules exemplified in lists are the most important of these because they either index a subject position or do so by moving a subject through space and time. Taken together they can therefore evoke the *sequence* inherent to instruction, as each pedagogical form in some way pivots from the teacher's position to the student's response. The movement achieved by such sequencing is perhaps clearest in the variation on the kinds of queries and responses I have already described as they appear in the *Catholicon*:

> Queritur que nomina discernant numeros et quae non. Ad hoc dico quod substantiva ut *homo* et *homines*...discrecionem quantitatis in rebus suppositis faciunt ut *est homo* ergo unum. *Et sunt homines* ergo plura...
>
> [It is asked which nouns distinguish number and which do not. And to this I say that a substantive such as *man* and *men*...make a distinction of quantity in the referents, for example, *he is a man* therefore one. And *these men* therefore are many...] (*Catholicon*, 27v b)

The question here is impersonal ("it is asked") and the response is in a first person that could very well be the voice of the teacher, since it actually provides the grammatical knowledge these statements teach, but it could just as easily be the question a curious or confused student could pose ("which nouns distinguish number and which do not?"). Conversely, what follows the impersonal query could be the correct response the teacher provides as part of the lesson ("if I were asked 'to this I [would] say'") just as it could be the student's response to the question once he has learned this lesson ("since it is asked...I say"). Although I did not call attention to this aspect of its pedagogy when I discussed it in Chapter 1, it is worth noting here that John of Cornwall's *Speculum grammaticale* not only combines and employs these elements of the grammar-school style ("Item si queratur...ad istud respondeo at dico..." [If it should be asked...I respond and say...]), it uses this form with such frequency across its great length that it can also be said that this element of the grammar-school style characterizes the style of that text on the whole.

Mention of the *Speculum grammaticale* makes it necessary to notice that the movement of knowledge from teacher to student tracked so vividly in and by the grammar-school style was rendered that much *more* vivid in the English grammar school by the movement from Latin to English that inevitably lay behind it. This movement is explicit in the *Speculum* where the examples employed in the text are in both Latin and English:

> Item querendum est quot sunt persone in verbo dicendum quod tres sunt prima seconda et tertia unde prima persona est que significat rem de se loquentem ut *lego* y rede *legimus* we rede *legis* þu redis *legitis* ʒe redin vel ʒe redith *iste legit* þis redith *isti legunt* þei redyn.
>
> [If it should be asked how many persons of verb there are, it ought to be said that there are three: first, second, and third, whereof the first person is that which refers to the person who is speaking, such as *Lego*, I read, *Legimus*, we read, *legis*, you read, *legitis*, you read, *iste legit*, he reads, *isti legunt*, they read.]
> (MS Auctarium F.3.9, p. 9)

There is, first, the impersonal question and the answer that are, at once, a version of the teacher's demonstration and the student's answer, there is, second, the set of examples which also may be the teacher's script or the student's learned response. The English that accompanies the Latin in each of these examples could be understood as an explanatory gloss, but it is also an increase in what might be described as the depth of the indexing of the student's position: as the grammar here moves from teacher to student it shows (again, at once) the teacher extending himself into the competence in English grammar that his student has brought to the classroom the better to teach him, speaking the student's language ("I read") thereby doubling the angles from which his own position is evoked. As I suggested in Chapter 1, the English additions to the *Speculum grammaticale* amount to elaborations of a general tendency toward realism in elementary teaching, but here both this technique and that realism can be seen as an intensification of all the tendencies of the grammar-school style I have so far described.

This movement from teacher to student and back again, both sequentially and simultaneously, as a cycle and as a repetition, is a particular feature of these exemplifications. For obvious reasons this element is omnipresent, but it also gathers up all that this style is and can do, and concentrates the style's defining principles in the one word that usually forms a hinge between the declarative rule and the example or list of them, the adverb "sic" or the conjunction "ut" [thus]. So central are these adverbs to the grammar-school style, in fact, that "ut" moves precept into example in the passages from the *Graecismus* I analyzed earlier ("ut '*uocor Ebrardus*'"), as well as passages in the *Ars minor* ("sic: *lego legis legit*") and the *Catholicon* ("ut *homo* et *homines*"). Since it is the adverbial function of the hinge that matters more than any particular word, not only will "ut" or "sic" do, but they are sometimes used together (as we will see in what follows) and the *Graecismus* sometimes uses "scilicet," "sicut," or "unde" for exactly the same purpose.[30] In the passage from the *Formula* I analyzed at the beginning of the chapter, the word "exemplum" also forms such a hinge. Each of these terms might be seen to perform a function rather than to constitute an element of the grammar-school style in themselves, but it is also the case that these terms do not merely assist in the movement that defines this style, they bring it about.

As it condenses the grammar-school style's characteristic movement from teacher to student (and vice versa) this element of the style also condenses all of this style's unique effects. Insofar as this movement always traces an angle of 180 degrees—as knowledge is moved from a teacher addressing a student, or as the student assumes the teacher's position by giving the correct answer, or as pedagogy moves from the teacher's question to scripting the student's response, or as the teacher extends himself into the student's linguistic competence—and not least because this movement is so frequently cyclical and swaps two otherwise fixed positions—it could also be said that the characteristic movement of the grammar-school style is a *rotation*. Insofar as that rotation moves knowledge between and into the subject positions that it simultaneously creates (the teacher teaching, the student learning) we can also call it a technique that everywhere brings a dry body of knowledge—rules and paradigmatic examples—to *life*. Such deployments of the resources of grammar are more appropriately described as the elements of a style than as a pedagogic method because they use language not only to explain grammar but to add a certain affect to that explanation. The texts that employ this style not only teach grammar, in other words, they teach it compellingly: they absorb any reader to a version of the grammar-school classroom built in the text, clarifying grammar's rules and putting them into active use by means of that vivacity. Small wonder that such a style was noticed by and useful to a poet.

---

[30] See, for example, *Graecismus*, ed. Wrobel, ch. 13, 248 (for "unde"), ch. 4, 65 (for "scilicet"), ch. 15, 5 (for "sicut"). For six other instances of this use of the word "exemplum" see *Formula* [Text Z], ed. Thomson, 135–6.

BREAD AND MILK FOR CHILDREN

As I noted at the start, the genealogy that connects the style of the basic grammars and its effects to Chaucer's style is surprisingly easy to trace because Chaucer obliged any such project by writing a work of elementary pedagogy himself, the *Treatise on the Astrolabe*, undertaken, as this text reports, at the behest of "lyte Lowys" (Pro. 1), a child of the "tendir age of ten yeer" (Pro. 24). The *Treatise* describes its own style in pedagogic terms, with Chaucer at some pains to insist that he has striven for simplicity ("for that curious endityng and hard sentence is ful hevy at onys for such a child to lerne," Pro. 45–6) and has often repeated himself for clarity's sake (for "to writen unto a child twyes a god sentence . . . semith bettter . . . than he forgete it onys" [to write a good sentence twice for a child seems better than that he should forget it once], Pro. 48–50). Because the *Treatise* says that the astrolabe it is describing is "compowned after the latitude of Oxenforde" [designed for the latitude of Oxford] (Pro. 10), scholars have sometimes ignored Chaucer's account of the text's intended audience and recruited the *Treatise* for hypotheses about Chaucer's university learning.[31] Chaucer and all of his writing has in this way been associated with Oxford and with the "Oxford calculators" at Merton College more particularly, an important site of astronomical research in the fourteenth century, and a college of which Ralph Strode, one of the dedicatees of Chaucer's *Troilus and Criseyde* (V.1857), was a fellow.[32] This is a more local version of the kind of confusion that I said in my introduction tends to surround the concept of *grammatica* whereby the duplication of a subject of elementary learning in the university syllabus encourages the substitution of sophisticated for elementary forms (although here the issue is not the duplication of grammar in the *trivium* but astronomy in the *quadrivium*).[33] But three surviving

---

[31] "Chaucer, to be sure, indicates that he bought an astrolabe to give to his 'little Lewis' before he had learnt much Latin. But 'Lewis' may be a fiction, to justify the simplicity with which the poet describes 'a certein noumbre of conclusiouns' appertaining to the same instrument," J. A. W. Bennett, *Chaucer at Oxford and at Cambridge* (Oxford: Oxford University Press, 1974), 33.

[32] See Bennett, *Chaucer at Oxford and at Cambridge*, 63–75; J. D. North, *Chaucer's Universe* (Oxford: Clarendon Press, 1988), 286; Edgar Laird, "Chaucer and Friends: The Audience for the *Treatise on the Astrolabe*," *The Chaucer Review* 41 (2007): 441.

[33] On "astronomy" as part of the *quadrivium* see Ernst Robert Curtius, *European Literature and the Latin Middle Ages* (Princeton, NJ: Princeton University Press, 1953), 37; Paul Abelson, *The Seven Liberal Arts: A Study in Mediaeval Culture*, Columbia University Teachers' College Contributions to Education 11 (New York, NY: Teachers' College Columbia University, 1906), esp. 119–27; David Wagner, "The Seven Liberal Arts

manuscripts of the *Treatise* endorse Chaucer's insistence that it was an elementary work: Oxford, Bodleian Library, MS Bodley 619, Oxford, Bodleian Library, MS E Musaeo 54, and Aberdeen, University Library, MS 123 all describe their copies of the *Treatise on the Astrolabe* as "brede and milke for children."[34]

The structural complexity of the astrolabe also makes any treatise on the subject seem too "forbiddingly technical" to be a work of elementary instruction.[35] Although it is a device whose main function is referential— to determine the time of day, or the date on a calendar, or a particular position on the surface of the earth—it provides such information as its parts move in three dimensions. In mechanical terms it consists of three (usually metal) plates, one containing two-dimensional representations of star locations in the heavens, another containing a two-dimensional projection of the earth's surface (in a fretwork of latitudinal and long-itudinal lines) from a particular location, the third containing a variety of metrics for measuring time; the first two of these plates are fixed to the third by a pin, and can therefore be turned in relation to each other as well as the third (see Fig. 3.1).[36]

In conceptual terms, these three plates act together to project the three dimensions of the earth's surface and the heavens above it into two dimensions thereby modeling every moment during the day and night

---

and Classical Scholarship," 1–23 in *The Seven Liberal Arts in the Middle Ages*, ed. David L. Wagner (Bloomington, IN: Indiana University Press, 1983).

[34] For the Oxford manuscripts see R. W. Hunt, *A Summary Catalogue of Western Manuscripts in the Bodleian Library at Oxford*, 7 vols. in 9 (Oxford: Clarendon Press, 1895–1953), 2, Part 1: 232 (for Bodley 619) and 2, Part 2: 679 (for E Musaeo 54). For the Aberdeen manuscript see N. R. Ker, *Medieval Manuscripts in British Libraries*, 5 vols. (Oxford, Clarendon Press, 1969–2002), 2: 4–11. I give the Bodley 619 reading (E Musaeo 54 has "bred and mylk for children" and the Aberdeen MS has "bred and mylk for chyldryn"). All of these manuscripts were copied in the fifteenth century. For the strong connections of these manuscripts to Oxford see M. C. Seymour, *A Catalogue of Chaucer Manuscripts*: Vol. 1: *Works before the* Canterbury Tales (Brookfield, VT: Ashgate, 1995), 107 (Bodley 619) and 109–10 (E Musaeo 54). Bodley 619 has marginalia in its scribe's hand that connect it to Merton College, although Simon Horobin has argued that this language may have been copied by a professional scribe (himself a Carthusian monk) from his exemplar. See Simon Horobin, "The Scribe of Bodleian Library MS Bodley 619 and the Circulation of Chaucer's Treatise on the Astrolabe," *Studies in the Age of Chaucer* 31 (2009): 109–24.

[35] Thomas J. Jambeck and Karen K. Jambeck, "Chaucer's *Treatise on the Astrolabe*: A Handbook for the Medieval Child," *Children's Literature* 3 (1974): 117. For a concise summary of those who have found the *Treatise* difficult see *A Variorum Edition of the Works of Geoffrey Chaucer*, vol. 6: *The Prose Treatises*, Part 1: *A Treatise on the Astrolabe*, ed. Sigmund Eisner (Norman, OK: University of Oklahoma Press, 2002), 36.

[36] For a more detailed description of an astrolabe's structure see North, *Chaucer's Universe*, 38–42.

Fig. 3.1. "The Painswick Astrolabe," *c.*1370, Museum of the History of Science, Oxford, 121 mm in diameter.

(as the plates, like the spheres, are turned).[37] However intimidating all of this may seem to us, the *Treatise on the Astrolabe* was clearly popular and accessible to many in Chaucer's day: it survives in more manuscript copies than any one of Chaucer's works other than the *Canterbury Tales*.[38] And, for all its spatial and computational complexity, the astrolabe is an oddly homely tool: unlike most reference works it tells whoever is using it about him or herself and, in particular, just where and when he or she actually is. The medieval custom was to insist on this homeliness by calling the stationary plate that holds the others the *mater*, or "moder" [mother] as Chaucer has it in his translation (I.2, I.3, I.4); Chaucer extends this image by calling the depression in the "mother" that makes it possible to attach this plate to the other two its "wombe" (I.3).[39]

Attempts to construe a relationship between the *Treatise on the Astrolabe* and Chaucer's other writings have almost always seized on such imagery, seeing it as yet another instance of Chaucerian realism, here turned to the vivid evocation of a "domestic moment."[40] The techniques of this domestication include that tendency toward simplification and a reduction of "the fussy erudition of the expert" to accommodate "the child's homelier vocabulary."[41] There are also two images that more broadly align the treatise with Chaucer's poetry because they are so imaginative and precise: in the first of these Chaucer likens the fretwork of the "riet" (the plate constructed as a kind of fretwork that allows the markings on the plate below to be partly visible) to the "web of a loppe" [a spider's web] (I.3); in the second he describes the curved and

---

[37] North provides progressively more complex descriptions of the astrolabe's function in his second chapter as well as helpful diagrams explaining the key principles of planispheric projection (*Chaucer's Universe*, 46–86, esp. 52–7).

[38] Edgar Laird, "A Previously Unnoticed Manuscript of Chaucer's *Treatise on the Astrolabe*," *Chaucer Review* 34 (2000): 410.

[39] Chaucer's probable source for this text is discussed in what follows but I cite it throughout from the edition and translation in R. T. Gunther, *Chaucer and the Messahalla on the Astrolabe* (Oxford: Oxford University Press, 1929), 137–92 (for the translation) and 195–231 (for the Latin text). For the term *mater* see Gunther (217). The first plate of the astrolabe containing the projection of the heavens, was usually called the "rete [net]" (Gunther, 217 and 221), a term that Chaucer more or less retains as "reet" (I.3) or "riet" (I.21). The second plate is referred to more generally in both Chaucer's source and his *Treatise* as the "tabulas climatum" (Gunther 217) or "tables of the clymates" (I.14).

[40] Jambeck and Jambeck, "Chaucer's *Treatise on the Astrolabe*," 117. On the general issue of Chaucer's "withdrawal from direct political statement" (40) see Lee Patterson, *Chaucer and the Subject of History* (Madison, WI: University of Wisconsin Press, 1991), esp. chapters 5 (244–79) and 7 (322–66) on The Shipman's Tale and The Miller's Tale respectively. See also Lee Patterson, "The 'Parson's Tale' and the Quitting of the 'Canterbury Tales,'" *Tradito* 34 (1978): 331–80 (esp. pp. 370–80).

[41] Seth Lerer, "Chaucer's Sons," *University of Toronto Quarterly* 73 (2004): 908 (see also 912–14). North makes a similar point, "Chaucer was fascinated by the sciences, but he saw in them a moral as well as an intellectual hierarchy" (*Chaucer's Universe*, 255).

overlapping lines marking latitude and longitude on the "table of climates" as the "clawes of a loppe" [a spider's legs], or the "werk of a wommans calle" [a hair net] (I.19–20). As an act "of paternal self-definition" the *Treatise* has also been connected to the tendency of Chaucer's most passionate poetry to deflect the political into more local matters of moral conduct or subjectivity (the domestication of the problem of war in the Melibee, say, or the Parson's penitential quitting of all the literary ambitions of the *Canterbury Tales*).[42] Connections have also been proposed between the subject of the astrolabe and the elaborate cosmological descriptions at the beginning of the General Prologue to the *Canterbury Tales*, The Introduction to the Man of Law's Tale, and The Parson's Prologue.[43] Chaucer, however, links the domestic much more mechanically to issues of language, placing "lyte Lowys" in much clearer relation to his linguistic competence than to his family (it is very hard to tell from the treatise if "Lowys" really *is* Chaucer's "son," rather than a young boy referred to in this paternal way), insisting above all that Lewis has not yet learned much Latin ("this tretis...wol I shewe the under full light reules and naked wordes in Englissh, for Latyn canst thou yit but small," Pro. 25–7). While the *Treatise* is anything but a grammar, insofar as it moves knowledge from Latin into English, the *Treatise* was parallel to the basic grammars in its function, as Chaucer makes clear in its prologue:

> And Lowys, yf so be that I shewe the in my lighte Englissh as trewe conclusions touching this mater, and not oonly as trewe but as many and as subtile conclusiouns, as ben shewid in Latyn in eny commune tretys of the Astrelabie, konne me the more thank (Pro. 50–6)
>
> [*yf so be*: if it happens; *konne me the more thank*: give me greater thanks]

Perhaps not surprisingly, Chaucer's understanding of the rendering of Latin in "naked words" resembles nothing so much as the account of translation given in the "General Prologue" to the Wycliffite Bible.[44] Such

---

[42] Jambeck and Jambeck, "Chaucer's *Treatise on the Astrolabe*," 118.

[43] This is Chaucer "in the country of the stars," in Chauncey Wood's redolent phrase, a poet who, like Boethius, found consolation in the universe's stabilities both a rationale and a correlative for the "steadfastnesse" he so generally prized in human affairs. See *Chaucer in the Country of the Stars: Poetic Uses of Astrological Imagery* (Princeton, NJ: Princeton University Press, 1970). As North puts this point, "the theme of mutability that runs through all of Chaucer's poetry, is possible only because his moral and religious convictions are firm enough to provide the plane of reference with respect to which up-so-doun can be judged. There are few signs that this moral confidence ever seriously wavered, and his portrayals of steadfastness have his own *Retraction* as an epilogue, removing from us the temptation to say otherwise" (*Chaucer's Universe*, 255).

[44] See Andrew Cole, *Literature and Heresy in the Age of Chaucer* (Cambridge: Cambridge University Press, 2008), 84–92 and 96.

purposes are well served by the simplicity and repetition Chaucer also says in this prologue that he has striven for throughout. On the other hand, if "showing" in "light English" the subtleties that are otherwise trapped in Latin was Chaucer's main purpose, the striking images that have garnered so much attention are unrepresentative of Chaucer's general practice in the *Treatise* as a whole.

As it shared a pedagogical task with the basic grammars and addressed a student at exactly the same stage, the *Treatise* quite naturally partook of the style of those grammars, and, for this reason too, however complex its subject matter may now seem, it was, like these grammars, an elementary work. Although he drew a few descriptions in the first part of his treatise from the *De sphera mundi* by John Sacro Bosco, the *Treatise* is, in most particulars, an expanded translation of the extremely popular text sometimes called the "De compositione et operatione astrolabii" [On the making and operation of an astrolabe] but more usually the "*Messahalla*" after "the medieval Latin transliteration of the famous Arabic astrologer and astronomer Māšā'allāh."[45] As the following example makes clear, the *Messahalla* also employs elements of the grammar-school style, particularly rules in the second person ("cum volveris" [when you wish to know]) and rules as commands ("pone" [set]) that index the position of the teacher:

De gradu solis inveniendo capitulum
Cum volueris scire gradum solis, pone regulam super diem mensis presentis, et gradus a summitate eius tactus erit gradus solis, qui cuius signi sit videbis, et eum ex alia parte nota in zodiaco in rethi. Notabis et nadayz eius, quod est simul gradus "7" signi. Diem quoque mensis per gradum solis invenies; posita enim regula super gradum solis diem quesitum ostendet.

[45] S. W. Harvey, "Chaucer's Debt to Sacrobosco," *Journal of English and Germanic Philology* 34 (1935): 34–8; Paul Kunitzsch, "On the Authenticity of the Treatise on the Composition and Use of the Astrolabe Ascribed to Messahalla," *Arvchives Internationales d'Histoire des Sciences* 31 (1981): 42. The "Messahalla" survives in over 200 manuscripts. See Francis J. Carmody, *Arabic Astronomical and Astrological Sciences in Latin Translation: A Critical Bibliography* (Berkeley, CA: University of California Press, 1956), 24–5. A number of thirteenth- and fourteenth-century manuscripts clearly attribute the text to Māšā'allāh, including the copy in Cambridge, University Library, MS Ii.3.3 (which calls the treatise "Tractatus Astrolabii edicionis Messehillath") and Oxford, Bodleian Library, Ashmole MS 1522 and MS 1796. This puts before us the unexplored possibility that Chaucer understood himself to be translating and disseminating a text that had originated in Arabic. On these manuscripts see Kunitzsch, "On the Authenticity of the Treatise on the Composition and Use of the Astrolabe Ascribed to Messahalla," 42 n. 6; *A Catalogue of the Manuscripts Preserved in the Library of the University of Cambridge*, ed. H. R. Luard, 6 vols. (Cambridge: Cambridge University Press, 1856–67), 3: 404–6; and the *Descriptive, Analytical and Critical Catalogue of the Manuscripts bequeathed unto the University of Oxford by Elias Ashmole*, ed. William Henry Black (Oxford: Oxford University Press, 1845), cols. 1426–30 (for Ashmole 1522) and cols. 1505–9 (for Ashmole 1796).

[To find the true motion of the sun
When you wish to know the degree of the sun, set the alidade upon the day of the present month: then the degree touched by its tip will be the degree of the sun. Look to see of what Sign it is, and note it on the zodiac of the rete on the other side. Also note its nadir, which is likewise the degree of the 7th Sign. And you may also find the day of the month from the degree of the sun; for the alidade, when once set upon the degree of the sun, will point out the desired day.][46]

Although "grammar-school style" may begin to seem like a less appropriate designation if it was also used in astronomical treatises like the *Messahalla*, it is useful that the pedagogical positions evoked are the same, and the style may still be said to be rooted in literacy training insofar as it uses grammar to evoke the positions of teacher and student for pedagogical effect. There is also a significant difference between the occasional use of some elements of the grammar-school style and the more vivid evocation of the whole scene of instruction produced when all of its elements are employed together or elaborated. In fact, the pedagogical positions produced here are kept some distance from the classroom by their tense, which projects the imagined activities into the future ("when" at some point "you wish to know... then the degree touched by its tip will be").

Chaucer also brings his version of the *Messahalla* closer to the basic grammars by eliminating the whole of the *Messahalla*'s first part and its elaborate description of how to construct an astrolabe, creating a new first part in which he describes the instrument of the astrolabe and all its parts instead. This first part is necessarily simple, moreover, because Chaucer generates it from the brief, declarative sentences that form the introductory paragraph of the *Messahalla*'s second part. Here, for example, is the first sentence of that first paragraph:

Primum est armila suspensoria ad capiendam altitudinem, et dicitur arabice *alhahucia*.

[The First is the suspending-ring for use when taking an altitude; in Arabic it is called *alhahucia*.] (168/217)

Chaucer tends to flesh out such sentences with the kind of repetition he identifies as basic to an elementary style in his prologue ("the heighte of thinges" is repeated as "the heighte of any thing" to prevent any confusion

---

[46] Messahalla, "On the Astrolabe," ed. Gunther, 169–70 (translation, with minor corrections), 218 (Latin). Hereafter this text and its translation will be cited from this edition in the text in the following form: page number of translation/page number of Latin.

about referents) but in this sense these descriptions grow simpler as they get longer:

> Thyn Astrolabie hath a ring to putten on the thumbe of thi right hond in taking the height of thinges. And tak kep, for from henes forthward I wol clepen the heighte of any thing that is taken by the rewle 'the altitude', withoute moo wordes. (I.1.1–6)
>
> [*tak kep*: take care; *clepen*: call]

Chaucer also shapes and elaborates these simple declaratives by introducing the more particular elements of the grammar-school style throughout. Here, in these two sentences, we find the rule in the second person ("thi"), the rule as command ("tak kep") and the authoritative first person ("I wol clepen"). These forms are intensifying and vivifying when joined together—elaborating a scene of instruction in typical form—but Chaucer also intensifies their effects by fleshing out one of the positions they so firmly index, giving the second person something like a body ("thi right hond") as if this implied student is *actually* holding an astrolabe while receiving these instructions.

Such intensification also describes Chaucer's method when he comes to translate the second part of the *Messahalla* where, generally speaking, he renders the contents of his source faithfully. As in its first part, the Latin of the *Messahalla* continues to use the rule as commands ("scito" [determine], "diuide" [divide]), in the perfect subjunctive ("si volueris" [if you should wish]), and the future tense ("habebis" [you will have]) that I have already noted:

> Si volueris reducere horas inequales in horas equales, scito gradus horarum inequalium, quot sint; et diuide eos per. 15., et habebis horas equales.
>
> [If you should wish to reduce the unequal hours into the equal hours, determine the divisions of the unequal hours, how many there are, and divide them by 15 and you will have the equal hours.] (173/220)

When translating an instruction such as this one, however, Chaucer simplifies the syntax of the *Messahalla*, removing the perfect subjunctive implying a condition and the future tense describing the result, leaving only a punchy sequence of imperatives:

> Know the nombre of the degrees in the hours inequales, and depart hem by 15, and tak there thin houres equales. (II.8)
>
> [*depart hem*: divide them]

Chaucer systematically reduces syntactic complexity in the *Messahalla* throughout this second part in just this way, as here, reeling in the subjunctives that make any use of the astrolabe hypothetical, converting conditions and possibilities into marching orders, as if a teacher were barking out commands to "rekne" (II.1, II.21), "put" (II.2), "tak" (II.3, II.17, II.24, II.29, II.34, II.35, II.37, II.38), "set" (II.6, II.7, II.13, II.18, II.19, II.20, II.27, II.28, II.36), "know" (II.8, II.9, II.22, II.40), "understond" (II.10, II.12, II.16, II.25), "sek" (II.14), "loke" (II.15, II.30), and "considre" (II.32) the astrolabe or the principles he wants his student to know. Where the *Messahalla* regularly evokes that student with rules in the second person, as in the passage just quoted, Chaucer regularly intensifies the evocation by adding a possessive pronoun to this construction ("thin" [thine]), again and again, putting the astrolabe right in the evoked student's hand ("thyn Astrelabie," II.2). In Chaucer's version of the *Messahalla*, this increasingly vivid subject not only holds this instrument, however, he has in his personal possession the information the astrolabe disposes ("thin houres equales") and his location in time ("thy month," II.5) and space ("thy sonne" [sun], II.5).

Chaucer's most extensive use of the grammar-school style in reshaping the *Messahalla*—and, for that very reason, the most determinate of his revisions—is concentrated in five extraordinary passages in the second part of the *Treatise*, each of which can be described as an extended practical example (II.1, II.3.15, II.12.7, II.17.29, II.23), and each of which can also be understood as the vivid evocation of a schoolroom scene. These passages and scenes are marked out as such *practica* because they are inaugurated by, not just one, but a whole host of the terms that I identified earlier as central to the grammar-school style and its effects, "as" (the English equivalent of *ut*), "thus" [*sic*] and "ensaumple" [*exemplum*]. More important than these terms or their profusion, however, is the way that the careful deployment of indices throughout these examples not only implies a classroom, but creates a whole narrative with a beginning, a middle, and an end. The first of these passages translates, but also significantly expands, the first passage I analyzed from the *Messahalla* (169–70/218):

> Ensaumple as thus: The yeer of oure Lord 1391, the 12 day of March at midday, I wolde knowe the degre of the sonne. I soughte in the bakhalf of myn Astelabie and fond the cercle of the daies, the whiche I knowe by the names of the monthes writen under the same cercle. Tho leyde I my reule over this foreseide day, and fond the point of my reule in the bordure upon the firste degre of Aries, a litel within the degre. And thus knowe I this conclusion.
>
> Anothir day I wolde knowen the degre of my sonne, and this was at midday in the 13 day of Decembre. I fond the day of the month in manere as I seide; tho leide I my rewle upon this foreseide 13 day, and fond the point of my

rewle in the bordure upon the firste degre of Capricorne a lite within the
degre. And than had I of this conlusioun the ful experience. (II.1)

[*I wolde knowe*: I want to know; *the whiche*: which; *Tho*: then]

As in the basic grammars, the adverbs that introduce this passage make all
aspects of the subsequent description indexical, ensuring that its every
word is "as," or an "example" of, what a teacher demonstrates in order to
teach his student "thus," *or* an elaboration of what the student can do with
the astrolabe after he has learned this lesson. As in similar examples in the
basic grammars, the "I" of the passage indexes both the teacher who is
showing a student how to employ the astrolabe as well as the student who
might put that teaching to use. As it moves, simultaneously, though the
evoked position of teacher and student this passage also executes the
defining rotation of the grammar-school style. Although such doubling
of positions was a basic mode of liveliness in the *Ars minor* and the *Speculum
grammaticale*, Chaucer renders them the more vivacious here by anchoring
all of the subject positions created here in calendrical time ("the yeer of oure
Lord 1391, the 12 day of March at midday") and tense ("I wolde know")
and then sequencing the scripted action syntactically ("I soughte . . . and
fond . . . thos leyde I . . . anothir day I wolde knowen . . . I fond . . . tho leide
I . . . and fond"). The degree and clarity of this movement so increases the
depth of field by which these rules and precepts evoke the positions of
teacher and student that it is as if they are both in motion, not just in a
classroom, but in some narrative.

It is this narrative depth that also gives this passage and the other four
like it in the *Treatise* the quality usually described by literary criticism as
"realism." Chaucer encourages such a characterization when he suggests (as
his source does not) that the "conclusioun" of the kind of practical training
this "ensaumple" provides is a "ful experience." "Experience" has played an
important role in modern discussions of learning, not least because John
Dewey insisted on the conjunction of "experience and education" (as he
put it in the title of one of his more important books) and generally
understood learning as "a transaction . . . between an individual and what,
at the time, constitutes his environment."[47] Dewey eventually decided
that the term "experience" was unhelpful because "it was so routinely
misappropriated," and the concept has more recently been described as a
"black box . . . used to discuss or define other problems while itself remaining impervious to definition or perhaps strategically vague."[48] On the

---

[47] John Dewey, *Experience and Education* (New York, NY: Macmillan, 1938), 44.
[48] Jayson Seaman and Peter J. Nelsen, "An Overburdened Term: Dewey's Concept of
'Experience' as Curriculum Theory," *Education and Culture* 27 (2011): 5 ("routinely");

other hand, modern thinkers such as Dilthey and Benjamin have insisted on the validity of what Raymond Williams later called "lived experience," and the mode of pedagogy usually called "experiential learning" still roots itself, unapologetically, in Dewey's use of the term.[49] It is this modern mode that Chaucer's terminology seems most to anticipate, and it is hardly surprising then that a description of its tenets also sounds like a characterization of the operations of the grammar-school style:

> In experiential learning theory, the transactional relationship between the person and the environment is symbolized in the dual meanings of the term *experience*—one subjective and personal, referring to the person's internal state, as in "the experience of joy and happiness" and the other objective and environmental, as in "He has 20 years of experience on this job."[50]

"Experience" here describes both of the positions I have said the grammar-school style allows basic pedagogy to index and move between. But the term "experience" not only offers another way to understand grammar-school pedagogy's characteristic movements, it makes it possible to re-describe those movements as a rotation through *perspectives* rather than subject positions, from the objective to the subjective, from the impersonal to the personal. Such a description also helps to make clear just how Chaucer may have noticed in such pedagogy's effects a set of techniques that could be recruited for more poetic ends. As the experience produced by any text could become as "full" as the experience of reading the *Treatise on the Astrolabe*, as the rotations made possible by the grammar-school style richly evoked, not just positions in a scene of instruction, but peopled varied and more complicated narratives, both those people and those stories could be made to rotate right out of the page. At this degree of fullness, in other words, the rotation the grammar-school style made possible simply *is* the vivacity we sometimes attribute to narrative, with the basic elements of that vivacity laid bare, as if the writing of the *Treatise*

Dominick La Capra, *History in Transit: Experience, Identity, Critical Theory* (Ithaca, NY: Cornell University Press, 2004), 38 ("black box"). For the landmark redefinition of "experience" as "not the origin of our explanation, not the authoritative (because seen or felt) evidence that grounds what is known, but rather that which we seek to explain," see Joan W. Scott, "The Evidence of Experience," *Critical Inquiry* 17 (1991): 773–97.

[49] On Dilthey, Benjamin, and Williams see Elizabeth J. Bellamy and Artemis Leontis, "A Genealogy of Experience: From Epistemology to Politics," *The Yale Journal of Criticism* 6 (1993): 168–9. For a defense of "experience" as a "term that cannot be effortlessly dissolved in a network of discursive relations" see Martin Jay, "The Limits of Limit-Experience: Bataille and Foucault," *Constellations* 2 (1995): 168. For Dewey's concept of experience as foundational for experiential learning theory see David A. Kolb, *Experiential Learning: Experience as the Source of Learning and Development* (Englewood Cliffs, NJ: Prentice-Hall, 1984), 27.

[50] Kolb, *Experiential Learning*, 35.

were a practicum, putting to use what Chaucer had learned grammar could do. This practicum not only shows Chaucer to have been well-schooled in these techniques but fully aware of the effects they produced.

THE GRAMMAR OF CHAUCERIAN REALISM

The postures of the grammar-school style appear in Chaucer's writing where we might least imagine pedagogy to be his subject. Although *Troilus and Criseyde* is a poem about two "lovers," for example, it proliferates scenes of instruction because its characters are so frequently teaching one another about some aspect of love. In Book 1, Troilus adopts the postures of a schoolmaster when he addresses all "loveres" (1.330) in the second person ("ye loveres ofte eschwe"), and gives them a rule, in the imperative, insisting that they "take" a particular point:

> "But take this: that* ye loveres ofte eschuwe*,   given that/ eschew
> Or elles* doon, of good entencioun,   else
> Ful ofte* thi lady wol it mysconstruwe...   very often
>
> (1.344–6)

Criseyde adopts the same posture with a similar imperative ("sette a caas") when she instructs herself in how to react to the news that Troilus wishes to woo her:

> "Now sette a caas*: the hardest is, ywys,   take [as a hypothetical] case
> Men myghten demen* that he loveth me.   believe
> What dishonour were it unto me, this?
>
> (2.729–31)

In the richest of these pedagogical moments, late in the poem, Troilus tries to understand what Boethius calls "conditional necessity" [necessitas con-dicionis] in order to see his tragic circumstances as compelled.[51] With commands that place him firmly in the position of the teacher ("lo," and "herkne") he then moves, by way of the conventional syntactic join

---

[51] In Chaucer's translation of the passage in Boethius that Troilus is paraphrasing he has already transformed a much looser Latin grammar ("veluti" for the first example, "ut" for the second) into the exact forms employed in the grammars ("veluti" and "ut" both become the reduplicated form "as thus"): "For certes ther ben two maneris of necessites: that oon necessite is symple, as thus: that it byhovith by necessite that alle men ben mortal or dedly; anothir necessite is condicionel, as thus: yif thow wost that a man walketh, it byhovith by necessite that he walke" (V.pr6.177–83) [Duae sunt etenim necessitates, simplex una, veluti quod necesse est omnes homines esse mortales, altera condicionis, ut, si aliquem ambulare scias, eum ambulare necesse est]. I take the Latin here from *Boethius Philosophiae Con-solationis Libri Quinque*, ed. Karl Büchner (Heidelberg: Carl Winter, 1977), V.pr6.2–8.

("as thus"), into a practical example that executes the characteristic rotation, inhabiting the "I" of the teacher, but also demonstrating what he, in the position of the student, will "sey" once he has learned this lesson:

> Lo, right so is it of the part contrarie,
> > now herkne*, for I wol nat tarie: listen
>
> "I sey that if the opynoun of the*   you
> Be soth*, for that* he sitte, than sey I this: true/ because
> That he mot sitten by necessite.
> And thus necessite in eyther is.

> > > > (4.1028–33)

It is not necessary to place any of these passages in a genealogy with the grammars to see how they achieve the same sort of vivacity as those texts by a similar means. A conversational scene is summoned up, not through description (as one person is said to be standing in front of someone else, addressing him) but as the positions of both addressor and addressee are evoked, secured, and filled out by the carefully articulated grammar of instruction.

The genealogy that need not be insisted upon in *Troilus and Criseyde* is firmly secured in one of Chaucer's earliest, most ambitious, and most self-referential works, *The House of Fame*. This poem is about many things, but if we say, with Sheila Delaney, that its main subject is "the body of traditional knowledge that confronted the educated fourteenth-century reader," then that subject was in a direct line with the fourteenth-century grammar school, whose subject matter was the body of traditional knowledge that produced such readers.[52] If we say, with John Dewey, that the purpose of education is to "translat[e]" the "achievements of the past" into "a potent instrumentality for the future" then we can also say that the relationship of *The House of Fame* to traditional knowledge that was its focus was pedagogical.[53] And if we say, finally, that the traditional knowledge on which *The House of Fame* focused was the knowledge "established by the grammarians," then *The House of Fame* was, at least at its center (that is in the second of its three books), using the style of the basic grammars to convey the grammatical knowledge that was also their subject.[54] If we stand back from these relationships we might also say—as Chaucer surely would have—that his largest aim in this poem was to

[52] Sheila Delany, *Chaucer's House of Fame: The Poetics of Skeptical Fideism* (Chicago, IL: University of Chicago Press, 1972), 3.
[53] Dewey, *Experience and Education*, 23.
[54] Martin Irvine, "Medieval Grammatical Theory and Chaucer's *House of Fame*," *Speculum* 60 (1985): 859.

negotiate his relationship to the great poets of Latin antiquity who embodied the amorphous "fame" he sought ("Stace" [1460], "Guydo... de Columpnis" [1469], "Virgile" [1483], "Ovide" [1487], "Lucan" [1499]). But if *The House of Fame* negotiated that relationship by showing how Latin could be translated into English—beginning, in Book 1, with Virgil and then moving to Ovid's account of Dido—we are right back to the tasks and techniques of the grammar school.[55]

The second book of *The House of Fame* describes the narrator's encounter with an eagle and their flight toward the houses of Fame and Rumor, but, while the eagle introduces himself as a messenger from Jupiter sent to carry the poet into the heavens and provide him with "som maner thing" (670) to write about, he also represents himself as a teacher, insisting that he has come, above all, to instruct:

"First shalt thou here* where she duelleth,	hear
And so thyn oune* bok hyt tellith:	own
Hir paleys stant, as I shal seye,	
Ryght even in myddes* of the weye	in the middle
Betwixen hevene and erthe and see,	
That what so ever in al these three	
Is spoken, either privy or apert*,	secretly or openly
The way therto ys so overt,	
And stant eke* in so juste a place	also
That every soun mot to hyt pace*;	approach
Or what so cometh from any tonge,	
Be hyt rouned*, red*, or songe,	whispered/ spoken
Or spoke in suerte* or in drede,	certainty
Certeyn, hyt moste thider nede*.	it must go there
Now herkene* wel, for why I wille	listen
Tellen the a propre skile*	reason
And a worthy demonstracion	
In myn ymaginacioun ...	

(*The House of Fame*, 711–28)

Since the eagle understands fame as a function not just of what "is spoken" but of "soun" in general, and the "first subject in the *artes grammaticae* is *vox*" or "sound," his teaching is couched from the start "in grammatical ... terms" and he tends to function throughout "like a grammarian" providing a "dazzling piece of exegesis."[56] The eagle draws his grammatical knowledge,

---

[55] For an analysis of this translation and its relationship to grammar-school activities see Chapter 4 in the present volume, p. 143.

[56] Irvine, "Grammatical Theory and the *House of Fame*," 854 ("first"), 859 ("grammatical"), and 862 ("grammarian").

not from the "elementary level of *grammatica*," but "from the extensive
middle range...where common assumptions and ways of talking about
language, writing and texts were widely disseminated."[57] His exposition
draws from commentaries on Priscian, by Peter Helias, among others, and
from John of Dacia's *Summa Grammatica*, and is therefore much more
theoretical than the mechanical and practical accounts of morphology,
conjugation, and declension that fill the basic grammars I have so far
discussed.[58] However, in much the same way as Chaucer simplifies the
complexities of the *Messahalla* in the *Treatise on the Astrolabe*, or of Boethius's
account of necessity in *Troilus and Criseyde*, the eagle's style of pedagogy is
much more basic than the material it disposes.

If the eagle draws his teaching from the middle range of *grammatica*, in
other words, he teaches by means of the grammar-school style. For
example, in an account of the nature of gravity and its relation to sound
the eagle establishes his authority and adopts the grammatical position
of the teacher with a few brisk commands ("loo," "lat go").[59] He transforms the narrator into a student by couching the rules of gravity in the
second person ("thou wost," "thou maist alday se"). And he unfolds a long
set of physical and cosmological principles in the form of a hands-on
practicum, rotating through the positions of teacher and student (who
would, in turn, "lat go" and "alday se," first as a demonstration, then as a
proof of a lesson learned) by means of the terms that routinely create this
double movement, "as thus":

> "Geffrey, thou wost* ryght wel this,   you know
> That every kyndely* thyng that is   natural
> Hath a kyndely stede* ther he*   place/ it
> May best in hyt conserved be;
> Unto which place every thyng
> Thorgh his* kyndely enclynyng*   its/ inclination
> Moveth for to come to
> Whan that hyt is awey therfro:
> As thus: loo, thou maist alday se
> That any thing that hevy be,
> As stoon, or led, or thyng of wighte*,   weight

---

[57] Irvine, "Grammatical Theory and the *House of Fame*," 852 ("elementary") and 852–3
("from").

[58] See Irvine, "Grammatical Theory and the *House of Fame*," 863–6 for a detailed
comparison of the commentaries that shed light on the grammatical theory Chaucer had
in mind.

[59] "Lo" is, technically, an "interjection" but, as here, was frequently used as the
imperative form of the verb "loken." See *MED*, s.v. "lo interj." (especially the etymology).
For a fuller explanation see the etymology in *OED* s.v. "lo interj1."

And bere hyt never so hye on highte,
Lat goo thyn hand, hit falleth doun.
Ryght* so seye I be* fyr or soun,   just/ about
Or some or other thynges lyghte,
Alwey they seke upward on highte,
While each of hem is at his large."

(The House of Fame, 729–45)

The best example of the style of pedagogy that the eagle employs can be found, fittingly, just when he takes up the theoretical basis of grammar ("soun") and explains how it is also the physical basis of fame. The lesson is typical in its grammatical positioning of teacher and student, but the scene is unusual in the way that Chaucer once again identifies the effects of the eagle's teaching in ways that make clear, not only why this teaching is so effective, but the grammar-school style was so useful to literature:

"Now hennesforth y wol the teche*   teach
How every speche, or noyse, or soun,
Thurgh hys* multiplicacioun,   its
Thogh hyt were piped of a mous,
Mot nede* come to Fames Hous.   must of necessity
I preve* hyt thus—take hede now—   prove
Be experience; for yf* that thow   if
Throwe on water now a stoon,
Wel wost* thou hyt wol make anoon   know
A litel roundell as a sercle*,   circle
Paraunter* brod as a covercle*;   perhaps/ lid of a pot

(The House of Fame, 787–92)

The eagle's analogy between the ever-widening ripples caused by a stone in water to the spreading of what we would call sound waves continues for many more lines than I have given here, but what I have quoted is enough, I think, to see that the eagle again produces a scene of instruction in the characteristic way: there is a rule in the first person coupled with a rule in the second person ("y wol the teche / How every speche, or noyse, or soun, . . . / Mot nede come to Fames Hous"); there is also a command ("take hede now"); most importantly, however, there is, again, the proof, "thus," which initiates the practical example which can be rotated through a practical demonstration and proof, a set of instructions that describe both what the person teaching will show and the person learning will discover when he repeats the same steps. As grammar creates these positions and moves through them the eagle also describes the resulting scene in something very like the language of experiential learning, understanding "experience" to be both objective and subjective, an acquired knowledge that can now be learned again and anew. The eagle has slightly modified the grammar of this pedagogic style by using the second person in his example, but he has clung closely enough to its principal elements to reveal that their consequence was not in fact teaching but the vivacity that served pedagogy so well—the investment of such potency in an idea that it could not but move across subject positions. The eagle's practical example also shows how this method is fundamentally grammatical rather than rhetorical— intersubjective rather than simply persuasive—because it achieves its effects by means of particular linguistic forms (specific adverbs, pronouns, or sequences of tense and aspect). This method is useful to pedagogy insofar as it makes a subject know more than he did; but—as the eagle, on Chaucer's behalf, reveals here—it is also fundamentally literary because, in just the way it rotates knowledge across subject positions in grammar and the *Treatise on the Astrolabe*, it rotates that knowledge right out of the text into the subject position of a reader. The largest proof of this last point is the whole of the poem we call *The House of Fame*, for as the eagle's knowledge becomes the narrator's, as the teacher's rule becomes the student's practice, as the scene of instruction becomes the reader's experience, what is made vivacious is not just a lesson about sound and its operations—though the stone and the ripples and the sound spreading like them is equally vivid—but "Geffrey," and, above all, his voluble teacher, the eagle. It is this last figure, in fact, who bursts out of the static tableaux that otherwise comprise the texture of this poem, becoming not just an anthropomorphized animal, not just a teacher, but a *character*—not just an eagle, but *the* Eagle.

This particular function of the grammar-school style is registered here, as it always is in its poetic manifestations, not just in the text (by, say, the narrator), but retrospectively, in the sequential reactions of readers and critics who find the eagle so vivacious that they treat him in any description or analysis of the poem as if he were a person Chaucer actually knew. Such a reaction has traditionally focused on a passage at the beginning of Book 2 which has certain attributes of autobiography, where, upon hearing the Eagle speak for the first time, the narrator describes his voice as unusually familiar:

Thus I longe in hys clawes lay,	
Til at the laste he to me spak*	spoke
In mannes vois, and seyde, "Awak!*	Wake up!
And be not agast* so, for shame!"	afraid
And called me tho* by my name,	then
And for I shulde the bet abreyde*,	wake up
Me mette* "Awak," to me he seyde	I dreamed
Ryght in the same vois and stevene*	manner of speaking
That useth oon I koude nevene;*	could name
And with that vois, soth for to seyn*,	truth be told

My mynde cam to me ageyn*,	again
For hyt was goodly seyd* to me,	kindly said
So nas hyt never* wont to be.	as it was not ever

(The House of Fame 553–66)

It was Skeat who first felt Chaucer could indeed "nevene" [name] the person described here and insisted that the Eagle spoke with the strident, familiar, and imperious voice of the nagging wife Skeat also assumed Chaucer had.[60] The relationship construed with an historical person—it would have to be Philippa Chaucer—is less relevant, however, than the assumption that this passage refers to one, and the way that assumption becomes tenacious enough to survive the error involved in insisting that a voice so clearly masculine ("he seyde") sounds like a shrill woman. Given that the "vois" is so masterful, and given also that it sounds imperious by virtue of the elements of the grammar-school style—not least as it explodes into the text here with a characteristic imperative ("awak!")—and given, finally that this is a figure who immediately launches into a lesson about grammar, it seems much more likely that the person the eagle resembled most was Chaucer's grammar-school teacher. But even if this supposition is unpersuasive, even to *disagree* with it—and, say that this voice resembles some other person or persons Chaucer knew—is to register the effects of the grammar-school style by succumbing to its grip: it is to discover in the discourse of the Eagle and Geoffrey an experience so "full" (to recur to the language of the *Treatise on the Astrolabe*) that it has become *our* experience.

Pedagogic scenes of the kind narrated at such length in *The House of Fame* fill Middle English literature. Indeed, if we were to measure the influence of the basic grammars on such literature by the frequency with which we find Will in the position of a student in *Piers Plowman* (before an authoritative personification who he begs to "kenne" him "to know" [teach him] [B 2.4]), or Genius in the *Confessio Amantis* in the position of a schoolmaster ("techen" Amans throughout "to knowe and understonde" [B 1.271; 287]) such enumerations would be enough to prove the wide influence of the grammar school on sophisticated literary production in the last decades of the fourteenth century. But the teaching in *Piers Plowman* remains in what I called at the start of this chapter the paradigmatic mode of simple declaratives, with Study stating general truths

---

[60] "The familiar 'vois' and 'stevene' no doubt belong to Chaucer's wife (as Skeat suggests)," *The Riverside Chaucer*, ed. Larry D. Benson, 3rd edn. (Boston, MA: Houghton Mifflin, 1987), 982; "The personal allusion can hardly refer to anyone but Chaucer's wife. The familiar tone recalls him to himself; yet the eagle's voice sounded kindly, whereas the poet sadly tells us that his wife's voice sounded far otherwise: 'So was it never wont to be,'" *The Complete Works of Geoffrey Chaucer*, ed. W. W. Skeat, 6 vols. (Oxford: Clarendon Press, 1899), 3: 255–6.

("Wisdom and wit now is noght worth a kerse [cress] / But if it be carded with coveitise as clotheres kemben hir [comb their] wolle," B 10.17–18) never producing the defining rotation of the grammar-school style because such teaching sticks so stringently to description and explanation. And while Genius speaks often of "examples" and sometimes invokes the position of the student ("thou"), what he produces with these terms is not a subject position, but an exemplary narrative that remains in the voice of the teacher ("I finde a tale") whose point, above all, is the meaning of that narrative as a whole ("what whilom fell in this matiere"):

And for to proeven* it is so	proven
Ensamples ther ben manyon*,	many a one
Of whiche if thou wolt knowen on*,	would like to know one
It is behovely* for to hiere	profitable
What whilom* fell* in this matiere:	once upon a time/happened
Among the kinges in the Bible	
I finde a tale, and is credible,	
Of him that whilom Achab hihte*,	called
Which hadde al Irahel to rihte*.	govern

(7.2522–30)

If we move outward from poetry to devotional prose, say, it is possible to see that elements of the grammar-school style spread itself across great tracts of fourteenth-century English writing. Julian of Norwich uses "thus" as a calque of "sic" or "ut" everywhere in the longer version of her text, the *Revelation*, usually to join topics ("I understood thus: Man is changeabil in this life") or to move from the description of a vision to her own reactions ("Thus saw I and felt...").[61] Her account is always compelling but it does not produce the species of vivacity found in the grammars or Chaucer's *Treatise on the Astrolabe* because Julian does not use this technique to create subject positions either. Rather than tracing the movement of knowledge from one such position to another, Julian uses the technique to bind consecutive thoughts:

Than thinketh this pore creature thus: "Lo, what might this noble lorde do more wurshippe and joy to me than to shew to me, that am so litille, this marvelous homelyhede."[62]

---

[61] Julian of Norwich, *A Revelation of Love*, 61–381 in *The Writings of Julian of Norwich*, ed. Nicholas Watson and Jacqueline Jenkins (University Park, PA: Pennsylvania State University Press, 2006), ch. 47, p. 265. I am grateful to Vincent Gillespie for pointing me toward Julian's rich use of this grammar-school technique.

[62] Julian of Norwich, *A Revelation of Love*, ch. 7, p. 147. I take it that the *Revelation* "may have been finished...after 1416," but include mention of it here, both because of Julian's insistent use of this key conjunction and the likelihood that the *Vision* was begun in

Chaucer's use also stands out from all of these others because he used elements of the grammar-school style that no other fourteenth-century English writer did: for example, the fussy phrase "as thus" that authenticates the pedagogy of the *Treatise on the Astrolabe* and marks the Eagle's pedantry in *The House of Fame* can be found nowhere else in the fourteenth century except in Chaucer's *Boece* and the *Equatorie of Planets*.[63]

The prominence of the grammar-school style in an elementary work such as the *Treatise on the Astrolabe* and its close association with pedagogy in *The House of Fame* suggest, as I have said, that Chaucer had a unique understanding of this style's value because it was pressed upon him from an early age—but it seems most likely that these techniques became so important to Chaucer because he found them so useful. To put it a different way, a poet so generally committed to techniques of realism of such variety and in so many texts—for whom vivacity in poetry was not just an achievement but a defining aspiration—could hardly have ignored these particular techniques when they had been so deeply drilled into him. The grammar-school style was, in this sense, purpose built for the poet Chaucer became. This centrality and its value can be observed nowhere

---

"the middle of the 1390s" and may largely have been written then (Nicholas Watson and Jacqueline Jenkins, "Introduction," 1–59 in Julian of Norwich, *A Revelation of Love*, ed. Watson and Jenkins, 1).

[63] This claim is based on the data yielded in a proximity search for "as" followed by "thus" (or "þus") in the whole of the online version of the *MED* (University of Michigan Digital Library Production Service [Dec. 18, 2001], accessed July 30, 2015). The uses in the *Boece* can be found at Book 1, prose 4, line 288, and Book 2, prose 5, line 163 and in *The Equatorie of the Planetis*, ed. D. J. Price and R. M. Wilson (Cambridge: Cambridge University Press, 1955), p. 40 line 16. Fifteenth-century uses are, for the most part, in instructional texts such as *The Master of Game* (*c.*1410), John Mirk's *Instructions for Parish Priests* (*c.*1425), Guy de Chauliac's *Grande Chirurgie* (*c.*1425) and, most often, in *The Craft of Numbering* (*c.*1425). There are also a few uses of the phrase in the *Fall of Princes* (*c.*1439), the *Pilgrimage of the Life of Man* (*c.*1430), and *The Saying of the Nightingale* (*c.*1449), as well as *Jacob's Well* (*c.*1425), the *Life of Saint Edith of Wilton* (*c.*1450), and *The Orchard of Sion* (*c.*1425). I do not give exhaustive references here but see *The Master of Game by Edward, Second Duke of York*, ed. W. A. Baillie-Grohman and F. Baillie-Grohman (London: Ballantine, 1904), 1–112 (p. 101); John Mirk, *Instructions for Parish Priests*, ed. G. Kristensson, *Lund Studies in English* 49 (1974): 67–103, p. 98 lines 570 and 578 and p. 99 line 597; *The Cyrurgie of Guy de Chauliac*, ed. M. S. Ogden, EETS o.s. 265 (1971), p. 13 line 12; *The Craft of Numbering*, 3–32 in *The Earliest Arithmetics in English*, ed. R. Steele, EETS e.s. 118 (1922; reprint 1988), p. 5 line 21; John Lydgate, *The Fall of Princes*, ed. H. Bergen, 4 vols., EETS e.s. 121–24 (1924–7), Book 3 line 8 (2: 329); John Lydgate, *The Pilgrimage of the Life of Man*, ed. F. J. Furnivall and K. B. Locock, EETS e.s. 77, 83, 92 (1899, 1901, 1904), p. 111 line 4195; John Lydgate, *The Saying of the Nightingale*, 221–34 in *The Minor Poems of John Lydgate*, ed. H. N. MacCracken, vol. 1, EETS e.s. 107 (1911; reprint 1961), p. 234 line 370; *Jacob's Well*, ed. A. Brandeis, part 1, EETS o.s. 115 (1900; reprint 1973), p. 39 line 32 and p. 105 line 11; *S. Editha Sive Chronicon Vilodunense*, ed. C. Horstmann (Heilbronn: Henninger, 1883), p. 55 line 2431; *The Orcherd of Syon*, ed. P. Hodgson and G. M. Liegey, EETS o.s. 258 (1966), p. 70 line 17.

more clearly than in the portraits of the pilgrims in the General Prologue
to the *Canterbury Tales*. These are the particular figures that Dryden saw
so "perfectly before" him and that Manly took to be people so "real" that
he tried to find them in the historical record, and this is where Chaucer
not only relies on the basic elements of this style, but also elaborates and
extends its so as to enhance the subjective rotation that is that style's
principal effect. Among these figures, there is probably none more vivacious than the Monk, not least because Chaucer deploys the elements of
the grammar-school style throughout to transform the narrator's description of the Monk into something like a *self*-description:

This ilke* Monk leet olde thynges pace*,	same/ go by
And heelde after the newe world the space.*	
	customs of the modern world
He yaf nat of that text a pulled* hen,	plucked
That seith that hunters ben nat hooly men,	
Ne that a monk, when he is recchelees*,	reckless
Is likned til* a fissh that is waterlees—	to
This is to seyn, a monk out of his cloystre.	
But thilke* text heeld he nat worth an oystre;	this same
And I seyde his opinion was good.	
What shulde he studie and make hymselven wood*,	crazy
Upon a book in cloystre alwey to poure*,	pore over
Or swynken* with his handes, and laboure,	work
As Austyn bit*? How shal the world be served?	commands
Lat Austyn have his swynk* to hym reserved!	work

(I.175–88)

This rotation is clearest in the last line of the passage where the imperative
comes as the authoritative pronouncement of the narrator ("I seyde his
opinion was good... Lat Austyn have his swynk to hym reserved"), but
because that pronouncement is so clearly the Monk's, the description is no
longer *about* the Monk ("this ilke Monk") but emerging *from* him ("[I say]
lat Austyn have...").[64] Chaucer layers the perspective of narrator and

---

[64] It was Jill Mann who first described this absorption: "We might say that whereas
other satirists play off the cleric's view of a certain piece of behaviour against their own views
as orthodox moralists, Chaucer in this instance unites his point of view with the Monk's to
the extent that we lose the opportunity for any other standpoint. To say this is not the same
as to claim that Chaucer (or the 'naïve narrator') takes the Monk at face value. But it is to
suggest that Chaucer's method is frequently to remind us of traditional satire while
discouraging or circumventing the moral judgments it aimed to elicit. And one way in
which Chaucer circumvents moral judgment is to show us the Monk from his own point of
view," *Chaucer and Medieval Estates Satire: The Literature of Social Classes and the* General
Prologue *to the* Canterbury Tales (Cambridge: Cambridge University Press, 1973), 27.

Monk throughout this description just as the grammars layer the perspectives of teacher and student, because, just as the grammatical practicum could be the teacher's explanation of a point of grammar or the student's demonstration of his mastery, the Monk is described throughout his portrait from the narrator's position, but always as if in his *own* words. Entwined in the passages' very grammar, in other words, is the supposition that the Monk is being described here as he described himself earlier when the narrator had "spoken" (I.31) with each of the pilgrims and discovered his or her "condicioun" (I.38). The intimacy of the language and the colloquialism also suggest that it was the Monk who earlier said that he didn't "give a pulled hen" for the Benedictine Rule, and that he "held after the new world the space." It is also clear that it was in this earlier conversation that the Monk (in parts of the portrait I haven't quoted here) took pride in the "many a deyntee hors" he had in his stable (I.167) and the bell-like jingling of his bridle in the wind (I.170). The doubled perspective derives from this retrospection built into the General Prologue's narrative, but it also depends, grammatically, on the transformation of a first person description into a third person description, a rotation of 180 degrees that ensures that the one form of statement is always implied by the other. To demonstrate how simple the necessary changes are I have reversed them with the appropriate pronouns where it is possible to do so in the following extracts from the portrait of the Monk:

> Ful many a deyntee hors hadde [I] in stable,
> And whan [I] rood, men myghte [my] brydel heere
> Gynglen in a whistlynge wynd als* cleere   as
> And eek* as loude as dooth the chapel belle   also
> Ther as [I] was* kepere of the celle.   where [I] was
> The reule of Seint Maure or of Seint Beneit—
> By cause that it was old and somdel streit*   strict
> [I] leet olde thynges pace,
> [I hold] after the newe world the space.
> [I give] nat of that text a pulled hen,
> That seith that hunters ben nat hooly men,
> Ne that a monk, when he is recchelees,
> Is likned til a fissh that is waterlees . . .
> [I hold] thilke text . . . nat worth an oystre;
> [Why should I] studie and make [myself] wood,
> Upon a book in cloystre alwey to poure,
> Or swynken with [my] handes, and laboure,

As Mann puts it succinctly, later in this discussion, Chaucer's array of techniques in the portrait of the Monk give it a unique "sense of depth" (37).

As Austyn bit? How shal the world be served?
Lat Austyn have his swynk to hym reserved!

(I.168–80; 182–8)

What Chaucer has done here, we might say, is to have understood the grammar-school style as an idea fully as much as it was a technique, noting the elements of that style that allowed an "example" to be phrased in terms that could move through two subject positions, recruiting still other elements of grammar (in particular the substitution of the third for the first person) to elaborate that style. The result could be described as free indirect discourse many centuries *avant la lettre*, but it is "free" because it is a style that recasts the same idea in different grammatical forms, and it is "indirect" because it employs the third person to convey statements in the first person. One final way to describe this is to say that Chaucer has taken a detailed description and grammaticalized it, using deft manipulations of the simplest grammar to render the Monk (like the Eagle) sufficiently vivacious for us to seem to hear his voice—or, as we might imagine Chaucer would say, for us to feel that we have fully experienced it.

Such experiences are general for readers of The General Prologue to the *Canterbury Tales* because we know the narrator has spoken with "ever-ichon" (I.31) of the pilgrims and on every occasion when we are told what the Knight, Franklin, Plowman, or Summoner "loved" (I.45, I.334, I.533, I.634), what the Squire lived "in hope" for (I.88), what the Yeoman "liste" (I.102), what the Friar "wiste" (I.228), what the Merchant "wolde" (I.276), or what the Clerk would "levere have" (I.293), we are also made to understand that these opinions have been rotated from the first person in which these characters described themselves to the third person of the narrator's account. Likewise, when the pilgrim is described in some activity the narrator could never have observed, as, say, the Sargent of Law reciting "everi statut... by rote" (I.327) or the Franklin with his "table dormant in his halle always" (I.353–4), or the Wife of Bath in what she habitually wore "on a Sonday" (I.455), or the Manciple's skill "in his achaat [purchasing]" (I.571), we are invited to imagine the narrator having heard a first person account of activities that long preceded the arrival of any of these pilgrims in the Tabard. As in the portrait of the Monk, in other words, the rotation of a description from first to third person is always inherent in a given portrait's content, which everywhere signals that this must be an "opinion" that, as the narrator says of the Friar, he "seyde himself" (I.219), shifted into the third person from the first person in which it originated (here I again restore the first person pronouns that I think we are asked to imagine in the portrait of the Friar):

[I] was an esy man to yeve* penaunce,	give
For unto a povre ordre for to yive*	give
Is signe that a man is wel yshryve*;	confessed
For if he yaf*, [I would dare to] make avaunt*,	gave/ boast
[I knew] that a man was repentaunt;	
For many a man so hard is of his herte,	
He may nat wepe, although hym soore smerte.	
Therefore in stede of wepynge and preyeres	
Men moote yeve silver to the povre freres.	

(I.223–32)[65]

It is similarly clear that the Parson "taught" (I.497) with the following "wordes" (1.498):

. . . if gold ruste, what shal iren do?	
For if a preest be foul, on whom we truste,	
No wonder is a lewed* man to ruste;	layman
And shame [I say] it is, if a prest take keep*,	take note
A shiten* shepherde and a clene sheep	shit-covered
Wel oghte a preest ensample for to yive,	
By his clennesse, how that his sheep sholde lyve.	

(I.500–6)

As if to authenticate all of the rotations that precede it, near the conclusion of the last of these portraits Chaucer finally uses the defining "thus" of the grammar-school style to mark the key rotation, although it is already well under way in the portrait by that point:

For in [my] male [I] hadde a pilwe-beer*,	pillow-case
Which that [I seyde] was Oure Lady veyl*:	veil
[I] seyde [I] hadde a gobet of the seyl*	sail
That Seint Peter hadde, whan that he wente	
Upon the see, til Jhesu Crist hym hente* . . .	summoned
. . .	
And *thus*, with feyned flaterye and japes*,	jokes
[I] made the person and the peple [my] apes.	

(I.694–8; 705–6)[66]

---

[65] The unaltered lines here are: "He was an esy man to yeve penaunce, / Ther as he wiste to have a good pitaunce. / For unto a povre ordre for to yive/Is signe that a man is wel yshryve; / For if he yaf, he dorste make avaunt, / He wiste that a man was repentaunt; / For many a man so hard is of his herte, / He may nat wepe, althogh hym soore smerte. / Therfore in stede of wepynge and preyeres / Men moote yeve silver to the povre freres" (I.223–32).

[66] The unaltered lines here are: "For in his male he hadde a pilwe-beer, / Which that he seyde was Oure Lady veyl; / He seyde he hadde a gobet of the seyl / That Seint Peter hadde, whan that he wente / Upon the see, til Jehesu Crist hym hente . . . And thus, with feyned flaterye and japes, / He made the person and the peple his apes" (I.694–8; 705–6).

While the narrative unfolded in and around this portrait is, again, sufficient to make clear that the whole of this passage is the Pardoner's self-description presented in the third person of the narrator, the "thus" not only makes clear that the description that follows it is fully internal to the Pardoner's experience but it gives that internalization emphasis. To conclude all the portraits in this way is to conclude a stylistic procedure as much as the sequential account of the "condicioun" of each of the pilgrims, as if this strategic and precise use of the defining element of the grammar-school style is not only meant to render the Pardoner's subjective position the more vivid, but also to acknowledge the stylistic procedure employed throughout the whole of the General Prologue for achieving its characteristic effects.

Such grammaticalization, if not each or all of its elements, was basic to the writing of all the Ricardian poets insofar as they turned literacy training in Latin to ambitious literary production in English. Chaucer also formulates this larger purpose with some forthrightness at the beginning and end of *The House of Fame*, and, also, memorably, at the end of *Troilus and Criseyde* when he sets his "litel book" on steps near the great Latin poets of antiquity (V.1786–92). What he documents in the *Treatise on the Astrolabe* and Book 2 of *The House of Fame*, however, is the realization, more particular to him, that a deft use of pedagogical technique can create a vivid subjectivity. This repurposing of the grammar-school style as a literary style is probably the most subtle and complex grammaticalization in the work of the Ricardian poets, but there were also other, equally pervasive, versions of this process whose effects must now be traced, not just phrase by phrase or sentence by sentence, but across the whole of literary forms.

4

Grammaticalization and Literary Form

Although I suggested in Chapter 1 that John of Trevisa was wrong when he said that John of Cornwall revolutionized grammar-school teaching by introducing English into the classroom, it is possible that John of Cornwall's practices still made a more subtle change. Although no one has ever read his oft-quoted description of grammar-school teaching as about anything other than the teaching of Latin, Trevisa's phrasing also suggests an alteration in the method for the teaching of *English*:

> ... now, þe ʒere of oure Lorde a þowsand þre hundred and foure score and fyue, and of þe secounde kyng Richard after þe conquest nyne, in alle þe gramere scoles of Engelond, children leueþ Frensche and construeþ and lerneþ an Englische.[1]

> [*leueþ*: leave; *an Englische*: in English]

I also discussed the evidentiary problems with Trevisa's claim that children "left French" in grammar schools (they never seem to have used French in the first place) but, if part of the claim here is that children now "learn" in English, it also seems that they "*construe*" in English. Middle English *construen* generally meant "translate," but Latin *construere* could mean "parse" or "analyze grammatically" and John of Trevisa almost certainly meant "construe" in that sense here.[2] He may therefore be suggesting that

---

[1] *Polychronicon Ranulphi Higden monachi Cestrensis*, vol. 2, ed. Churchill Babington, Rolls Series 41 (London: Kraus Reprint, 1964; first published 1869), 160–1.

[2] The *MED* takes the verb in this passage of Trevisa to mean "to write a text or composition correctly," but the *OED* takes it to mean "to analyse or trace the grammatical construction of a sentence." Similarly, though Langland uses "construe" in all three texts of *Piers Plowman* to describe how a Latin phrase might be understood by a "clerk," the *MED* takes Langland's use of the verb to mean "to give a translation" while the *OED* takes it to mean grammatical analysis. The *OED* is clearly right in this case, not least because the A-text of *Piers Plowman* uses "construe" to refer to grammatical analysis when the clerks called "for to construe þis clause declynede faste" (*Piers Plowman: The A-Version*, ed. Geoge Kane [London: Athlone Press, 1960] 4.133), as the *MED* acknowledges in its definition of "declynede" in this passage ("to give the inflectional forms of a word"). The same passage is ambiguous in the B-text where clerks "construe" a "clause ... for þe Kynges profit" (B 4.150) as well as in the C-text where they "construe" by saying "kyndeliche what it meneth" (C 4.147). See *MED*, s.vv. "construen v." 2 and "declinen v." 6 and *OED*, s.v.

schoolboys were taught *English* grammar in grammar schools as an adjunct to Latin teaching. There is also support for this view in John of Cornwall's *Speculum grammaticale* where English "examples" are often really glosses on Latin paradigms, in each such case showing how English words can be conjugated or declined. When the point is to illustrate the "three persons...in the verb" [tres sunt...persone in verbo], for example, and what follows is not only the forms for the conjugation of *lego* in the present tense but the same forms for *reden*, the schoolboy is learning as much about the English verb as he is about the Latin: "*lego* y rede *legimus* we rede *legis* þu redis *legitis* ȝe redin vel ȝe redith *iste legit* þis redith *isti legunt* þei redyn."[3]

The knowledge produced by such parsing was clearly localized for much of the fourteenth century, but the shadowing of Latin grammatical teaching with English eventually produced a much more general change whereby not just the forms of grammar but all the tools of grammatical analysis had to be absorbed from Latin to English. These absorptions were often recorded most fully where the process of translation was at issue, as in the discussion of how the "ablatif case absolute" can be "resoluid... into English" in the Prologue to the Wycliffite Bible (1395–6) mentioned at the beginning of Chapter 3.[4] Translation was another engine behind such change, particularly where Latin employed grammatical metaphor, as Bartholomaeus often does in the *De proprietatibus rerum*. John of Trevisa's translation of the analogy Bartholomaeus makes between the rigor of grammatical agreement and incorruptibility of the bodies of angels shows how extensive such borrowing could be:

> As if a childe knoweþ þat if þe nominatif case and þe verbe discordith in persone and in noumbre, þanne þe resoun is incongrue, as in þis manere: *puer sumus bonus.* Þanne take for on premis: no reason is conger in þe whiche þe nominatif case and þe verbe discordith in noumbre and in persone. And take for þe oþir premis: in þis resoun, *puer sumus bonus,* þe nominatif case and þe verbe discordeth in noumbre and in persone. And make þi conclusioun in þis maner: ergo þis resoun is not conger, puer sumus bonus.[5]

> [discordith: *do not agree;* incongrue: *incorrect;* conger: *congruent (sensible)*]

"construe v." 3a. See also Charlton Thomas Lewis and Charles Short, *A Latin Dictionary* (Oxford: Clarendon Press, 1993; first published 1879), s.v. "construo," B.

[3] Oxford, Bodleian Library, MS Auctarium F.3.9, p. 9.

[4] *The Holy Bible,* 4 vols., ed. Josiah Forshall and Frederic Madden (Oxford: Oxford University Press, 1850), 1: 57.

[5] *On the Properties of Things: John Trevisa's Translation of Bartholomaeus Anglicus, De Proprietatibus Rerum: A Critical Text,* ed. M. C. Seymour, 3 vols. (Oxford: Oxford University Press, 1975–2000), 1: 60; Bartholomaeus Anglicus, *De proprietatibus rerum* (Lyons: Pierre Hongre, 1482), 5r.

Where grammatical discussion was this extensive, borrowing often occurred at the level of the word as well as the idea, since English often lacked the grammatical term employed to make a key point in Latin. Elsewhere in his translation of the *De proprietatibus*, for example, Trevisa must borrow the noun "partitive" [partitiva] in order to make Bartholomaeus's point that the essence of God is as indivisible as the word "deus" (it is never "some God" [aliquis deus] but always, "one God" [unus deus]).[6] Innovation of this kind was doubtless common in fourteenth-century schoolrooms in ways that the textual record could never preserve, but the Trinity Grammar records the fruits of a great variety of such activity just over the divide of the century's turn. There, in the oldest surviving grammar we have that construes extensively in English, what had been only a trickle of new terms becomes a flood, and sixty words for grammar's parts and operations are recorded for the first time in the English, including "declension," "comparison," "demonstrative," "deponent," "expletive," "imperative," "infinitive," "optative," "pronoun," and "supine."[7]

Ambition alone ensured that literature was often out in front of the grammars in providing English with such grammatical tools, as the C-text of *Piers Plowman* well demonstrates. In what is sometimes described as Conscience's "grammar lesson," Langland tries to resolve some of the problems that bedeviled his account of "mede" in the A- and B-texts of this poem by introducing a second term for reward, "mercede," going on to relate these two concepts by means of an extended grammatical metaphor on "direct" and "indirect" agreement:[8]

---

[6] See *MED*, s.v. "partitif adj." For the passages in question see Bartholomaeus Anglicus, *De proprietatibus rerum*, 2v–3r. *On the Properties of Things*, ed. Seymour, 1: 47–50.

[7] For a list of these terms see Sanford Brown Meech, "An Early Treatise in English Concerning Latin Grammar," in *Essays and Studies in English and Comparative Literature*, University of Michigan Publications, Language and Literature 13 (1935): 95–7. For the terms I list see *MED*, s.vv. "declinson n."; "comparisoun n.," 5; "demonstratif adj. and n.," b; "deponent adj."; "expletif adj." "imperatif adj.". "infinitif adj."; "optatif n." and "optatif adj.," "pronoune n.," "supin n." Since the *MED* follows Meech's date of *c*.1450 for the Trinity Grammar (see "An Early Treatise," 83), many of these words seem to be used in other English texts earlier. But I follow Thomson in dating the manuscript to the first quarter of the fifteenth century and the treatise to an even earlier date, well before any other text cited in the *MED*. See David Thomson, *A Descriptive Catalogue of Middle English Grammatical Texts* (New York, NY: Garland, 1979), 158.

[8] Margaret Amassian and J. Sadowsky. "Mede and Mercede: A Study of the Grammatical Metaphor in *Piers Plowman*," *Neuphilologische Mitteilungen* 72 (1971): 473. On the complexities of this passage and the variety of interpretations proposed for them see Andrew Galloway, *The Penn Commentary on Piers Plowman*, vol. 1: *C Prologue-Passus 4; B Prologue-Passus 4; A Prologue-Passus 4* (Philadelphia, PA: University of Pennsylvania Press, 2006), 340–59.

> Thus is mede and mercede as two maner relacions,
> Rect and indirect, reninde bothe
> On a sad and a siker semblable to hemsuluen.
> Ac adiectif and sustantif vnite asken
> And acordaunce in kynde, in case and nombre.[9]

[Thus are reward and wages two kinds of relation, direct and indirect, each one requiring something both secure and stable, similar to themselves. But adjective and substantive require unity and agreement by gender, in case and number.]

The illustration continues for another seventy lines, and many commentators have criticized its complexity ("barely intelligible and very dull," in the words of Skeat) and, at times, Langland's grasp of grammar (his representation of the agreement between an adjective and a substantive as a "likeness" has been judged a mistake).[10] But it is also clear that a certain strain is central to Langland's point: he reaches for what are likely to have been new English words ("adjective" and "substantive"), and uses "indirect" and "rect" in ways never previously recorded, because the difficulties of syntactic relationships so perfectly capture the conceptual difficulties inherent in the idea of "reward."[11] The meaning of the comparison is, then, not only that "mede" and "mercede" are both alike ("sad and siker" [secure and stable]) and different (with one in complete and the other in partial "acordaunce" [agreement]), but that this relationship is hard to understand. The longer discussion from which the passage just quoted is taken insists on this difficulty lexically, using nine words other than "rect" and "indirect" for the first time in a grammatical sense as well "relatif" (to refer to a "relative pronoun") for the first time in recorded English.[12]

As I tried to make clear in the previous chapter, Chaucer put much that he learned from the basic grammars to significant use in his poetry, but, as this last example makes clearer still, whereas a genealogy is required to see the connections between the technique of the grammars and Chaucer's

---

[9] William Langland, *Piers Plowman: A New Annotated Edition of the C-text*, ed. Derek Pearsall (Exeter: University of Exeter Press, 2008), 3.332–7. Hereafter quotations from the C-text will be taken from this edition and cited by passus and line number in the text.

[10] William Langland, *The Vision of William Concerning Piers the Plowman in Three Parallel Texts*, ed. W. W. Skeat, 2 vols. (Oxford: Clarendon Press, 1886), 2: 50. On the mistake in his characterization see Langland, *Piers Plowman: A New Annotated Edition of the C-text*, ed. Pearsall, 93.

[11] *MED*, s.vv. "adjectif adj. and n.," "indirect adj.," "rect adj," "relatif n.," and "substantif n."

[12] This is a point made by Katherine Breen (*Imagining an English Reading Public, 1150–1400* [Cambridge: Cambridge University Press, 2010], 255 n. 32). The nine terms in addition to "rect" and "indirect," as Breen surveys them in the *MED*, are "relacioun 2b," "accordaunce 3b," "kinde 14b," "cas 10," "nombre 5," "unite 4e," "antecedent 3," "accorden 8," and "termison n." Of these, "termison" is a *hapax legomena* never recorded again in Middle English. See also *MED*, s.v. "relatif n."

style, Langland's grammaticalizations hewed much more closely to the forms of grammar-school teaching which he often simply repurposed wholesale. It is hardly an accident that Langland refers to the putative author of the most basic of the grammar-school texts, the *Distichs of Cato*, more than any other authority in *Piers Plowman*, nor that most of these references occur at climactic moments in the poem (as, for example, when Conscience is finally sent by the king to fetch Reason at the conclusion of the debate over the marriage of Lady Meed, and, right at Reason's side, saddling up his horse, is "Caton, his knave" [B 4.16–19]).[13] Langland is also the only English poet to quote one of the basic grammars directly, as Trajan does, attributing the words to "Reason" as confirmation of the view that poverty is the "best lif" [best life] (B 11.255):

> And wel sikerer he slepeth, the segge that is povere,
> And lasse he dredeth deeth and in derke to ben yrobbed
> Than he that is right riche—Reson bereth witnesse:
> *Pauper ego ludo dum tu diues meditaris.*

[The man who is poor sleeps more soundly, and dreads death, and being robbed in the dark, less, than he who is very rich—Reason bears witness, *As a poor man I can play while you, a rich man, worry.*]

(B 11.265–7a)[14]

Although this line illustrates the relationship between pronoun (*ego* versus *tu*) and verb (*ludo* versus *meditor*) in Alexander of Villa-Dei's *Doctrinale*, Langland seems much less interested in these subtleties than in equating the wisdom of a basic grammar with the passages drawn from Scripture and scriptural commentary that are his more usual Latin sources.[15] That equation alone makes it much less likely, I think, that

---

[13] For a summary of all the lines from Cato that Langland works into the various versions of *Piers* see John A. Alford, *Guide to the Quotations*, 26. Cato is quoted on eight separate occasions in the B-text, and one additional instance each in the A- and C-texts (though neither of these texts include all the citations in B): B 6.315 (C 8.336a) B 7.73 (C 9.69), B 7.156 (A 8.134a), A 10.98, B 10.195–6 (A 11.147–8), B 10.343a, B 11.404 (C 13.212), C 13.224b, B 12.22a, B 19.296a (C 21.296a). To these quotations must be added the occasions when "Cato" is mentioned but the *Distichs* are not actually cited which include the passage I have just mentioned (B 4.17 [A 4.17, C 4.17]) as well as B 10.201 (A 11.150), and C 7.34. Particularly because C adds citations and allusions or references to B, I think Galloway overstates the case when he sees "a seemingly programmatic excision of Cato from the final C-text," Andrew Galloway, "Two Notes on Langland's Cato: *Piers Plowman* B 1.88–91; 4.20–23," *English Language Notes* 25 (1987–8): 11.

[14] The line, also quoted in C (12.154a), is Alexander of Villa-Dei, *Doctrinale*, ed. Theodore Reichling (Berlin: A. Hofmann, 1893]), line 1091.

[15] On Langland's scriptural quotations see Alford, *Guide to the Quotations*, 17–23.

Langland was deeply influenced by the "semi-logical, speculative" forms of grammar found in "English university curricula," despite the wide influence of that claim.[16] Although Langland sometimes relies on grammar's conceptual difficulties to capture difficulties in other arenas of thought, he is only sophisticated in the manner of his deployment, since that grammar can almost always be traced to the texts of basic literacy training.

In fact, as I will detail in this chapter, the *whole* of the form of *Piers Plowman* constitutes the most extensive grammaticalization in Middle English literature insofar as it reproduces the most basic of grammar-school exercises while overlaying this larger form, in the latter two-thirds of the poem, with an allegory structured by the most basic of grammatical relationships. This poem is therefore both measure of, and guide to, the broader importance of elementary grammar to Middle English poets. Langland's grammaticalizations also amount to a kind of *ars grammatica* that shows that it was not only grammar (as I described in the previous chapter), but also the exercises used to teach it that provided rich resources for meaning-making and ornamentation in poetry. Since those exercises so often involved teaching schoolboys to write in Latin, one consequence of this relationship that has been almost entirely missed is the extent to which the most celebrated and iconic of our "Middle English poets" wrote some of his poetry in Latin. But the distinction between grammar-school exercises and the mature writer's work was inevitably blurred because, as I began by noticing in Chapter 2, and will continue to explore here, it was really the *point* of the grammar-school teaching to train the schoolboy, not just how to read and write, but how to write poetry.

---

[16] Anne Middleton, "Two Infinites: Grammatical Metaphor in *Piers Plowman*," *ELH* 39 (1972): 174–5. This tendency is particularly marked when Andrew Galloway locates the riddles he discovers in what I would categorize as grammar-school books, Manchester, John Rylands University Library, MS Latin 394 and London, British Library, Harley MS 3362, in the "English university," and, specifically, "at Oxford" (70): Andrew Galloway, "The Rhetoric of Riddling in Late-Medieval England: The 'Oxford' Riddles, the *Secretum philosophorum*, and the Riddles in *Piers Plowman*," *Speculum* 70 (1995): 68–105. On the grammar-school contents of the first of these manuscripts see Chapter 2, pp. 75–9, and, on the second, see p. 133 n. 23 below. Alford documents the trend toward crediting Langland with a certain scholasticism in "Langland's Learning" (*Yearbook of Langland Studies* 9 [1995]: 1–8), but, while noting the tendency to complicate the poem in this way ("with every new book on Langland, it seems, the poem gets more and more difficult" [2]), he concludes by generally endorsing the trend: "to understand *Piers Plowman* we must go to school, not only with medieval grammarians, as Donaldson said, but also with medieval logicians, lawyers, theologians, philosophers, political thinkers" (8).

EX VI TRANSICIONIS

The most substantial discussion of grammar in *Piers Plowman* seems to be anything but elementary since it includes, at its explanatory center, the phrase, "half a laumpe lyne," which has been described as the "most striking single crux in a poem studded with difficult passages."[17] Langland makes that phrase even harder to understand by continuing the line with a Latin phrase that is neither glossed nor translated but also deeply embedded in the syntax of the English that surrounds it (it "carries some force as a modifier of both the verb 'bere' and the participle 'ybounde' in line 152"):[18]

> For he that loveth thee leelly, lite of thyne coveiteth,
> Kynde love coveiteth noght no catel but speche.
> With half a laumpe lyne in Latyn, *Ex vi transicionis*
> I bere therinne about faste ybounde Dowel,
> In a signe of the Saterday that sette first the kalender,
> And al the wit of the Wodnesday of the next wike after;
> The myddel of the moone is the myghte of bothe.

[For he who loves truly, covets little of yours, for natural love covets nothing you have but your speech. With a half-a-lamp line in Latin, *by the power of transitivity*, I carry therein, bound firmly, Dowell, in a sign of the Saturday that established the starting point of the calendar, and all the wit of the Wednesday of the following week; the middle of the moon is the strength of both.]

(B 13.150–6)

The phrase "ex vi transicionis" [by the power of transitivity] restates a simple principle of Christian belief in a grammatical metaphor ("just as a transitive verb rules its object … so also love ought to rule the Christian with certain analogous effects").[19] But the rest of the line could not be translated until Andrew Galloway discovered how the phrase "half a laumpe" referred to a crescent moon by way of an allusion to a Latin riddle in which the "moon" represented a "C" and the "myddel of the moone" represented an "O" so that the whole of the riddle spelled out the

---

[17] Edward C. Schweitzer, "'Half a laumpe lyne in Latyne' and Patience's Riddle in Piers Plowman," *Journal of English and Germanic Philology* 73 (1974): 313. Cited in Galloway, "Rhetoric of Riddling in Late-Medieval England," 91. Something of this passage remains in the C-text (XV.154–76) but the grammatical analogy has been removed.

[18] R. E. Kaske, "'Ex Vi Transicionis' and Its Passage in 'Piers Plowman,'" *Journal of English and Germanic Philology* 62 (1963): 51. See also Cynthia Bland, "Langland's Use of the Term *Ex Vi Transicionis*," *Yearbook of Langland Studies* 2 (1988): 125–35.

[19] John A. Alford, "The Grammatical Metaphor: A Survey of Its Use in the Middle Ages," *Speculum* 57 (1982): 755.

word "C-O-R" [heart].[20] These phrases, and the image of the heart they invoke, could then be seen to elaborate the claims this passage more generally makes about "true love" (or "loving leelly" [loving truly]) in such a way as to insist on the inherent difficulty of such love.

This passage sits at the heart of an episode usually described as the Feast of Patience, and the success of this scene and its principal figures at modeling hermeneutic difficulty has always suggested to commentators that Langland was drawing on the most sophisticated forms of learning throughout it. Certainly the feast seems to place itself very close to the university when its guest of honor ("maad sitte for the mooste worthi" [positioned at the table as the most honored] B 13.33) is introduced as a "meister" [master] (B 13.25), and referred to as a "doctour" (B 13.99) when he first speaks. While the focus of mealtime conversation is the simple phase "do well," ever since that phrase first emerged in the priest's translation of the pardon that Piers the Plowman and his fellow pilgrims received from Truth (urging all to "do wel and have wel" [B 7.112]), it has perplexed Will in its very generality. He also immediately complicated matters by hearing the phrase, not as an injunction to action, but as a kind of allegory "coined . . . using several parts of speech," which posits a figure named "Dowel" (B 7.2) who Will must seek.[21] The phrase as well as its grammar are complicated still further by Thought who treats the compounded form as if its adverbial component implied both comparative and superlative, thereby insisting that, if Will wanted to find Dowell, he also needed to search for "Dobet and Dobest the thridde" (B 8.79). The discussion of these terms in this scene also seems to be located in higher learning by Clergy who describes Dowell and Dobetter as "two infinites":

> . . . Dowel and Dobet aren two infinites
> Whiche infinites, with a feith fynden oute Dobest.
>
> [Dowell and Dobetter are two infinites, which, along with belief, discover Dobest.]
>
> (B 13.127–8)

According to Anne Middleton this phrase was best explained by discussions in the advanced grammars used in universities such as Priscian's *Institutiones Grammaticae* and Duns Scotus's *Grammatica Speculativa*, with the resulting metaphor so "complicated and obscure" that it finally "defeats its own purpose."[22]

---

[20] Galloway, "Rhetoric of Riddling," 86–91.

[21] Middleton, "Two Infinites," 171.

[22] Middleton, "Two Infinites," 181. On Priscian's discussion of the "infinite" see 174–9. Middleton's reference to the *Grammatica Speculativa* is indirect and she relies upon its discussion of transitivity and intransitivity (179 n. 13) as it is summarized in

And yet, it is not necessary to enter the precincts of higher learning to be confused by grammar (any child can manage it), and however complicated these metaphors may seem to those of us who have never spent time in a medieval grammar school, the Feast of Patience draws on elementary grammar's most basic texts again and again. Galloway discovered the riddle that explained the meaning of the phrase "half a laumpe lyne" in a schoolbook, London, British Library, MS Harley 3362.[23] And, however obscure that riddle may be to us, it references the "heart" by spelling it out ("C-O-R"), in this way taking the explanation back to literacy training's very first subject, the abc's. The complicating phrase "ex vi transicionis" is, for its part, common in the basic grammars.[24] It derived from an understanding of syntax usually described as *regimen* in its medieval form but of a piece with that modern method of construing syntax in which a verb is said to "govern" the noun or nouns that are its object.[25] As good an example as any of this theory can in fact be found in Alexander of Villa-Dei's *Doctrinale*, the basic grammar that, as I noted before, Langland knew well enough to quote:[26]

> Hinc datur exemplum tibi triplex: "Dico magistrum
> Discipulos mores placidos de iure docere."
> Infinitivi natura regit praeeuntem
> Doctrinam capiens regitur vi transitionis.

[Here a third example is given to you: "I say that the teacher teaches students peaceful habits according to the law." The nature of the infinitive governs the preceding subject, taking hold of the subject, it is governed by the force of transitivity.][27]

In the twelfth and thirteenth centuries, there was an extensive expansion of what is sometimes called "*ex vi* terminology" (although it could also be

---

Ben H. Smith, *Traditional Imagery of Charity in Piers Plowman* (The Hague: Mouton, 1966), 46.

[23] For the solution Galloway finds in MS Harley 3362 see "Rhetoric of Riddling," 87–8. Alongside its riddles this book contains the basic reading text the *Stans puer ad mensam* (on this text see Chapter 2 in the present volume, pp. 64–6) as well as the kind of ad hoc grammatical text (a "treatise on synonyms") that characterizes all basic grammars of the period. See *Catalogue of the Harleian Manuscripts in the British Museum*, 3 vols. (London: British Museum, 1808), 3: 20.

[24] See Kaske, "'Ex vi transicionis' and Its Passage in 'Piers Plowman,'" 38.

[25] On "*regimen*" and "*regimen*-theory" see Michael A. Covington, *Syntactic Theory in the High Middle Ages: Modistic Models of Sentence Structure* (Cambridge: Cambridge University Press, 1984), 12–19.

[26] Kaske does not, notice that Langland certifies his familiarity with passages like this from the *Doctrinale* by quoting from this text, and therefore cannot also notice that Langland takes the quotation in passus 11 from exactly this key section on *regimen*.

[27] Alexander of Villa-Dei, *Doctrinale*, ed. Reichling, lines 1245–8.

described as "*ex natura* terminology" since *natura* is often substituted for "*vi*" in its common phrases) because transitivity was insufficient as a concept to explain all of the ways that one word might be "ruled" by another, so grammarians developed a whole vocabulary based on this phrase to specify other grammatical relationships.[28] The *Catholicon* (1286), another of the basic grammars, devotes a whole section to *regimen* where it explains that the genitive case is ruled "ex natura possessionis" [by virtue of possession], "ex natura verbalis significacionis" [by virtue of the word's meaning], "ex natura particionis" [by virtue of the division], "ex vi accentis" [by virtue of the emphasis], "ex vi cause materialis" [by virtue of the material cause], "ex natura transicionis" [by virtue of transitivity]; the dative is ruled "principaliter, ex natura acquisicionis" [principally by virtue of acquisition] as well as "ex vi transicionis" [by virtue of transitivity]; the accusative is ruled "ex natura transicionis" [by virtue of transitivity]; and the ablative is ruled "ex vi accidentis" [by virtue of accidence].[29] This terminology remained important in the fourteenth century (John of Cornwall's *Speculum grammaticale* uses *ex vi* terminology to explain that all "causal statements" are ruled by verbs not only by the force of transitivity but by the force of intransitivity [omnis dictio casualis quo habet regi at debet regi ex vi transicionis vel ex vi intransicionis]).[30] In the fifteenth century, the Trinity Grammar devotes one of its five sections to the concept of *regimen* and its terminology.[31]

Basic grammar also explains Clergy's understanding of Dowell and Dobetter as "infinites" in a number of ways that Langland criticism has generally overlooked. It is not necessary to consult Prisician to discover that the "'infinite' verb is the citation-form or name of the verb" for any schoolboy would have met the "infinitivus" [infinitive] as one of the six basic "modes" [modi] in the most elementary of grammars, Donatus's *Ars minor*.[32] Clergy's understanding of an "infinite" would also have been

---

[28] Bland, "Langland's Use of the Term *Ex vi transicionis*," 131.

[29] Joannes Balbus, *Catholicon* (Mainz, 1460), 53r–54v.

[30] Oxford, Bodleian Library, Auctarium F.3.9, p. 5. Bland first noted this passage "on the regimen of the nominative case" in the *Speculum grammaticale* and its relevance to the metaphors of *Piers Plowman* ("Langland's Use of the Term *Ex vi transicionis*," 132–3).

[31] See Meech, "An Early Treatise in English Concerning Latin Grammar," 121–5. On the Trinity Grammar in general see Chapter 2 in the present volume, pp. 71–2.

[32] Middleton, "Two Infinites," 175 citing Priscian, *Institutiones Grammaticae*, ed. Heinrich Keil, *Grammatici Latini*, vols. 2 and 3 (Leipzig: Teubner, 1855–8), XVIII.40. The relevant passage in Donatus is as follows: "Modi qui sunt? Indicatiuus, ut lego; imperatiuus, ut lege; optatiuus, ut utinam legerem; coniunctiuus, ut cum legam; infinitiuus, ut legere; inpersonalis, ut legitur." [What are the moods? Indicative, such as *lego*; imperative, such as *lege*; optative, such as *utinam legerem*; subjunctive, such as *cum legam*; infinitive, such as *legere*; impersonal, such as *legitur*], Donatus, *Ars Minor*, 585–612 in Louis Holtz, *Donat et la tradition de l'enseignement grammatical* (Paris: Centre National de la Recherche Scientifique,

clarified by the allusion Patience makes to the theory of regimen, for one
of its basic principles was that it was in the "nature of the infinitive"
[infinitivi natura] to be governed "by the force of transitivity" [vi transi-
tionis] (1246–8). The association of the infinitive and transitivity also
helps to explain why Clergy would have insisted that Dowell and Dobetter
were "two infinites." The phrasing suggests he is counting these forms
(first, "to do well" and, second, "to do better"), but it seems more likely
that he means to say that, as the theory of *regimen* also held, *each* of these
"infinites" comes in two distinct forms. A thirteenth-century commentary
on the *Doctrinale* puts the key point in language very similar to Clergy's
when it observes that "words of the infinitive mode" [verbum infinitivi
modi] can be understood "in two ways" [dupliciter], either governing
an object by "completing" a finite verb, or as the subject of the finite verb
that follows it:

> Potest enim considerari dupliciter: ut secundum rationem quam habet ad
> verbum precedens, cuius motum recipit et terminat, et secundum hoc
> dicitur transitivus; aut potest considerari secundum comparationem imme-
> diatam ad verbum subsequens, tanquam subiectum in quo radicatur actus
> verbi sequentis, et secundum hanc comparationem est intransitivus. Ad hoc
> ergo quod obicitur quod obliqui sunt transitivi, hoc intelligitur secundum
> comparationem quam habent ad precedens, a quo reguntur...Cum ergo
> verbum indicativi modi exigat nominativum, et hoc ratione modi finiti, et
> verbum infinitivi modi exiget maxime obliquum, et ita accusativum, in
> ratione modi infinitivi.[33]

> [For it can be considered in two ways: either according to the relationship it
> has to the preceding verb, whose action it receives and completes, and
> according to this it is to be called transitive; or it can be considered according
> to the verb immediately following it, as the subject in the action of the
> following verb, and according to this comparison it is intransitive...Should
> the objection to this be that the oblique (cases) are transitive, it should be
> understood by their similarity to the preceding by which they are governed.
> When, therefore, a verb of the indicative mood requires a nominative, and
> this, by virtue of the finite mode, and the verb of the infinitive mode greatly
> requires an oblique, it is therefore accusative by reason of the infinitive mode.]

1981), 590. The term "infinitive" is also regularly used in the parsing exercises found in the
Informacio, one of the earliest Middle English grammars: e.g. "*Ire*: what mode? Infinitif mode.
Why soo? For when ij verbus comyn togedur wtowt a relatif or a coniunction comyng
betwene, þe later verbe shal be infinitif mode," David Thomson, *An Edition of the Middle
English Grammatical Texts* (New York, NY: Garland, 1984), 86.

[33] Charles Thurot, *Extraits de Divers Manuscrits Latins pour Servir a l'Histoire de Doctrines
Grammaticales au Moyen-Age* (Frankfurt am Main: Minerva, 1964; first published, Paris,
1869), 310.

Both Dowell and Dobetter can be understood, *ex vi transicionis*, as *either* transitive or intransitive.[34]

To insist on the elementary nature of the grammatical knowledge required to understand the discourse in the Feast of Patience makes it possible to notice too that the lessons Will learns in this scene are simple. Although the doctor is meant to represent university learning, the first question Will addresses to him could hardly be less ambitious ("What is dowel, sire doctour?," B 13.103) and the doctor's initial response ("do noon yvel to thyn evencristen" [do no evil to your fellow Christian] B13.105) is almost ostentatiously basic, since it takes Will right back to the precept that constituted the second line of the pardon from Truth that first introduced this concept to Will and the poem. The doctor then defines the sequence of Dowell, Dobetter, and Dobest as three kinds of teaching: Dowell is to "do as clerekes techeth" ([do as clerks teach] B 13.116); Dobetter is "he that techeth and travailleth to teche othere" ([he who teaches and works to teach others], B 13.117), and Dobest is he who "doth hymself so as he seith and precheth" ([does himself what he says and preaches], B 13.118). Patience then repeats the doctor's definition by reducing it to four words, a "school maxim" (in Alford's helpful phrase) whose endpoint is the monosyllable "love":[35]

> "*Disce*," quod he, "*doce; dilige inimicos*.
> *Disce*, and Dowel; *doce*, and Dobet;
> *Dilige*, and Dobest—thus taughte me ones
> A lemman that I lovede—Love was hir name."

["*Learn*," he said, "*teach; love your enemies*. *Learn*, and Dowell; *teach* and Dobetter; *love* and Dobest—thus I was once taught by a sweetheart I loved: Love was her name."]

(B 13.137–9)

Understood as a lesson about this one word, it also becomes clear why Clergy should have insisted that Dowell and Dobetter are "two infinites," since to understand the verb "love" as both transitive (as in "to love your enemies") and intransitive ("lerne to love" [learn to love], B 20.208, as

---

[34] Covington shows in some detail how medieval grammatical theory could understand a construction as Janus-like in this way: transitive from one perspective but intransitive in the other. In the sentence *Socrates videt Platonem* [Socrates sees Plato], for example, "the construction *Socrates videt* is clearly intransitive, since the dependency goes back to the *primum* [Socrates], while *videt Platonem* is clearly transitive, since in it, the dependency is terminated by something distinct from the *primum*" (*Syntactic Theory* 54). This view is underpinned by a searching exploration by medieval grammarians of the concept of "transitivity" (see Covington, *Syntactic Theory*, 44–61).

[35] Alford, *Guide to the Quotations*, 84.

Kynde puts it at the end of the poem), is to understand exactly why "love" is the best thing to do:

> "With wordes and with werkes," quod she, "and wil of thyn herte,
> Thow love leelly thi soule al thi lif tyme.
> And so thow lere the to lovye, for the Lordes love of hevene,
> Thyn enemy in alle wise eveneforth with thiselve.
> Cast coles on his heed of alle kynde speche,
> Bothe with werkes and with wordes fonde he his love to wynne,
> And leye on him thus with love til he laughe on the."

["Love your soul truly, with words and deeds and all your desire," she said, "all of your life. And so learn to love your enemy equally with yourself in every way for the sake of the Lord of heaven's love. Cast coals on his head (i.e. burn with passion) in every form of speech to try to win his love with both deeds and words, and bear him down thus with love until he laughs at you."]

(B 13.141–4)

Patience packs the key grammatical relationship into a single phrase in which the infinitive, "to lovye" [to love] is both transitive, "to lovye . . . thyn enemy" [to love your enemy], and intransitive, "to lovye for the Lordes love of hevene" [to love for the sake of the Lord of heaven's love], a love that has no immediate object because it is absolute, what one should do (to do well, better, and best) as a Christian in imitation of a Lord who simply *is* Love.

The lessons of the Feast of Patience are also simple enough to clarify the shape of Will's journey after the arrival of the pardon in passus 7. This reflexivity—the extent to which this scene has a synechdocal relationship to the larger structure of *Piers Plowman*—is also referenced throughout its teaching. When the language of the doctor's first definition of Dowell takes Will right back to the pardon and the starting point of his current search, for example, he is also recapitulating the "reiterative rather than progressive" structure of every key scene in the poem, and providing one of the many "new starts" that constitute the poem's "episodic form."[36] When the doctor envisions Dowell, Dobetter, and Dobest as tutelary figures, and Patience then condenses those figures into a pithy lesson that is both about teaching and learning, in the form of the kind of maxim schoolboys learned, he is condensing the way so many of the episodes in the poem, from Will's encounter with Holy Church (B 1.3–251) to his climactic encounter with Need (B 20.3–51), are fundamentally scenes of

---

[36] Anne Middleton, "Narration and the Invention of Experience: Episodic Form in *Piers Plowman*," 91–122 in *The Wisdom of Poetry: Essays in Early English Literature in Honor of Morton W. Bloomfield* (Kalamazoo, MI: Medieval Institute Publications, Western Michigan University, 1982), 92 ("reiterative") and "new" (94).

instruction.[37] But what most ensures that the lesson taught in this scene becomes a structuring principle for the passūs that both precede and follow it—that the grammar of Dowell, Dobetter and Dobest will grammaticalize so much of the poem—is the way its tutelary figures so generally insist that it is only possible to understand *what* Dowell, Dobetter, and Dobest mean by understanding *how* they mean, by construing these terms by means of their grammar. Will clearly understands this since he is still looking for "Dowel" when he wakes from this vision (B 15.2). And so too did a significant proportion of *Piers Plowman*'s medieval readers, since, from the earliest stages of the poem's copying, passūs 8–20 in the B-text were routinely divided into three sections labeled "Dowel," "Dobet," and "Dobest," each corresponding to "recognizable concentrations of interest" in the visions these sections contained.[38] As Katherine Breen describes the general formal consequence, the latter two-thirds of *Piers Plowman* can be seen as "an extended grammatical exercise... explained in terms of a brand-new English grammatical vocabulary."[39]

GRAMMAR-SCHOOL POETRY

The complexity of the forms invented by a poet such as William Langland always hide the simplicity of the grammar on which they are based, but, as I have already suggested, grammar-school training treated poetry as simple enough, asking the schoolboy to recite it as the first step in literacy training, and, soon enough, to write it as part of translation exercises. While this poetry was often in Latin, wherever English made inroads into grammatical teaching, schoolboys also wrote in English too, and so, as part of the exercises designed to teach them Latin, the fourteenth-century schoolboy was often asked to make English poetry. Oxford, Bodleian Library, MS Rawlinson D 328, the schoolbook whose Latin translations I looked at in some detail in Chapter 2, illustrates the general practice well, showing how the making of versified "Latins" could easily be reversed so that Latin prompts became the points of departure for English poetry:

---

[37] James Simpson has shown how Langland continually and variously "invokes the discourses of education," *Piers Plowman: An Introduction*, 2nd rev. edn. (Exeter: University of Exeter Press, 2007), 84. For a careful anatomization of these discourses see this volume 93–105 and 116–23.

[38] William Langland, *The Vision of Piers Plowman: A Complete Edition of the B-text*, ed. A. V. C Schmidt, 2nd edn. (London: J. M. Dent, 1995), xxxii–xxxiii.

[39] Breen, *Imagining an English Reading Public*, 182–3.

Brume tempestas vorat hoc quod procreat estas.
Whynter etyt þat somer getyt.
[*A storm in the winter eats what summer produces.*
Winter eats what summer gets.][40]

Quod cor subcelat lingua sepe reuelat.
That the hert þynkyt the mowte spekyt.
[*What the heart conceals the tongue often reveals.*
What the heart thinks the mouth speaks.] (119)

Cum fueris Rome Romane viuito more
Cum tu sis alibi viuito more loci.
Whan tho herde hat Rome
Do so of ther þe dome
Whan þu herd hels are
Do of ther as þe dothe thare.

[*When you are in Rome, live in the Roman manner,*
When you are elsewhere, live in the manner of that place.
When you are at Rome follow the local convention.
When you are elsewhere do as they do there.] (122)[41]

Within the context of such exercises, however, and generally concealed in even the most momentous instance by its resemblance to the writing that surrounded it, was a hugely significant literary-historical change: when the schoolboy, etching his translations dutifully with his stylus on his wax tablet, or writing them out on a bit of parchment, decided to move beyond the lines of Latin verse set him for translation to write a line or two of his own invention, Middle English poetry was born. Such a transition could never be located in time or the actions of a particular person because it would have occurred again and again, in a variety of schoolrooms, all over England. And every one of these moments and actions would also have gone unnoticed and certainly uncelebrated. On the other hand, to the extent that such schoolroom invention followed the same course as the invention that produced the most formally ambitious early Middle English poems—a set of texts characterized by the degree to which they depart from the models before them (by the extent to which they are isolated by their formal originality)—it emerged in exactly the same way as

---

[40] Sanford B. Meech, "A Collection of Proverbs in Rawlinson MS D 328," *Modern Philology* 38 (1940): 118. Hereafter quotations from this manuscript will be given by page number to the edition in this article.

[41] The Latin couplet in this example survives elsewhere. See *Thesaurus proverbiorum medii aevi: Lexikon der Sprichwörter des romanisch-germanischen Mittelalters*, ed. Samuel Singer et al., 13 vols. (Berlin: W. de Gruyter, 1995–2002), IX: 355. I thank Traugott Lawler for this reference.

the poetry that has been celebrated.[42] It has become traditional to understand the beginnings of Middle English literature as the consequence of some significant historical change (the yielding of the linguistic forms we call Old English to those we call Middle English), or, alternatively, to insist that "Middle English" only exists as the consequence of an arbitrary division and its earliest texts are best understood as Old English "rewritten."[43] Viewed from the perspective of the classroom, however, neither of these historical narratives can be true, since the emergence of Middle English poetry must always have been a step taken away from—with its origins in—Latin, and was therefore a practice everywhere produced by grammar-school norms.

Just as some of the "Latins" produced by such norms survive, some instances of this English invention also survive, and, like those Latins, these texts have sometimes been collected in modern anthologies by the catachresis that understands the schoolroom exercise as a macaronic poem. Where the English or some part of it goes beyond mere translation, moreover, the significance of the departure has been wholly concealed from literary history since it is so small in scale. Still, it is possible to see a different sort of birth for Middle English poetry in the text Robbins printed from Cambridge, St John's College, MS 37 as one of his *Historical Poems of the Fourteenth and Fifteenth Centuries*.[44] This text clearly acquired a certain canonicity in the Middle Ages since it survives (with variations) in a number of manuscripts.[45] Its Latin may have been the product of a

---

[42] The freedom of early Middle English writing of all kinds from formal models in English is a defining aspect of the period that I explore in my *Grounds of English Literature* ([Oxford: Oxford University Press, 2004], see esp. pp. 11–15).

[43] For one of the more nuanced accounts of early Middle English as a "transition" see Thomas Hahn, "Early Middle English," 61–91 in *The Cambridge History of Medieval English Literature*, ed. David Wallace (Cambridge: Cambridge University Press, 1999). On "continuity" the classic essay is R. W. Chambers, *On the Continuity of English Prose*, EETS o.s. 191A (1932). For a more recent set of arguments of this kind see *Rewriting Old English in the Twelfth Century*, ed. Mary Swan and Elaine Treharne (Cambridge: Cambridge University Press, 2000) as well as Elaine Treharne, *Living Through Conquest: The Politics of Early English, 1020 to 1220* (Oxford: Oxford University Press, 2012).

[44] *Historical Poems of the XIVth and XVth Centuries*, ed. Rossell Hope Robbins (New York, NY: Columbia University Press, 1959), pp. 143–4 (#55). Brackets in the poem as printed here indicate my emendation. There is some discussion of this poem, and its Latin is printed, in Rossell Hope Robbins, "Poems Dealing with Contemporary Conditions," 1389–1536 in *A Manual of the Writings in Middle English*, ed. Albert E. Hartung (New Haven, CT: Connecticut Academy of Arts and Sciences, 1975), 5: 1432–4. There is also a brief discussion in Cameron Louis, "Proverbs, Precepts and Monitory Pieces," 2057–3048 in *A Manual of the Writings in Middle English*, ed. Albert E. Hartung (New Haven, CT: Connecticut Academy of Arts and Sciences, 1993), 9: 3011 and 3380–1 (where Louis notes that a four-line "variant" of this poem can be found on fol. 15b of Manchester, John Rylands, MS Latin 394, the schoolbook I have already described in this chapter and in Chapter 2, pp. 75–9).

[45] These are Oxford, Bodleian Library, MS Douce 95 (fol. 23v), London, British Library, Additional MS 8151 (fol. 200v); London, British Library, Additional MS 9066 (fol. 54v);

classroom exercise since it rings a variety of changes on the description of the "state of the world" [status mundi actualis] provided by the "four wisest philosophers" [quatuor philosophi sapientissimi] in authoritative manuscripts of the *Gesta Romanorum*.[46] For the most part, its English faithfully reproduces this Latin line by line:[47]

> Munus fit iudex, fraus est mercator in urbe
> Non est lex domin[i]s, nec timor est pueris.
> Ingenium dolus est, amor omnis ceca voluptas,
> Ludus rusticitas, et gula festa dies.
> Senex ridetur, sapiens mendosus habetur,
> Dives laudatur, pauper ubique iacet.
> Prudentes ceci, cognati degeneres sunt;
> Mortuus inmemor est, nullus amicus erit.

[Bribery is judge, dishonesty is tradesman in the city; / Noblemen know no law, nor (school)boys any fear / Cleverness is deceit, and love is blind desire, / Boorishness is playfulness, and gluttony is a feast. / Old age is ridiculed, and the wise man is treated like a liar, / The rich man is praised and the poor man is despised. / Those with foresight are blind, and kindred are degenerate; / A dead man is forgotten; he will be no friend (to anyone).]

> ӡeft is Domesman, & gyle is chapman;
> Lordys ben owtyn lawe, & chylderen ben withowtyn awe;
> Wyth is trechery, & loue is lecherye;
> & pley turnyt to vylanye, & holyday to glotonye.
> Eld man in scornyng, wyse man in lesyng,
> Ryche man in levyng, & pore man in losyng;
> Sly men ben blynd, & kenred is onkynd;
> Þe ded is owtyn of mynd, for he may [noo frond fynd].[48]

London, British Library, MS Harley 2251 (fol. 153); London, British Library, MS Royal 17 B. XVII (fol. 2v); Worcester, Cathedral Library, MS F.154 (fol. 110va); Dublin, Trinity College, MS 509 (pp. 7–8); New Haven, Yale University, Beinecke Library, MS Takamiya Deposit 61 (fol. 56). See *The DIMEV: An Open-Access, Digital Edition of the Index of Middle English Verse: Based on the Index of Middle English Verse (1943) and its Supplement (1965)*, ed. Linne R. Mooney, Daniel W. Mosser, Elizabeth Solopova with Deborah Thorpe and David Hill Radcliffe, <http://www.dimev.net> (accessed June 12, 2014), #1506.

[46] *Gesta Romanorum*, ed. Hermann Osterley (Berlin: Wiedermannsche, 1872), cap. 144 (p. 500). On the relationship of the Latin the English translates here to the Latin of the *Gesta* see *The Early English Versions of the Gesta Romanorum*, ed. Sidney J. H. Herrtage, Early English Text Society 33 (1879): 499–500. For a version of the English as it appears in the context of English versions of the *Gesta Romanorum* see this edition (360). For a description of these textual relationships see also *Historical Poems of the XIVth and XVth Centuries*, ed. Robbins (326–7).

[47] The translation is close enough, in fact, that the version of this text in Oxford, Bodleian Library, Douce 95 alternates Latin and English lines. See *DIMEV*, ed. Mooney et al., #1506.

[48] *Historical Poems of the XIVth and XVth Centuries*, ed. Robbins, 143–4 (#55). I have emended Robbins's reading in the last line for the sake of rhyme.

[Bribery is judge, and trickery is merchant; lords are without law, and children disrespectful; wit is treachery and love is lechery. / and play turns to villainy, and holidays to gluttony. / the old man is scorned and the wise man treated like a liar, / The rich man is praised, and the poor man is dying; / Wise men are blind, and kin are unkind. / The dead are put out of mind, for he may not find a friend.]

After the English I have just quoted, the version of this text preserved in Cambridge, St John's 37 includes two Latin lines in a similar vein, although they are taken from an entirely different source:[49]

Virtus	Ecclesia	Clerus Demon	Simonia
cessat.	calcatur.	errat. regnat.	dominatur.

[Virtue dies. The Church is trampled. The clerk errs. The devil reigns. Simony rules.]

These lines are then carefully translated into English, although, in a manner that could not be quieter about the originality involved, since it is, at once, completely faithful to the original, while also introducing small and progressive expansions:

> Now men leuyn good thewis,
> & holy chyrch is led with schrewys,
> Clergie goth owt of þe wey,
> þe fend among hem hath hys prey,
> Symony is aboue, & awey is trwloue.

[Now men abandon good manners, and holy church is governed by rogues, and clergy wander from the right way, and the fiend among them finds his prey, simony holds sway, and true love is gone.]

The English faithfully reproduces the meaning and lexis of the first half-line of the Latin ("virtus" > "thewis," "holy church" > "ecclesia," "clerus" > "clergie," "demon" > "þe fend," "simonia" > "symony"), but each successive line of English also stretches just a little further beyond the Latin of the second half-line, providing perpetrators of abuse ("schrewys") or victims ("prey") not in the Latin, until, finally, in the last line, a wholly new idea is added: "awey is trwloue." This last extension provides a balancing rhyme for "aboue," and is the inevitable consequence of the attempt to transform Latin verses about five distinct abuses into three English couplets. But identifying the grounds for this departure is only another way of registering its defining modesty, since, however much it was rooted in formal

---

[49] These lines survive as a stanza of the collection we now call the *Carmina Burana* (Munich: Bayerische Staatsbibliothek, clm 4660). For this text as it is collected there see *Carmina Burana*, ed. Alfons Hilka and Otto Schumann, 2 vols. (Heidelberg: Carl Winter, 1930–41), vol. 3, ed. Bernard Bischoff (Heidelberg: Carl Winter, 1971), 1: 5 (#5, st. 3). I am grateful to David Carlson for bringing this source to my attention.

considerations, that form, fully as much as the phrase that completes it, constituted an imaginative leap, a wholesale English invention.

Reconstructing the kinds of invention such schoolroom translation encouraged makes it possible to see how the practice might have shaped more familiar Ricardian poems, although the modesty that is so much part of the technique means that it is often just as hard to discern in the English we know well. A representative example here is the transcription in Book 1 of Chaucer's *House of Fame* of what was "writen" on the "table of bras" (142) that the dreamer finds "on a wall" (141) which is also an exact translation, in verse, of the first two lines of Virgil's *Aeneid*:

> "I wol now synge, yif* I kan,   if
> The armes and also the man
> That first cam, thrugh his destinee,
> Fugityf of Troy contree,
> In Itayle, with ful moche pyne*   very great trouble
> Unto the strondes* of Lavyne."   shores

(The House of Fame, 140–8)[50]

The scope of this grammaticalization is as easy to miss as the schoolroom form embedded in the dream-vision, for, as the first lines of the *Aeneid* expand from this straightforward translation into a summary of that poem's narrative ("First sawgh I the destruction / Of Troye," 151–2), as the events central to the *Aeneid* become the events central to the *House of Fame*, the activity of the schoolroom exercise is thematized, so that the relationship of the Latin literary tradition in and to English poetic invention becomes what this poem is very generally about. To this extent, and according to these relations, the whole form of the *House of Fame* is an inventive expansion of a schoolroom exercise. The same schoolroom exercise is absorbed to The Nun's Priest's Tale, although here the modesty is part of that absorption's meaning, since what matters most in this case—and is the source of its humor—is that Chauntecleer, the rooster, plays the part of the errant schoolboy who inverts the meaning of the Latin proverb he claims to have translated:

> "*Mulier est hominis confusio.*"
> Madame, the sentence of this Latyn is:
> "Womman is mannes joye and al his blis."

["*Woman is man's ruin*": Madam, the meaning of this Latin is: "Woman is man's joy and all his bliss."]

(VII.3164–6)

---

[50] The lines translated here are "Arma virumque cano, Troiae qui primus ab oris / Italiam, fato profugus, Laviniaque venit litora" [I sing of arms and the man, he who, exiled by fate, first came from the coast of Troy to Italy, and to Lavinian shores], Virgil, *Aeneid*, 261–597, in *Eclogues, Georgics, Aeneid, 1–6*, ed. and trans. H. Ruston Fairclough, rev. G. P. Goold (Cambridge, MA: Harvard University Press, 1999; first published 1916), I.1–3.

Chauntecleer's confusion about the meaning of Latin stands in for his confusion about all the learning he parades before his doubtful "wife," Pertolote, particularly his confusion about the validity of dreams. Moreover, by reversing the meaning of the Latin proverb, Chauntecleer fails to heed the useful warning it might have supplied (against Pertelote's "confusing" insistence that his frightening dream could not be prophetic), and then extends this contradiction into his own actions, when he decides to "deffye" the warning of the dream that he has just insisted at great length must be heeded (VII.3171). Chauntecleer's mistranslation mocks the proposition that chickens know Latin (that the beasts in this beast fable are as learned as they claim to be), but the mistake is so generally of a piece with the way words fail to work in the first half of this tale, and it is so ceremoniously marked (here, Chauntecleer says, with such dramatic authority, is what these words teach you) that a schoolroom exercise again carries enormous thematic weight. This grammaticalization not only absorbs the schoolroom exercise, however, but also its performance, since, in any classroom in which the point was to teach children who did not know Latin how to translate properly, mistranslation must have been a necessary step to success, just as it turns out to be in The Nun's Priest's Tale. For when the chips are down (and Chauntecleer has been seized by the fox) words work so well for Chauntecleer that they save his life.[51]

Where grammaticalization shapes still larger forms in Ricardian literature, it becomes even harder to see, in part because the relationship is so disproportionate, but, also, because the ambition of the poem tends to ally its Latinity with higher learning. This paradox certainly governs the one major Middle English poem whose Latinity we now honor most often by referring to it with a Latin name, Gower's *Confessio Amantis*. Although the bulk of this poem consists of English octosyllabic couplets, in both medieval manuscripts and modern editions, Latin elegiac verses introduce each of its major sections, and shorter Latin prose sentences, usually described as "commentaries" or "glosses," run alongside the English of each section or are sometimes (in certain manuscripts) interleaved with it.[52] When

---

[51] On the understanding of language played out in The Nun's Priest's Tale see my "The Language Group of the *Canterbury Tales*," 25–40 in *Medieval Latin and Middle English Literature: Essays in Honour of Jill Mann*, ed. Christopher Cannon and Maura Nolan (Cambridge: D. S. Brewer, 2011).

[52] R. F. Yeager, "'Oure englisshe' and Everyone's Latin: The Fasciculus Morum and Gower's '*Confessio* Amantis,'" *South Atlantic Review* 46 (1981): 45 ("approximate"); Derek Pearsall, "Gower's Latin in the *Confessio Amantis*," 13–25 in *Latin and Vernacular: Studies in Late-Medieval Texts and Manuscripts*, ed. A. J. Minnis (Cambridge: D. S. Brewer, 1989), 13 (on Latin "commentaries"); Robert F. Yeager, "English, Latin, and the Text as 'Other': The Page as Sign in the Work of John Gower," *Text* 3 (1987): 251–67 ("glosses," pp. 254–5).

viewed as supplement to the poem's English, all of this Latin can be understood as a "scholastic apparatus" whose chief function is to aggrandize that English as well as Gower as an author, conferring authority to the extent that Latin in the fourteenth century had a "status" both higher than and "*different* from that of the English text."[53] Certainly the elegiac verse can be different in meaning from the English that follows it, but in many cases it is exactly equivalent, giving the English the character of a poetic paraphrase, and giving the Latin and English together, once again, the form a schoolroom exercise. Here, for example, are the first elegiacs introducing the section on "boasting" or "avantance" (as it is termed in Middle English) in Book 1 of the *Confessio Amantis* as well as the English that follows it:

> Magniloque propriam minuit iactancia lingue
>   Famam, quam stabilem firmat honore cilens.
> Ipse sui laudem meriti non percipit, vnde
>   Se sua per verba iactat in orbe palam.

[The boasting of a bombastic tongue diminishes its own fame which being silent would, with honor, confirm as stable. He who does not receive the praise for his merit, openly extolls himself in his own words to the world.]

"The vice cleped* Avantance*	called/ Boasting
With Pride hath take his aqueintance,	
So that his oghne pris* he lasseth*,	own value/ lessens
When he such mesure overpasseth*	exceeds
That he his oghne herald is.	
That ferst was* wel is thanne mis*,	what was first/ amiss
That was thankworth* is thanne blame,	worthy of thanks
And thus the worschipe* of his name	value
Thurgh pride of his avantarie*	boasting
He torneth into vilenie.	

(1.2399–419)

The different metrical needs of verse in each language are more than enough to account for the small differences in meaning here. Such equivalencies are even more consistent between the Latin "glosses" or "commentaries" and the English verse it is often assumed to analyze. In general, this

---

[53] Pearsall, "Gower's Latin," 16 ("status" and "different"; emphasis Pearsall's) and 20 ("scholastic apparatus"). A. J. Minnis also argues that Gower "attempted to provide for his own works that apparatus which medieval readers believed to be appropriate for an *auctor*," *Medieval Theory of Authorship: Scholastic Literary Attitudes in the later Middle Ages* (London: Scholar Press, 1984), 275. For a similar view see Yeager, "English, Latin, and the Text as 'Other,'" 256. On the "tension" between the English and the attempt this Latin may seem to make to "contain" it see Rita Copeland, *Rhetoric, Hermeneutics, and Translation in the Middle Ages: Academic Traditions and Vernacular Texts* (Cambridge: Cambridge University Press, 1991), 217.

Latin prose introduces a narrative example (e.g. "hic ponit Confessor exemplum" [here the Confessor offers an example]), and then summarizes it fully, so that English and Latin are best described as translations of one another, as for example, when the tale of Narcissus is used to illustrate the sin of pride:

> Ubi ipse faciem suam pulcherrimam in aqua percipiens, putabat se per hoc illam Nimpham, quam Poete Ekko vocant, in flumine coram suis oculis pocius conspexisse.
>
> [There, perceiving in the water his own most beautiful face, he thought instead that he was regarding that nymph whom poets call Echo, in the river before his eyes.]

. . . As he caste his lok*	attention
Into the welle and hiede tok*,	took heed
He sih* the like* of his visage,	saw/ likeness
And wende* ther were an ymage	thought
Of such a nimphe as tho* was faie*,	then/ enchanted
Wherof that love his herte assaie*	press upon
Began, as it was after sene,	
Of his sotie*, and made him wene*	foolishness/ think
It were a womman that he syh.	

(1.2313–21)

The equivalence in meaning also means there is nothing in these passages, nor in the relationship between the Latin elegiacs set against the octosyllabics just shown, that indicates their priority: the Latin could be a version of the English; the English could be a version of the Latin; and therefore either version might be a translation of the other. Such equivalencies do not necessarily confound the general presumption that Gower was using the Latin to situate the whole of this poem—its English as well as its Latin—"within the context of the learned Latin tradition," not least because the Latin verse signals its ambition with an extravagance of diction and imagery that has been described as a kind of "fireworks."[54] And yet, even where Gower's hopes for the status of the *Confessio Amantis* are at their most aspirational, the material of those aspirations was not fundamentally "scholastic" but, rather, the translation exercise that was one of the grammar school's most basic pedagogical forms.

---

[54] Pearsall, "Gower's Latin," 18. On the difficulty of Gower's Latin in the verses see also Siân Echard and Claire Fanger, "Introduction," pp. xxv–liv in *Latin Verses in the Confessio Amantis: An Annotated Translation*, trans. Siân Echard and Claire Fanger (East Lansing, MI: Colleagues Press, 1991), p. xxxix.

The modern decision to see the *Confessio Amantis* as the most substantial of Gower's "English works," and then to separate this poem in editions from Gower's "Latin works," has not only made the *Confessio*'s Latin secondary, but virtually removed it from critical consideration of the poem as a whole.[55] This occlusion is abetted by the common decision to place the Latin prose in editions of the poem, not just in smaller type in the margins of the text (as Macaulay always did), but in the footnotes (as in the TEAMS edition). Gower's medieval readers, however, clearly saw— and we might imagine read—this Latin as integral to the English that we now take as all that constitutes this poem's "text." In fact, like many of the later manuscripts of the poem, London, British Library, MS Harley 3490 moves the Latin prose into the main column of the English text.[56] In New York, Pierpont Morgan Library & Museum, MS M 126 this Latin is given such priority that it seems as though "the English text is to be read as a commentary on the Latin and on the illuminations rather than vice versa."[57] Such *mise en page* not only reflects a very different understanding of the poem's form from our own, it insists that that form is a grammaticalization, returning it to the shape of those schoolbook exercises in which Latin prose and poetry alternated with the English prose or poetry that translated it, and in which a schoolboy such Gower would have first learned to produce the kind of English verse and Latin prose and verse that now comprise the whole of the *Confessio Amantis*.

To see the Latin of the *Confessio Amantis* as integral to its form is also to see just how much it resembles the form of *Piers Plowman*. Although these two poems emerge from two wholly distinct metrical traditions—the octosyllabic verse common in Middle English romance in the case of the

[55] The distinction was basic to G. C. Macaulay's edition of Gower's *Complete Works* two volumes of which contained his "English Works" (issued as both EETS, e.s. 81–2 [1900–1] and as vols. 2–3 of the Oxford edition), and another of which contained his "Latin works" (vol. 4). The durability of the distinction is best illustrated by the observation, in remarks describing the place of Gower in Anglo-Latin literature, that Gower, "faced with a choice of three langauges . . . used English for the *Confessio Amantis*," A. G. Rigg, "Preface," pp. xiii–xxiv in *Latin Verses in the Confessio Amantis*, trans. Echard and Fanger, p. xv.

[56] Pearsall notes this tendency but attributes it to the carelessness of "scribes who decided it was too complicated for them to arrange to put the prose in the margin" ("Gower's Latin," 14). On "the practice of inserting marginal prose summaries into the text itself . . . common in many of the later MSS" see John Gower *Confessio Amantis*, ed. Russell A. Peck, 2nd edn., 3 vols. (Kalamazoo, MI: Medieval Institute Publications, Western Michigan University, 2006–13), notes to lines *34–*35 (1: 241).

[57] Echard and Fanger "Introduction," *Latin Verses in the Confessio Amantis*, trans. Echard and Fanger, p. xxviiii. Echard and Fanger are describing Pierpont Morgan Library & Museum MS M 126, fols. 1ra–204va.

Confessio, the variety of "alliterative" traditions in the case of *Piers Plowman*—the Latin in both poems ensures that every manuscript of *Piers Plowman* looks exactly like those manuscripts of the *Confessio* I have just described in which English and Latin consistently alternate. The frequency with which the Latin of *Piers Plowman* is attributed ("for thise ben wordes writen in the Euaaungelie," B 1.200) or attributable (most often to Scripture) has ensured that it is routinely referred to as a set of "quotations," a borrowing from another text rather than a native part of *Piers Plowman*.[58] But it is also clear that these quotations were of such importance that they were "the matrix out of which the poetry developed," an integral substrate or foundation for the thinking that constitutes Langland's English.[59] Moreover, as Tim Machan has observed, the shift between Latin and English in *Piers Plowman* is never a semantic necessity ("not regularly determined by context, speaker, interlocutor, topic, lexical inadequacy or alliteration") but, rather, "stylistic," a shift that has a particular meaning in a given context in and of itself.[60]

Perhaps to an even greater degree than in the *Confessio Amantis*, then, the Latin of *Piers Plowman* is integral to the poem's local and general meanings. This does sometimes mean that such Latin stands in for— effectively means—its own opacity to the unschooled, as if the form grammaticalization takes is to absorb schoolroom training, as if every reader were no more competent than Chauntecleer and still needed help with his Latin.[61] For example, when Reason cites the kind of Latin proverb common in schoolbooks,

---

[58] As John Alford put this point, "the feature that most obviously sets *Piers Plowman* apart from other Middle English poems is its extensive use of quotations" (*A Guide to the Quotations*, 1).

[59] John A. Alford, "The Role of the Quotations in *Piers Plowman*," *Speculum* 52 (1977): 96. On the complexities inherent in using the category "quotation" for these Latin lines see also Katherine Zieman, *Singing the New Song: Literacy and Liturgy in Late Medieval England* (Philadelphia, PA: University of Pennsylvania Press, 2008), 156–7. Sarah Kay also describes the ways that the many medieval texts that quote troubadour poetry "are similar to Latin pedagogical or didactic works, particularly those concerned with the teaching of Latin grammar and poetry" (*Parrots and Nightingales: Troubadour Quotations and the Development of European Poetry* [Philadelphia, PA: University of Pennsylvania Press, 2013], 197).

[60] Tim William Machan, "Language Contact in *Piers Plowman*," *Speculum* 69 (1994): 375. See also Helena Halmari and Robert Adams, "On the Grammar and Rhetoric of Language Mixing in *Piers Plowman*," *Neuphilologische Mitteilungen* 103 (2002): 73–92.

[61] In addition to the example I give here, other examples of relatively straightforward translation of Latin into English in the B-text are: 3.72a–4, 3.234a–5, 3.237a–9, 8.91a–2, 10.88a–90, 10.201a–4, 10.240a–1, 10.255a–7, 10.262a–4a, 10.429a–31, 10.455–62, 11.175a–6, 12.13a–15, 12.29a–30, 13.433a–5, 14.275a–86a, 15.55a–9, 18.410a–14.

> Qui parcit virge odit filium.
> [Who spares the rod hates his son.]

(B 5.39a)

he then quickly gives that proverb in English—with some slight modifications—as if the Latin were not immediately intelligible:

> Whoso spareth the spryng spilleth hise children.
> [Who spares the switch ruins his children.]

(B 5.40)

This is the logic that governs the large-scale grammaticalization I have already discussed in which a priest translates the Latin pardon sent from Truth, but it is worth noting here that part of what the priest uncovers by his efforts is a certain irreducible obscurity. The rest of the poem is grammaticalized according to this phrase—becomes, in this sense, an extended effort to parse it—because it turns out that understanding the meaning of its Latin is not nearly enough to understand how this is a pardon or, indeed, what this "pardon" means:

> *Et qui bona egerunt ibunt in vitam eternam;*
> *Qui vero mala, in ignem eternum.*
> "Peter!" quod the preest thoo, "I kan no pardon fynde
> But 'Do wel and have wel, and God shal have thi soule,'
> And 'Do yvel and have yvel and hope thow noon oother
> That after thi deeth day the devel shal have thi soule!'"

> [*And he who does well will enter into eternal life: he who does evil will enter into eternal fire*; "Peter," said the priest then, "I can find no pardon except 'Do well and it will go well for you, and God will receive your soul.' And 'Do evil and it will go ill for you and expect nothing else but that the devil will have your soul when you die!'"]

(B 7.110a–14)

But *Piers Plowman* more often proceeds as if its Latin was completely intelligible to its readers. When Repentance offers a prayer on behalf of the sins who have just confessed to him, he embeds bits of the Latin liturgy into that prayer, drawing immediately and directly on the meaning of that Latin, without ever translating it:

> "Now God," quod he, "who that of Thi goodnesse gonne the world make,
> And of naught madest aught and man moost lik to Thiselve,
> And sithen sufredest hym to synne, a siknesse to us alle—
> And al for the beste, as I bileve, whatevere the Book telleth:
> *O felix culpa! O necessarium peccatum Ade!*
> For thorugh that synne Thi sone sent was to this erthe
> And bicam man of a maide mankynde to save."

["Now God," he said, "made the world out of Your goodness, and made something from nothing and man most like Yourself, and then allowed him to sin, a sickness to us all—and all for the best, so I believe, whatever the Book says: '*O happy fall! O necessary sin of Adam!*' For through that sin Your son was sent to this earth and became man from a maid in order to save mankind."]

(B 5.481–6)

Latin may also be so embedded in English syntax that it is necessary to understand the Latin in order to understand the English, as, for example, when Holy Church quotes God in direct speech at the beginning of passus 1:

> "*Reddite Cesari*," quod God, "that *Cesari* bifalleth,
> *Et que sunt Dei Deo*, or ellis ye don ille."

["*Render to Caesar*," said God, "that which belongs *to Caesar, and to God that which belongs to God,* or else you do ill."]

(B 1.52–3)

Where Latin is not this deeply embedded in the syntax of an English sentence, it can still be attached to the surrounding English syntactically, as, for example, when Holy Church's observations about the relationship of chastity and charity is predicated on the assertion from James 2:26 on the relationship of faith and works, given in untranslated Latin:[62]

> *Fides sine operibus mortua est*
> Forthi chastite withouten charite worth cheyned in helle.

[*Faith without works is dead*, therefore chastity without charity will be chained in hell.]

(B 1.187a–8)

Langland ensured that every aspect of schoolroom practice was involved in this grammaticalization on those many occasions when he gives the English version of a given set of Latin lines first. In some cases, this means that the Latin authenticates the idea expressed in English as it returned, by way of translation, to its source (here, Genesis 6:7):

> Til God wrathed for hir werkes, and swich a word seide,
> "That I makede man, now it me forthynketh:
> *Penitet me fecisse hominem.*"

[Until God became angry over what they did, and said, "I am now sorry that I made man": *I repent that I made man.*]

(B 9.129–30a)

---

[62] Another good example of this method of quotation can be found at B 9.143–7 where, in Wit's account of biblical history (and the descent of the curse of Cain) he says that the son bears the sins of the father and then quotes a line from Ezekiel "against" it, which he does not translate, even though he then continues with a qualification that only makes sense if the content of that Latin is clear ("Ac I fynd..." [but I find...]).

But the Latin that becomes the target language for the English need not be scriptural, nor even from some other authoritative source, but, rather, the linguistic ground to which the English has been simply but firmly returned:

> And al the wikkednesse in this world that man myghte werche or thynke
> Nis na moore to the mercy of God than inmiddes the see a gleede:
> *Omnis iniquitas quantum ad misericordiam Dei est quasi scintilla in medio maris.*
> [And all the wickedness in this world that man might do or think is no more to the mercy of God than an ember in the sea; *Every wickedness is as much to the mercy of God as a spark in the middle of the sea.*]
>
> (B 5.283–4a)

In the twenty-seven instances in which this last pattern can be found in the B-text, it is as if *Piers Plowman* unfolds as if it *were* a schoolroom exercise, the making of so many "Latins."[63]

These last examples also suggest with some force that it is just as wrong to call *Piers Plowman* "the greatest English poem of the Middle Ages" as it is to call the *Confessio Amantis* an "English work."[64] Scale matters here, and it is worth acknowledging, alongside the patterns I have identified that, roughly speaking, only 1,200 of the B- and C-text's 7,200 lines, or 15 percent, are in Latin. And yet, if it seems extraordinary that even this much of an "English" poem could have been written in a language that was unintelligible to its intended audience, the obvious conclusion is that Langland assumed that it was not—that any audience literate enough to read the English of his poem necessarily knew enough to puzzle out its Latin. But, as in the *Confessio Amantis*, and those instances where Latin is translated for figures in *Piers Plowman* as if they don't understand it—as, particularly, in the general confusion generated by the Latin of the pardon—puzzlement was clearly an important aspect of this grammaticalization too. Since it was the method of English grammar schools to immerse a schoolboy in Latin in order to teach him to read and write—and to present him with progressively harder Latin to improve his mastery—learning grammar often consisted of being baffled by Latin sentences, many of them proverbs or scriptural quotations. Without in any way claiming that the *Confessio Amantis* or *Piers Plowman* taught their readers some Latin (though, surely, this must have happened), these texts

---

[63] For this pattern see also B Pro. 194–5a, 1.186–7a, 3.240–1a, 3.305–8a, 3.334–5a, 5.273–a, 5.281–a, 5.283–4a, 5.567–a, 7.41–2a, 7.43–4a, 7.83–a, 9.62–a, 9.133–a, 9.185–6a, 10.261–a, 10.342–a, 11.81–a, 11.82–a, 11.397–8a, 12.57–a, 14.76–7a, 14.305–7a, 18.109–a, 18.160–2a, 18.262–a, 20.256–a.

[64] A. V. C. Schmidt, "Introduction," pp. xvii–lxxxvi in Langland, *The Vision of Piers Plowman*, ed. Schmidt, p. xix.

could also be described as schoolroom forms to the very extent that they presented readers with Latin they could not easily or immediately or completely understand.

LANGLAND'S LATIN

The claim implicit in all that I have said about the extensive use of Latin in both the *Confessio Amantis* and *Piers Plowman*, is that, like the good schoolboys they generally were, Gower and Langland *wrote* the Latin— or at least some of the Latin—in their poems. This is only a modest claim to make for the *Confessio*, since, from Macaulay onward, most have simply presumed that Gower wrote the Latin verses in his poem.[65] Many who have written about the Latin prose "associated" with the text have hedged their bets, tending to describe Gower as the "origin" rather than the "author" of this material (in this way preserving the possibility that he arranged for its writing but did not write this Latin himself), but such hesitation has also generally yielded to the presumption that this Latin is Gower's "own composition" too.[66] The most recent edition of the *Confessio Amantis* even describes it as a "bilingual poem."[67] The proposal that Langland wrote some of the Latin in *Piers Plowman* is audacious enough, however, to be entirely new. The many differences between the lines of Scripture quoted in surviving texts of *Piers Plowman* and the accepted version of the Vulgate have usually been thought to derive from differences in the text of Scripture Langland had to hand ("during the Middle Ages the biblical text existed in a variety of forms").[68] Even when the text

---

[65] See, for example, the attribution of the "Latin verses" in the Prologue to "the author" (Gower, *Complete Works*, ed. Macaulay, 2: 457). A. J. Minnis is less certain and says that Gower "may even have written" the Latin of the "apparatus" (*Medieval Theory of Authorship*, 274–5 n. 45).

[66] All the phrases I quote here are Pearsall's in "Gower's Latin," 14 ("associated" and "origin") and 15 ("own"). R. F. Yeager also says that Gower chose to "include" the Latin prose in the *Confessio*, though he also says that "Gower apparently wrote . . . these . . . himself, or at least oversaw their inclusion in manuscripts" ("'Oure englisshe' and Everyone's Latin: The *Fasciculus Morum* and Gower's *Confessio Amantis*," *South Atlantic Review* 46 [1981]: 41–53 ["include," 41 and "Gower," 46]). Although it prints the Latin prose in its notes rather than alongside the English, the TEAMS edition of the *Confessio Amantis* assumes throughout that all the poem's Latin "*marginalia*" are by Gower (see especially Gower, *Confessio Amantis*, ed. Peck, 1: 16 and 23).

[67] Gower, *Confessio Amantis*, ed. Peck, 1: 238 (note to Latin verses).

[68] Alford, *Guide to the Quotations*, 17.

from which Langland took a given "quotation" cannot be found, that source is understood to be "unidentified" or "unknown."[69]

There are a number of reasons, internal to the form of *Piers Plowman*, that might be used to query such a view, however, not least the extent to which referring all of Langland's Latin to texts and authors outside of *Piers* tends to obscure the relationship much of that Latin has to *itself*. That is, a certain proportion of Langland's Latin can be understood as a quotation of a Latin line used earlier in *Piers*, often with long stretches of text intervening between initial and subsequent uses. There are seven such lines in all, although their repetition means that they account for twenty-five different occurrences (in the B-text):

> *Heu michi quod sterilem duxi vitam iuvenilem.* [Alas, what a useless life I led in my youth.] B 1.141a (C 1.140a), B 5.440a (C 7.54a)
>
> *Date et dabitur vobis.* [Give and it will be given to you.] B 1.201(Z 1.124, A 1.175, C.1.196) B 12.54
>
> *Ponam pedem in aquilone, et similis ero Altissimo* [I shall set my foot in the north, and I will be like the Most High.] B 1.119 (C.1.111a), B 15.51a (C 16.213a)
>
> *Misericordia eius super omnia opera eius.* [His mercy is over all his works.] B 5.282a, 11.139a (C 12.74a), B 17.318a (C 19.298a)
>
> *Michi vindictam et ego retribuam.* [Vengeance is mine and I will repay.] (Romans 12:19), B 6.225a, B 10.209a, B 10.374 (A 11.255; C 17.235a), B 9.446a (C 21.446a)
>
> *Patientes vincunt.* [The patient ones conquer.] B 13.135a (C.15.137), B 13.171a (C 15.156a), B 14.33c, 14.54 (C 15.253), B 15.268, 15.598a
>
> *Redde quod debes.* [Pay what you owe.], B 19.187 (C 21.187), B 19.259 (C 21.259), B 19.390 (C 21.390), B 20.308 (C 22.308), and as "reddit quod debet," B 19.193 (C 21.193)
>
> *Homo proponit et deus disponit.* [Man proposes and God disposes.] B 11.37–8 (C 11.303–4), B 20.33a

Two of these lines are taken from the Vulgate: "Date et dabitur vobis" is from Luke 6:38 and "Redde quod debes" is from Matthew 18:28. "Misericordia eius super omnia opera eius" resembles a line from the Psalms (144: 9) but the Vulgate regularly has "Miserationes" where *Piers Plowman* always has "Misericordia." "Ponam pedem in aquilone, et similis ero Altissimo" closely resembles a sentence in Augustine's *Enarrationes in Psalmos*, but the accepted version of this text has "sedem meum" for "pedem" and "ero similis altissimo" for "similis ero altissimo."[70] The

---

[69] See, for example, Alford on C 3.190a as "unidentified" (*Guide to the Quotations*, 38) and B 13.50 and 13.73a as "unknown" (*Guide to the Quotations*, 82–3).

[70] Augustine, *Enarrationes in Psalmos*, ed. E. Dekkers and I. Fraipont, 3 vols., Corpus Christianorum Series Latina 38–40 (Turnhout: Brepols, 1956), I, 4 (38: 2). The phrase in

line "Heu michi quod sterilem duxi vitam iuvenilem" is a regular dactylic hexameter that has been found in no authoritative source, but can be found in a schoolbook I described at some length in Chapter 2, Manchester, John Rylands University Library, Latin MS 394.[71] "Homo proponit et deus disponit" can be found in a number of other texts, but, because it is a common proverb, it is never seen as originating in any of them. "Patientes vincunt" [the patient ones conquer] resembles another common proverb, "patientia vincit" [patience conquers], but the proverb has only been found with *patientes* in place of *patientia* in one other text. When Anna Baldwin discovered this use in the apocryphal Testament of Job, it was quickly assumed to be the source for "patientes vincunt" in *Piers Plowman*, and adopted as such by Schmidt in the revision of his edition of the B-text.[72]

The variety of the trajectories by which these lines entered *Piers*, and the degree to which so many of them have been reworked, suggests just how free Langland felt to vary any Latin he found in a book, and the presence of one of these lines in the kind of book that would have taught a schoolboy like Langland how to compose in Latin clarifies the grounds of such freedom: Langland was clearly prepared to make his own Latin, even if that making consisted of no more of the small changes in lexis or morphology that were common in school exercises. Looking more closely

Augustine is a version of Isaiah 14:13–14, but, as Alford notes, this quotation was probably known to Langland via commentary on the *Fables* of Avianus. See Alford, *Guide to the Quotations*, 35 and R. G. Risse, "The Augustinian Paraphrase of Isaiah 14:13–14 in *Piers Plowman* and the Commentary on the *Fables* of Avianus," *Philological Quarterly* 45 (1966): 712–17, and A. L. Kellogg, "Langland and Two Scriptural Texts," *Traditio* 14 (1958): 385–98.

[71] The discovery of this line in this volume was first reported in a letter to the *TLS* by A. H. Bright as cited by Alford (*Guide to the Quotations*, 35). Alford also notes that the first line of the phrase Langland quotes at B 10.266a–b ("Si culpare velis culpabilis esse cauebis; / Dogma tuum sordet cum te tua culpa remordet" [If you wish to blame others make sure you are not blameworthy / Your teaching is sullied when your own faults come back to haunt you]) also appears in this schoolbook (*Guide to the Quotations*, 65). Alford does not say where this phrase appears, but it can be found at fol. 3r. As I have noted, the manuscript is described and transcriptions of most of its English lines (but not the bulk of its Latin) are provided in W. A. Pantin, "A Medieval Collection of Latin and English Proverbs and Riddles, from the Rylands Latin MS 394," *Bulletin of the John Rylands Library* 14 (1930): 81–114. See also Alford, *Guide to the Quotations*, 71–2. It was Traugott Lawler who noticed that the line is in "verse" and related it to the training Langland must have been giving in the writing of Latin poetry ("Langland Versificator," *Yearbook of Langland Studies* 25 [2011]: 54). For the earlier discussion of the contents of this book see pp. 75–8 in the present volume.

[72] Anna P. Baldwin, "The Triumph of Patience in Julian of Norwich and Langland," 71–83 in *Langland, the Mystics and the Medieval Religious Tradition: Essays in Honour of S. S. Hussey*, ed. Helen Phillips (Cambridge: D. S. Brewer, 1990), 72. See also Langland, *Vision of Piers Plowman*, ed. Schmidt, 460.

at the way some of these lines were treated in context also makes clear that Langland often treated them of a piece with his English, not only working them into its syntax, as I have suggested previously, but treating them as if they were indistinct from that English. When he splits the proverb "Homo proponit, deus disponit" in half, for example, he presents it as if it is a report, in direct speech, of what "a poete" said:

> "*Homo proponit*" quod a poete tho, and Plato he highte,
> "And *Deus disponit*" quod he; "lat god doon his wille."

["*Man proposes*," said a poet, and Plato was his name, "And *God disposes*," he said, "let God do as he wishes,"]

(B 11.37–8)

The line is therefore also worked into the poem's alliterative verse form (each phrase provides two of the alliterative staves in a line) and becomes the undifferentiated equivalent of the English that concludes what the poet is claimed to have "said" ("lat god doon his wille"). On another occasion, the phrase "redde quod debes" occurs just after it appears in its Gospel form, again worked into the surrounding English syntax, but this time recast grammatically for the purpose as a declarative rather than an imperative ("reddit" instead of "redde"):

> And whan this dede was doon, do best he þoughte,
> And yaf Piers power, and pardon he grauntede:
> To alle maner men, mercy and foryifnesse;
> To hym, myghte men to assoille of alle manere synnes,
> In couenaunt that thei come and kneweliche to paye
> To Piers pardon thee Plowman—*Redde quod debes*.
> Thus hath Piers power, be his pardon paied,
> To bynde and unbynde bothe here and ellis,
> And assoille men of alle synnes save of dette one.
> Anoon after an heigh up into hevene
> He wente, and wonyeth there, and wol come at the laste,
> And rewarde hym right wel that *reddit quod debet*—
> Paieth parfitly, as pure truthe wolde.

[And when this deed was done, he thought to do best and gave Piers power, and granted him a pardon: to everyone there would be mercy and forgiveness; to him, the power to absolve all manner of sins on the condition that they come and acknowledge what is due for Piers Plowman's pardon: *Pay what you owe*. Thus Piers has the power, by satisfaction of his pardon, to bind and unbind here and elsewhere, and absolve men of all sins except one. Soon thereafter he went on high up to heaven and dwells there and will come at the end and reward him well who *pays what he owes*—pays fully, as pure truth would wish it.]

(B 19.183–95)

Without the repetition to make clear that Langland knew the original, the second of these variations could be taken as a phrase from a different version of the Vulgate or, among the corruptions also thought to have occurred when Langland quoted from a secondary source that had undertaken what Alford has called "exegetical revision."[73] The more likely explanation, however—since he could only have learned to write in *English* by means of such exercises—is that Langland was adapting the grammar of a Latin model, ringing the necessary changes on its forms to fit it into a given syntax, in a manner that had become routine for him in school. Minor as such a change may be in the context of all the English invention in *Piers Plowman*, it may well extend to *all* those cases where Langland's Latin does not resemble the sources we still tend to insist he was quoting, as well as in those many cases where, on the same grounds, we say that Langland is quoting from an "unknown" or "unidentified source."

Grammaticalization of the sort I have been exploring could extend no further than this, as the techniques of the schoolroom have been so thoroughly absorbed to the form of an English poem that that poem is, in effect—if only briefly and sporadically—made in Latin. And the largest payoff for such a discovery in Middle English poetry is a much better explanation for the origins of the phrase "patientes vincunt," a modest phrase to be sure, and yet one that is repeated so often, and with such increasing intensity (because with frequency toward the end of the poem) that it becomes something like an overarching precept for *Piers Plowman* as a whole, one of the most important lessons this pedagogical poem was designed to teach. This phrase is not always embedded in the surrounding English syntax, but it often is, as, for example, when Patience uses it to explain to Haukyn that simple forms of Christian devotion will protect him (here figured as "eating" a piece of the *Paternoster*) "because" such patience overcomes hardship:

> "Have, Haukyn," quod Pacience, "and et this whan the hungreth,
> Or whan thow clomsest for cold or clyngest for drought;
> And shul nevere gyves thee greve ne gret lordes wrathe,
> Prison ne peyne, for *pacientes vincunt*."

["Take this, Haukyn," said Patience, "and eat this when you are hungry, or when you are numb with cold or parched with drought. Fetters will never grieve you nor great lords anger you, neither prison nor pain, because *the patient ones overcome*."]

(B 14.51–4)

---

[73] Alford, *Guide to the Quotations*, 19. Alford documents a wide range of these revisions, pp. 19–20 n. 33.

The phrase is also embedded in the English syntax when Anima uses it to make the point that human suffering imitates Christ's suffering (and is therefore a debt that we owe and must bear willingly for our sins), where it *must* be in the plural since Anima is describing all Christians:

> Ac he suffrede in ensample that we sholde suffren also,
> And seide to swiche that suffer wolde that *Pacientes vincunt.*
> "*Verba gratia,*" quod he—and verray ensamples manye.

[But he suffered to show us that we must also suffer, and said to those who willingly suffer that *the patient ones overcome.* "*For example,*" he said—and many true examples more.]

(B 15.266–8)[74]

As I have already noted, the phrase "patientes vincunt" can be found in the apocryphal Testament of Job, but there is no evidence that Langland knew this text (he does not otherwise quote from it), and not only are there similar phrases in the common school text, the *Distichs of Cato* which Langland might have adapted (for example, "Parentem patientia vince" [overcome your parents with patience]), but the phrase "patientia vincit" was the most common of proverbs.[75] If the transformation of the phrase "redde quod debes" into "reddit quod debet" shows the sort of invention Langland would have had to employ in order to transform "patientia vincit" into "patientes vincunt," it is only concealed from us because Langland never used the proverb in its more familiar form. Rather than assume that Langland was referencing something other than this proverb, we might take more seriously his insistence that this proverb was only meaningful in *Piers Plowman* in the plural: what he wants to say when he

---

[74] Kane and Donaldson emend these lines as follows: "Ac he suffrede in ensample þat we sholde suffren also, / And seide to swiche þat suffre wolde, / *Pacientes Vincunt verbi gracia,* and [verred] ensamples manye" (B 15.266–7). Quality not quantity of the readings in a manuscript tradition matters most of course, but it is still worth noting, I think, that twelve of the seventeen manuscripts on which Kane and Donaldson rely embed this Latin phrase in the English sentence, and arguing in favor of those twelve readings are exactly those habits of style on which Kane and Donaldson say they normally rely in their judgments. That is, the embedding of Latin in an English syntax is one of those "characteristic mannerisms" that make Langland's verse "distinctive." On this criterion see George Kane and E. Talbot Donaldson, "Introduction," 1–220 in William Langland, *Piers Plowman: The B Version,* ed. George Kane and E. Talbot Donaldson, rev. edn. (London: Athlone Press; Berkeley and Los Angeles, CA: University of California Press, 1988, first published 1975), 130.

[75] *The Distichs of Cato* (as *Dicta Catonis*), 585–63 in *Minor Latin Poets,* ed. J. Wight Duff and Arnold M. Duff (Cambridge, MA: Harvard University Press, 1961; first published 1934), pro. This parallel has not, to my knowledge, been noticed before. Chaucer uses the proverb in its common form in The Franklin's Tale where the narrator insists that "pacience ... venquysseth" (V.773–4), although here it is transformed by translation and thereby made into a "vulgar" by the most basic schoolroom procedure. See also Alford, *Guide to the Quotations,* 84.

has Conscience use it the first time (B 13.135a), and then wants to insist upon again and again as he repeats the phrase to describe the ideal form of the active life (B 14.36a, B 14.53, B 15.51–4, B 15.172a), or to describe both Christ's sacrifice (B 15.266–8) and his power (B 15.598), is that "patience" is never an abstraction—some quality or virtue a person can possess—but an activity that not only each person but *all* people must engage in in order to produce a Christian community worthy of the name. To this extent the phrase—enjoining all his readers to become "patient ones"—is the most explicit definition Langland ever gives of what he thinks it is to Do well, Do better, and Do best. And nothing could be more formally appropriate to *Piers Plowman* as a whole, nor more deeply in tune with the spiritual forms that so often preoccupy Langland, than the recasting of a common proverb so that an abstraction takes on human form. This is the form Christ and his sacrifice take in passus 18 (when "Jesus of his gentries wol juste in Piers armes / in his helm and in his haubergeon, *humana natura*" [Jesus in his gentility will joust in Piers's arms, in his helm and mail coat, *human nature*] B 18.22–3) because this is the form of Christ himself, a God who becomes so material, as Langland imagines the transformation in passus 1, that "hevene myghte nat holden it" [heaven might not hold it] (B 1.153) because "it hadde of this fold flessh and blood taken" [it had taken flesh and blood from this earth] (B 1.155). In having made a common Latin phrase so completely his own in this way Langland also retraces in little the general contours of all the grammaticalizations I have been describing, using the most basic grammar-school exercise as a method for formulating his poem's most ardent thought. Such habits of invention make it right to say that, just as in the *Confessio Amantis*, the Latin in *Piers Plowman* is not a supplement but central, not a carapace but a backbone; and just as in so many grammar-school exercises, *Piers Plowman*, just like the *Confessio Amantis*, is a truly macaronic poem, written, just as it was meant to be read, in Latin as well as English.

5

The Basic Reading Texts and Literary Work

The subject of *grammatica* is language, but in the medieval schoolroom such knowledge was acquired, not only in "grammars" or in the exercises in which that knowledge was put to use, but also in the basic reading texts where grammar could be seen in active use. The schoolboy memorized declensions, conjugations, and syntax and wrote his own sentences, but he also relied on that knowledge to understand sentences and sequences of sentences in texts. Surviving schoolbooks suggest that grammar-school students were asked to read almost as soon as they began to learn grammar's rules. Moreover, just as he memorized those rules the schoolboy was clearly asked to memorize what he read as well. Many of these texts were chosen for their simplicity, but, like any active use of language, they immediately plunged the student into difficulties: ambiguities of phrasing, unexpected words and irregular forms, idioms, and gray areas of tone and emphasis. This is clearly why, as I noted at the beginning of this book, Rabanus Maurus defined *grammatica* as a "science," not of grammatical forms and relations, but "of interpretation" [scientia interpretandi].[1] If learning to write proceeded with surprising speed to what Quintilian called a "figure of speech" [figura verborum], reading advanced even more quickly to the abstractions he called a "figure of thought" [figura sententiae].[2]

The first reading text of any length that the schoolboy met was almost certainly the *Distichs of Cato*, not least because it was so easy. Its first two injunctions are two words each: "Deo supplica" [Pray to God] and "Parentes ama" [Love your parents]. After fifty rules of equal pith, the

---

[1] Rabanus Maurus, *De Clericorum Institutione*, III.18 (*Patrologiae cursus completus, series latina*, ed. J.-P. Migne, 221 vols. [Paris, 1844–64], 107, col. 395b): "Grammatica est scientia interpretandi poetas atque historicos, et recte scribendi loquendique ratio." See also p. 3 n. 11 in the introduction to the present volume.

[2] For the distinction see Quintilian, *The Orator's Education*, ed. and trans. Donald A Russell, 5 vols. (Cambridge: MA: Harvard University Press, 2001), 4: 18–19 (IX. i.15–16).

Distichs also moved the schoolboy smartly into longer sentences in verse, the couplets that give the "distichs" their name. Since it retained a certain classical sensibility, these verse sentences also required the Christian schoolboy to come to grips, instantly, with polytheism (e.g. "ask not if the Gods exist" [an di sint... ne quere doceri]) and a decidedly un-Christian ethics (e.g. "do... good to others so that no serious injury befalls you" [Sic bonus esto bonis, ne te mala damna sequantur], *Distichs* I.11). In a similar way, although the fifteen- or twenty-line *Fables* of Avianus could hardly be simpler narratologically, they so often mix animals, natural objects, and deities with people that they immediately asked the schoolboy to negotiate "the relationship between fiction and truth."[3] While the default mode of these stories is to analyze human attitudes by projecting them onto animals—so, for example, a calf demonstrates the callowness of youth when he taunts a toiling ox, unaware that he is himself heading for disaster—the *Fables* gain ethical force by disrupting the very anthropomorphism they otherwise lead a reader to expect.[4] So, for example, in the fable called "De alite et messione" [The bird and the harvest] birds speak and understand human speech, but their worries are avian (they fear the harm a farmer might do to their nest), while, at the same time, the farmer in the story only interacts with other people, twice entrusting the task of reaping to his "friends" [amicis]. Nor is the generic tension between beast fable and morality tale ever resolved, for, when the mother bird finally grows fearful because the farmer realizes he must do the job himself if it is to get done, the story's lesson must be that birds are wiser than humans:

> "Nunc," ait, "o miseri, dilecta relinquite rura,
> cum spem de propriis viribus ille petit."

["Now, "she said," my poor dears, abandon the fields you love so well, now that he seeks the fulfillment of his hopes from his own powers."]

(Avianus, Fables, XIX.13–14)

Although the standard medieval introduction to these *Fables* understood them as either "Libystic" (in which "conversation between men talking to beasts, or beasts talking to men is feigned" [cum hominum cum bestiis vel bestiarum cum hominibus fingitur esse vocis commercium]), or "Aesopic"

---

[3] Vincent Gillespie, "From the Twelfth Century to c.1450," 145–235 in *The Cambridge History of Literary Criticism*, vol. 2: *The Middle Ages*, ed. Alastair Minnis and Ian Johnson (Cambridge: Cambridge University Press, 2005), 155. Gillespie suggests that students had their "first contact... with figurative language" as well as "allegorical interpretation and the relation between fiction and truth" in such texts.

[4] See Avianus, *Fables*, XIX ("De Abiete ac Dumis" [The pine and the bramble bush]) and XXXVI ("De Vitulo et Bove" [The calf and the ox]).

(in which "animals or else inanimate objects, such as trees and the like are feigned talking about themselves" [cum animalia inter se sermocinari finguntur vel quae animata non sunt, ut arbores et similia]), this distinction bears no relation to the complexities of these stories.[5] In fact, any reading of the *Fables* of Avianus, no matter elementary, must call into question immediately what a "fable" [fabula] actually is.

The basic reading texts did not grow progressively more difficult as literacy training advanced toward literary making then; they began in complexity. These complexities and the kinds of training they provided will be the primary focus of this chapter, although the importance of the reading texts turns out to be so great that this shift away from the basic grammars governs all the remaining chapters of this book. Fundamental to such an exploration is a more careful description of the *forms* of the reading texts since it is clear that those forms acted as an implicit set of instructions—precepts in action—showing the schoolboy, even as he learned to read, how a poem or literary prose should be shaped. This description is itself no small task because the presumption that basic literacy training has little to do with sophisticated literary making has also ensured that these texts have almost never been treated by modern criticism as works of literature.[6] And yet it could not be clearer that the major Ricardian poets continued to look to them for definitive models, not only as starting points, but, again and again, for guidance and material. Langland cites the *Distichs of Cato* or its putative author more often than any other authority in his poem.[7] Chaucer makes reference to or quotes directly from all but one of the six texts in the *libri Catoniani*.[8]

---

[5] *Medieval Literary Theory and Criticism, c.1100–c.1375: The Commentary Tradition*, ed. A. J. Minnis and A. B. Scott, with the assistance of David Wallace (Oxford: Clarendon Press, 1988), 16; *Accessus ad auctores; Bernard d'Utrecht; Conrad d'Hirsau*, ed. R. B. C. Huygens (Leiden: E. J. Brill, 1970), 22. As Minnis points out, these categories are drawn from Isidore of Seville, *Etymologiarum sive originum libri XX*, 2 vols., ed. W. M. Lindsay (Oxford: Clarendon Press, 1911), 1.40.2.

[6] Tony Hunt identified this lacuna some decades ago. "Regrettably little has been done to investigate the links between the characteristics of literary production in the Middle Ages and the nature of the reading and exposition which were taking place in the schools," *Teaching and Learning Latin in Thirteenth Century England*, 3 vols. (Woodbridge: D. S. Brewer, 1991), 1: 59.

[7] I also mentioned this crucial fact in Chapter 4. See p. 129 and n. 13.

[8] Many of these citations and uses are explored in this chapter but they are, in sum, citations of the *Distichs of Cato* in The Miller's Tale (I.3227), The Reeve's Tale (I.4321), The Merchant's Tale (IV.1377), The Nun's Priest's Tale (VII.2940), and The Canon's Yeoman's Tale (VIII.688) and three quotations in The Manciple's Tale (IX.327–8, 332–3, and 359–60), a version of a story found in the *Fables* of Avianus in The Wife of Bath's Prologue (III.692), mention of "daun Pseustis," a figure in the *Eclogue* of Theodulus, in *The House of Fame* (1227), a direct quotation from Maximian's *Elegies* in The Pardoner's Tale (VI.728–38), and mention of Claudian's *On the Rape of Proserpina* in The Merchant's Tale

And, in the *Confessio Amantis*, Gower draws the stories of Achilles and Chiron (4.1963–2013) and Achilles and Deidamia (5.2961–3202) from the *Achilleid*, follows Matthew of Vendôme's *Tobias* in describing the chaste marriage of Tobias and Sara (7. 5307–71), and takes the fable of the mouse and the mountain (7. 3553–75) from the elegiac *Romulus*, a collection of fables similar in content and schoolroom use to the *Fables* of Avianus.[9] These direct references demonstrate just how well Ricardian writers remembered these texts, but, as I will also try to make clear in what follows, it is only the most visible part of a knowledge so broad and so deep that it could shape the whole of a poetic form.

The teaching these basic school texts have usually been thought to provide is ethical, what the *Liber cartule* nicely calls a "pattern for living" [vivendi norma] (col. 1312a/p. 63) traced out in stern precepts or by narrative example. This was certainly true in the Middle Ages where the common *accesūs* to the *Distichs of Cato* and the *Fables* of Avianus define the "subject matter" [materia] of the former as "precepts for living a good and moral life" [precepta bene et caste vivendi] and suggest that the "useful-ness" [utilitas] of the latter lies in "the correction of behavior" [correctio morum].[10] The medieval *accessus* to Theodulus's *Eclogue* says that it "pertains to ethics" [ethicae subponitur].[11] For their part, modern histor-ians of the schoolroom have continued to say that these texts imparted the "skills of perspicacity and balance... that were readily transferred... to the complexities of moral decisions to be found in the real world."[12] But scholars have also registered surprise that moral teachings should describe

<hr />

(VI.2232) where Proserpina and Pluto are also speaking characters. For a thorough analysis of all of these passages see Jill Mann, "'He Knew Nat Catoun': Medieval School-Texts and Middle English Literature," 53–65 in *The Text in the Community: Essays on Medieval Works, Manuscripts, Authors and Readers*, ed. Jill Mann and Maura Nolan (Notre Dame, IN: University of Notre Dame, 2006).

[9] See Statius, *Achilleid*, 1.198–960 (for the story of Achilles and Chiron) and 2.110–28 (for the story of Achilles and Deidamia). For the fable of the mouse and the mountain (or of the earth and the mouse, as it is called in this edition) see *L'Esopus attribuito a Gualtero Anglico*, ed. Paola Busdraghi, vol. 10 (2005) in *Favolisti latini medievali e umanistici*, ed. Ferruccio Bertini (Genoa: Università di Genova, Pubblicazioni del Dipartimento di Archeologia, Filologia Classica e Loro Tradizioni, 1984–2005), 98. The elegiac *Romulus* is also widely available in a single-text edition in *The Fables of "Walter of England": edited from Wolfenbüttel, Herzog August Bibliothek, Codex Guelferbytanus 185 Helmstadiensis* ed. Aaron Eugene Wright, (Toronto: Pontifical Institute of Mediaeval Studies, 1997). For the fable, here called "Mons peperit murem" [The mountain gave birth to a mouse], see this edition, 76–7. For Matthew of Vendôme's *Tobias* see the "Note on Texts," p. xiv in the present volume.

[10] *Medieval Literary Theory and Criticism*, ed. Minnis and Scott, 16 (for both the *Distichs* and *Fables*); *Accessus ad auctores*, ed. Huygens, 21 (*Distichs*) and 22 (*Fables*).

[11] *Medieval Literary Theory and Criticism*, ed. Minnis and Scott, 18; *Accessus ad auctores*, ed. Huygens, 27.

[12] Gillespie, "From the Twelfth Century to *c.*1450," 157.

the kinds of erotic adventures that fill the *Elegies* of Maximian or the sexual violence that is a key episode in the *Achilleid* and the central subject of *On the Rape of Proserpina*. Many medieval schoolmasters seem to have shared these reservations since so many schoolbooks replaced the racier texts with more overtly Christian teachings such as the *Liber parabolarum*, *Liber cartule* (sometimes known as the *De contemptu mundi* and attributed to Bernard of Clairvaux) and the *Liber penitencialis*.[13] But the addition of these Christian texts often produced exactly the sorts of complexity in a given syllabus that I have just suggested governed even its most basic texts. If a schoolboy was to fashion his "life" according to the rules or examples set down in his first schoolbooks, his first challenge would have been to figure out what sort of "pattern" they actually traced.

On the other hand, the basic readings provided very clear patterns for *literary* activity, not least because elements in these texts that would provide such training were inevitably reinforced in the schoolboy's life, as a part of a daily pedagogy that was also variously as well as intensely involved in the making of literature. Although we have come to this realization late, there is nothing culturally specific about the tendency for literacy training to glide right over the contents of the texts it purports to teach. As John Guillory's penetrating study of the process has shown, canonical works are almost of necessity bad at teaching their contents because the durability that makes a work canonical also insists that it reach across great cultural change in order to teach successive generations of students.[14] As I have already noted, a teaching that employed as many classical texts as the medieval curriculum did was bound to make ethical recommendations that a medieval instructor would have had to tell his pupils to ignore. As a result, the basic reading texts in the Middle Ages demonstrate the corollary Guillory finds for the surprising ineffectiveness of any literary canon's contents: literature is usually at its most "pedagogic" when it shapes *linguistic* practice.[15] As I will try to make clear in the following pages, this effect was enabled in medieval literacy training by the degree to which the ethics its texts tried to teach took language and its

---

[13] See Hunt, *Teaching and Learning Latin*, 1: 70; Marjorie Curry Woods and Rita Copeland, "Classroom and Confession," 376–406 in *The Cambridge History of Medieval English Literature* (Cambridge: Cambridge University Press, 1999), 380; and John M. Miner, *The Grammar Schools of Medieval England: A. F. Leach in Historiographical Perspective* (Montreal & Kingston: McGill-Queen's University Press, 1990), 172–3. In Jill Mann's view, the new texts in the grammar-school curriculum "followed the old model," often recasting a set of concerns in a different form, but still fulfilling "similar functions to the originals," "'He Knew Nat Catoun,'" 51.

[14] John Guillory, *Cultural Capital: The Problem of Literary Canon Formation* (Chicago, IL: University of Chicago Press, 1993), 63.

[15] Guillory, *Cultural Capital*, 62.

proper use as a central topic. It helped that these texts often set out their ethics by means of literary devices that foregrounded language use ("quotations" of other texts, "writings" that had to be read, "speech" that had to be carefully interpreted). But the patterns these texts most strongly recommended cannot be summarized or even grasped by a paraphrase of their contents because they consisted *of* the forms of these texts both individually and in aggregate. The medieval schoolboy learned those forms—and how to retrace them—not only as he read these texts again and again, but as the similarities between them proposed their shapes as normative for poetry.

THE FORMS OF THE TEXTS

The first step in characterizing the kinds of guidance these texts provided for a poet, then, is a careful characterization of their forms. On the few occasions when they have been seen as providing some literary training those forms have usually been seen as various, providing a tour for the schoolboy through the "genres of poetry" as well as a "graded series of relatively short texts of increasing narrative complexity" which he might imitate progressively as the "building blocks" for his first compositions.[16] In this view, these texts provide lessons in the writing of aphorisms or epigrams (the *Distichs* and the *Liber parabolarum*), simple narratives (the *Fables* of Avianus), debate (the *Eclogue* of Theodulus), elegy (Maximanus), epic (the *Achillead*), and tragedy (*On the Rape of Proserpina*). But as important as their variety must have been to the formal training these texts provided were their similarities. Taken together, they could be said to converge on only two genres, collections of precepts (the *Distichs of Cato*, the *Liber parabolarum*, the *Facetus* ["cum [est] nihil utilius"], the *Peniteas cito*, and the *Liber cartule*) and narratives (the *Fables* of Avianus, the *Eclogue* of Theodulus, the *Achilleid*, *On the Rape of Proserpina*). If we were willing to recognize "pedagogy" as a genre of text, these texts could even be said to converge on a *single* form since so many of them take shape as scenes of instruction. The immediacy of these scenes must have made their form compelling in much the way that form of grammatical teaching was made compelling by the absorption of schoolroom postures and activities to the grammars. But this generic convergence seems to have acted most of all as a mode of emphasis, ensuring that the reading of each

---

[16] Nicholas Orme, *Medieval Schools: From Roman Britain to Medieval England* (New Haven, CT: Yale University Press, 2006), 100 ("genres"); Woods and Copeland, "Classroom and Confession," 381 ("building blocks") and 384 ("graded series").

of these texts together and in succession amounted to so many repetitions of a single formal imperative.

The shape of this imperative is clearest in the *Distichs of Cato* which, as one of the oldest of the reading texts, must have acted as a formal model for some of the later ones. It begins with a gesture that converts the whole of the rest of the text into knowledge conveyed from a teacher to a student, domesticated slightly in the form of address, so that the student becomes the teacher's "son":

> Nunc te, fili karissime, docebo quo pacto morem animi tui componas.

> [Now I will teach you dearest son, how to fashion a system for your mind.]

> (Prologue [unlineated prose])

Although the *Liber parabolarum* has no such introduction, its precepts are converted into a teaching in its penultimate stanza, where an aside makes clear that they have all been addressed to a "pitiable boy" [miserandus puer] (line 619/p. 174). Although the *Facetus* does not address its precepts to some student at the start, it effectively makes the prologue of the *Distichs* its own by presenting its instruction as an extension of "Cato's":

> Quod minus exsequitur morosum dogma Catonis,
> supplebo pro posse meo monitu rationis.

> [I shall furnish what the teaching of the wise Cato did not address, as far as I can through the counsel of reason.]

> (*Facetus* 2/p. 43)

As these precepts unfold, a number of asides make clear that they too are addressed to a boy ("learn my boy" [disce puer], 171 and 185).[17] The *Liber cartule* offers its precepts to a "brother" [frater] rather than boy, but as an education in a "life" [vita] that "would please Christ" [ut placeas Christo], it also unfolds as a set of elementary instructions (1304b/p. 58). The lessons of the *Liber penitencialis* are focused throughout on confession and therefore seems to reproduce an exchange between a priest and some penitent ("Sinner, you ought to quickly repent so that the Judge may be merciful" [Peniteas cito peccator cum sit miserator iudex] (lines 2–3/p. 116) but this text also guides by means of stern rules that give the priest the role of teacher and position the "sinner" as his student ("Omnia peccata plangat contritio vera" [True contrition should lament every sin] (14/p. 118).[18]

Although they never describe a grammar school or its students, the narrative texts among these basic readings also tend to unfold as scenes of

---

[17] Pepin does not translate these two precepts.

[18] Woods and Copeland have noted how "pedagogical texts and classroom practices have their natural counterparts in confessional texts and practices," not least as "the confessional operates in the manner of the classroom," "Classroom and Confession," 376–7.

instruction by making teaching central to the stories they tell. The *Tobias* is in many ways about the way a man reproduces himself in his son (both are fittingly named Tobias) by teaching him virtue ("Nate, precor, mea iussa libens intellige: patris / Expedit in factum fructifare preces" [Son, listen willingly to my commands, I pray; It is expedient / That the prayers of your father bear fruit in deeds] [lines 515–16/p. 98]), and the instruction the elder Tobias provides is so lengthy that it transforms this narrative, for a large proportion of its lines, into a collection of precepts for which that narrative is but a frame.[19] A large number of the *Fables* of Avianus describe teaching too: I have already mentioned the narrative in which the bird teaches her chicks the importance of self-reliance (XXI, "De alite et messione"), but there is also a crab instructed by its mother (III, "De cancro et matre eius" [The crab and its mother]), an assembly of gods "taught" [docuit] by Phoebus (line 15 in IV, "De vento et sole" [The wind and the sun]), a farmer teaching a donkey (V, "De asino pelle leonis induto" [The donkey and the lion's skin]), a vixen who "disclosed the futility of giving credence to words" [verborum vacuam prodidit esse fidem] (line 10 in VI, "De rana et vulpe" [The frog and the fox]), an older dog "warning" [monens] a younger dog (line 14 in VII, "De cane qui noluit latrare" [The dog that would not bark]), Jupiter teaching a camel (VIII, "De camelo et Iove" [The camel and Jupter]), a bear who "warned" [monuit] a traveler (IX, "De Duobus sociis et ursa" [The two companions and the bear]), Fortune admonishing [admonet] a peasant (line 8 in XII, "De rustico et thesauro" [The peasant and the treasure]), an ox who says that others may "learn" [discere] from the nature of his death (line 16 in XVIII, "De quattuor iuvencis et leone" [The four oxen and the lion]), a lion teaching a hunter the role of perspective in art (XXIV, "De venatore et leone" [The hunter and the lion]), a mouse commanding an ox to "learn" [disce] (line 11 in XXXI, "De mure et bove" [The mouse and the ox]), a ploughman commanding an oxen to "learn" [disce] (line 11 in XXXII, "De aratore et bobus" [The ploughman and his oxen]), an ant teaching a grasshopper (XXXIV, "De formica et cicada" [The ant and the grasshopper]), a lion teaching a pampered dog the value of independence (XXXVII, "De cane et leone" [The dog and the lion]), and a fox who commends the value of "counsel" [consilium] over "bodily charms" [corporeis bonis] (lines 10 and 12 in XL, "De pardo et vulpe" [The leopard and the fox]). Even the

---

[19] In a further merging of reproduction and instruction these precepts are also said to produce a man so exemplary that his virtues are themselves a "teaching" for others ("Exemplo legitur doctrina: quod edocet, actu / Consolidat mentis expositiva manus" [teaching is seen in his example; what he teaches, his hand, acting as a gloss for his mind, confirms in action]) (lines 101–2/p. 86).

Achilleid, epic in conception, and meant to describe the whole of the life of Achilles, focuses on the hero's youth when he is not yet a warrior, but a "pupil" [alumnus] in the book and a half read in medieval classrooms (Statius, *Achilleid,* 1.118). The central episode of this text as it stands is therefore devoted, not to Achilles's martial triumphs, but to his relationship with his tutor, Chiron, often described in the most emotional terms:

> ... saxo collabitur ingens
> Centaurus blandusque umeris se innectit Achilles,
> quamquam ibi fida parens, assuetaque pectora mavult.

[The huge centaur [Chiron] collapses on stone and Achilles fondly twines himself about his shoulders, though his faithful mother is there, preferring the familiar bosom.]

(Statius, *Achilleid,* 1.195–7)

Much of the activity in the text seems, on its face, anything but instructional, particularly a long episode in which Achilles is dressed as a woman (with his appearance magically altered by Thetis), but that episode concludes when Achilles betrays his disguise by showing inordinate interest in a spear and a shield, and it is, therefore, in sum, an elaborate procedure for teaching Achilles about his "true" warrior nature ("Then, ay, then, above all is Achilles manifest" [tunc vero, tunc praecipue manifestus Achilles], l.835).

Set alongside reading texts as overtly and generally pedagogical as those I have just described, texts with strong generic affiliations of a very different kind can seem to bend those genres to the purposes of elementary instruction. We might be inclined to describe the *Eclogue* of Theodulus as a pastoral in which a boy and girl sublimate sexual tension in the "game" [ludus] of "debate" [lis] or as an allegory in which the verbal "arts" [artes] of the shepherdess Alithia, who represents Christian "truth," prevail over those of the shepherd Pseustis, who represents the "falsehood" of classical mythology, in the judgment of "mother Phronesis" [mater Fronesis] who represents "understanding."[20] But we could also say that both pastoral and allegory not only convene a scene of instruction in which two students— one good, the other errant—demonstrate their learning before a tutelary figure, but a scene in which this teacher sets each student the task of making verse ("in your series let there be four songs" [sit tetras in ordine vestro]) (29/p. 35) and then sits "in judgment" [pro iudice] on the quality of such arts. In even more subtle ways the nostalgia of the *Elegies* of Maximian creates a schoolroom scene by conjuring up something like

---

[20] Theodulus, *Eclogue,* lines 29 ("ludus"), 33 ("lis"), and 325 ("artes"). I have altered Pepin's translation here (Pepin has "sport" for "game" [p. 28], "contest" for "debate" [p. 29], and "skills" for "arts" [p. 40]).

the subject position of the schoolboy. This form travels with some stealth beneath an eroticism vivid enough to include detailed memories of love affairs,

> dum licuit, votum tacite compressimus ambo
>   et varia dulces teximus arte dolos.
> at postquam teneram rupit verecundia frontem
>   nec valuit penitus flamma recepta tegi.
>
> [While we could we suppressed our love in silence
> And wove with varied art sweet stratagems.
> But after our shyness burst its tender cover
> And the flame that burned within could not be concealed.]
>
> (Maximian, *Elegies*, III.21–24)

and sensational enough to conclude with a paean to the penis ("Penis, the busy provider of festive days, / Once the delight of my heart and a treasure to me" [mentula, festorum cultrix operosa dierum, / quondam deliciae divitiaeque meae] [V.87–8]). But, since these "elegies" lament a misspent youth from the perspective of age they everywhere imply a set of recommendations—they are, in effect, a set of implicit precepts—for a young boy like Maximian once was ("I cannot do what I was unable not to want" [nec quod non possum, non voluisse meum est]) (Maximian, *Elegies*, IV.54). Because the older voice is always reminiscing, these recommendations always inhabit the perspective of that boy:

> has inter virtutis opes tolerantia rerum
>   spernebat cunctas insuperata minas:
> vertice nudato ventos pluviasque ferebam,
>   non mihi solstitium, non grave frigus erat:
>
> [My patience, unconquered amid these resources of virtue,
> Scorned all the menacing crises of daily life.
> Bareheaded I bore the assaults of wind and rain.
> Neither the heat nor the cold was oppressive to me.]
>
> (Maximian, *Elegies*, I.33–6)

As accounts of love affairs take their place alongside such "patience" the text provides an ethics of redemption in which dissolution is always redeemed by later (or greater) virtue—what the *Elegies* neatly describe as "an alternate grace" [decus alternum] (I.32) Since this ethics is so regularly rotated into the subject position of Maximian's younger self, the more sensational details of Maximian's errors are finally in the service of the vivacity that is this ethics' most memorable and pertinent quality, a set of recommendations made compelling by the extent to which they seem to have been discovered from the perspective of the sort of boy to whom they are being made.

Such texts, like all the standard elements of the canon of basic reading texts, could even be described as extraordinarily unimaginative, both initially and then repeatedly, since the quality that seems to have marked them out for inclusion in that canon was the degree to which they each seemed to represent the classroom in which they were to be used. A text's pedagogical form was therefore much more important than anything that text taught. But contents could matter where they too were representational, and texts were clearly also chosen with an eye to the ways—and the extent to which—the ethics they tried to teach also reflected back activities and habits common in the grammar-school classroom:

> Read books [Libros lege] (*Distichs*, pro. 26).
>
> Come then and learn and, as you read, learn what wisdom is [ergo ades et quae sit sapientia disce legendo] (*Distichs*, II.pro).
>
> Fail not to learn; equip your mind with rules [Instrue praeceptis animum, ne discere cessa] (*Distichs*, III.1).
>
> Read much [Multa legas] (*Distichs*, III.18).
>
> At school you sometimes suffer the teacher's blows [Verbera cum tuleris discens aliquando magistri] (*Distichs*, IV.6).
>
> Learn something [Disce aliquid] (*Distichs*, IV.19).
>
> Fail not to learn [Discere ne cessa] (*Distichs*, IV.27).
>
> Thus a good mind keeps what has been learned, and a dull one spills it [sic audita tenet mens bona, fundit hebes] (*Liber parabolarum*, line 80 [p. 155]).
>
> Thus, if you want to retain the lessons of your teacher, / Call to mind often what you received once by ear [sic, documenta tui si vis retinere magistri, / sepe recorderis quod semel aure capis] (*Liber parabolarum*, lines 167–8 [p. 159]).
>
> Learning does not present itself to our minds in just one way [non uno doctrina modo se mentibus infert] (*Liber parabolarum*, line 303 [p. 163]).

The representation of the classroom could also amount to little more than the ventriloquizing of the teacher's voice, as in these examples from the *Distichs* and the *Liber parabolarum*, in which it is as if the basic reading text absorbed the injunctions a schoolmaster could often be heard to give. But such representation could also stand at some remove from schoolroom activities and, rather than record them, to observe or reflect upon them:

> One man can offer draughts of learning to many [prebere potest... pocula doctrine pluribus unus homo] (*Liber parabolarum*, lines 25–6/p. 153).
>
> A teacher's doctrine enters hearts through little ears [corda per auriculas dogma docentis init] (*Liber parabolarum*, line 56/p. 154).
>
> The rod compels the boy to find time for study [cogit... / puerum studio virga vacare suo] (*Liber parabolarum*, lines 65–6/p. 154).

From a small boy there often comes a skilled man [de parvo puero sepe peritus homo] (*Liber parabolarum*, line 82/p. 155).

Now it pleases us to teach before we have learned [ante docere modo quam didicisse iuvat] (*Liber parabolarum*, line 160/p. 158).

Those who frequent schools everywhere do not learn. / For many come so that they might be seen there [non discunt quicumque scholas ubicumque frequentant, / nam plures veniunt ut videantur ibi] (*Liber parabolarum*, lines 373–4/p. 166).

Thus, while he is a boy, let a man be taught to keep the right [sic homo dum puer est doceatur recta tenere] (*Liber parabolarum*, line 589/p. 173).

This ventriloquism could also take the more complicated form I have just described in Maximian's *Elegies* in which instructions move into the perspective of the boy who is then asked to learn from an adult's youthful errors. This is particularly true when a single injunction moves all the way from youth to age ("why is a man twice a boy when he ought to be once" [cur homo bis puer est, quem licet esse semel], *Liber parabolarum*, line 376/ p. 166), or when a boy is asked to take an adult's perspective or feelings into consideration:

Love both your parents equally: To please your father never wound your mother [Aequa diligito caros pietate parentes, / nec matrem offendas, dum vis bonus esse parenti] (*Distichs*, III.24).

Don't strain against a father's angry words [fer patris imperium, cum verbis exit in iram] (*Distichs*, IV.6).

So while a youth has time suited for sweat, let him seek how he can enjoy weary old age [sic iuvenis, dum tempus habet sudoribus aptum, querat quo possit lassa senecta frui] (*Liber parabolarum*, lines 151–2/p. 158).

Such representation also occurs when the instructions of a text seem to address the whole of a class, not just the schoolboy but his "kin" [cognati] (*Distichs*, I.pro. 3), "partner" [socius] (*Distichs* IV.15), "comrade" [sodalis] (*Distichs* II.22), or "friend" [amicus] (*Distichs* I.23, I.26, I.34, I.40, II.1, IV.13, IV.41, IV.47), as if it were not only teaching a boy, but, also, the boy sitting right next to him.

The intimacy of these absorptions of the classroom's activities and subjects, like the pedagogical forms that produce them, were underscored by the extent to which the lessons these texts taught so frequently circled back to grammar-school subjects, to language and the nature of speech. Thus, the *Distichs* would doubtless have seemed to its schoolroom readers overwhelmingly concerned with how to "rule the tongue" [compescere linguam] (*Distichs*, I.3), "tattling" [rumores] (*Distichs*, I.12), "what folk do or say" [multorum dicta] (*Distichs*, I.16), "whispering" [tacitus sermo]

(*Distichs*, I.17), "talk" [dici] (*Distichs*, I.17), "flattery" [sermo blandus] (*Distichs*, I.27), "words" [verba] (*Distichs* II.11), "bitter words" [maledicta] (*Distichs*, II.15), "those who talk excessively" [qui multa loquuntur] (*Distichs*, II.20), "the comment of the wicked" [verba malorum] (*Distichs*, III.2), "softly whispered flatteries" [sermones blandi blaesi] (*Distichs*, III.4), "another's word" [alterius dictum] (*Distichs*, III.7), "counsel" [consilium] (*Distichs*, III.10), "meal time talk" [inter convivas sermo] (*Distichs*, III.19), "talk of men" [sermo hominum] (*Distichs*, IV.20), or, again, "words" [verba] (*Distichs*, III.20). The *Fables* of Avianus return with equal insistence, not only to "what is said" [dictum] (I.15), "speech" [vox] (XVII.14)/[sermo] (XXXI.7), "speaking" [loqui] (XVII.13), and "words" [verba] (XXIV.10), but also to the relationship between language and truth—the "untruthful tongue" [perfida lingua] (II.8), "the futility of giving credence to words" [verborum vacuam esse fidem] (VI.10), "fallacious words" [verba fallacia] (XVIII.17) versus "credible words" [vox credita] (XXI.5), "deceitful blubbering" [supervacui rictus] (XXV.2), "correct" [recta] versus "suspect" [suspecta] "words" [verba] (XXVI.11–12), "falsehoods" [vana mendacia] and "affected language" [laborata dicta] (XXXVIII.7)—as well as the quality of utterances, whether speech is "imitated" [imitatum] (V.17), "insulting" [insultans] (XV.10), or "reluctant" [piger] (XXXII.11). Although it is hardly surprising that a guide to confession should focus on the nature of what is said to a confessor, in the context of the schoolroom canon the extent to which the *Liber penitencialis* insisted that a penitent's speech should be "true" [vera], "complete" [integra], "clean" [munda], "quick" [cita], "firm" [firma], "often" [frequens], "humble" [humilis], "spontaneous" [spontanea], and "unadorned" [nuda] (lines 21–2) would have made this text seem to be, above all, yet another rigorous analysis of language.

When the basic reading texts look beyond the boundaries of the schoolroom, their gaze is very narrow in social terms, focusing on marriage above all, as if this were the one relationship all schoolboys would need to understand. This seems odd if the presumption is that basic literacy training often prepared boys for careers in the church, and yet the real object of such training must have been the schoolboy's emergent sexuality, and the view spread throughout these texts is that marriage is the only appropriate social field in which to channel such desire. That channeling is often basic and practical. For example, there are some very detailed recommendations about marriage choice ("Do not for dowry's sake espouse a wife" [Uxorem fuge ne ducas sub nomine dotis] (*Distichs*, III.12); "Do not marry the daughter or widow of usurers, robbers, priests, moneylenders, or canons, since to them are given ill-gotten goods which are rightly brought to nothing" [Usuratorum, praedonum, canonicorum, assignatorum nummorum, presbiterorum, natam vel viduam ducas non, his quia dantur res male quaesitae, quae iustis adnihilantur] (*Facetus*, 63/ p. 45)). There are also rules for how the schoolboy should conduct himself in marriage, although, as so often in medieval accounts of this kind, misogyny is part of the point of such counsel:

> When you have a wife, do not trouble yourself over possessions and fame [Cum coniunx tibi sit, ne res et fama laboret] (*Distichs*, IV.47).
>
> Do not make known your secrets to your wife; whatever you do
> From this life's hazards can arise for you [Quicquid agis, ne pande tuae secreta maritae, unde tibi possunt nasci discrimina vitae] (*Facetus*, 65/p. 46).
>
> If you have a wife always ready to obey, let your grateful good will honor, respect, and love her [Si tibi sit coniunx semper parere parata, excolat hanc, veneretur eam tua gratia grata] (*Facetus*, 100/p. 46).
>
> If you have a wife who is rebellious in word and deed, you should reject her according to the law lest you be condemned with her [Si nequam tibi sit linguaque manuque rebellis, ne secum damnaris, eam de iure repellis] (*Facetus*, 101/p. 47).

In the narrative texts, marriage is often equated with rescue from youthful error, as if "the consummate joy of marriage" [coniugii gratia summa] (Maximian, *Elegies*, V.114) was the most appropriate reward for a well-lived life. Misogyny rears its head here as well, since this error often takes the form of rape, although sexual violence is always understood in these texts as a wrong that must be redressed.[21] In the *Achilleid*, for example, the young Achilles satisfies "his desire by force" [vi potitur, I.642] but Statius is clear that the action is "monstrous" [tantis monstris, I.662] and that, by such actions, Achilles courts "cruel punishment" [acerbas poenas, I.666–7]. Claudian's *On the Rape of Proserpina* suggests that a happy marriage may follow such violence ("Joy fills the gray land, the buried throng holds high festival, and the ghosts sport them at the nuptial feast" [Pallida laetatur regio gentesque sepultae / luxuriant epulisque vacant genialibus umbrae], II.326–7), but it also represents sexual violence with metaphorical precision as an unheard cry ("Proserpine is borne away in the winged car, her hair streaming before the wind, beating her arms in lamentation, and calling in vain remonstrance to the clouds" [volucri

---

[21] Marjorie Curry Woods has studied "the long-standing schoolroom tradition of teaching texts describing rape" and argued that they provided a way of exorcising the anxieties produced by discipline as such, providing imaginative opportunities in which "those who control the boy" were transformed into "those whom he might be able to control," "Rape and the Pedagogical Rhetoric of Sexual Violence," 56–86 in *Criticism and Dissent in the Middle Ages*, ed. Rita Copeland (Cambridge: Cambridge University Press, 1996), 60 ("long-standing") and 69 ("those whom").

fertur Proserpina curru / caesariem diffusa Noto planctuque lacertos / verberat et questus ad nubila tendit inanes], II.242–4), and it sees the happiness of the subsequent marriage as a function, not of Proserpina's subjection, but of Pluto's newfound subservience ("Whatever you wish will be done" [sitque ratum quodcumque voles], II.306). Proserpina's plight would have been particularly easy for a schoolboy to compassionate, since Pluto's actions are shown to be horrifying because they separate parent from child ("Give her back" [reddite], II.364) is Ceres's mordant cry), just as the schoolboy would have been separated from his parents either in general or on a daily basis.[22] The tendency of these texts to ask schoolboys to identify with a victimized women would have been further encouraged by their tendency to insist, even in the context of their misogyny, that it was important to treat women well ("Never say bad things about the female sex, but respect whatever woman you see as much as you can" [Femineo nunquam de sexu prava loquaris, / sed, quacumque vides, pro posse tuo verearis], *Facetus*, 99/p. 46]). This general fearfulness of women also meant, of course, that marriage was sometimes understood as a sublimation rather than an expression of sexuality. The marriage most celebrated in the *Tobias* is successful because it is for the purpose of reproduction, not sex:

> Non incentivo Veneris, sed prolis amore
> Uxoratur, amat fructifare Deo.
>
> [Not by the inducement of Venus does he take a wife, but
> For love of offspring; he loves to be fruitful for God].
>
> (Matthew of Vendôme, *Tobias*, lines 121–2/p. 86)

Such a marriage ensures that the husband is "dutiful" [pius] because his wife is, for all intents and purposes, "chaste" [casta] (lines 1231–2/p. 119).

Taken together these reading texts must have seemed especially appropriate for the grammar school because they seem to be *about* nothing so much as the grammar-school boy, piecing out the pattern of his life as if they were a single text whose defining formal principal was the treatment of this one subject from a variety of angles. It is a significant attribute of this aggregated form that it had no maker, since those who wrote each of its texts, however much they might have thought of a schoolboy audience, did not set out to write a text for a canon that included the others. The agent of this making was the collectivity of schoolmasters whose decisions

---

[22] "The school that separated boys from their mothers physically and linguistically could also preserve the figure, and emotions, of precisely those its students were forced to leave behind," Lynn Enterline, *Shakespeare's Schoolroom: Rhetoric, Discipline, Emotion* (Philadelphia, PA: University of Pennsylvania Press, 2012), 139.

converged on these resources. The result was a form produced by a social practice that tended to reproduce that practice in the classrooms in which it was used. Such reproduction is what we usually describe as "teaching" of course, but it is worth putting it in such schematic terms in this instance since it helps to make clear that it was as much the form of this teaching as its content that the grammar-school student was taught. For the same reason, just as each of the similar texts in the canon converged on a formal model for the schoolboy, the whole of the canon became the most influential form of all. What that form finally taught best was not how to reproduce each of the similar forms that constituted it, but, rather, how to reproduce the *canon* by piecing together a form out of variegated parts.

THE POETRY OF PATCHWORK

In the *De praescriptione haereticorum* Tertullian (160–225) identified the *cento* as a poem "patched together into one piece from many verses drawn together... from the works of Homer."[23] A variety of canonical poets replaced Homer as the source of material for this antique compositional practice, and that development seems to have culminated in the fourth century with Ausonius's *Cento Nuptialis*, which repurposes lines of Virgil to describe a wedding and its consummation, and Proba's *Cento Vergilianus de laudibus Christi*, which uses lines of Virgil to construct a scriptural history.[24] The terminology used to describe these forms is barely metaphorical since the Latin word *cento* referred, at root, to a garment sewed together out of disparate pieces, and therefore always kept in view that the

---

[23] Tertullian, *De praescriptione haereticorum*, Brepols Library of Latin Texts (Turnhout: Brepols, 2010), cap. 39, l. 4: "Homerocentones etiam uocari solent qui de carminibus homeri propria opera more centonario ex multis hinc inde compositis in unum sarciunt corpus." On the foundations of *cento* as a form see Scott McGill, *Virgil Recomposed: The Mythological and Secular Centos in Antiquity* (Oxford: Oxford University Press, 2005), esp. 1–30. On the relationship of the technique of *cento* to other sorts of quotation in the Middle Ages, particularly of the troubadours, see Sarah Kay, *Parrots and Nightingales: Troubadour Quotations and the Development of European Poetry* (Philadelphia, PA: University of Pennsylvania Press, 2013), 1 (and see, also, her whole introduction, 1–23 on the varieties and functions of medieval quotation). For a helpful history of the *cento* in relation to a Ricardian poet see R. F. Yeager, "Did Gower Write Cento?" 113–32 in *John Gower: Recent Readings* (Kalamazoo, MI: Western Michigan University, 1989), 113–14.

[24] Isidore mentions Proba when expanding Tertullian's definition so that *cento* may be assembled from the works of Virgil: "Centones apud Grammaticos uocari solent, qui de carminibus Homeri seu Vergilii ad propria opera more centonario ex multis hinc inde conpositis in unum sarciunt corpus, ad facultatem cuiusque materiam," *Etymologiarum siue originum libri XX*, ed. W. M. Lindsay, 2 vols. (Oxford: Oxford University Press, 1971), Book 1, cap. 39, par. 25.

whole of this form, its body or "corpus" (in Tertullian's phrasing), was comprised of separable parts.[25] The bravura of such a form lies in the way scraps that have a meaningful function in one whole are given new meaning when brought together in another. Proba's *Cento Vergilianus* gives such refashioning doctrinal purpose when she takes lines that tell a pagan story and makes them yield scriptural truths. But the process need not always be so complete in its repurposing nor so comprehensive in its piecing together of parts. While many of the poems in the grammar-school syllabus were not *cento* on the whole, they can be described as *cento-like*, since their forms are often defined by the scraps taken from canonical poems that are then pieced together with newer material. Sometimes this sort of patchwork dramatically repurposes these scraps, as, for example, when the resonant words Lucan uses to describe Caesar's power in the *De Bello Civili*—"Caesar was everything" [omnia Caesar erat]—becomes an exemplary instance of human transience in the *Liber parabolarum*:[26]

> Omnia Cesar erat, sed gloria Cesar esse
> desiit et tumulus vix erat octo pedum.
>
> [Caesar was everything, but Caesar's glory ceased to be,
> And his tomb was scarcely eight feet high.]
>
> (Alain of Lille, *Liber parabolarum*, lines 109–10/p. 156)

Most commonly, however, school texts re-used memorable phrases from canonical literature, not as quotations, but for the precision of their metaphor as, for example, when the "anchor's bite" [ancora morsu] said to keep a ship in port in Book 1 of the *Aeneid* becomes the way that "hope" [spes] anchors someone "in purpose" [in proposito], in the *Liber parabolarum* (line 38/p. 153).[27] The *Fables* of Avianus are full of similarly apt "reminiscences of Virgil and . . . Ovid," as is the *Eclogue* of Theodulus, which takes many phrases from Lucan, Statius, Calpurnius, and Claudian.[28] Since such scraps were taken from texts the grammar-school boy, almost by definition, had had no opportunity to read, such references and allusions would have been

[25] Charlton T. Lewis and Charles Short, *A Latin Dictionary* (Oxford: Clarendon Press, 1993; first published 1879), s.v. "*cento, onis* m."

[26] Lucan, *De Bello Civili* (or the *Pharsalia*) in *Lucan*, ed. and trans. J. D. Duff (Cambridge, MA: Harvard University Press, 1962), III.108 (p. 122). The reference is noted by Limone in *Liber parabolarum*, n. to l. 109.

[27] Virgil, *Aeneid*, 261–597, in *Eclogues, Georgics, Aeneid, 1–6*, ed. and trans. H. Ruston Fairclough, rev. G. P. Goold (Cambridge, MA: Harvard University Press, 1999; first published 1916), Book I, line 169. This parallel is also noted by Limone (in *Liber parabolarum* n. to l. 38).

[28] Gillespie, "From the Twelfth Century to c.1450," 155; R. P. H. Green, "The Genesis of a Medieval Textbook: The Models and Sources of the *Ecloga Theoduli*," *Viator* 13 (1982): 49–106 (esp. 105).

invisible to him. But, since the schoolboy also tended to acquire his reading texts permanently—committing them to memory as he learned them— these reminiscences would have become increasingly visible to him, the more he read.

The basic reading texts would also have seemed *cento*-like to the schoolboy too because they converge on a single form by bringing together precept and narrative in different proportions. For example, texts that are primarily preceptive such as the *Distichs of Cato* and the *Facetus* ("cum [est] nihil utilius"), which consist on the whole of a sequence of injunctions about how to live well, orient those injunctions with a scrap of narrative that emplots them as if they are being uttered by characters (a teacher issuing commands and a student learning them) in a setting (in which teaching is occurring). Conversely, each of the narratives in the *Fables* of Avianus is presented as the illustration or proof of a precept that is made part of that story. Stanza by stanza, the *Eclogue* of Theodulus summarizes a classical story or a book of Scripture in four lines, but, as the following summary of a central episode in the Book of Joshua makes clear, each one of these narratives is exemplary and tends to gather itself into a preceptive conclusion:

> Victrici populo ne quondam vivida bello
> Deficeret virtus Gabaon ad proelia, Phoebus
> Imperio Josuae stabat defixus in arce:
> Quae sanctae fidei sint praemia, discite cuncti.
>
> [Lest the once-vigorous strength in war should fail
> A victorious people at the battle of Gibaon, the sun
> Stood motionless on high at the command of Joshua.
> Learn, All, what the rewards of holy faith are.]
>
> (Theodulus, *Eclogue*, 169–72/p. 34)

In ways that I have already touched upon, the *Tobias* is effectively a narrative that creates both a reason and a scene for the precept collection it frames. The *Elegies* of Maximian lament a past time through retrospective narration ("I was a speaker renowned throughout the world" [orator toto clarus in orbe fui], I.10) but these stories are intermixed with maxims about the relationship between youth and age ("The boy delights in games, old age in sternness" [exultat levitate puer, gravitate senectus], I.105). The *Liber penitencialis* constructs a confessional scene and narrates the proper conduct of confession, but it also proceeds in the preceptive manner of the incipit that gives the poem its name ("repent quickly") unfolding as a collection of rules about how confession should occur ("True contrition should lament every sin, / examining the age, feelings, location, time, each part" [omnia peccata plangat contritio vero / Scrutans etates, sensus, loca, tempora, membra], lines 14–15).

An obvious and direct consequence of such formal interweaving is that these texts signify by means of this patchwork, making meaning by the manner in which precept and narrative are combined. This method is most schematically illustrated in the *Fables* of Avianus where the precept often arrives as a summary of the preceding narrative's lesson ("this teaches us..." [haec nos dicta monent...] [XVI.19] or "this is applicable to those who..." [convenit hoc illis quibus...] [XXIII.13]), but these stories often suggest that it is their events that are most instructive, a lesson absorbed *to* a narrative rather than a retrospective interpretation of it. So the precept may come at the end of the fable, not in some authorial voice, but as the utterance of one of the fable's characters:

> tunc victor docuit praesentia numina Titan,
> nullum praemissis vincere posse minis.

[Then in his triumph the Titan taught the assembled gods that no one can win victory by an advance guard of threats.]
(Avianus, *Fables*, IV.15–16)[29]

On other occasions what a figure in a story says calls attention to the way a story's action teaches a lesson. Here, for example, a young crab provides a version of the injunction to "judge not (lest you be judged)" by noticing that his mother has rebuked him for walking in exactly the same way she has:

> nam stultum nimis est, cum tu pravissima temptes,
> alterius censor si vitiosa notes.

[For it is exceedingly foolish of you, when you are attempting the most crooked of courses yourself, to set up as censor and criticize the faults of another.]
(Avianus, *Fables*, III.11–12)

Such absorption of precept to narrative sometimes goes so far that the narrative simply *is* a precept. When a farmer says to a donkey who has tried and failed to disguise himself with a lion's skin, "to me you will always be a donkey as before" [at mihi, qui quondam, semper asellus eris] (Avianus, *Fables*,V.18), for example, he is making the point of the story—that animal nature cannot be changed—by summarizing it.

In the more preceptive texts there is a similar sort of patchwork when a rule or command carries an implied story within it. This is a pervasive formal feature of the *Liber parabolarum*, particularly enabled there by the way its precepts always take the form of "comparisons" [parabolae]. The structure provided the schoolboy with training in the making of

---

[29] For another example see Avianus, *Fables*, XXI.11–12 and XXXII.11–12.

metaphor while also providing a stock of metaphors ripe for repurposing, but, because many of these comparisons relate natural activities or processes to human behaviors, they also form short narratives or sequences of them:

> De nuce fit corilus, de glande fit ardua quercus,
> de parvo puero sepe peritus homo.
>
> [From a nut comes a shrub, from an acorn comes a tall oak;
> From a small boy there often comes a skilled man.]
>
> (Alain of Lille, *Liber parabolarum*, lines 81–2/p. 155)

Some comparisons are themselves stories in which the similarity in a sequence of events becomes the point of contact between the natural world and the human:

> A Phoebo Phebe lumen capit, a sapiente
> insipiens sensum quo quasi luce micat.
>
> [The moon takes her brightness from the sun, and from a wise man
> The fool takes an opinion by which he shines as if by a light.]
>
> (Alain of Lille, *Liber parabolarum*, lines 1–2/p. 152)

Such narrative shapes also grow in length, since each successive section of the poem contains stanzas two lines longer than the section before (so the second section has four line stanzas, the third has six line stanzas, and so on, until the sixth and last section has twelve). Sometimes this growth is by multiplication (with more short narratives, or implied narratives) in a given stanza (a hare is hard to catch *and* an eel slips away easily so friends slip away unless you look after them) (lines 271–6/p. 162), but this expansion also provides room enough for some of these maxims to bloom into something like a short fable:

> Cum curvare potes vel curvam tendere virgam,
> Faxis ut ad libitum stet tua planta tuum,
> cum vetus in magnum fuerit solidata vigorem
> non leviter flectes imperiale caput;
> rursus si tortam patieris surgere primum,
> semper ut est primo torta manebit ea;
> sic homo dum puer est doceatur recte tenere
> ne cor consuetis imbuet ille malis.
>
> [While it is possible to train or to bend a curved twig,
> Do so, in order that your shoot might stand to your liking.
> When the old tree has grown firm in its great strength,
> You will not easily bend its stately head.
> Again, if you first allow a shoot to grow twisted, it will
> Always remain twisted as it is at first.

Thus, while he is a boy, let a man be taught to keep the right,
And let him not stain his heart with habitual evils.]
(Alain of Lille, *Liber parabolarum*, lines 583–90/p. 173)

So thoroughly do the scraps of story here swamp the precepts interspersed
with them, it is as if, in this stanza at least, the *Liber parabolarum* has
become a collection of fables that include maxims rather than vice versa, a
form that does not just borrow from texts like the *Fables* of Avianus but
has become such a text.

What might be elevated to a type and described as preceptive narrative
is not only frequent in the *Liber parabolarum* but found throughout the
larger schoolroom canon. The *Tobias* not only interrupts its narrative for
the long precept collection I have already mentioned (in this sense, falling
into two distinct—patched together—parts), but that narrative is regularly
interrupted by moralizing precepts that recapitulate the events of the story
but in a generalized form. After a lengthy account of the virtues of Tobias
and his father, for example, their similarities are summarized thus:

Sanctum sancta patrem soboles imitatur, honesta
Innocuum, stabilem sobria, iusta pium.

[The holy child imitates the holy father, the honorable the innocent,
The sober imitates the steady, the just the merciful.]
(Matthew of Vendôme, *Tobias*, lines 2095–6/p. 144)

Preceptive narrative can also be found in Maximian's *Elegies*, where much
of the speaker's lamentation describes the diminished capacities of the
elderly in the first person ("I'm conquered by an infirm body" [vincimur
infirmi defectu corporis], Maximian, *Elegies*, I.257), but that diminish-
ment is also generalized in metaphors couched as general rules:

Deficiunt validi longaevo tempore tauri
et quondam pulcer fit modo turpis equus.
Fracta diu rabidi conpescitur ira leonis,
lentaque per senium aspera tigris erit.

[Strong bulls grow weak within course of time,
The once handsome horse grows ugly presently.
The lion's anger is checked when its day is done,
The tiger's pace is slowed with harsh old age.]
(Maximian, *Elegies*, I.269–72)

This last movement occurs by means of that rotation of subject position
from first to third person that I mentioned earlier and claimed in
Chapter 3 was the defining characteristic of the grammar-school style.
So this is probably the place to notice too that the connection between

formal kinds is often made by the same adverb used to link precept and
practical demonstration in the grammars, "thus" [sic].[30] This is often true
in the linking of summarizing precept to story in the *Fables* of Avianus and
even more common in the linking of example and precept in the *Liber
parabolarum*.[31] In each of these cases the borderline between formal
kinds—across the join of the patched together scraps—is the pedagogical
moment, when the knowledge inherent in the one form is drawn out more
emphatically by its appearance in another.

The lesson taught again and again by such forms, regardless of precepts
or stories patched together, or even the nature and kind of the aggregate
patchwork, was that texts could be made—might even appear *always* to be
made—by aggregation, by the patching together of otherwise distinct and
separable parts. That point is made with the least subtlety in the way that
so many individual schoolroom texts are patchworks of the *same* form
repeated over and over—precept joined to precept again and in a long
chain in the *Distichs* and the *Facetus*, and narrative after narrative in a
similar chain in the *Fables* of Avianus. Such patchwork nominated these
texts for schoolroom use since it made them so formally simple (once two
lines of the *Distichs* are understood the shape of the whole poem is clear).
The *Eclogue* of Theodulus can also be said to be about this formal principle
to a considerable extent, since the poem's purpose is to pit pagan falsehood
against Christian truth point for point, in constant alternation, with each
view couched in a parallel stanza the better for the truth to refute the
whole of the lie:

> P.   Venit ab Oceano summergens cuncta vorago;
> tellus cessit acquae, periit quod vixerat omne.
> Deucalion homines, preter quem nemo superstes,
> cum Pirra iactis renovavit coniuge saxis.
> A.   Ultio digna Dei fontes dirupit abissi
> octavum Noe servans in partibus arche;
> amodo ne talem patiantur saecula cladem,
> visibus humanis per nubila panditur Iris.

[Pseustis (Falsehood):]
From Ocean came a gulf submerging all things.
The Earth gave way to the water, and everything which had been alive perished.
Deucalion—there was no survivor besides him—with his wife,
Pyrrha, restored mankind when stones were thrown behind them.

---

[30] See, Avianus, *Fables*, II.15, XXX.13, XXXV.15, and XLII.15.
[31] For "sic" see *Liber parabolarum*, lines 4, 10, 14, 22, 28, 36, 38, 40, 42, 46, 52, 62, 64,
80, 115, 122, 127, 135, 139, 147, 151, 167, 175, 179, 183, 195, 214, 255, 275, 348.
"A simili" is used in line 420 for a similar purpose, and "per exemplum" in line 551.

Alithia (Truth):
God's fitting vengeance burst the streams of the abyss
While saving Noah, the eighth person on the decks of his ark.
From this time on, lest the ages suffer such destruction,
The rainbow displayed itself through the clouds to the sight of men.]

(Theodulus, Eclogue, lines 69–76/p. 34)

These stories are so pithy as to approximate the kind of preceptive narrative I described in the *Fables* of Avianus and the *Liber parabolarum*. But the more obvious lesson of the juxtaposition of these two creation stories in two identical forms—the recapitulation of so much similarity in stanzas meant to be distinguished by their difference—is that a certain truthfulness inheres in patchwork, that literature says most (or says what it has to say most clearly) when it achieves the richness of perspective inherent in the aggregated form.

This formal recommendation would have been further emphasized by the way that the canon of reading texts consists of so many of the same forms treating so many of the same subjects that each of these texts can seem to be made from pieces of one of the others. Thus, the fable of Avianus, "De mure et bove" [The mouse and the ox] (XXXI), in which we learn that a mouse is agile enough to harass an ox because of its small size, might seem to find its moral, not in its own conclusion, but in the *Distichs* of Cato:

> Corporis exigui vires contemnere noli:
> consilio pollet cui vim natura negavit.
>
> [Do not underestimate the strength housed in a small frame
> For nature may deny strength to the wise.]

(Distichs of Cato, II.9)[32]

Similarly, the *Distichs* might seem to provide a pithier version of the preceptive observation made by the bear in the fable "De duobus sociis et ursa" [The two companions and the bear] (IX), when one man is abandoned by his quicker "friend" [socium] the instant he sees this bear approaching:

> Cum tibi praeponas animalia bruta timore,
> unum hominem scito tibi praecipue esse timendum.

---

[32] The fable concludes with the mouse offering a similar observation, though with less preceptive pith: "Because your parents transmitted strong limbs to you, it does not follow that they added efficiency to your strength. Learn, however the self-reliance that our tiny mouths possess, and learn how our pigmy band does whatever it wants" [Non quia magna tibi tribuerunt membra parentes, / viribus effectum constitutere tuis / disce tamen brevibus quae sit fiducia rostris, / ut faciat quicquid parvula turba cupit] (Avianus, *Fables*, XXXI.9–12).

[When fear of brute beasts preoccupies you
Know what you most should dread is human kind.]
                    (*Distichs of Cato* IV.11)[33]

The *Liber cartule*'s relentless contempt for the world not only makes it a chain of injunctions to "reflect always upon the future with watchful care" [pervigili cura semper meditare futura] (col. 1312d/p. 64), but a series of precepts that, however general, are designed to guide the watchful toward a better life:

> Sacred reading shows the way to the soul seeking eternal life [vitam quaerenti dat iter sacra lectio menti] (*Liber cartule*, 1314a/p. 65).

> Guide your mind and make it wise, believing correctly and observing holy admonitions [ipse tuam mentem regat, et faciat sapientem, / Recte credentem, monitusque bonos retinentem] (*Liber cartule*, 1314c/p. 65).

The pervasiveness of this theme also means that the preceptive moments of the *Tobias* provide nearly identical statements:

> Carnis vita labor, carnis conceptio tabes
>   Menstrua, putredo finis, origo lutum
> Sperma prius, modo saccus olens, post vermibus esca
>   In tumulo: qua, qua dote superbit homo?
> Es sapiens? marcet sapientia morte; redundas
>   Divitiis? lapsu mobiliore fluunt.

> [The life of flesh is toil, the conception of the flesh is menstrual
> Corruption, its end is rottenness, its origin is mud.
> First semen, now a smelly sack, afterward food for worms
> In the tomb: for what, for what endowment is Man proud?
> Are you wise? Wisdom droops in death. Do you abound in
> Riches? They flow away in swift flight.]

                    (Matthew of Vendôme, *Tobias*, lines 653–8/p. 102)

Much of this interchangeability is a consequence of the detachability of the parts of individual forms. Vincent Gillespie has suggested that "the primacy of the aphoristic 'sentence' as the basic unit of ethical teaching in these elementary reading texts" allowed them to provide a kind of "portable piety," easily carried away from the text and, thus, just as easily from one text to the next.[34] The relentless focus in each of these parts, as well as in all of these formal wholes, on the subjects and social circumstances of

---

[33] In the fable, the bear says "'Be chary of returning to partnership with another,' she said, 'lest a rabid beast get hold of you a second time'" [Ne facile alterius repetas consortia," dixit, "rursus ab insana ne capiare fera Avianus] (*Fables*, IX.23–4).

[34] Gillespie, "From the Twelfth Century to c.1450," 156.

elementary pedagogy would have contributed to this portability. But the larger consequence was not only that the whole of the schoolroom canon would have seemed made of detachable pieces, but, as an assemblage of patchwork forms, the canon itself would have seemed to *be* a patchwork.

It was, then, the repetition of such a formal principle at so many levels of this canon that would have transformed it into something like a precept about literary form, an emphatic (because endlessly repeated) insistence that the form of the canon was the best, if not only, way to make poetry. The variety of patchwork that could be found within that insistence would also have provided a very fine-grained training in how to construct such a form: as he did no more than learn to read, the schoolboy would have also learned how to mix precept and narrative; he would have learned how to couch the same idea in different forms as well as how to use the same form to say a variety of things; and he would have learned most of all how to treat a single, large, and complex subject in a chain of detachable, but homologous, parts. The canon was hardly assembled to provide such instruction and it is nowhere explicit about providing it. But the repetition also involved in learning Latin from these texts would have added a different layer of insistence to the form of the canon even as it clarified its finer and larger contours. In both its shape and the practices that that shape fostered, the canon of basic reading texts would have blurred the distinction between literacy training and literary work, always tending to ensure that the former became, or led directly to, the latter.

THE MIDDLE ENGLISH POET AS SCHOOLBOY

The most obvious way Middle English poets reproduced the form of the syllabus in their own work was by incorporating passages from the basic readings in a manner so familiar to us from other contexts that we have almost always described it as "quotation." Perhaps because it was the first text schoolboys tended to read (and therefore the text they best remembered), but doubtless because it falls into the simplest and most detachable pieces, the *Distichs of Cato* is the school text most commonly so "quoted" by the Ricardian poets. Langland takes lines from the *Distichs* to describe the fecklessness of the workmen charged with ploughing Piers the Plowman's half acre,[35] to support Scripture's view that money should not be

---

[35] "Ayeins Catons counseil comseth he to jangle: / *Paupertatis onus pacienter ferre memento*" [Against Cato's counsel he begins to quarrel: *Remember to bear the burden of poverty patiently*] (B 6.313–13a). Langland is here citing *Distichs* I.21.

coveted,[36] to formulate Wit's view (in the A-text) that one should ignore slander or backbiting "words,"[37] for Ymaginatif's belief in the inevitability of sin,[38] on the care necessary in giving,[39] and for Will's attempt to justify his "meddling" with "making."[40] Cato is also used to characterize the kind of strength contained in the seed containing the cardinal virtue of "fortitude" sown by Piers the Plowman.[41] Langland folds the process of quoting from Cato into the very allegory of *Piers*, so that when Conscience is sent by the king to fetch Reason, right at Reason's side, saddling up his horse, as if he personified schoolroom learning itself is "Caton, his knave" (B 4.16–19). But the grounds for calling this process something other than "quotation" become clearer where Chaucer cites the distich from "Cato" denouncing the knowledge learned in dreams, since Chaucer works it into The Nun's Priest's Tale by translating it ("Ne do no fors of dremes").[42]

---

[36] "And Catoun kenneth us to coveiten it [silver] naught but at [nede]; / *Dilige denarium set parce dilige formam*" [And Cato teaches us to desire silver only when we have need; *Love money but do not love it for its own sake*] (B 10.335–37a). Langland has substituted "denarius" [money] here for "te ornari" [to adorn oneself]. The original reads "Dilige te ornari, sed parce dilige formam" [Take care to look after yourself, but do not love beauty alone] (*Distichs* IV.4).

[37] "Ac gif thou werche be Godis word, I warne the the best, / Whatso men worden of the, wraththe the nevere; / Catoun counseillith so—tak kep of his teching— / *Cum recte viuas ne cures verba malorum.* / But suffre and sit stille and sek thou no ferthere, / And be glad of the grace that God hath isent the" [But if you proceed according to God's word, I warn you well, whatever people say about you, never grow angry; Cato advises this—heed his teaching—*if you are living righteously pay no attention to criticism*] (A 10.95–100). For the original see *Distichs* III.2.

[38] "For man was maad of swich a matere he may noght wel asterte / That som tyme hym bitit to folwen his kynde. / Caton acordeth therwith—*Nemo sine crimine vivit!*" [Because man was made of matter he may not escape the possibility of committing sin according to his nature; Cato agrees with this—*no one lives without sin*] (B 11.400–2). For the original see *Distichs* I.5.

[39] " . . . the nedieste sholde be holpe. / Caton kenneth men thus, and the Clerc of Stories; *Cui des videto* is Catons techyng" [The neediest should be helped. Cato teaches men thus, as does Peter Comestor, *Take care to whom you give*]. The original is *Distichs*, Pro 17. Langland reworks this passage and the meaning he takes from this injunction in the *Distichs* in the C-text (*Piers Plowman: A New Annotated Edition of the C-text*, ed. Derek Pearsall [Exeter: University of Exeter Press, 2008], C IX.69). On the relationship between these two passages, see Chapter 7 in the present volume, pp. 248–51.

[40] "I seigh wel he seide me sooth and, somwhat me to excuse, / Seide, 'Caton conforted his sone that, clerk though he were, / To solacen hym som tyme—as I do whan I make; / *Interpone tuis interdum gaudia curis*'" [I saw clearly that he told me the truth and to excuse me a little he said, "Cato comforted his son by saying, though he was a clerk, he should enjoy himself sometimes—as I do when I write poetry; *intermix pleasure sometimes with your worries*"] (B 12.20–2a). See *Distichs*, III.6.

[41] "And covered hym under conseille of Caton the wise: / *Esto forti animo cum sis dampnatus inique*" [And was governed by the counsel of Cato, the wise: *Be strong in spirit when you are unjustly condemned*] (B 19.299–a). See *Distichs*, II.14.

[42] Pertelote cites the passage to support her claim that Chauntecleer is a coward for fearing the vision of disaster he has just had in a dream: "Lo, Catoun, which that was so wis

In The Merchant's Tale Chaucer translates another of the *Distichs* on the need to put up with a wife's nagging as he also does in The Canon's Yeoman's Prologue when suggesting that a person with a guilty conscience will always feel that he is being talked about.[43] In The Miller's Tale Chaucer condescends to John, the carpenter, when he says that he is simply too uneducated to know what the *Distichs* say about the danger of marrying someone unlike oneself:

> He knew nat* Catoun, for his wit was rude,   not
> That bad men sholde wedde his simylitude.
> Men sholde wedden after hire* estaat,   their
> For youthe and elde* is often at debaat.   age
>
> (I.3227–32)

As Brusendorff first pointed out, this advice cannot be found in the *Distichs* but, rather, in the *Facetus* ("Take a wife who is your peer in birth and beautified by moral excellence if you want to lead a righteous life in peace" [Duc tibi prole parem moremque vigore venustam, / Si cum pace velis vitam deducere iustam]).[44] Chaucer may even have meant this mistake to be obvious, layering his joke so that the Miller telling this tale would look as ignorant as the carpenter he is criticizing. But, the ambiguity is revealing, since it only exists because Chaucer has absorbed the scrap of the school text so thoroughly that it is not so much inserted into

---

a man, / Seide he nat thus, 'Ne do no fors of dremes?'" (VII.2940–1). This distich is also cited in Latin by Will in *Piers Plowman*, in one his very few waking moments, as a warning against just the sort of visions he has been having: "Caton and canonistres counseillen us to leve / To sette sadnesse in songewarie—for *sompnia ne cures*" [Cato and canonists advise us to refrain from placing faith in the interpretation of dreams—*for you should pay no attention to dreams*] (B 7.150–1).

[43] The passage in The Merchant's Tale is "Suffre thy wives tonge, as Caton bit; / She shal comaunde, and thow shalt suffren it," IV.1377–8. See *Distichs*, III.23: "Uxoris linguam, si frugi est, ferre memento; / namque malum est non velle pati nec posse tacere" [Make sure to endure a wife's tongue if she is frugal; for it is wrong not to be patient nor able to keep silent]. The passage in The Canon Yeoman's Tale is "For Catoun seyth, that he that gilty is / Demeth al thing be spoke of him, iwys" (VIII.688–9). See *Distichs* I.17: "Ne cures, si quis tacito sermone loquatur: conscius ipse sibi de se putat omnia dici" [Pay no attention what is whispered: the self-conscious think that everything said is about them]. For Chaucer's reliance on Cato in general see Richard Hazelton, "Chaucer and Cato," *Speculum* 35 (1960): 357–80.

[44] Aage Brusendorff, "'He Knew Nat Catoun For His Wit Was Rude,'" 320–39 in *Studies in English Philology: A Miscellany in Honor of Frederick Klaeber* (Minneapolis: University of Minnesota Press, 1929), 337–8. It is certainly possible that Chaucer expected the *Distichs* to be so well known that his readers would recognize the mistake. As I noted earlier (p. 165), moreover, the *Facetus* represents itself as a continuation of the *Distichs* so it may be that Chaucer meant "Cato" in the broader sense of the wisdom associated with him rather than a particular text. On this use of the *Distichs* see also Mann, "'He Knew Nat Catoun,'" 42–3.

the larger form he is making but a part of that form (a patch, to return to the formal metaphor here, that makes the fabric whole). Just as the Latin Langland absorbs from the *Distichs* was worked into a texture that consisted in substantial part of lines absorbed from many other texts as well as both English and (as I suggested in the last chapter) Latin written by Langland himself, Chaucer's absorptions from the *Distichs* and the *Facetus* are not just pieces taken from the schoolroom canon but the piecing out of an English poem by the formal means demonstrated in and by that canon.

It is hard to measure the extent of this formal procedure because Middle English poems are often patched together from bits of schoolroom learning in ways that call no attention to the origin of the line or lines that have been so absorbed. Gower, for example, was particularly fond of the claim in the *Distichs* that "inactivity is the food of vice" (nam diuturna quies vitiis alimenta ministrat, I.2) and, while he cites Cato when he employs it in the *Miroir de l'omme*,

> Car danz Catouns ce nous aprent,
> Que long repos de songement
> Norrist les vices au dessus.

> [For in Cato we learn that lengthy dream-filled rest nourishes vices above all].[45]

by the time he is writing Book 4 of the *Confessio Amantis*, the name Cato has vanished:

> For Slowthe, which as moder is
> The forthdrawere* and the norrice*   producer/nurse
> To man of many a dredful vice,
> Hath yit* another laste of alle ...   yet
>
> (4.3381–4)

There is also no reference to Cato when Gower repeats the maxim twice in Book 7 of the *Confessio*:

> Ther is yit on*, which Ydelnesse*   one/Idleness
> Is cleped*, and is the norrice   called
> In mannes kinde* of every vice.   among mankind
>
> (7.1086–8)

> And worldes ese*, as it is told,   leisure
> Be weie of kinde* is the norrice   naturally
> Of every lust*.   desire
>
> (7.4384–6)

---

[45] John Gower, "Mirour de L'Omme," 1–334 in *The Complete Works of John Gower: The French Works*, ed. G. C. Macaulay (Oxford: Clarendon Press, 1899), lines 5266–8.

It may be that Cato's authority is assumed in the last of these passages—"as it is told" could be understood to refer to the *Distichs* by virtue of their familiarity—but it is also another instance in which the meaning and language of the schoolroom text have been absorbed deeply enough to emerge as if they were the Ricardian poet's own words. And this is exactly Chaucer's manner in the first four lines of the Prologue to The Second Nun's Tale which paraphrase this maxim on idleness as if the idea were Chaucer's alone:

The ministre* and norice unto vices,	attendant
Which that men clepe* in Englissh Ydelnesse,	call
That porter of the gate is of delices*, pleasuress	
To eschue, and by hir contrarie* hire oppresse—	opposite
That is to seyn, by leveful bisynesse*—	dutiful application
Wel oughten we to doon al our entente.	

(VIII.1–6)[46]

In all such instances the basic reading texts accomplish the literary work of the Ricardian poet, providing him with the language of his poem before it is even written, showing him how to work that language into his poem as the kind of detachable piece it is in the poem and canon in which he found it.

The seamlessness of such absorption is a further function of the schoolroom origin of such texts, since it was unnecessary for Chaucer and Gower to say that a given maxim was drawn from a particular school text since every literate person was bound to know that. But such assumptions meant that a poet could work the piece of a schoolroom text so completely into the texture of his English that it not only seemed to be his own formulation but something like a defining thought. That process can

---

[46] There is a similar view of idleness in Ecclesiasticus ("multam enim malitiam docuit otiositas" [for idleness teaches much mischief], 33:29); this maxim appears in Chaucer's source for The Tale of Melibee ("Car Salemon dit que oisiveté enseigne faire moult de maulx," J. Burke Severs, "The Tale of Melibeus," 560–614 in *Sources and Analogues of Chaucer's Canterbury Tales*, ed. W. F. Bryan and Germaine Dempster [Chicago, IL: University of Chicago Press, 1941], 602) and then in the Melibee ("For Salomon seyth that idelnesse techeth a man to do manye iveles," VII.1589). It is attributed in both cases to Solomon because Ecclesiasticus was traditionally thought to have been written by him. These similarities sometimes cause editors to see the source of lines in the Melibee as scriptural (e.g. *The Riverside Chaucer*, ed. Larry D. Benson [Boston, MA: Houghton Mifflin, 1987], 927 and Geoffrey Chaucer, *The Canterbury Tales*, ed. Jill Mann [Harmondsworth: Penguin, 2005], 1012) and the beginning of The Second Nun's Tale as "conventional" (*Riverside Chaucer*, ed. Benson, 943) or "proverbial" (*Canterbury Tales*, ed. Mann, 1055), but the strong image of idleness as food is not part of either the scriptural or proverbial formation and here, as often elsewhere, it is probably most accurate to say that the explicit citation of Cato was not required because the text was so familiar.

be traced in the uses Middle English poets made of the distich on the way
a trickster may be outfoxed by his own tactics:

> Qui simulat verbis nec corde est fidus amicus,
> tuo quoque fac simules: sic ars deluditur arte.
>
> [He who dissembles in words is not a faithful friend at heart,
> See that you copy: thus art beguiles art.]

(Distichs of Cato, I.26)

In *Piers Plowman*, Dame Study cites this distich in the most straightforward way, carefully attributing it to Cato, to confute Theology's view that
the best way to deal with "enemies" is to love them:

> In oother science it seith—I seigh it in Catoun—
> *Qui simulat verbis, nec corde est fidus amicus,*
> *Tuo quoque fac simile; sic ars deluditur arte.*
> Whoso gloseth as gylours doon, go me to the same.
>
> [In other kinds of learning it says—I saw it in Cato—*who pretends in words
> but is not a true friend in his heart, imitate him likewise; thus art is beguiled by
> art.* Whenever anyone lies, as tricksters do, you do the same.]

(B 10.191–2)

When Genius offers this wisdom in the same language to Amans in
Book 6 of the *Confessio Amantis*, Gower not only absorbs the maxim
but also the form in which it is couched in the *Distichs*, presenting it as
knowledge conveyed from a teacher to a pupil addressed as "my son."
Unlike Langland, however, Gower mentions neither Cato nor any other
source for the view:

> Mi sone, that goth wonder streite*,   is very difficult
> For this I mai wel tele soth*,   truth
> Ther is no man the which* so doth,   who
> For al the craft* that he can caste*,   skill/ employ
> That he n'abeith it* ate laste.   does not pay for it
> For often he that wol beguile
> Is guiled with the same guile,
> And thus the guilour* is beguiled.   beguiler

(6.1374–81)[47]

---

[47] One consequence of the complete absorption is that Macaulay does not even note the
quotation (see Gower, *English Works*, 2: 516). The TEAMS edition describes these lines as
"proverbial" and refers readers to *Piers Plowman*, although it references B 15.340 in error for
B 10.191–2 (John Gower, *Confessio Amantis*, ed. Russell Peck, 3 vols. [Kalamazoo, MI:
Medieval Institute Publications, Western Michigan University, 2000], 3: 430).

When Chaucer cites the text in the person of the Reeve, pointing the moral of the whole of The Reeve's Tale, he does not cite Cato, but he does say that the idea is "proverbial":

> And therfore this proverbe is seyd ful sooth*:   in truth
> Hym thar nat wene wel that yvele dooth*.
> He should not expect good who does evil
> A gylour* shal himself bigyled be.   beguiler
>
> (I.4319–21)[48]

The maxim pulls away from the *Distichs* entirely in the passage, late in *Piers Plowman*, when Mercy uses an English translation of it (without attribution) to describe the trickster tricked, but then translates it into a *different* Latin form than it has in the *Distichs*, using what is in fact the phrasing of a hymn by Venantius Fortunatus:

> And right as thorugh gilours gile bigiled was man formest,
> So shal grace that al bigan make a good ende
> And bigile the gilour—and that is good sleighte:
> *Ars ut artem falleret.*

[And just as through the trickster's tricks man was first tricked, so shall the grace that began all things make a good end and trick the trickster—and that is a good sleight of hand: *so art shall foil art.*]

(B 18.159–61)[49]

What may seem to be the bravura invention whereby Langland finds the meaning of the Latin distich that condenses the point he has just made in English in the phrasing of another Latin poem is, in fact, a schoolroom technique (where, as I noted in the previous chapter, translation from Latin to English verse and then from English to Latin verse was a standard exercise). But it could also be said that bravura invention of this particular kind was the defining characteristic of what might be called the poetics of patchwork: the repurposing of lines written by another poet for the ringing formulation of the Middle English poet's own thinking.

The distinctive quality of this poetics might be best described as its finish, an absorption so easy that citation was unnecessary and so complete that it was almost inaccurate to say that citation had occurred—a

---

[48] Chaucer's source here is usually understood as "proverbial." See, for example, *Riverside Chaucer*, ed. Benson, 852 and *Canterbury Tales*, ed. Mann, 856. Mann notes elsewhere, however, that "this proverb is represented in 'Cato,'" "'He Knew Nat Catoun,'" 65.

[49] For the passage in Fortunatus's famous hymn "Pange lingua" see Venantius Honorius Clemenianus Fortunatus, *Opera Poetica*, ed. Friedrich Leo (Berlin: Weidmann, 1881), Carmina, Book 2, number 2 (p. 28).

technique whose distinguishing mark was, paradoxically, its invisibility. This meant that, in some cases, the school text could be referenced by mention of its contents or its prominent characters without any mention of the text itself, as, for example, when, in *The House of Fame*, Chaucer associates the fame of Statius with the fame he achieved for Achilles without ever mentioning the *Achilleid*:

> There saugh* I stonden ...   saw
> The Tholosan that highte* Stace,   called
> That bar of Thebes up the fame*   increased the fame of Thebes
> Upon his shouldres, and the name
> Also of cruel Achilles.
>
> (*The House of Fame*, 1456–63)

The mention of "daun Pseustis" (1228) among a troop of shepherds that "maden lowde mynstralcies" (1217) in *The House of Fame* references the *Eclogue* of Theodulus by way of the shepherd who represents "falsehood" there, just as the mention of Claudian for his portrayal of "Pluto, and of Proserpyne" later in the poem (1509–11) references *On the Rape of Proserpina* without ever mentioning the poem itself.[50] In the *Confessio Amantis*, summaries of the fable of Avianus "De Cupido et Invido" [The greedy man and the jealous man] (XXII) in Book 2 of the *Confessio Amantis* (291–364), of the education of Achilles by Chiron from the *Achilleid* (2.110–28) in Book 4 (1963–2044), and of Achilles's coupling with Deidamia from the *Achilleid* (1.198–960) in Book 5 (2961–3246) reference both of these texts at length without mentioning them either. The most finely finished of all such absorptions is the arrival of Pluto and Proserpina in January's garden in Chaucer's Merchant's Tale as characters who finally determine that tale's conclusion. Chaucer does mention *On the Rape of Prosperina* by way of introducing these figures ("Pluto, that is kyng of Fayerye / And many a lady in his compaignye / Folwynge his wyf, the queene Proserpyna, / Which that he ravysshed out of Ethna," IV.2227–30), but they are borne forward in the text, not by translation or paraphrase of passages from Claudian, but as if *On the Rape of Proserpina* had described the past that determined the tale's present actions: Pluto addresses Proserpina as his "wyf" (IV.2238), as if the marriage envisioned near the end of the school text had occurred, and the rancor that governs that marriage, as well as Prosperina's general

---

[50] The reference to Theodulus was first described by Ferdinand Holthausen, "Chaucer und Theodulus," *Anglia* 16 (1894): 264–6 (see esp. p. 264), but his argument is not always adopted with enthusiasm by editors of Chaucer. See, for example, *Riverside Chaucer*, ed. Benson, 986.

stridency ("'Ye shal?' quod Proserpyne, 'wol ye so? / Now by my moodres
sires soule I swere / That I shel yeven her sufficient answere,'" IV.2264–6),
are very clearly rooted in the horror of the *raptus* Claudian describes.

A confounding but inevitable consequence of patchwork so seamless is
that the informing school text can be all but impossible for those trained
outside medieval schoolrooms to identify, and the frequency with which
certain patches are used tends to make them seem more and more like
common sayings. A revealing case in point is the Samaritan's claim in *Piers
Plowman* that there are "thre thynges ther ben that doon a man . . . / For to
fleen his owene hous" [three things there are that cause a man to flee his
own house] (B 17.317–18):

> That oon is a wikkede wif that wol noght be chasted:
> Hir feere fleeth hire for feere of hir tonge.
> And if his hous be unhiled, and reyne on his bedde,
> He seketh and seketh til he slepe drye.
> And whan smoke and smolder smyt in his sighte,
> It dooth hym worse than his wif or wete to slepe.

[The first is a wicked wife who refuses to be reprimanded: her spouse flees
her for fear of her tongue. And if his house has no roof and it rains on his
bed, he searches until he sleeps dry. And when smoke and smoldering wood
obscures his sight it is worse for him than his wife or his wet bed.]

(B 17.319–25)

Because most commentators can find strong, but not exact, parallels to
this formulation in Innocent III's *De miseria* as well as a number of verses
in Proverbs they routinely describe this list as "proverbial."[51] Chaucer's
Wife of Bath seems to confirm this presumption since she says her
husband complains about the shrewishness of wives by means of a similar
list ("Thow seyst that dropping houses, and eek [also] smoke, / And
chiding wives maken men to flee / Out of hir [their] owene house,"

---

[51] See, for example, William Langland, *The Vision of Piers Plowman: A Complete Edition
of the B-text.*, ed. A. V. C Schmidt, 2nd edn. (London: J. M. Dent, 1995), 477; Langland,
Piers Plowman: The C-Text, ed. Pearsall, 317 n. to 19.297; and William Langland, *The
Vision of William Concerning Piers the Plowman in Three Parallel Texts*, ed. W. W. Skeat, 2
vols. (Oxford: Clarendon Press, 1886), 2: 246. The passages in Proverbs are 19:13 ("tecta
iugiter perstillantia litigiosa mulier" [a wrangling wife is like a roof continually dropping
through]), 10:26 ("sicut acetum dentibus et fumus oculis sic piger his qui miserunt eum"
[as vinegar to the teeth, and smoke to the eyes, so is the sluggard to them that sent him],
and, especially, 27:15 ("tecta perstillantia in die frigoris et litigiosa mulier conparantur"
[roofs dripping through in a cold day, and a contentious woman are alike]). For the use of
these verses see Lotario dei Segni (Innocent III), *De Miseria Condicionis Humane*, ed. and
trans. Robert E. Lewis (Athens, GA: University of Georgia Press, 1978), I.18.

III.278–80).[52] Commentators on this passage also note the parallel in the *De miseria* and another in the *Lamentations* of Matheolus, a text the Wife of Bath cites elsewhere.[53] But the only one of these putative source-texts that closely resembles what the Wife of Bath says is Proverbs 27:15 ("tecta perstillantia in die frigoris et litigiosa mulier conparantur" [roofs dripping through in a cold day, and a contentious woman are alike]), and, since it lacks one of the three things she mentions (the fire), it does not provide the "three thynges" that gives her list (and the Samaritan's in Langland) its distinctive identity. A list that exactly parallels what she and the Samaritan say can, however, be found in the school text, the *Tobias*:

> Asserit ut Salamon, tria sunt confusio quorum
> Excludit fragiles commodiore domo:
> Hec tria sunt fumus, aqua stillans, noxia coniunx.
>
> [As Solomon declares, there are three things whose
> Disorder drives out weak men from their own house:
> These three are smoke, dripping water and a noxious wife.]
>
> (Matthew of Vendôme, *Tobias*, lines 631–3/p. 101)

The Samaritan slightly complicates this relationship by saying that his list of "three things" comes from "Holy Writ" (17.318), although it is easy to see that such an attribution could derive from the claim that this is Solomon's wisdom. It is, moreover, the absence of direct citation more than anything else that confirms the connection of the words of the Samaritan and the Wife of Bath to the *Tobias*, since it is in the nature of the poetics of patchwork to absorb the school text so fully that the Middle English text will seem to have no source at all.

At its most accomplished the poetics of patchwork is not only an art that conceals artfulness, a patchwork so carefully stitched that it seems to have no seams, but borrowed words that seem *particularly* characteristic of the poet who did not invent them. Examples of this kind would include use of the *Liber parabolarum*'s metaphor for deceptive appearances ("Do not consider gold everything that shines like gold, / Nor think that each and every lovely fruit is good" [Non teneas aurum totum quod splendet ut aurum / nec pulchrum pomum quodlibet esse bonum], III.217–18/p. 160) as a description of the Canon's deceptiveness in Chaucer's

---

[52] This is the implication of the citation in *Proverbs, Sentences, and Proverbial Phrases from English Writings Mainly before 1500*, ed. Bartlett Jere Whiting, with Helen Wescott Whiting (Cambridge, MA: Harvard University Press, 1968), T187, although Whiting notes that the "three things" that cause "a man to flee" are often "varied."

[53] *Les Lamentations de Matheolus et le Liver de Leesce de Jehan le Fèvre*, ed. A. G. Van Hamel, 2 vols. (Paris, 1893–1905), ll. 68–76. Cited in Chaucer, *Canterbury Tales*, ed. Mann, 886–7.

Canon's Yeoman's Tale which, in that context, seems "Chaucerian" in its homely precision:

Every man semeth* a Salomon;	seems
But al thing* which that shineth as the gold	everything
Ne is nat gold*, as that I have herd told,	is not gold
Ne very appul that is fair at eye	
Ne is nat good*, whatso men clappe* or crye.	is not good/ say

(VIII.962–5)[54]

The *Liber parabolarum*'s warning about the wolf in sheep's clothing ("When the shepherd is meek, the wolf shits wool, / And the unguarded flock is torn apart by him" [Sub molli pastore lupus lanam cacat, et grex, / incustoditus, dilaceratur eo] (I.31–2/p. 153 [I.31]) lends Ymaginatif's characterization of corrupt "bischops" (B 9.256) a typically Langlandian disgust ("Thy shep ben ner al shabbede, the wolf shyt the wolle, *Sub milli pastore* &c," C 9.265–a).[55] Slightly softened by Chaucer, however, the phrase provides a typically wry description of the violence coiled under authority in the Physician's Tale:

> Under a shepherde softe and necligent
> The wolf hath many a sheep and lamb torent*.   torn apart

(VI.101–2)[56]

But no schoolroom text is more fully worked into the text of a Middle English poem than what appears for all the world as a rhetorical question, not only typical of Chaucer, but of the Wife of Bath's aggressive interrogation of the bias built into the authoritative texts of medieval misogyny. "Who peynted the lion, tell me who?" (III.692) is a question that, at once, summarizes the Wife's view of how men misrepresent all women, and reproduces the observation made by a lion in one of the *Fables* of Avianus (XXIV, "De venatore et leone" [The hunter and the lion]) when shown a tombstone depicting a lion being defeated by a man:

> "quod si nostra novum caperet sollertia sensum,
> sculperet ut docili pollice saxa leo,

---

[54] Mann calls the *Liber parabolarum* the "immediate source" here (*Canterbury Tales*, 1075) as does the *Riverside Chaucer*, ed. Benson (950).

[55] Pearsall says the phrase is "proverbial" with "capit" or "rapit" [seizes], but also notes that the verb Langland translates here, "cacat" [shits], is the verb that appears in the version of this saying in the *Liber parabolarum* (*Piers Plowman*, ed. Pearsall, 181–2 n. to l. 265a). On the meaning of this saying see John Burrow, "'The Wolf Shits Wool': *Piers Plowman* C IX 265–265a," *Notes and Queries* n.s. 57 (2010): 168–9.

[56] Mann describes this as "a gentler version of the proverb 'Under a weak shepherd, the wolf shits wool'" (*Canterbury Tales*, 963). The *Riverside Chaucer* also describes this phrase as "proverbial" (903).

tunc hominem adspiceres oppressum murmure magno
conderet ut rabidis ultima fata genis"

[If our ingenuity gave us other outlets, allowing a lion to engrave stones with
a fine touch, then you would see how the man, overwhelmed by a loud roar,
met his fate in a greedy mouth.]

(Avianus, *Fables*, XXIV.13–16)[57]

A similarly complete absorption governs Chaucer's nearly verbatim quotation in The Pardoner's Tale of the passage from Maximian's *Elegies* in which
its narrator produces a memorable account of the privations of old age:

"Suscipe me, genetrix, nati miserere laborum:
    membra peto gremio fessa fovere tuo.
Horrent me pueri, nequeo velut ante videri:
    horrendos partus cur sinis esse tuos?
Nil mihi cum superis: explevi munera vitae:
    Redde precor patrio mortua membra solo.
Quid miseros variis prodest extendere poenis?
    Non est materni pectoris ista pati."

[Take me, my mother, pity your child that suffers:
I seek to nourish my tired limbs upon your breast.
Children abhor me, my appearance has so changed.
Why do you allow your offspring to look so horrible?
I've nothing to do with life, I've fulfilled its chores:
Restore dead limbs, I pray, to their native soil.
Why torture miserable men with added pain?
No mother's heart can allow such things.]

(Maximian, *Elegies*, I.227–34)

In the *Elegies* these views are part of a minatory teaching—a bitter warning
against the squandering of opportunities—but in the very process of

---

[57] Chaucer could also be referencing the version of this common fable in the prose
Romulus where the lion points to a painting in which a man defeats a lion ("pictura
quomodo leo ab homine suffocatur") rather than the sculpture described in Avianus.
When the man shows the lion the picture in the *Romulus*, the lion says "si leo pingere
nosset, pinxisset quomodo leo suffocasset hominem" [if a lion knew how to paint, he would
paint how a lion overcame a man]. This fable is edited as IV.17 of the *Romulus vulgaris* 2:
176–328 in *Les Fabulistes Latins*, ed Léopold Hervieux, 2nd edn., 2 vols. (Paris: Firmin-
Dido, 1893–99), 2: 227. The prose *Romulus* was used in schoolrooms and the closeness of
the parallel makes this the more likely source—if it is right to assume that this line had only
one source for Chaucer. On the other hand, the *Fables* of Avianus were so much more
common in the English schoolbooks examined in Chapter 2 that it seems certain that
Chaucer knew the corresponding fable there very well too, and had to be influenced by the
parallel, if he was not wholly relying on it. On the various versions of this fable as well as its
dissemination in Marie de France and Chrétien de Troyes's *Yvain* see Jill Mann, *From Aesop
to Reynard: Beast Fable in Medieval Britain* (Oxford: Oxford University Press, 2009), 92–3.

stripping these images out of their context, of turning them into a scrap for his patchwork, Chaucer renders them all the more powerful in their effects, projecting out of the images the old man uses a figure so hostile to life that he is not only suicidal but murderous (happy to direct the rioters he has just met directly to "Deeth"):

Ne Deeth, allas, ne wol nat han* my lif!	will not have
Thus walke I, lyk a restelees kaityf*,	wretch
And on the ground, which is my moodres* gate,	mother's
I knokke with my staf, bothe erly and late,	
And seye, "Leeve* moder, leet me in!	dear
Lo, how I vanysshe, flessh and blood and skyn!	
Allas, whan shul my bones been at reste?	
Mooder, with yow wolde I chaunge my cheste*	trunk
That in my chambre* longe tyme hath be,	room
Ye, for an heyre clowt* to wrappe me!"	haircloth
But yet to me she wol* nat do that grace,	will
For which ful pale and welked* is my face.	withered

(VI.727–38)

In this case, the scrap of the schoolroom text becomes Chaucerian as it is enlivened by the texture into which it has been placed, made not only more vivid in its imagery but somehow more *apt*—as if schoolroom text somehow anticipated the Middle English poet's purpose—as if the repurposed context and texture were somehow *more* suitable for these lines than the poem in which they first occurred. This is therefore a poetics that firmly rounded the circle elementary learning typically traced for the Middle English poet, ensuring that the earliest poetry he read contained some of the more memorable lines he later seemed to write.

The broadest effects of the poetry of patchwork on the Ricardian poets are to be found, however, not in the quantities of lines or images or topics borrowed from the school texts, nor in the fineness of the finish in the resulting patchwork, but in the extent to which the most ambitious forms these poets made tend toward patchwork on the whole, as if the form of the schoolroom canon and its constituent parts was not only the first formal model for these poets, but their *only* model. Even when Gower does not take the stories he tells in the *Confessio Amantis* from school texts, he pieces that advice together *as* the *Confessio* from a set of narratives he takes from other texts. Although Langland brings such patchwork down to the level of the line rather than the narrative, and he sometimes makes no gesture toward concealing the joins—not only citing texts very clearly but splicing the Latin of their original into his own English—*Piers Plowman* is nothing other than a sequence of Langland's lines pieced together with thousands of lines written by others. Although Chaucer absorbs this

formal fact to the narrative that constitutes its frame tale—making his text
not a patchwork of texts but a collection of characters and a chorus of their
voices—Chaucer's *magnum opus*, the *Canterbury Tales*, is a patchwork of
stories, most of which are taken from other texts, sometimes by direct and
faithful translation. As is well known, Gower is deploying exempla in the
tradition of confessional literature, just as Langland's citational habits were
influenced by the sermon tradition, and Chaucer doubtless had Boccac-
cio's *Decameron* in mind as a model for a collection of stories. But it must
also have mattered in the choice of these models—and the extent to which
all the major Ricardian poets chose a model of this kind—that these poets
were trained to read and write by so much patchwork. To adopt any of
these other forms was, in effect, to decide again that the form of literature
was the form of the grammar-school canon of basic reading texts. In
this sense, that canon was not only a repository of lines and narratives
and the poetics from which larger poems could be made, but an active,
extensive, and deeply practical definition of patchwork as the form of
poetry itself.[58]

CODA: THE *GAWAIN*-POET'S EXCEPTIONALISM

Although the point could be made by means of many of the topics
already taken up in this book, these conclusions about the schoolroom
canon and its effects make this the best place to note that one of the
more surprising discoveries of tracing the movement from fourteenth-
century literacy training to Ricardian poetry is just how little there is to
say about the work of the *Gawain*-poet. Pedagogy does figure in
significant ways in this poet's poems, as I explore in the next chapter.
Cleanness is a narrative patchwork pieced together out of a variety of
biblical stories. And the claim in *Sir Gawain and the Green Knight* that
the "forme to the fynisment foldes ful selden" [the beginning seldom
accords with the end] could be seen to rework the second half of one of
the *Distichs of Cato*:[59]

---

[58] Wendy Scase has also shown how Middle English poems themselves came to furnish
material for the patchwork of later poets trained by the same schoolroom readings: "Just as
schoolboys were taught to imitate their text-book models when composing on themes set by
their schoolmaster . . . so the Piers-tradition poets characteristically borrow fragments of
Piers and redeploy them to develop their own distinctive themes," "Latin Composition
Lessons, *Piers Plowman*, and the *Piers Plowman* Tradition," 34–53 in *Answerable Style: The
Idea of the Literary in Medieval England*, ed. Frank Grady and Andrew Galloway
(Columbus, OH: Ohio State University Press, 2013), 42.
[59] *Sir Gawain and the Green Knight*, 239–406 in *The Works of the Gawain Poet: Sir
Gawain and the Green Knight, Pearl, Cleanness, Patience*, ed. Ad Putter and Myra Stokes

Cum fueris felix, quae sunt adversa caveto:
non eodem cursu respondent ultima primis.

[When you are happy beware adversity:
Since what the start promises, the end is not.]

(*Distichs of Cato*, I.18)

But this connection is frail not least because the *Gawain*-poet never betrays knowledge of any of the other distichs, nor, in fact, of *any* of the other basic reading texts.

The grounds for this exceptionalism are easy enough to imagine, however: the *Gawain*-poet must have had a very different sort of education from the other major Middle English poets, and indeed from the majority of fourteenth-century English schoolboys. Certainly there is a strong suggestion that his social origins differed significantly from Chaucer's, Langland's, or Gower's. The tantalizing coincidence that the *Gawain*-poet's poems survive in the Cheshire dialect and Richard II had particularly strong connections with that region, including an "innovative and aggressive campaign of recruitment" for personnel, have caused some to suppose that this poet was closely connected to the court of the king.[60] This would not entirely distinguish him from Chaucer, who was in the king's employ, most notably, from 1389–91, as Clerk of the King's Works.[61] But, as Michael Bennett has argued, the *Gawain*-poet may have been, not just connected to the court of the king, but "an insider, a courtier's courtier," a poet who adopted the "view-point" of the royal court because he was a member of the royal household.[62] Such an attachment would in no way rule out the possibility that the poet was a cleric, as has also sometimes been claimed, since it was not uncommon for clerics in minor orders to work in an administrative capacity "in the service

(London: Penguin Books, 2014), line 499. Putter and Stokes say that "this sententia was current in a variety of forms" (p. 636) and cite the *Distichs*, and quote several other examples, including Orderic Vitalis, *Historia Ecclesiastica*, ed. Marjorie Chibnall, 6 vols. (Oxford: Oxford University Press, 1969–80), 6: 314 (XII.xx). If the writers of these other texts had typical elementary school training, however, the currency of the saying could derive entirely from the frequency with which such training began with the *Distichs*.

[60] John M. Bowers, *The Politics of Pearl: Court Poetry in the Age of Richard II* (Cambridge: D. S. Brewer, 2001), 13. See also his chapter 5, "Richard II's Cheshire Connection" (69–76).

[61] Derek Pearsall, *The Life of Geoffrey Chaucer: A Critical Biography* (Oxford: Blackwell, 1992), 210–14.

[62] Michael J. Bennett, "*Sir Gawain and the Green Knight* and the Literary Achievement of the Northwest Midlands: The Historical Background," *Journal of Medieval History* 5 (1979): 63–88 (p. 81).

of a nobleman."[63] And even the concerns, settings, and imagery of the *Gawain*-poet's more overtly religious poems reflect a person who has had a great deal of what Jonathan Nicholls called "court experience."[64]

The strong implication, then, is that the *Gawain*-poet's education was unique because he was tutored in an aristocratic household rather than by way of typical arrangements (ad hoc though these so often were) or by means of the canon of typical schoolroom texts (variable as any grammar-school teacher's selection from that canon might be), perhaps by one of the "masters" Nicholas Orme says were "employed from the twelfth century onwards to look after and teach the younger sons of the royal family and the sons of the rest of the aristocracy."[65] Orme has some difficulty marshaling evidence of such household tutoring much beyond the royal court, but this absence provides another sort of evidence for connecting the equally elusive *Gawain*-poet with the royal household.[66] There is no strong argument to be made from these absences of course. But all of the evidence I have marshaled in this and the preceding chapters showing how profoundly the poetry of the Era of Grammaticalization was shaped by grammar-school pedagogy also suggests that the *Gawain*-poet was a *sui generis* poet because his elementary education was *sui generis* too.

[63] Ad Putter, *Introduction to the Gawain Poet* (London: Longman, 1996), 37. For a careful exploration of the strong indications that the *Gawain*-poet was a cleric working within an aristocratic household see Putter, 14–23.

[64] Jonathan Nicholls, *The Matter of Courtesy: Medieval Courtesy Books and the* Gawain-*Poet* (Woodbridge: D. S. Brewer, 1985), 1.

[65] Nicholas Orme, *From Childhood to Chivalry: The Education of the English Kings and Aristocracy, 1066–1530* (London: Methuen, 1984), 24. See also Richard Firth Green, *Poets and Princepleasers: Literature and the English Court in the Late Middle Ages* (Toronto: University of Toronto Press, 1980), 72–91.

[66] The one exception seems to be "Ralph the *magister* of the children of Aubrey de Vere, earl of Oxford" who "attested a charter not later than 1187" (Orme, *From Childhood to Chivalry*, 24).

6

Equipment for Living

What did the medieval schoolboy learn from his school texts other than how to read and write? Previous chapters have explored the nature of grammatical knowledge and its influence on literary practice as well as the shaping pressures exerted by the form of the basic reading texts and the canon of those texts as a whole. But could it really be that the contents of these texts were completely inert? Did the basic reading texts *ever* teach anything other than principles of grammar and form? The degree to which they could turns on questions rarely asked about the kinds of knowledge these texts contained.[1] That knowledge is usually assumed to be a simple and practical ethics, but the extent to which these texts could ever have provided what Kenneth Burke helpfully called "equipment for living" turns out to be largely chimerical.[2] As I will try to show in the next chapter, such knowledge had certain cognitive effects, since the degree to which it was internalized transformed it into a perceptual grid that shaped what it is probably best to call "experience." But, as I want to show here, this knowledge could not guide behavior because it was fundamentally useless. I will try to explain how so much learning could add up to so little, but, in so doing, I hope to show how such an intellectual void also had a profoundly *affective* component, instilling certain feelings, shaping passions if not actions, in this way becoming an important, if unusual, resource for literature.

The medieval term for this knowledge was not *ethice* or *ethica* but *sapientia*, or "wisdom," although one of the first confusions attending this subject is that most school texts define *sapientia* as something very like a practical ethics—as the *Distichs of Cato* put it, a "wisdom" that "you live with" [ut sapiens vivas] (II.pro). The paradigmatic form such knowledge

---

[1] Katherine Breen has argued that the "grammar of declensions and conjugations, agreement and syntax lays the foundation for the more delicate modulation of personal and collective morality...in the medieval discipline of ethics," *Imagining an English Reading Public, 1150–1400* (Cambridge: Cambridge University Press, 2010), 83 (and, see generally, her chapter on "The grammatical paradigm," 80–121).

[2] Kenneth Burke, "Literature as Equipment for Living," 293–304 in his *The Philosophy of Literary Form: Studies in Symbolic Action* (Louisiana, LA: Louisiana State University Press, 1941).

takes in the canon of schoolroom texts, as in many others, is the "maxim," "apothegm," "adage," "aphorism," "precept," or, as it is most commonly called in the Middle Ages and now, the "proverb." This form is not only aggregated to constitute the whole of the *Distichs* but, also the *Facetus*, the *Liber parabolarum*, as well as a substantial part of the *Tobias* (in its inset proverb collection), not to mention the maxims that appear so frequently in the *Fables* of Avianus. "Wisdom literature," as we might also describe these texts, is one of the oldest literary kinds.[3] The category usually includes five books of the Hebrew Bible—the Book of Proverbs, Job, Ecclesiastes, Ecclesiasticus, and Wisdom—as well as an array of even more ancient texts that these books of Scripture drew upon.[4] Because such texts are by definition both short and pithy, almost all wisdom literature began as elementary learning; even the wisdom books of the Bible were probably first written as school texts.[5]

Since the *Distichs of Cato*, the *Facetus* ("cum [est] nihil utilius"), the *Fables* of Avianus, the *Liber parabolarum*, and the *Tobias* have certain literary ambitions (they are all in verse, if nothing else), it is probably well to be clear here that the knowledge they contained did *not* provide the utility sometimes attributed to the aesthetic, what Horace understood in the *Ars poetica* as the way poetry mixed the "useful" with the "sweet" [miscuit utile dulci], its characteristic joining of what is "likewise pleasurable and helpful in life" [simul et iucunda et idonea...uitae].[6] This is certainly a well-attested view in the Middle Ages. The Host in the *Canterbury Tales*, for example, wraps such criteria around every one of the tales by defining the "best" tale as the one that conveys the most "sentence" [teaching] and "solaas" [comfort] (I.798). But if, as I will argue

[3] One example, surviving on Egyptian papyri, closer to a mirror for princes, but still practical in its orientation, probably dates from 2000 BC. See *The Instruction for King Meri-ka-re*, 155–61 in *Documents from Old Testament Times*, ed. D. Winton Thomas et al. (London: T. Nelson, 1958).

[4] For a survey of this literature in Middle English literature see Cameron Louis, "Proverbs, Precepts, and Monitory Pieces," 2957–3048 in *A Manual of the Writings in Middle English*, gen. ed. Albert E. Hartung, vol. 9 (New Haven, CT: Connecticut Academy of Arts and Sciences, 1993–). On the genre in the Bible see W. Baumgartner, "The Wisdom Literature," 210–37 in *The Old Testament and Modern Study: A Generation of Discovery and Research*, ed. H. H. Rowley (Oxford: Clarendon Press, 1951). On the kinds of ancient wisdom on which these texts draw see E. W. Heaton, *The School Tradition of the Old Testament* (Oxford: Oxford University Press, 1994). For a detailed account of the particular texts on which the Book of Proverbs draws see R. N. Whybray, *The Composition of the Book of Proverbs* (Sheffield: Sheffield Academic Press, 1994) and R. N. Whybray, *The Book of Proverbs: A Survey of Modern Study* (Leiden: E. J. Brill, 1995), esp. 1–28.

[5] See Heaton, *School Tradition of the Old Testament*, esp. 24–64.

[6] Horace, *Ars poetica* 442–89 in *Satires, Epistles and Ars poetica*, ed. and trans. H. Fairclough (New York, NY: G. P. Putnam, 1942), lines 334 ("simul") and 343 ("miscuit").

here, "comfort" is one of the principal effects of wisdom literature "sentence" is not.[7] Nor is such literature "equipment for living" if such equipment must be an admixture of learning and affect as Burke also defined it, of "strategies for dealing with situations," on the one hand, or "attitudes" toward "a pattern of experience" on the other.[8] As I will suggest in all that follows, any equation between the practical and affective qualities of the contents of wisdom literature mistakes the fundamental degree to which this particular species of wisdom could not, by definition, ever be put to practical use.

To put this last point in a more positive way, the proverb and, by extension, the large part of schoolroom learning consisting of such wisdom, was valuable, not because it provided wisdom that informed behavior, but because it pleased by providing the knowledge that made whoever possessed it feel wise. Such an observation not only flies in the face of definitions of poetry provided by Horace, Chaucer, and Burke, but, as I will make clear in the next section of this chapter, most modern scholarship on the proverb. As I will go on to suggest in subsequent sections, however Ricardian poets, like all medieval writers trained to read and write by means of the standard schoolroom canon, understood wisdom literature as both practically useless but deeply comforting *for that reason*. Tracing this understanding as it unfolds in the actions of medieval narrative makes clear how the proverb even now is affective rather than informative, but also why literature generally has such an affinity for this ancient form (why all literature can be understood, as Burke also puts it boldly, as "proverbs writ large").[9] In this sense, what the Middle English writer learned most of all from his basic literacy training was how to deploy the *utile* so that it was *dulce*, how to ensure, not that "sentence" was always accompanied by "solaas," but that it was equivalent to it, how to use a wisdom that provided happiness to the extent that its possessor could be sure that it was always *there*.

SCHOOLROOM WISDOM

There is a large scholarly literature on the proverb, although that scholarship emerges from so many different disciplines that it is very hard to say whether this form of knowledge is more precisely defined by its form or by the nature of its contents. It has been understood as a verbal structure

---

[7] *MED*, s.vv. "sentence 2a" and "solas 2b."
[8] Burke, "Literature as Equipment for Living," 296 ("strategies"), 297 ("attitudes"), and 300 ("pattern").
[9] Burke, "Literature as Equipment for Living," 296.

characteristic of everyday conversation ("the strategic social use of meta-phor"),[10] as an unusually condensed "ethics" ("pithy, memorable phrases and sentences that encapsulate guidance for behaviour in ethical situa-tions"),[11] and as a political device (a "linguistic instrument... by which people attempt to get other members of their culture and society to see the world and behave in a common way").[12] The proverb has also been seen as the precise marrying of verbal and ideational shape (according to "the symmetrical structure of its form and content").[13] Aside from the last of these, however, the common assumption of all such definitions is that the proverb offers useful advice: it provides teaching that can be put into action, knowledge that betters—because it can provide guidance for—daily life.

It is significant, then, that most of what constitutes proverbial know-ledge in medieval school texts cannot teach in this way for two reasons. First, proverbs rarely define the "good" they insist upon. A paradigmatic instance here is the demand in the prologue of the *Distichs* that we all "practice virtue" [virtute utere] (*Distichs of Cato*, pro). As one of fifty-five, short instructions at the start of the *Distichs* (what is sometimes called the "parva" or "little" Cato) the emptiness here might seem a consequence of the proverb's pith, and it does seem possible to follow similarly short injunctions to "pray to God" [Deo supplica], "love your parents" [parentes ama], or "be tidy" [mundus esto]. And yet, insofar as such injunctions fail to explain how to pray, or what "love" of this kind consists of, or what it is to be "tidy," their pith empties them of the very practical knowledge on which they seem also to rely. Proverbs are by definition short forms, but this also means that they are actually formally committed to omissions of this kind. The inset proverb collection in the *Tobias* provides further illustration of this pith in its injunctions ("sow virtues" [insere virtutes], line 550/p. 99), but its longer injunctions also illustrate the more subtle formal means by which proverbs disable their own advice:

> Cavenda cave, sectare sequenda, relega
> Crimina, vas mentis purificare stude.

> [Avoid what should be avoided, pursue what should be pursued,
> Banish sins, strive to purify the vessel of your soul.]

> (Matthew of Vendôme, *Tobias* 517–18/p. 98)

---

[10] Peter Seitel, "Proverbs: A Social Use of Metaphor," *Genre* 2 (1969): 143.
[11] Cameron Louis, "Authority in Middle English Proverb Literature," *Florilegium* 15 (1998): 85.
[12] Cameron Louis, "Proverbs and the Politics of Language," *Proverbium* 17 (2000): 177.
[13] G. B. Milner, "What is A Proverb?," *New Society* 332 (1969): 200.

Quicquid agas, numquam vicio mergatur honestum.
[Whatever you do, never let virtue be drowned by vice.]

      (Matthew of Vendôme, *Tobias* 589/p. 103)

Ut Domino placeas, noli peccare.
[So that you might please the Lord, do not sin.]

      (Matthew of Vendôme, *Tobias*, 911/p. 109)[14]

The first line of the first of these is a perfect tautology, but its second line as well as all of the other proverbs could be described as *functional* tautologies, since they each define the good as the opposite of the not-good ("crime" [crimen] is what should be banished, "virtue" [honestas] is the opposite of "vice" [vitium], doing good is failing to "sin" [peccatum]). Such proverbs fail to instruct by failing to define the terms that must be understood if they are to be followed. As one of the proverbs in the *Liber parabolarum* also demonstrates, such tautology could occur even in the context of what is, otherwise, (what is formally) the most careful of explanations:

Munda manus mundum vas quod lavat efficit atque
Sordida sordidius quam fuit ante facit.

[A clean hand makes that vessel clean which it washes;
A dirty hand makes it dirtier than it was before.]

      (Alan of Lille, *Liber parabolarum*, lines 455–6/p. 169)

It is the repetition of the term to be defined in the definition (the "clean" makes something "clean" just as the "dirty" makes something "dirty") that nullifies these statements, each intensifying the emptiness of the other in their mirroring structure.

A second problem with the advice that proverbs might be understood to provide is the extent to which so many of them are "linked to another ... which appears to give it the lie."[15] This is a principle easy to illustrate with proverbs common today ("fools rush in where angels fear to tread" versus "the early bird catches the worm"), but it virtually defines any schoolroom syllabus that drew from the standard canon, since the contradictions inherent in the form meant that the texts a given schoolmaster brought together often undermined one another. The *Tobias*, for example, includes a profusion of injunctions that are versions of the Golden Rule:

---

[14] A similar sort of instruction can also be found in the *Liber cartule*, "Si vis salvari, semper studeas imitari / Vitam justorum, fugiens exempla malorum" [If you wish to be saved, always strive to imitate the life of the just, fleeing the examples of the wicked] (*Liber Cartule*, col. 1312c/p. 63).

[15] Milner, "What is a Proverb?," 199.

> Da miseris, potum sitienti funde, molestum
>   Letifica: parcus semine parca metes.
> Est ancilla Dei simplex elemosina, mortis
>   Antidotum, venie porta, salutis iter.
>
> [Give to the unfortunate, pour forth drink for the thirsty, cheer
>   the troubled; sparing of your seed you will harvest little.
> The handmaid of God is sincere alms, the remedy of
>   Death, the gate of pardon, the way of salvation.]
>
>   (Matthew of Vendôme, *Tobias* 913–16/p. 110)[16]

While the *Distichs* insist that alms should always take a back seat to personal interest:

> Dapsilis interdum notis et largus amicis
> cum fueris, dando semper tibi proximus esto.
>
> [Though you are sometimes generous to friends with great gifts,
> In giving always keep yourself close.]
>
>   (*Distichs of Cato* 1.40)

Some of this contradiction must be the consequence of the additive nature of proverb collections—itself a consequence of the proverb's brevity (which always made it possible to add another proverb)—with the result that such collections often conflate the assumptions and keenly held principles of very different cultures. It is for this reason that, as I noticed in the last chapter, the *Distichs* are, at once, resolutely polytheistic:

> An di sint caelumque regant, ne quaere doceri.
> [Do not seek to know whether the Gods exist or rule the heavens.]
>
>   (*Distichs of Cato*, II.2)

> Incusare deos noli, sed te ipse coerce.
> [Do not blame the gods but correct yourself.]
>
>   (*Distichs of Cato*, I.23)

but also resolutely monotheistic:

> Quid deus intendat, noli perquirere sorte:
> quid statuat de te, sine te deliberat ille.
>
> [Do not seek too much what God plans:
> What he plans for you, he does without your advice.]
>
>   (*Distichs of Cato*, II.12)

---

[16] Although phrased in the negative there is also a version of the Golden Rule in the *Facetus*: "Ne facias alii, tibi quod minime fieri vis; / sic Christo placidus et amatus habebere cuivis" [Do not do to others what you would not want done to you; so will you be pleasing to Christ and a friend to anyone] (13/p. 44).

This is also why the *Distichs* can insist that self-interest trumps generosity, as in the proverb just mentioned, and the line I also quoted in Chapter 4:

> Sic bonus esto bonis, ne te mala damna sequantur.
> [Do . . . good to others so that no serious injury befalls you.]
>
> (*Distichs of Cato*, I.11)

but can also insist on the most Christian forms of charity:

> Si potes, ignotis etiam prodesse memento:
> utilius regno est meritis acquirere amicos.
>
> [Take pains to help even strangers, if you can:
> To gain friends with kindness is more useful than power.]
>
> (*Distichs of Cato*, II.1)

Some of these contradictions could be understood as a particularly rich education, furnishing the schoolboy with a range of possibilities for responding to a given situation or for making an equally wide range of ethical choices. In this sense, when the *Distichs* urge the schoolboy to be confident in his opinions,

> Laudaris quodcumque palam, quodcumque probaris,
> hoc vide ne rursus levitatis crimine damnes.
>
> [What you've approved and openly praised,
> Do not casually reproach.]
>
> (*Distichs of Cato*, IV.25)

as well as urging him to be circumspect,

> Quod pudeat, socios prudens celare memento,
> ne plures culpent id quod tibi displicet uni.
>
> [What makes you blush before friends be careful to conceal,
> Lest many blame what displeases you alone.]
>
> (*Distichs of Cato*, II.7)

they are freeing him to choose between these positions, while also supporting him in whatever decision he makes. This may not be an ethics worthy of the name, since it may define as good any action a person chooses, and yet the point of such instruction cannot be sifting the bad from the good, but, rather, the activity of instruction itself, the provision of advice so copious and varied that a person always has some rule to follow.

And yet proverbs have long been understood to dispense knowledge of great value. B. J. Whiting, one of the most dedicated modern scholars of the form, defined it as "a short saying of philosophic nature . . . constantly applicable, and appealing because it bears a semblance of universal truth," and he traced this view back to Aristotle, who was said by Synesius to have defined the proverb as "the remnants of man's early philosophy which had managed to escape destruction because of their brevity and cleverness."[17] Since the Renaissance it has been more common to insist, as James Howells did in the *Paroimiographia or Old Sayed Sawes* (1659), that such philosophy had its origins, not in ancient times, but in "the peeple's voice / Coin'd first, and current made by common choice."[18] Such an insistence on the "common" qualities of the proverb has almost always generated an attendant condescension, whereby the proverb's "truth" is, as Whiting also put it, "apparently... fundamental."[19] A touchstone for this attitude must be John Heywood's apology, in a prefatory poem addressing "the reader," for the offense he might give "fine tender eares" by the "rough rude termes of homely honestie" of the proverbs he expands as his *First Hundred Epigrams* (1549).[20] And yet, even where the proverb was condescended to in this way it was always assumed to have taught something useful. As John Heywood put it in the prefatory poem to his *Dialogue Containing Proverbs* (1546), "common plaine pithie proverbes olde /... include so large a reache / That almost in all thinges good lessons they teache."[21] Even as the sphere of its operation was devalued, in other words, the proverb was seen to have use-value for those with little learning. As Natalie Zemon Davis put the point, summing up a long tradition of such views, the proverb is "an essential resource... recommending different courses of action... for... peasants... in their primarily unlettered and still quite local world."[22]

The attitude governing all of these formulations may well have been the unintended consequence of Erasmus's herculean effort to collect ancient

[17] Synesius is quoted in Greek and paraphrased in English in B. J. Whiting, "The Nature of the Proverb," *Harvard Studies and Notes in Philology and Literature* 14 (1932): 278. See also *Proverbs, Sentences and Proverbial Phrases from English Writings Mainly before 1500*, ed. Bartlett Jere Whiting and Helen Wescott Whiting (Cambridge, MA: Harvard University Press, 1968), p. xi. Natalie Zemon Davis quotes this view as if from Aristotle's *Rhetoric* in "Proverbial Wisdom and Popular Errors," 227–67 and 336–46 (notes) in her *Society and Culture in Early Modern France* (Stanford, CA: Stanford University Press, 1975), 234.

[18] James Howell, *ΠΑΡΟΙΜΙΟΓΡΑΦΙΑ. Proverbs, or Old sayed sawes & adages in English (or the Saxon Toung), Italian, French and Spanish, whereunto the British for their great Antiquity and weight are added* (J. G., 1659), A, 1v., as cited in Whiting, "The Nature of the Proverb," 294.

[19] Whiting, "Nature of the Proverb," 302.

[20] John Heywood, "The First Hundred Epigrams," 103–39 in *John Heywood's Works and Miscellaneous Short Poems*, ed. Burton A. Milligan, Illinois Studies in Language and Literature 41 (Urbana, IL: University of Illinois Press, 1956), 104.

[21] John Heywood, "A Dialogue Containing Proverbs," 17–101 in *John Heywood's Works*, ed. Milligan, 18.

[22] Davis, "Proverbial Wisdom and Popular Errors," 243.

"adages" or what he often terms *proverbia* in the introduction to his *Adagia* (1500–30).[23] Erasmus could not have valued the proverb more, and he amassed his collection of sayings from the works of the most revered philosophers and writers (Plato, Euripides, Terence, Cicero, Aristotle) in all the languages of learning (not only Greek and Latin, but Hebrew as well). But the very process of collecting so much wisdom inevitably prompted Erasmus to order it, and one of the criteria he used was quality ("I think the best of them are those which equally give pleasure by their figurative coloring and profit by the value of their ideas" [Tum optimas fateor eas, quae pariter et translationis pigmento delectent et sententiae prosint utilitate].[24] This qualitative distinction was installed into Erasmus's definition of the proverb, which he understood as a "saying" characterized above all by its "originality" [novitas]: "A proverb is a saying in popular use, remarkable for some shrewd and novel turn" [Paroemia est celebre dictum, scita quapiam novitate insigne].[25] Erasmus may have been documenting a contemporary view rather than bringing about a large-scale shift, but, either way, the *Adagia* make it possible to observe and date with some precision the moment when a great deal of what had passed for proverbial wisdom passed out of the precincts of learning and into a new category of what we still sometimes call "common" or "popular" wisdom. Such wisdom was neither "learned" nor "eloquent" and therefore understood as a product of lived experience rather than books, a status and origin confirmed by the extent to which it circulated in the vernacular.[26]

It is both convenient and logical, then, that the best account of such proverbs and their function prior to this sixteenth-century transformation

---

[23] Erasmus, *Adagiorum Chilias Prima*, ed. M. L. van Poll-van de Lisdonk, M. Mann Phillips, and Chr. Robinson, Ordo 2, vol. 1 in Desiderius Erasmus, *Opera Omnia* (Amsterdam: North-Holland, 1969–) and Erasmus, *Adages*, trans. Margaret Mann Phillips, annotated R. A. B. Mynors, vol. 31 in *Collected Works of Erasmus* (Toronto: University of Toronto Press, 1974–). Erasmus generally refers to the texts he is collecting as *paroemiae*, rather than *adagia* (a term he uses sparingly), but he frequently cites definitions of the *proverbium* (e.g. *Adagia*, Prolegomena, i [p. 45, ll. 10 and 12], *Adages*, Introduction, i [p. 3, ll. 6 and 8]), entitles one section of his introduction "Commendatio proverbiorum a dignitate" [Proverbs are to be respected for their value] (*Adagia*, Prolegomena, v [p. 52, l. 77]), and refers, interchangeably to *proverbia* and *paroemia* in a section called "Ad persuadendum conducere" [Proverbs as a means to persuasion] (*Adagia*, Prolegomena, vii [pp. 62–4, ll. 319, 330, 331, 350, 354, 358, 367 ["proverbia" and its declined forms], ll. 333, 346, 372 ["paroemia" and its declined forms]; for this section in the translation, see *Adages*, pp. 15–17). *Paroemia* is also the common term for the proverb in rhetorical treatises; see, for example, Quintilian, *The Orator's Education*, ed. Donald Russell, 5 vols. (Cambridge, MA: Harvard University Press, 2001), V.11.21 and VIII.6.58.
[24] *Adagia*, Prolegomena, i (p. 46, ll. 39–40); *Adages*, Introduction, i (p. 4, ll. 37–9).
[25] *Adagia*, Prolegomena, i (p. 46, ll. 44–5); *Adages*, Introduction i (p. 4, ll. 43–4).
[26] Davis discusses this shift in "Proverbial Wisdom and Popular Errors," esp. 230–6.

can be found in vernacular literature, and one of the best reflections of these functions in schoolroom learning can be found in Chaucer's Nun's Priest's Tale. This tale has schoolroom wisdom at its core, since it is the kind of beast fable that was a staple of the grammar-school syllabus, and, like many beast fables, it embeds proverbs near its conclusion as a summary of the lesson the animals have learned (and therefore that the fable teaches).[27] The Nun's Priest's Tale is much more than a fable too, and its manner has also been associated with beast epics like the *Roman de Reynart* from which it derives its central narrative.[28] But the events at its core remains as simple as any one of the *Fables* of Avianus (a rooster is seized in a farmyard by a fox and, with a trick, saves his own life), and its lessons are offered in the form of what Chaucer also calls "common" proverbs.[29] So far from recommending courses of action, however, these proverbs look back toward and reflect upon decisions that have already been made.

The Nun's Priest's Tale works toward these reflections by focusing on, and generating much of its humor from, a series of spectacular errors. The rooster, Chauntecleer, has a dream in which he sees himself snatched by a predator in the farmyard, but, even as he insists on the predictive value of dreams, he defies his prediction, and descends into the farmyard, where, in due course, a fox snatches him. As the fox carries him off on his back, Chauntecleer persuades him to turn to his pursuers and gloat, but when the fox opens his mouth to do so, he releases Chauntecleer who flies into a tree well out of reach. Each animal then uses a proverb to berate himself for the wisdom he so signally lacked. Chauntecleer, realizing that he should have been more cautious after having had such a dream, observes:

> For he that wynketh*, whan he sholde see,   blinks
> Al wilfully, God lat him nevere thee*!   thrive
>
> (VII.3431–2)[30]

The fox, realizing that he should have kept his mouth shut, says:

[27] For an account of the beast fable and the Nun's Priest's Tale as "wisdom literature" see Morton W. Bloomfield, "The Wisdom of the Nun's Priest's Tale," 70–82 in *Chaucerian Problems and Perspectives: Essays Presented to Paul E. Beichner*, ed. Edward Vasta and Zacharias P. Thundy (Notre Dame, IN: University of Notre Dame Press, 1979).

[28] On the relationship between the tale and the *Roman de Reynart* and its significance to its style and the scope of its meanings see Jill Mann, *From Aesop to Reynard: Beast Literature in Medieval Britain* (Oxford: Oxford University Press, 2009), 251–61 (for a discussion of the deeper sources of the episodes Chaucer borrows from the *Reynart* see 238–43).

[29] On Chaucer's use of the phrase "common proverb" see the discussion on p. 215.

[30] See *Proverbs, Sentences and Proverbial Phrases*, ed. Whiting and Whiting, W367.

... God yeve* hym meschaunce*   give/bad luck
That is so undiscreet* of governaunce*   careless/behavior
That jangleth whan he sholde holde his pees.

(VII.3433–5)[31]

Both of these nuggets of wisdom are also completely useless because they
are deployed after they could be applied. Such positioning could be seen as
typical of many ethical lessons and of fables in general: the concluding
moral extracts the "good" out of the exemplary disaster. But, however
typical, this order demonstrates the fundamental problem with any such
teaching. Where a lesson is drawn from prior error what it cannot do is
guide, and where that lesson is a well-known proverb—wisdom "common"
enough, or learned early enough, to have been known long before the error
occurred—what that lesson insists upon most of all is that such wisdom is
exactly what those who erred should *already* have known. Such knowledge
shows itself to be the very inversion of an ethics, not a way of knowing how
to act but a way of coming to terms with an event once it has occurred, not a
guide to the future, but an *interpretation of the past*.

Most proverbs are preceptive, even hortatory, insisting in their very
form that they instruct, and yet the belatedness of the proverbs in The
Nun's Priest's Tale is typical of their use in medieval literature. Examples
abound, but another particularly useful illustration can be found at the
conclusion of the tale of Actaeon narrated in Book 1 of John Gower's
Confessio Amantis. Actaeon has "caste his yhe" [eye] (361) and "syh" [saw]
(362) Diana bathing naked in the fountain, and he has already been
punished by his transformation into a hart. Genius then draws a moral
from this story with a proverb that resembles Chauntecleer's in both
language and imagery, but also inverts it (providing the mirror-image
that almost every proverb seems to have) insisting it is far better to
shut one's eyes than "to look":

Lo now, my sone, what it is
A man to caste his yhe* amis, !   eye
Which Actaeon hath dere aboght*;   dearly purchased
Be war* forthi* and do it noght.   wary/ therefore
For ofte, who that hiede toke*,   took heed
Betre is to winke* than to look.   blink

(1.379–84)

[31] See *Proverbs, Sentences and Proverbial Phrases*, T366, T367, and T373. These lines
may also be a variation of the distich that Chaucer quotes at the end of the Manciple's Tale:
"Virtutem primam esse puto, compescere linguam" [I think that the first virtue is to restrain
one's tongue] (*Distichs* I.3), as "The firste vertu, sone, if thow wolt leere, / Is to restreine and
kepe wel thy tonge" (IX.332–4).

This sequence offers the customary insistence that the proverb is a story's teaching, and this would be in keeping with Genius's general practice in the *Confessio*, since he routinely offers stories as "examples" of a particular ethical rule (in this case, he introduces the narrative of Acteon as "a tale, to be war [mindful] therby / Thin yhe [eye] for to kepe and warde [guard]," 1.331–2). And yet, since this is a story, not of the good that comes from "winking" but, rather, of the dangers incurred by looking, this proverb is also the retrospective interpretation of a mistake. It is not too much to say in fact, that what this proverb provides is the wisdom the actions of this narrative have failed to impart. Since Genius insists that Amans learn from Actaeon's mistake exactly what Chauntecleer understood to be his mistake in The Nun's Priest's Tale, this story also helps to make clear just how little proverbs *could* teach.

Since such wisdom could not possibly constitute a map that would help whoever possessed it to avoid error, its use-value lay in its circumstantial constancy, its general availability for any ethical need. The proverbs in The Nun's Priest's Tale and the tale of Actaeon are cited as a consequence of the errors made by the rooster, the fox, and Actaeon and so, while they specify those errors, rather than teach those who cite them what to do, they formulate the lesson that has just been learned. In pedagogical terms, such deployments require that some distinction be made between possessing knowledge and employing it, as well as a general acknowledgment that knowing a rule does not ensure that it will be followed at the crucial juncture. The "wisdom" or *sapientia* of the schoolroom proverb is more properly understood, then, as a relation to knowledge rather than a body of facts or principles. "Using" such knowledge entails learning what one already knew (discovering through the events in which the proverb finds its meaning, what the proverb "really" means). I think this is why Burke also defined the proverb as "medicine" or "consolation," since, as the narratives I have just rehearsed also make clear, the sudden recognition of the pertinence of an already-known knowledge inevitably has an affective component.[32] Its predicate is often a kind of trauma—Chauntecleer has had a scare, the fox has lost his coveted prey, and Actaeon has been dramatically punished—and the proverb emerges, first, wistfully, laden with regret that it was not remembered soon enough to avoid the mistake. As the pertinent wisdom hoves into view, however, it brings the erring figure into the community of all those who have cited this proverb in such circumstances before. The status of the proverb as a long-known and long-held "wisdom"—as an ancient knowledge, shared

---

[32] Burke, "Equipment for Living," 297.

by whole cultures and many past cultures too—means that, following the trauma that calls it out, and accompanying the knowledge it dispenses, comes the comforting realization, the relief, that this error has been made many times before. What the schoolroom proverb provides most of all, then, by means of its always-belated use, is the reassurance that he who has just been foolish has *finally* grown wise.

THE MERRIMENT OF THE MELIBEE

The patterns of use I have just described remain common I think—we are still much more likely to cite a proverb when its wisdom has been proven than prior to making a decision—but we fail to recognize these defining patterns because we still denigrate this knowledge according to the script provided by the early modern period (proverbs remain "common" in both senses of the term), and we therefore also ignore the pleasures that attend our own usage. If this is not the place to pursue this larger topic, the broader patterns of misrecognition can be explored in a single narrative, Chaucer's Tale of Melibee, which not only cites proverbs but often largely consists of them, and which, insists, at least on its face—and again and again and again—that what proverbs do, above all, is teach. The deadly seriousness of those who cite proverbs in this tale—and the seriousness of the grounds on which they cite them—also make it possible to see, as if in relief, how the comfort provided by such wisdom finally swamps its propositional content, and therefore how Ricardian writers could depend on this particular part of their elementary schoolroom learning to lend such affect to literature. The Melibee is also usefully examined for such relationships because it is not usually understood to resemble, or even to have been influenced by, a grammar-school text. It is usually described as a work of "counsel" or a "mirror for princes" focused on whether—and on what grounds—the figure called "Melibee" might avenge himself on his "olde foos [foes]" after they have "setten ladders to the walles of his hous and by windowes ben entred [have entered], and betten his wif and wounded his doghter with five mortal woundes in five sundry [different] places... and leften hire for deed and wenten away" (VII.970–1), or whether, as his wife Prudence insists at length, Melibee should sue for peace.[33] Many of its proverbs come directly from Scripture, or school texts

---

[33] For political readings of this tale see Lee Patterson, " 'What Man Artow?': Authorial Self-Definition in *The Tale of Sir Thopas* and *The Tale of Melibee,*" *Studies in the Age of Chaucer* 11 (1989): 117–76 (esp. 135–60); Judith Ferster, *Fictions of Advice: The Literature and Politics of Counsel in Late Medieval England* (Philadelphia, PA: University of

212	*From Literacy to Literature*

used in a different tradition than the one I have been tracing in this book, since the Melibee is a very close translation of Renaud de Louens's *Livre de Melibée et de Dame Prudence* (*c.*1336), which is in turn an abridgment and translation of the *Liber consolationis et consilii* by the lawyer, Albertano of Brescia. If Chaucer encountered these source texts as an adult writer, and the proverbs he translated differed from those he learned in his own grammar-school books, they were identical in function, and often in content, to the wisdom he learned in those books, and his identification with this material—the sense that this wisdom was *his* wisdom—is also carried in the fact that this is the one serious tale told by the narrator of the *Tales*, the "Chaucer" who seems to share much of Chaucer's biography and attitudes.

The Tale of Melibee is also a useful site for analyzing the use of proverbs because it so carefully inserts this tale in the larger context of the frame narrative of the tale-telling contest that it is possible to scrutinize the pilgrims' expectations for, and reactions to, wisdom literature of this kind. When the narrator introduces this "litel thing in prose" (VII.940) he

Pennsylvania Press, 1996), 89–107; Donald Howard, *The Idea of the Canterbury Tales* (Berkeley, CA: University of California Press, 1976), 309; and Richard Firth Green, *Poets and Princepleasers: Literature and the English Court in the Late Middle Ages* (Toronto: University of Toronto Press, 1980), 143. For historicist arguments which see the Melibee as an attempt to intervene in particular moments, or in particular issues, of late fourteenth-century politics see Gardiner Stillwell, "The Political Meaning of Chaucer's *Tale of Melibee,*" *Speculum* 19 (1944): 433–44; William Askins, "The *Tale of Melibee* and the Crisis at Westminster, November, 1387," *Studies in the Age of Chaucer, Proceedings* 2 (1986): 103–12; V. J. Scattergood, "Chaucer and the French War: *Sir Thompas* and *Melibee,*" 287–96 in *Court and Poet: Selected Proceedings of the Third Congress of the International Courtly Literature Society (Liverpool 1980),* ed. Glyn S. Burgess, with A. D. Deyermond, W. H. Jackson, A. D. Mills, and P. T. Ricketts (Liverpool: Francis Cairns, 1981); and Lynn Staley Johnson, "Inverse Counsel: Contexts for the Melibee," *Studies in Philology* 87 (1990): 137–55. David Wallace sees the Melibee as a work of "counsel" but for "he or she who must speak to powerful men," rather than for princes (*Chaucerian Polity: Absolutist Lineages and Associational Forms in England and Italy* [Stanford, CA: Stanford University Press, 1997], 221). David Aers finds a more subtle politics in the Melibee's embrace of forgiveness and repentance "without any mention of the Church in which the Catholic Christian was taught to fulfil the sacrament of penance," an absence that seems very carefully to avoid "traditions under pressure from Wycliffites." See his "Chaucer's *Tale of Melibee*: Whose Virtues?," 69–81 in *Medieval Literature and Historical Inquiry: Essays in Honour of Derek Pearsall,* ed. David Aers (Cambridge: D. S. Brewer, 2000), 81 (for the phrases I have quoted). Although the wide-ranging concerns of her argument do not really anticipate my own ("the analysis will contribute toward a fuller understanding of everybody's favourite Canterbury pilgrim, the Wife of Bath" [170]), a similar identification is made in Betsy Bowden, "Ubiquitous Format? What Ubiquitous Format?: Chaucer's *Tale of Melibee* as a Proverb Collection," *Oral Tradition* 17 (2002): 169–207. More pertinent is Mann's categorization of the Melibee as an instance of wisdom literature in the head note to her commentary on the tale in Chaucer, *The Canterbury Tales,* ed. Jill Mann (Harmondsworth: Penguin, 2005), 1000–1.

describes it as "moral," but he also insists that its main point will lie in the manner of its "telling" (VII.948) rather than its "sentence" (VII.947). Commentators have often recoiled from that manner—what Pearsall called its "remorseless good sense"—with some even suggesting that the tale is not "to be taken seriously" because it is "too pedantically elaborate."[34] Tatlock characterized its proverbs as "no more than the sayings of dead wiseacres," finding the whole production "unspeakably trite and dry."[35] And yet Chaucer signals his own seriousness of purpose, not only by assigning it, in effect, to himself, but by presenting it as one of the few tales all the other pilgrims heartily approve. Much more important, in other words, than the critical consensus that the tale is dreary is the narrator's claim that this rich collection of "sentence" would be, above all things, "mirye" [merry] (VII.944):

> ... though that I telle somwhat moore
> Of proverbes than ye han* herde bifoore   have
> Comprehended* in this litel tretys heere,   included
> To enforce* with th'effect of my mateere*;   fortify/ material
> And though I nat* the same wordes seye   do not
> As ye han herd, yet to yow alle I preye
> Blameth me nat; for, as in my sentence*,   meaning
> Shul* ye nowher fynden difference   shall
> Fro the sentence of this tretys lyte
> After the* which this murye tale I write.   according to
> And therfore herkneth* what that I shal seye,   listen to
> And lat me tellen al my tale, I preye.

(VII.955–66)

This promise of merriment is the more insistent and striking because the claim that the "litel tretise" contains "somwhat moore" of proverbs than other versions of this treatise turns out to be an exaggeration (careful

---

[34] Derek Pearsall, *The Canterbury Tales* (London: George Allen & Unwin, 1985), 287. Helen Cooper, *The Structure of the Canterbury Tales* (London: Duckworth, 1983), 173–6. Talbot Donaldson also observed that the Melibee was "a very popular story in the Middle Ages when readers did not entirely distinguish between pleasure in literature and pleasure in being edified" (*Chaucer's Poetry: An Anthology for the Modern Reader*, ed. Talbot Donaldson [New York: Ronald Press, 1975], 1101). See also Dolores Palomo, "What Chaucer Really Did to *Le Livre de Mellibee*," *Philological Quarterly* 53 (1974): 49–55 and Ralph W. V. Elliott, *Chaucer's English* (London: André Deutsch, 1974), 173–4.

[35] John S. P. Tatlock, *The Development and Chronology of Chaucer's Works*, Chaucer Society, 2nd series 37 (London: Kegan Paul, Trench, Trübner, 1907), 189. Tatlock was specifically countering the view that the Melibee was Chaucer's revenge on the Host for interrupting his Tale of Sir Thopas. For this view see *The Prologue from Chaucer's Canterbury Tales*, ed. Frank Jewett Mather (Boston, MA: Houghton Mifflin, 1899), p. xxxi and Robert M. Lumiansky, *Of Sondry Folk: The Dramatic Principle in* The Canterbury Tales (Austin, TX: University of Texas Press, 1955), 94.

scholarship has shown that Chaucer adds, at most, three proverbs to his source).[36]

The grounds on which these proverbs and their wisdom were meant to be taken seriously are also outlined with some care at the beginning of the *Melibee*, as if to guide any reader who might be in doubt about their purpose. The key passage could even be understood as a summary of the whole work, since "wisdom" seems to be personified there by one of *Melibee*'s putative advisors, a character referred to only as "oon of thise olde wise" (VII.1037). This old man is the first to speak out passionately against the war that a hastily convened counsel of flatterers and feigned friends has just urged upon Melibee, but the passage is significant here because it takes such careful notice of the affective nature of the old man's (of "Wisdom's") failure:

> And with his hand made contenaunce that men sholde holden hem stille and yeven him audience. "Lordynges," quod he, "ther is ful many a man that crieth 'Werre, werre!' that woot ful litel what werre amounteth. Werre at his bigynning hath so greet an entryng and so large, that every wight may entre whan hym liketh and lightly fynde were; but certes, what ende that shal therof bifalle, it is nat light to knowe. For soothly, whan that werre is ones bigonne, ther is ful many a child unborn of his moder that shal sterve yong by cause of thilke werre, or elles lyve in sorwe and dye in wrecchednesse. And therfore, er that any werre bigynne, men moste have greet conseil and greet deliberacioun." And whan this olde man wende to enforcen his tale by resons, wel ny alle atones bigonne they to rise for to breken his tale, and beden him ful ofte hise wordes for to abregge. For soothly, he that precheth to hem that listen nat heeren hise wordes, his sermon hem anoyeth. For Jhesus Syrak seith that "musik in weping is a noyous thing"; this is to seyn: as much availleth to speken bifore folk to whiche his speche anoyeth, as it is to synge biforn hym that wepeth. (VII.1037–45)

> [*countenance*: a sign; *yeven*: given; *woot*: knows; *his bigynning*: its beginning; *wight*: man; *hym liketh*: it pleases him; *certes*: certainly; *soothly*: truly; *sterve*: die; *thilke*: this very; *er*: before; *wende*: thought; *wel ny alle atones*: nearly all at once; *abregge*: cut short; *listen nat*: would rather not; *noyous*: irritating; *say*: saw]

This counsel is not in itself thick with proverbs, focusing, rather, on images of the futility and hopelessness of war. But, after he is completely shouted down by his audience and decides not to pursue his argument any further, the "old wise" produces two proverbs as if in summary of all that

---

[36] Mann finds such additions at VII.1054 and 1325–6 but notes that "even here we cannot be certain that the proverbs were not additions already present in the manuscript of the French text [Chaucer] was using," Chaucer, *The Canterbury Tales*, ed. Mann, 1001.

has been said, the first from Ecclesiasticus, the second, although described as a "common proverb," from a late antique collection very similar to the *Distichs of Cato*, usually called *Publilius Syrus*:[37]

> And whan this wise man saugh that hym wanted audience, al shamefast he sette hym doun agayn. For Salomon seith: "Ther as thou ne mayst have noon audience, enforce thee nat to speke." "I see wel," quod this wise man, "that the commune proverbe is sooth, that good conseil wanteth whan it is moost nede." (VII.1046–9)
>
> [*him wanted*: he lacked; *ther as thou ne mayst*: wherever you may not; *enforce thee nat*: do not try; *wanteth*: is lacking; *moost nede*: most needed]

As in The Nun's Priest's Tale and Gower's Tale of Actaeon, these proverbs come too late, the first sanctioning the decision that has just been made, the second describing the lesson the "old wise" has just learned. On this occasion, however, the emotional responses that accompany these belated citations are explored with equal care. In the large scene of instruction that the "old wise" had tried to convene, it is not simply that his advice was unheeded, but that those who heard what he had to say found it deeply "annoying" ("hem anoyeth"). More importantly, the "old wise" finds such a rejection of his words to be an immediate source of despair (he does not simply give up, but sits down "al shamefast"). Since he cannot provide any counsel—the point of the proverbs he has adduced is that his audience has stopped listening—the "old wise" uses his learning as a remedy for his *own* despair, using proverbs as a "medicine" that transform his fruitless efforts into a confirmation that *he* knows something. That is, if the "old wise" has been foolish to try to share his knowledge with those even more foolish than himself, he finds in the proverbs at which he finally arrives the comfort—the relief in knowing—that this is often true. Once again, proverbs are the source of a certain pleasure, snatched from the jaws of error, and the occasion for this "old wise" to celebrate quietly (since only to himself) that he has now become wiser still.

As it unfolds, The Tale of Melibee provides a similarly rich and informative collection of responses to the deployment of an extremely long chain of proverbs; indeed, the formal consequence of embedding so much proverbial wisdom in such an extended exchange of views—in so much

---

[37] "Where there is no hearing, pour not out words" [ubi auditus est non effundas sermonem] (Ecclesiasticus 32:6); "Counsel is always most lacking when it is most necessary" [Semper consilium tunc deest cum opus est maxime] (*Publilius Syrus*, l. 653). As cited in *The Canterbury Tales*, ed. Mann, 1003. For *Publilius Syrus* and a brief situating introduction see pp. 2–111 in *Minor Latin Poets*, ed. and trans. J. Wight Duff and Arnold M. Duff (Cambridge, MA: Harvard University Press, 1961; first published 1934). I will cite this text hereafter from this edition by line number in the text.

argument—is to make this, not just a collection of wisdom, but an exploration of the *extent* to which proverbs fail to teach The definitive moment here is, inevitably, the tale's conclusion, and, in particular, the moment when Melibee claims to have been fully persuaded by Prudence's arguments ("I assente and conferme me to have pees [peace]," VII.1777). Melibee's foes are then summoned in order to "trete of pees and of accord" (VII.1798), at which point they ask that Melibee grant them "foryevenesse of oure outrageous trespass and offense" (VII.1823). But when Prudence then asks Melibee what "vengeance" he proposes to take, he makes clear that he has not learned the lesson he just said he has: "I thynke and purpose me fully to desherite hem [dispossess them] of al that evere they han, and for to putte hem in exil for evere" (VII.1835). Lee Patterson described this moment as "devastating" because it indicates that "Prudence's teaching has been largely useless."[38] And it is worth underscoring Patterson's well-chosen phrasing here to note that this uselessness extends well beyond this moment, for the power of Prudence's wisdom is even called into question by the terms of its ultimate success. There are only three more paragraphs left in the tale (as we now tend to print it), and, in the second of these, Melibee changes his mind, and finally heeds Prudence's advice:

> For as muche as I se and biholde youre grete humylitee... it constreyneth me to doon yow grace and mercy. Wherefore I receyve yow to my grace, and foryeve yow outrely all the offenses, injuries, and wronges that ye have doon agayn me and myne. (VII.1878–81)
>
> [*outrely*: completely; *constreyneth*: moves]

All that has intervened between Melibee's waywardness and this *volte-face*, however, is a paragraph in which Prudence has tried once again to argue that the punishment Melibee intends for his enemies is a "cruel sentence" (VII.1846), including four more proverbs on the value of mercy and peace:

> For it is writen that "he that moost curteisly comandeth, to hym men mooste obeyen." And therefore I prey yow that in this necessitee and in this need ye caste yow to overcome youre herte. For Senec seith that "he that overcometh his herte, overcometh twies." And Tullius seith: "Ther is no thyng so comendable in a greet lord as whan he is debonaire and meeke, and appeseth him lightly." And I prey yow that ye wole forbere now to do vengeance, in swich a manere that youre goode name may be kept and conserved, and that men mowe have cause and mateere to preyse yow of pitee and mercy, and that ye have no cause to repente yow of thyng that ye doon. For Senec seith:

---

[38] Patterson, "'What Man Artow,'" 157.

"He overcometh in an yvel manere that repenteth him of his victorie."
(VII.1857–66)

[*caste yow*: choose; *debonaire*: gentle; *appeseth him lightly*: is easily calmed; *mowe*: might; *mateere*: reason; *that repenteth*: who repents]

As is common throughout The Tale of Melibee, the attributions here are largely inaccurate, and while the first, anonymous proverb ("it is writen that") is actually from Seneca, the two sayings attributed to Seneca come, again, from *Publilius Syrus*, with the fourth, attributed to "Tullius" drawn from the *De Officiis*.[39] More important than where these sayings come from, however, is the extent to which they continue the pedagogical program Prudence has been pursuing throughout the tale: she is citing exactly the same sort of wisdom, counseling exactly the same action, she recommended from the start. In other words, while Melibee was able to disregard the enormous quantity of wisdom urging peace in the first instance—a remorseless unfurling of good sense if ever there was one— he now accepts a proportionately infinitesimal quantity without hesitation. The structural logic here is stark: as if the proverb were inversely effective and fewer instances of this wisdom were actually more useful than many. But it is not even necessary to quantify this knowledge in order to make the simpler point that Melibee's behavior is wholly arbitrary with respect to Prudence's teaching. As always—but here with an emphasis constituted by almost the whole of this narrative—proverbial wisdom is shown to be ethically useless, a knowledge that seems *by definition* unable to shape action.

This uselessness is further illustrated by the extent to which Melibee's arguments against Prudence take the form of Prudence's arguments as if in a mirror: they are similarly ineffectual and similarly rife with proverbs. In fact, at the very beginning of the tale, when Melibee wishes to insist that nothing Prudence might have to say will be worth listening to, he cites two wisdom books from the Bible, Ecclesiastes and Ecclesiasticus (twice) in order to support his position:

This Melibee answerde unto his wyf Prudence: "I purpose nat," quod he, "to werke by thy conseil, for many causes and resons. For certes, every wight

---

[39] Seneca, *On Mercy*, 356–449 in *Moral Essays*, vol. 1, ed. and trans. John W. Basore (Cambridge, MA: Harvard University Press, 1994; first published 1928), I.xxiv.I ("Remissius imperanti melius paretur"); *Publilius Syrus*, l. 77 ("Bis vincit qui se vincit in victoria"); Cicero, *De Officiis*, ed. and trans. Walter Miller (Cambridge, MA: Harvard University Press, 1997; first published 1913), I.xxv.88 ("Nihil enim laudabilius, nihil magno et praeclaro viro dignius placabilitate atque clementia"); and *Publilius Syrus*, l. 407 ("Male vincit is quem paenitet victoriae"). These attributions are carefully sourced in Chaucer, *Canterbury Tales*, ed. Mann, 1015.

wolde holde me thanne a fool; this is to seyn, if I, for thy conseillyng, wolde
chaungen thynges that been ordeyned and affermed by so manye wyse.
Secoundely, I seye that alle wommen ben wikke, and noon good of hem
alle. For 'of a thousand men,' seith Salomon, 'I foond o good man, but
certes, of alle wommen, good womman foond I nevere.' And also, certes, if
I governed me by thy conseil, it sholde seme that I hadde yeve to thee over
me the maistrie, and God forbede that it so weere! For Jhesus Syrak seyth
that 'if the wif have maistrie, she is contrarious to hir housbonde.' And
Salamon seith: 'Nevere in thy lyf to thy wyf, ne to thy child, ne to thy freend,
ne yeve no power over thyself, for bettre it were that thy children aske of thy
persone thynges that hem nedeth, than thou see thyself in the handes of
thy children.'" (VII.1055–60)

[*purpose nat*: do not intend; *wight*: man; *by so manye wise*: by so many wise
men; *wikke*: wicked; *noon good of hem alle*: none of them any good; *yeve*: give;
maistrie: control; *hem nedeth*: they need]

Such a reliance on proverbs that not only confute Prudence's arguments
but insist that she is "wicked" ensures in a different way that Melibee's
change of heart at the end of the tale has no meaningful relationship to
such wisdom's contents. The very many antithetical positions supported
by such wisdom throughout the tale make the point about the proverb's
ethical generosity that the canon of basic reading texts also, repeatedly,
makes: "wisdom" of this kind may support *any* position. To this extent,
such wisdom is also always its opposite, since Prudence and Melibee, like
anyone who wants to cite a proverb, may adopt any stance, argue whatever
line they choose, and there will always be a proverb ready to hand to prove
the position they have chosen.

This may make it sound as if The Tale of Melibee criticizes such
wisdom, but, all in all, the tale conducts a very careful analysis of the
good such wisdom can do. In fact, what the Melibee as a narrative seems
both to know and demonstrate is that such knowledge, supple and self-
contradictory as the most flattering of counselors, never guides but therefore always reassures since it is always available to recast any position its
possessor chooses as "wise." It therefore matters very much that the most
common action in this tale is not waging war or suing for peace, or even
the making of arguments, but, rather, the act of citation itself (by Melibee,
Prudence, and all of their advisors). The tale's most frequently repeated
phrases are "Senec seyth" (eighteen instances), "Solomon seyth" (forty-
three instances), and "Tullyus seyth" (eighteen instances).[40] And the tale is

---

[40] For the phrase "Senec seyth" (or its equivalent) see VII.984, 991, 1071, 1127, 1147,
1185, 1226, 1320, 1324, 1437, 1448, 1450, 1455, 1488, 1531, 1775, 1859, 1866. For
the phrase "Salomon seyth" (or its equivalent) see VII.997, 1003, 1047, 1057, 1060, 1076,

also often clear that the consequences of such citation are emotional, not cognitive:

> Whanne Melibe hadde herd the grete skiles and resouns of dame Prudence, and hir wise informaciouns and techynges, his herte gan enclyne to the wil of his wif, considerynge hir trewe entente, and conformed hym anon, and assented fully to werken after hir conseil, and thonked God, of whom procedeth al vertu and al goodnesse, that hym sente a wyf of so greet discrecioun. (VII.1869–73)
>
> [*skiles*: arguments; *informaciouns*: advice; *gan enclyne* inclined; *conformed hym*: acquiesced; *werken after*: follow; *that hym sente*: who sent him]

When Melibee finally decides to yield to his wife's teaching he is, in the most technical sense, *moved* by it, as his "herte" is finally brought in line with the desires of his wife. But this change of heart is also very clearly not the result of something we would call learning, since Melibee knows nothing new when he suddenly decides to change his mind. What Prudence has offered in the "wisdom" of her "teaching" is the comfort of being wise in agreement rather than dispute, a set of tenets Melibee can cling to by deciding to "encline to the wil of his wif." As if its characteristic were finally friendliness rather than perspicacity, such wisdom does not instruct behavior but, rather, promises to accompany its bearer, like a steadfast and reassuring companion—like a wise and prudent spouse—bolstering whatever opinion that bearer "inclines" to think is right.

The Tale of Melibee is such a valuable site for learning this particular lesson because this view of proverbial wisdom is also insisted upon by the frame narrative, after this tale's conclusion, when Harry, the Host, suggests that Prudence's teaching would be of value to his wife, Goodelief:

> I hadde levere* than a barel ale   would rather
> That Goodelief, my wyf, hadde herd this tale!
>
> (VII.1984–5)

What Harry wishes Goodelief to learn, however, is how to curb a general aggressivity by emulating Prudence's "pacience" (e.g. VII.1064):

> And if that any neighebore of myne
> Wol nat in chirche to my wyf enclyne*,   bow

1078, 1087, 1113, 1158, 1167, 1171, 1173, 1178, 1186, 1194, 1317, 1416, 1485, 1512, 1514, 1539, 1542, 1550, 1571, 1571, 1572, 1578, 1589, 1590, 1628, 1638, 1639, 1653, 1664, 1671, 1696, 1704, 1707, 1709, 1719, 1739, 1754. For the phrase "Tullius seyth" (or its equivalent) see VII.1165, 1176, 1180, 1192, 1201, 1339, 1344, 1347, 1355, 1359, 1360, 1381, 1387, 1390, 1393, 1585, 1621, 1860.

Or be so hardy* to hire to trespace*,	bold/ offend
Whan she comth hoom she rampeth* in my face,	rages
And crieth, "False coward, wrek* they wyf!	avenge
By corpus bones*, I wol have thy knyf,	God's bones
And thou shalt have my distaf and go spynne!"	
Fro day to nyght right thus she wol bigynne.	

(VII.1901–8)

Harry could be responding to any of those early moments in the tale when Melibee says he will not listen to his wife's counsel, and yet, as an account of what his wife would have "herd" in "this tale" he has got it completely wrong. It ought to be one of the more ineffective narratives he could find for persuading Goodelief not to berate him since Prudence spends almost the whole of the tale berating Melibee, insisting that he "encline" to her will, and, in the end, wholly succeeds. Harry's reactions offer a more pedestrian demonstration of the uselessness of proverbial teaching, and yet, like all those who cite the wisdom that constitutes so much of this tale within it, Harry takes enormous pleasure in making his monumental mistake. Indeed, Adam Pinkhurst, the scribe thought to have written the Ellesmere MS, picks up on the prediction in the tale's prologue that the tale will be a "mirye" occasion and adds a rubric here describing Harry's reactions as "the murye wordes of the Hoost."[41] Even though it is only like a schoolroom collection of proverbs rather than a schoolroom text itself, the Host's reactions enter The Tale of Melibee into *The Canterbury Tales* as a homage to schoolroom learning, ensuring that the whole of the treatise can be seen, not as the kind of dreary instruction from which a schoolboy would have recoiled, but, rather, as a deep well of "informaciouns" that, whenever and wherever they were remembered in later life, would have made him merry. The largest point of the Melibee in the context of the *Tales*, then, is that even an ethical learning need not lead a schoolboy toward the good for him to have benefited from it. Even where his behavior was entirely unchanged by what he read in his school texts they furnished him with any number of opportunities for the unalloyed and repeatable pleasure of discovering, and repeatedly saying, that his behavior was "wise" because it had been endorsed by what was said in some book.

---

[41] See Geoffrey Chaucer, *The Canterbury Tales: The New Ellesmere Chaucer Monochromatic Facsimile (of Huntington Library MS EL 26 C 9)*, ed. Daniel Woodward and Martin Stevens (San Marino, CA: Huntington Library, 1997), fol. 168r. On Adam Pinkhurst see Lynne Mooney, "Chaucer's Scribe," *Speculum* 81 (2006): 97–138.

THE WISDOM OF MIDDLE ENGLISH
LITERATURE

Because The Tale of Melibee functions in the whole of *The Canterbury Tales* as the proverbs that comprise it function in the arguments made by each figure in that text—as if to prove Burke's claim that literature can be understood as a proverb "writ large" this tale is marshaled by Harry Baily as if it were itself a proverb—the Melibee also helps to specify, at both of these levels, just how wisdom of this kind could be useful to literature. As the citation of proverbial knowledge always seems to instill a certain feeling rather than communicate a particular content to characters in the Melibee as well as in *The Canterbury Tales* as a whole, so too did the citation of wisdom in other texts tend to produce affective rather than cognitive results in its readers. The corollary here also seems to have been widely true: a citation was never more useful to literature—never more purely affective—than when it was clear that it had taught nothing. Proverbs have long been thought to be valuable to literature, of course. In Roman schoolroom exercises, and clearly for some time afterwards (since both Quintilian and Priscian make reference to the practice), students were trained to deploy a proverb as something like a rhetorical figure for elaborating a particular topic or idea.[42] Middle English writers probably weren't working squarely within this tradition, since, as I now want to show, they tended to draw wisdom in fairly instrumental ways from the elementary readings they knew best. But as Quintilian and Priscian also recommend, they tend to use proverbs as something akin to a figure or ornament, a way of couching a thought that lent it a certain affective power.

Middle English writers created frequent opportunities for such elaboration, moreover, because they were generally committed to making the scenes of elementary instruction in which proverbial wisdom played such a

---

[42] Exercises that include a method of elaboration called "proverb" (or, sometimes, *sententia*) are described in Donald Lemen Clark, *Rhetoric in Greco-Roman Education* (New York, NY: Columbia University Press, 1957), 179–212 and James J. Murphy, "Roman Writing Instruction as Described by Quintilian," 36–76 in *A Short History of Writing Instruction: From Ancient Greece to Twentieth-Century America*, ed. James J. Murphy, 3rd edn. (New York: Routledge, 2012), 65. See also Ernst Robert Curtius, *European Literature and the Latin Middle Ages*, trans. Willard R. Trask, Bollingen Series 36 (Princeton, NJ: Princeton University Press, 1953), 442. For the exercises in Quintilian see *The Orator's Education*, ed. and trans. Donald A. Russell, 5 vols. (Cambridge, MA: Harvard University Press, 2001), V.11 (1: 441–3). For Priscian see his *Praeexercitamina*, 551–60 in *Rhetores Latini Minores*, ed. Carol Halm (Leipzig: Teubner, 1863), 551–60.

central part equally central to their texts. As I explored at some length in Chapter 3, the second book of *The House of Fame* consists almost entirely of a lesson on the physics of sound and the nature of fame taught by an eagle who sounds for all the world like an elementary schoolmaster. *Piers Plowman* begins with Will, personifying the desire to know, posing the kind of simple questions to Holy Church that we might expect any elementary school student to ask his teacher ("Mercy, Madame, what may this be to meene? [mean]," B 1.11), and it then proceeds to what is usually called an inward journey in which Will is taught by a sequence of allegorical figures representing the processes of learning ("Study"), the cognitive faculties ("Wit"), university learning ("Clergy"), and the disciplines ("Theology").[43] In the *Confessio Amantis*, despite a pervasive courtliness ("Ma dame, I am a man of thyne, / That in thy court have longe served," B 1.168–9) and a firmly confessional structure ("Come forth and hier this mannes schrifte [confession]," B 1.197), Amans sets himself to "scole" (1.63) in order to find someone to "teche" him (l. 40), a pursuit that becomes the more explicit in Book 7, where Amans stops learning in the "registre / Of Venus" (7.19.20) and turns, instead, to the "scole... / Of Aristotle" (7.4–6). Even the *Gawain*-poet, who is so generally atypical in his relationship to the syllabus of elementary learning, tends to configure each of the various genres he takes up pedagogically.[44] In *Sir Gawain and the Green Knight*, Gawain's main task is to learn something: the Green Knight's challenge is formulated as a promise to "teche" Gawain about his "house" and "home" and "name," and, as Bertilak later in the poem, he promises to "teche" Gawain how to find Green Chapel.[45] While *Pearl* uses the language of courtly love to configure the Pearl-maiden's relationship with the dreamer, the maiden instantly adopts the voice and posture of teacher, offering continuous correction ("Sir, ye haf your tale mysetente" [Sir, you are mistaken in what you say]) to the "unavysed" [ignorant] dreamer.[46] *Patience* begins with a version of the eighth beatitude in the

---

[43] For a careful anatomization of the "discourses of education" this inward journey invokes see James Simpson, *Piers Plowman: An Introduction*, 2nd rev. edn. (Exeter: University of Exeter Press, 2007), 93–105 and 116–23. On the cognitive nature of this part of the poem see, in particular, Nicolette Zeeman, *Piers Plowman and the Medieval Discourse of Desire* (Cambridge: Cambridge University Press, 2006).

[44] On the *Gawain*-poet's relationship to the schoolroom syllabus see Chapter 5 in the present volume, pp. 196–8.

[45] *Sir Gawain and the Green Knight*, 237–406 in *The Works of the Gawain Poet: Sir Gawain and the Green Knight, Pearl, Cleanness, Patience*, ed. Ad Putter and Myra Stokes (London: Penguin, 2014), lines 407–8 ("house," "home," and "name") and 1069 ("teche"). Hereafter this poem will be cited from this edition by line number in the text.

[46] *Pearl*, 3–81 in *Works of the Gawain Poet*, ed. Putter and Stokes, lines 257 ("Sir") and 292 ("unavysed").

form of schoolroom wisdom ("Pacience is a poynt, thagh hit displese ofte" [Patience is a virtue, although it often displeases]), and suggests that such wisdom was what Matthew—like this text—tried to "teche."[47]

The emplotment of pedagogy in each of these texts provides a rich field for the use of schoolroom wisdom since it always implies that a lesson will be learned, but—as if it also tracked the cognitive logic of this wisdom— that project usually fails. At every such point, however, schoolroom wisdom also serves to translate frustration into the comforts of realization. This structure is nowhere more schematically true than in *Patience*, which finds the perfect formal correlative for the failure of teaching by repeating the proverb introduced in the poem's first line as its last line:

> Forthy penaunce and payne to-preve hit in sighte
> That pacience is a noble poynt, thagh hit displese ofte.

[Therefore penance and pain conclusively prove it by demonstration that patience is a noble virtue, although it often displeases.] (530–1)

This circularity is a structure that the *Gawain*-poet favored (*Pearl* and *Sir Gawain and the Green Knight* also end, roughly speaking, with their first lines) in order to insist on the implacability of a particular problem (loss of a loved one in *Pearl*, the fearfulness hidden behind the façade of honor of Arthur's court in *Sir Gawain*). But *Patience* most fully absorbs the characteristics of proverbial wisdom to its form because the repetition of the poem's initial maxim as its last line makes the poem very much about the impossibility of learning this truth. The poem's central figure, Jonah, is a figure of unvarying *im*patience ("he wolde not suffer" [would not be patient], 113), no matter what God says or does to him. If the narrative of *Patience* concludes with God, like a good-natured schoolmaster, still trying to drive a lesson into the errant schoolboy ("Be noght so gryndel, goodman, bot go forth thy wayes; / Be preue and be pacient in payne and in joye" [Do not be so angry, my friend, but go your way / Be steadfast and

---

[47] *Patience* 195–235 in *Works of the Gawain Poet*, ed. Putter and Stokes, lines 1 ("Pacience") and 10 ("teche"). Hereafter this poem will be cited from this edition by line number in the text.

Whiting and Whiting categorize the first line of *Patience* as "proverbial" although they find the saying in no other witnesses (*Proverbs, Sentences and Proverbial Phrases*, ed. Whiting and Whiting, P54). "Patience is a virtue" also has a close and obvious parallel in the common proverb "patience conquers," which plays such an important role in The Franklin's Tale and *Piers Plowman* (see Chapter 4 of the present volume, pp. 153–8). The notion that patience is defined by a struggle against adversity is nowhere more common than in confessional manuals and handbooks (see Ralph Hanna, "Some Commonplaces of Late Medieval Patience Discussions: An Introduction," 65–87 in *The Triumph of Patience: Medieval and Renaissance Studies*, ed. Gerald J. Schiffhorst [Orlando, FL: University of Florida Press, 1977], esp. 68–9).

patient in the face of difficulties or good fortune], 524–5), it also insists on the permanence of the lesson Jonah has failed to learn, since a merciful God is always there to teach it ("Why schuld I wrath with hem, syn wys wil turne, / And come and know me for kyng and my carpe leve?" [Why should I be angry with them, since men will turn, and come, and know me for king, and believe my preaching?], 518–19). The repetition of the truth that Jonah's obstinacy prevents him from learning as the last line of the poem also insists on the comforting durability of that truth, a Christian principle couched as a proverb because this is the form so often taken by knowledge that is always available but often unlearned.

It is The Reeve's Tale, however, in a passage that I mentioned briefly in the previous chapter, that reveals best how the qualities of schoolroom wisdom could exert a shaping force on Middle English literary form. As in *Patience*—and as ever—wisdom in this tale arrives late, in a summary of the foolishness that has generated its plot, when that foolishness is reconstituted, as it is in all of Chaucer's fabliaux, as a lesson:

> Thus is the proude millere wel ybete*,   beaten
> And hath ylost* the gryndyng of the whete,   lost
> And payed for the soper everideel*   entirely
> Of Aleyn and of John, that bette hym weel;
> His wyf is swyved*, and his daughter als.   fucked
> Lo swich it is a millere to be fals!
> And therfore this proverbe is seyd ful sooth:
> "Hym thar nat wene wel that yvele dooth."
> A gylour shal himself bigyled be.[48]

(I.4313–21)

The whole of The Reeve's Tale directs itself toward this conclusion, since not only is its narrative very much about proverbial wisdom (both clerks cite variations of the proverb "nothing ventured nothing gained" as the grounds for key decisions near the conclusion of the tale), but that plot also demonstrates such wisdom's belatedness, since this last "proverbe" so firmly contradicts the rationale each character in the tale has given for his actions.[49] Such wisdom is also belated with respect to itself, since, after

---

[48] The last couplet is best translated: "He should not expect good who does evil / A trickster shall himself be tricked."

[49] These proverbs are "With empty hand men may na haukes tulle [no hawks lure]" (I.4134), "Unherdy is unsely" [Cowardly is unfortunate] (I.4210). See *Proverbs, Sentences and Proverbial Phrases*, ed. Whiting and Whiting, H89 (for the first of these proverbs) and N146 (for the second). All of the characters in the tale believe fervently in reciprocity but only as it may pertain to them, and so each is heedless of the consequences that might follow his or her own actions. This logic is introduced into the tale when the miller says "the moore quente crekes that they make, / The mooore wol I stele whan I take" (I.4050–1) and it

one statement of the "proverbe" here ("hym thar nat wene wel that yvele dooth"), we get that proverb again ("a gylour shal himself bigyled be"), in the formula that was so widely used for translating the phrase "sic ars deluditur arte" (1.26) from the *Distichs of Cato.*[50] As in the formulation in *Patience*—as generally in schoolroom wisdom as such—a proverb carries its familiarity within it (a proverb *is* a proverb to the extent that it conveys knowledge that has been long and widely known). To conclude a narrative with such knowledge, or even to arrive at it after a sequence of events, is always to give the narrative prior to that conclusion something of the form of *Patience* retrospectively (here, as if the schoolroom wisdom "a gylour shal himself bigyled be" was in fact The Reeve's Tale's first line), since it is in the nature of such knowledge to remind every literate reader that this is a truth he or she has long known. Such usage also tends to bring with it a certain flattery for every literate reader too, since the familiarity of the proverb shows him or her to be wiser than the narrative he or she has just read as well as every character in it. And such flattery leads once more to the comfort that comes from discovering that what seemed as if it would be something new—as the narrative unfolded toward some as-yet-unknown conclusion—turns out to be the most familiar ground.

The satisfaction such wisdom provides to any point of arrival also explains, I think, why so many of the most ambitious Middle English poems cite schoolroom wisdom at climactic or concluding moments. The Manciple's Tale is perhaps the most subtle but thematically dramatic of all of these. It is not, of course, the conclusion of *The Canterbury Tales*, since it comes before The Parson's Tale in all authoritative copies and manuscript traditions, and it is the Parson who says he will "make an ende" (X.47) to the pilgrimage narrative.[51] But the Parson refuses to tell a "tale" in any generic sense ("thou getest fable noon ytoold for me," X.31), and

---

governs what Aleyn calls a "law" ("That gif a man in a point be agreved, / That in another he sal be releved," I.4181–2). All of these proverbs are firmly corrected by the distich with which the tale concludes.

[50] Both the phrase "Him thar nat wene wel that ivele dooth" and the phrase "A gilour shal himself bigiled" are categorized as proverbs by Whiting and Whiting in *Proverbs, Sentences and Proverbial Phrases*, E185 and G491. On the latter as a common translation of *Distichs* 1.26 see Chapter 5 in the present volume, pp. 187–9.

[51] The consensus about The Manciple Tale's position in fifteenth-century copies of the *Canterbury Tales* is neatly set out in the first page of Germaine Dempster, "The Fifteenth-Century Editors of the *Canterbury Tales* and the Problem of Tale Order," *PMLA* 64 (1949): 1123–42. See also Germaine Dempster, "A Chapter of the Manuscript History of the *Canterbury Tales*," *PMLA* 63 (1948): 456–84 (esp. 470–1) and Larry D. Benson, "The Order of the Canterbury Tales," *Studies in the Age of Chaucer* 3 (1981): 77–120 (esp. 79 and 83–90).

offers, instead, a "handbook on penance."[52] As the last narrative or fable in the collection, then, The Manciple's Tale firmly concludes the tale-telling activity that generally defines the *Tales*, and it provides that conclusion in the form of proverbs dispensed, just as they are in the *Distichs of Cato*, as advice given to a "son" (in the instance of this tale as "taughte" to the narrator by his "dame").[53] Not all of the instructions addressed to this "son" in The Manciple's Tale are drawn from the *Distichs*, but three of the most important of them are. There is, first, a version of the line "nam nulli tacuisse nocet, nocet esse locutum" [it harms no one to keep silent, but speaking may be harmful, I.12b]:

My sone, ful ofte* for to muche speche	very often
Hath many a man ben spilt*, as clerkes teche,	ruined
But for litel speche, avysely*,	prudently
Is no man shent*, to speke generally.	harmed

(IX.325–8)

Second, there is a version of the distich "virtutem primam esse puto, compescere linguam: / proximus ille deo est qui scit ratione tacere" [I think the first among virtues is to govern one's tongue; he is nearest to God who knows enough to keep quiet, I.3]:

The firste vertu, sone, if thow wolt leere*,	learn
Is to restreyne and kepe wel thy tonge.	

(IX.332–3)

Finally, the tale's penultimate couplet is a version of the line "Rumores fuge neu studeas novus auctor haberi" [Don't gossip and be careful not to make up stories, I.12a], while its very last couplet repeats the wisdom of distich I.3 (as in IX.333 to "kepe wel" the "tonge"):

My sone, be war, and be noon auctour newe*	source
Of tidynges, wheither they been false or trewe.	
Wherso* thou come, amonges hye or lowe,	wherever
Kepe wel thy tonge, and think upon the crowe.	

(IX.359–62)

Each one of these proverbs recommends reticence at the conclusion of a tale in which speaking the truth provokes murder as well as serious injury to the messenger who speaks it, and the retreat from "speech" that results from these disasters can be understood as a kind of palinode for—even an implicit retraction of—the whole of the *Canterbury Tales*. By returning to

---

[52] On the genre of The Parson's Tale see Siegfried Wenzel, "Notes on the Parson's Tale," *Chaucer Review* 16 (1982): 237–56 (esp. 248–51).

[53] See *Distichs of Cato*, pro (pp. 592–3).

familiar knowledge to formulate this hard truth, by using proverbs to bolster the view that tale telling is, as a rule, a mistake, Chaucer leavens the profound regret that constitutes such a conclusion with the insistence that something positive has been achieved. By returning to one of the first texts he read (as the *Distichs* clearly were) to suggest that his greatest poetic achievement may have been a mistake, Chaucer is also insisting is that he has *always* known this—that the hard truth is also a fundamental truth, important enough to be worthy of such extensive elaboration.

Something very like this structure and meaning also governs *Piers Plowman*, although the key passage occurs, not at the very end of this poem, but at what might be described as its climax. The schoolroom text here is a single couplet from the *Liber parabolarum* cited just after the poem's description of Redemption, as the gates of hell burst open and angels sing and play the harp, while Peace celebrates Christ's victory:

> Thanne pipede Pees of poesie a note:
> "*Clarior est solito post maxima nebula Phebus;*
> *Post inimicicias clarior est et amor.*
> After sharpest shoures," quod Pees, "moost shene is the sonne;
> Is no weder warmer than after watry cloudes;
> Ne no love levere, ne lever frendes
> Than after were and wo, whan love and pees ben maistres.
> Was nevere were in this world, ne wikkednesse so kene,
> That Love, and hym liste, to laughynge ne broughte,
> And Pees, thorugh pacience, alle perils stoppede."
> "Trewes!" quod Truthe; "thow tellest us sooth, by Jesus!
> Clippe we in covenaunt and ech of us kisse oother."
>
> (B 18.410–19)[54]

[Then Peace sang some poetry: "*The sun is usually brighter after much cloudiness; Love is also brighter after enmity.* After the greatest showers," said Peace, "the sun is the brightest; no weather feels warmer than after rain-filled clouds; nor no love better, nor better friends than after war and woe, when love and peace are masters. There was never war in the world, nor such great wickedness that Love, when he chose, brought all to laughter, and Peace, by means of patience, put an end to all trouble." "Truce," said Truth, "you tell the truth, by Jesus! Let us embrace in agreement, and each of us kiss the other."]

Whether we accept the recent theory that passus 18 formed the conclusion of this poem's B-text—and these lines would therefore have concluded one of the text's definitive versions—this passage still marks the moment when Will finds the greatest cause for celebration in his searching, and the

---

[54] For the passage Langland is quoting see *Liber parabolarum*, lines 33–4/p. 153.

poem's most positive point of arrival before the slow unraveling in passūs
19 and 20, with Peace finally forced to admit the forces of corruption to
the Barn of Unity (B 20.349–55).[55] If it is in Langland's nature, as
projected into Will's, always to continue searching, and so, the conclusion
of the poem is inevitably constituted by a rededication to the search for
Piers the Plowman (as Conscience becomes a pilgrim to "seke" him [B
20.381–3]), the recognition by Truth that the citation from the *Liber
parabolarum* is "truth" constitutes the endpoint of the search inaugurated
when Will first sees the tower of Truth at the beginning of the poem
("Whan alle tresors arn [are] tried," Holy Church says, "treuth is the
beste," B 1.85), and begun again as the pilgrimage to St Truth guided by
Piers in passus 5 ("Knowestou aught a corsaint," quod thei "that men calle
Truthe? / Koudestow wissen us the wey wher that wye dwelleth?" [Do you
know of any shrine, (the pilgrims) said that men call Truth. Could you
show us the way to the place where that person lives?, B 5.532–3]). As Jill
Mann understands the meaning of such a form it is as if "to . . . Langland,
one of the best things about the Redemption is finding out that one's
schoolbooks are true."[56] But as important as such content I think is the
comfort that must be such a realization's coefficient: the schoolroom
proverb transforms the point of arrival into a return, and the pressing
need that inaugurated and impelled the search falls into the relief of
discovering that what has been so long sought was, in fact—can now be
recognized to have been—well known from the start.

Since schoolroom wisdom had such formal and thematic prominence
in the work of the Ricardian poets, it is odd in many ways that such use
needs to be pointed out. As I will show in the next chapter (where the
return also demonstrates another important quality of basic literacy training), like Chaucer and Langland, Gower also cites the basic reading texts at
the culminating moment of his *magnum opus* too. And yet, as I hope the
foregoing has demonstrated, such wisdom and its importance is likely to
elude us because it lies just outside modern categories and, therefore, of
our accounts of literary technique. Once we understand the nature of such

---

[55] On the possibility that B ended at passus 18 and what we currently take as the text's
last two passūs were, in fact, C-text additions which were retrospectively attached to an ur-
B-text, see Lawrence Warner, "The Ending, and End, of *Piers Plowman* B: The C-Version
Origins of the Final Two Passus," *Medium Aevum* 76 (2007), 225–50 (esp. pp. 226–7) and
Lawrence Warner, *The Lost History of Piers Plowman: The Earliest Transmission of Langland's
Work* (Philadelphia, PA: University of Pennsylvania Press, 2011), 49–61.

[56] Jill Mann, "'He Knew Nat Catoun': Medieval School-Texts and Middle English
Literature," 41–74 in *The Text in the Community: Essays on Medieval Works, Manuscripts,
Authors and Readers*, ed. Jill Mann and Maura Nolan (Notre Dame, IN: University of Notre
Dame, 2006), 66.

knowledge it becomes possible to see how wisdom had, above all, a characteristic shape—and it therefore offered medieval poets a variety of formal resources because it so generally transformed a point of departure into a destination. Understanding that shape is also to understand that it was a form that tended to produce a certain feeling, a way of transforming knowing into the comfort, the sheer relief, of moving, in a poem or by way of one, from doubt to realization, from error to wisdom.

7

The Experience of Learning

The previous chapter described how the contents of schoolroom learning could provide an affective resource that Middle English writers often found useful in their poetry (and prose). It would be simplest to say that the subject of that inquiry was the proverb and its uses, not least since proverbs were so often the substance of this learning and the instrument for such affect. But, as that discussion should have made clear, the repetition involved in this affect—the way the proverb meant most when it was re-encountered, after having been well-learned in school— defined all grammar-school learning: *everything* the schoolboy learned first seems to have become as familiar to him as any proverb is to us now. What I want to suggest now, then, is that a schoolroom learning that was constantly available for citation in later life also shaped the activities of cognition. Although, as ever in this book, this phenomenon must be observed through the optic of literature and the effects it produced in that forum, my concern here is really with how schoolroom learning made its way out of books: how it became so like what we often call "experience" in a lived life that it functioned as a grid through which subsequent events in that life were perceived and understood.[1] As I also noted in Chapter 3, it is by now a truism of many modes of investigation that "experience" is problematic as a category because it "establishes a realm of reality outside discourse" that can be appealed to as a grounding and unassailable "foundation."[2] As Althusser had it, what we take to be "the 'lived' experience of human existence itself" is often better called "ideology," since what we take to have happened is so often a set of imagined

---

[1] Mary Carruthers describes the key step in this process thus: "the medieval understanding of the complete process of reading does not observe in the same way the basic distinction we make between 'what I read in a book' and 'my experience' ... for 'what I read in a book' *is* 'my experience,'" *The Book of Memory: A Study of Memory in Medieval Culture*, 2nd edn. (Cambridge: Cambridge University Press, 2008; first published 1990), 211.

[2] Joan W. Scott, "The Evidence of Experience," *Critical Inquiry* 17 (1991): 790. See Martin Jay, "The Limits of Limit-Experience: Bataille and Foucault," *Constellations* 2 (1995): 155–74 (esp. 168).

relations.[3] And yet it is precisely on the grounds that "experience" has so often been critiqued in this philosophical tradition, as a cognitive structure so "like belief" that "we think *with* not *about*," that I want to suggest schoolroom learning was most valued and used by the medieval schoolboy once he was grown.[4] It turned out to be learning that was surprisingly useful to think with.

An example will help to specify this complex and subtle process more fully, and there is no more dramatic instance of such learning in medieval education than the account of Augustine's conversion in his *Confessions*. The key elements in this account begin with the visit, in a garden in Milan, by a Christian friend, Ponticianus. Having discovered Augustine and another of his friends, Alypius, with the epistle of Paul to the Romans open in front of them, Ponticianus tells them the story of someone who was converted by reading the Life of St Anthony. This story makes a great impression on Augustine, not just because he has already made Scripture a subject of the most "careful study" [scripturis curam maximam impendere] (VIII.vi [p. 432]) but because he has read Scripture with such an "avid intensity" [avidissime] (VII.xxi [p. 396]) that its words are "stuck fast" to his "heart" [inhaeserant praecordiis meis verba tua] (VIII.i [p. 402]). Although Augustine sets up this scene by saying that he has become dissatisfied with his career as a rhetor, something in Ponticianus's story makes him even more upset than he had been before: he "grows sick and is tormented" [aegrotabam et excruciabar] (VIII.xi [p. 456]). He is rescued, however, when he hears "a voice from a nearby house, as if it is singing over and over again, 'Pick up and read, Pick up and read'" [audio vocem de vicina domo cum cantu dicentis, et cebro repetentis... "tolle lege, tolle lege"] (VIIII.xii [p. 464]) and so he returns to the place where Alypius was sitting:

> For there I had placed the book of the Apostle when I had got up. I picked it up, opened it and read, in silence, the chapter on which my eyes first fell.
>
> [Itaque concitus redii in eum locum, ubi sedebat Alypius; ibi enim posueram codicem apostoli, cum inde surrexeram. Arripui, aperui et legi in silentio capitulum, quo primum coniecti sunt oculi mei.][5]

---

[3] Louis Althusser, "A Letter on Art in Reply to André Daspre," 221–7 in *Lenin and Philosophy and Other Essays*, trans. Ben Brewster (London: New Left Books, 1971), 223. Althusser's views are also helpfully discussed in Elizabeth J. Bellamy and Artemis Leontis, "A Genealogy of Experience: From Epistemology to Politics," *Yale Journal of Criticism* 6 (1993): 172–4.

[4] Bellamy and Leontis, "Genealogy of Experience," 168.

[5] Augustine, *Confessions*, ed. and trans. William Watts, 2 vols. (Cambridge, MA: Harvard University Press, 1995; first published 1912), 8.12. Hereafter citations to the

The passage he sees first is Romans 13:13–14: "Non in comissationibus et ebrietatibus, non in cubilibus et inpudicitiis, non in contentione et aemulatione, sed induite dominum Ieusm Christum" [Not in rioting and drunkenness, not in sleeping together and impurities, not in contention and envy, but put on the Lord Jesus Christ and make no provision for the flesh in its concupiscences] (VIII.xii [p. 464]). And it is as if "a light of comfort from all anxiety" suddenly suffused his heart "and all the shadows of doubt were dispelled" [quasi luce securitatis infusa cordi meo, omnes dubitationis tenebrae diffugerunt] (VIII.xii [p. 464]).

Although he does not describe it in these terms, what Augustine describes in this central passage of the *Confessions* is a scene of instruction, but it is an instruction that succeeds because Augustine *already* knows what he claims to have been taught. The generality of that scene—the pedagogic structure it shares with so many others—is also revealed in the command that causes Augustine to return to his reading. He hears the phrase "pick up and read" as "something divine" [aliud ... divinitus], but this voice is also a metonym for the classroom since it is spoken "*as if* by a boy or a girl" [quasi pueri an puellae], the very repetition is a schoolroom form (in the shape of a drill), and the demand is for exactly the sort of re-reading that was the basic task of literacy training. The sentence Augustine reads under such instruction could hardly be less compelling as a prompt for conversion: it lacks compelling imagery or forceful rhetoric, and focuses on none of the central tenets of Christian doctrine. It is decisive, however, because, as if these particular words were hooks that drew in every other word of Scripture—as if they described an episode vivid enough to remind him of every other episode in the gospels—it stands for all doctrine. The transformation is accompanied by the familiar affect (a source of "comfort" [securitas]) and described with the familiar term, "wisdom" [sapientia] (VIII.vii [p. 438]).[6] But, in this case, such affect not only accompanies a re-encounter with old knowledge, but a decisive change in Augustine's *ability* to know. Although he carries the text of Scripture within him—as he says, according to the still-familiar metaphor, he knows it "by heart"—looking at the passage from Romans now makes Augustine feels as if he has been "placed in front of [him]self" [retorquebas me ad me ipsum] (VIII.vii [p. 438]), as if the text he knew so well was really a part of him, as if, not that self, but the world that self perceived had been

---

Confessions will be to this edition by book, chapter, and page number in the text. The translations throughout are my own.

[6] For these terms and their referents see Chapter 6 in the present volume, pp. 199–201.

entirely altered by the depths of the absorption.[7] This is a sort of knowing defined by the fact that it is a knowing *again* (*re*-cognizing) but also a form of knowing that proceeds by *re*-understanding an old knowledge, seeing it anew and differently (a re-*cognizing*). Augustine's conversion, as it is mediated in and through the texts he has read and decided to read again, is knowing as *recognition* in the fullest sense of that term.[8]

Augustine can perceive and think by means of Scripture in this way because he can "read" it without needing to consult the words on any page.[9] Such learning as well as its pedigree in schoolrooms of the West is vividly depicted in another clarifying example, the "school scene" that can be found on a red-figure vase attributed to Douris (active *c.*500 to 460 BCE).[10] Its sides depict four distinct pairs of students demonstrating their learning in music or letters to a teacher; in the rightmost pair of Fig. 7.1, the student is showing that he has learned to read but he has no text in front of him. In fact, the text on the papyrus roll faces neither teacher nor student, and since it is clearly in possession of the teacher (if this is a stylized view showing the viewer of the vase what the person holding the text sees, it is the teacher who sees it), Eric Havelock thought it wrong to call this a representation of "reading" of any sort.[11] But the papyrus provides a recognizable text (the lines in the image scan as a hexameter conflating two lines from Homer, "Muse to me" and "I begin to sing of wide-flowing Scamander"), and, as even Havelock granted, the point of the image was to show that this student can accurately reproduce the contents of this text.[12] It is also true that, even if the student had a text facing him, it would not have represented "reading," since "merely running one's eyes

---

[7] Mary Carruthers has also said that the repetition of certain texts in medieval learning was so continuous and pervasive that it is as if, for the medieval student "this material ... [was] transformed into their very selves" (*Book of Memory*, 223).

[8] See *OED* s.v. "recognition n." especially 2 and 8a.

[9] I treated this phenomenon in an earlier version of this argument as a kind of "re-reading," but I have since come to think that "re-reading" is only one aspect of a cognitive process that once blurred the distinctions we now make between what is learned from a book and what is perceived in the phenomenal world. For this earlier argument see my "The Art of Rereading" *ELH* 80 (2013): 401–25. A briefer account of the kind of learning depicted on Douris's vase can be found in my "Reading as Knowing," *PMLA* 130 (2015): 711–17.

[10] Henry Immerwahr, "Book Rolls on Attic Vases," 17–48 in *Classical, Mediaeval and Renaissance Studies in Honor of Berthold Louis Ullman*, ed. Charles Henderson (Rome: Edizioni di Storia e Letteratura, 1964).

[11] Eric Havelock, *The Literate Revolution in Greece and its Cultural Consequences* (Princeton, NJ: Princeton University Press, 1982), 202–3.

[12] Immerwahr, "Book Rolls," 19; Havelock, *Literate Revolution*, 203.

Fig. 7.1. Side B of a red-figured drinking cup (kylix), from Cerveteri, 480 BCE, Berlin, Antikensammlung, Staatliche Museen (image by permission of Art Resource).

over the written pages is not reading at all" in ancient and medieval education.[13] Like Augustine with any passage of Scripture, the boy on the vase does not require a text in order to read it, because he knows the text he is reading as well as he knows himself.

Such learning and its significance is the harder to notice and its consequences the harder to scale because it sits behind an epistemic shift in the nature of education. It is sometimes now said that all reading is re-reading, "a process of continuous hypothesis building and revising."[14] Nabokov insisted in his *Lectures on Literature* that "one cannot read a book; one can only reread it."[15] But the importance re-reading has played in teaching has been transformed by changes in fundamental and material conditions. Prior to 1750 reading was "intensive" by necessity because of the relative scarcity of books available for private use; the paucity of reading matter meant that any given book had to be read "over and over

[13] Carruthers, *Book of Memory*, 11.

[14] Matei Calinescu, *Rereading* (New Haven, CT: Yale University Press, 1993), p. xiv.

[15] Vladimir Nabokov, *Lectures on Literature*, ed. Fredson Bowers (New York, NY: Harcourt Brace Jovanovich, 1980), 3, cited in David Galef, "Observations on Rereading," 17–33 in *Second Thoughts: A Focus on Rereading*, ed. David Galef (Detroit, MI: Wayne State University Press, 1998), 17.

again."[16] After 1800, however, people could afford to read "extensively," looking only once at a text because they were able to obtain new texts (newspapers and other periodicals in particular) daily, "read[ing] things only once before racing on to the next item."[17] Intensive reading took a very long time to die out, especially in the schoolroom. John Dewey's attempts to re-shape American education in the first half of the twentieth century were predicated on the assumption that "recitation" and the "repetition of lessons" remained the norm in American schools.[18] The assumption that such practices were a "mold for a cast-iron result," and the general shift to "process" away from such intensive absorption of contents has ensured that students are now rarely trained to re-read a text in the manner of the schoolboy depicted on the Douris vase.[19] Now "people normally reread to improve their comprehension of a difficult text."[20] The exercise is understood by educators as a way of improving "metacomprehension," the understanding, not of the contents of a text, but of how much of a given text has so far been understood.[21]

The subject of this chapter is the legacy of schoolroom practice before this flood, not just to literature or lives, but to thought; it will try to indicate the ways that intensive reading not only enlarged what the schoolboy knew but his capacity to know it. As I have already acknowledged, these operations are, by their nature, very difficult to capture, but the sequential versions in which *Piers Plowman* has survived offer an unusual opportunity to observe such thinking, not least because Langland revisited certain key issues by means of a schoolroom text, and then found in that text an entirely new perspective or idea. It is no accident in this connection that Langland configures the allegory of *Piers Plowman* as so many episodes in which a character called "Will" addresses himself to figures called Study (B 10.1–220) and Scripture (B 10.331–11.316) and

---

[16] Robert Darnton, "Toward a History of Reading," *The Wilson Quarterly* 13 (1989): 91. Darnton credits Rolf Engelsing with this term and the related distinction, for which see his "Die Perioden der Lesergeschichte in der Neuzeit," *Archiv für Geschichte des Buchwesens* 10 (1970): 945–1002.

[17] Darnton, "Toward a History of Reading," 91.

[18] John Dewey, *The School and Society* and *The Child and the Curriculum* (Chicago, IL: University of Chicago Press, 1990; first published 1900 and 1902; 1915, rev. edn.), 55–6. See also Catherine Robson, *Heart Beats: Everyday Life and the Memorized Poem* (Princeton, NJ: Princeton University Press, 2012).

[19] John Dewey, *Experience and Education* (New York, NY: Macmillan, 1938), 72.

[20] Keith K. Millis and Anne King, "Rereading Strategically: The Influences of Comprehension Ability and a Prior Reading on the Memory for Expository Text," *Reading Psychology* 22 (2001): 60.

[21] Katherine A. Rawson and John Dunlosky, "The Rereading Effect: Metacomprehension Accuracy Improves Across Reading Trials," *Memory and Cognition* 28 (2000): 1004–10.

Book (B 18.236–59)—as James Simpson puts it, "what else could we mean when we say 'Will confronts Scripture' than, in effect, 'Will reads Scripture'"—nor is it an accident that such an allegory everywhere insists that such reading is a "dynamic" process "whereby reader and text interact."[22] This is also why the outcome of such reading is so often described in *Piers Plowman* as "kynde knowing," a phrase that refers to an "experiential knowledge" in many ways indistinguishable from what has otherwise been learned by the "experience of years."[23] To understand such "knowing" in some detail in *Piers Plowman* will also make it possible to revisit such recognition where it occurs in less overt ways in some of the more reflexive uses of schoolroom texts I have mentioned in previous chapters.

LEARNING BY HEART

Learning in the Middle Ages shaped and re-shaped thought because, as Mary Carruthers has shown, it can be understood, from the start, as a "memory procedure."[24] The habit is written into language as old as Douris's vase, since "ancient Greek had no verb meaning 'to read' as such: the verb they used, *anagignósko*, means 'to know again', 'to recollect'"; the Latin verb that described reading, *lego*, was intimately related to this use since it "means literally 'to collect' or 'to gather', referring also to a memory procedure."[25] Such procedures were also written deeply into medieval monastic practice. As Hugh of St Victor understood it, the very first step in attaining "wisdom" [sapientia] through learning was "the practice of meditation" [studium meditationis] on Scripture.[26] According to Jean Leclercq "total meditation" resulted in a kind of "muscular memory" whereby key texts were, in effect, incorporated into

[22] James Simpson, "Desire and the Scriptural Text: Will as Reader in *Piers Plowman*," 215–43 in *Criticism and Dissent in the Middle Ages*, ed. Rita Copeland (Cambridge: Cambridge University Press, 1996), 232.

[23] Mary Clemente Davlin, "'Kynde Knowyng' as a Middle English Equivalent for 'Wisdom' in *Piers Plowman* B," *Medium Aevum* 50 (1981): 7 ("experiential") and 14 ("experience"). See also Mary Clemente Davlin, "'Kynde Knowyng' as a Major Theme in *Piers Plowman* B," *Review of English Studies* n.s. 22 (1971): 89–127. For a helpful summary of the most important scholarship on this phrase see Zeeman, *Piers Plowman and the Medieval Discourse of Desire* (Cambridge: Cambridge University Press, 2006), 7 n. 13.

[24] Carruthers, *Book of Memory*, 34.

[25] Carruthers, *Book of Memory*, 34.

[26] Hugh of St Victor, "De Arca Noe Mystica," cols. 681–702 in *Patrologia cursus completus, series Latina*, ed. J.-P. Migne (Paris, 1841–64), 17, col. 635a. Cited and discussed in Carruthers, *Book of Memory*, 203.

the body.[27] Such embodiment was captured best in medieval clerical life by the habit of describing reading as "rumination" [ruminatio], a term that still carried the strong sense of the cud-chewing of ruminants.[28] All of these attitudes are best captured now in phrasing that Augustine was already using in the *Confessions* when he referred to the Scripture he could read without recourse to its inscription on any surface as a text that he knew "by heart."[29]

As I have already suggested, such knowledge of the text was the common consequence of ancient and medieval literacy training because the kind of repetition or drill Augustine seems to reference in his account of his conversion constituted so much of the activity of basic literacy training.[30] In his *Institutio Oratoria* (*c*.95 AD) Quintilian recommends that boys "commit to memory selected passages of speeches or histories or some other type of book" [ediscere electos ex orationibus vel historiis aliove], but he also makes that recommendation using the unusual verb *ediscere*, a calque of *ànagignósko* which understands reading *as* re-reading and is therefore often translated as "to learn by heart."[31] Although Quintilian was largely lost in the Middle Ages, the oldest of the Roman rhetorical treatises, the *Ad Herennium* (*c*.90 BC), which circulated widely, contains a whole section devoted to rereading.[32] After explaining the "industry, devotion, toil and care" [industria, studio, labore, diligentia] necessary to "commit something to memory" [aliquid memoriae tradere], this section concludes with a kind of *mise en abyme* of this pedagogic

---

[27] Jean Leclercq, *The Love of Learning and the Desire for God*, trans. Catherine Misrahi (New York, NY: Fordham University Press, 1961), 90.

[28] Leclercq, *Love of Learning*, 90.

[29] For another example see the prologue to the *Fecunda Ratis* where Egbert of Liège writes of things being written down "[so that] they might be preserved better in a mindful heart" [quo magis memori pectore servarentur], *The Well-Laden Ship*, ed. and trans. Robert Gary Babcock (Cambridge, MA: Harvard University Press, 2013), 2–3.

[30] On Augustine and other such schoolboys see Carruthers, *Book of Memory*, esp. 204 and 271–3.

[31] Quintilian, *The Orator's Education*, ed. and trans. Donald A. Russell, 5 vols. (Cambridge, MA: Harvard University Press, 2001), II.7.1–4 (1: 314–15). Hereafter I will cite Quintilian from this edition by book, chapter, line, and page number in the text. I have altered Russell's translation in my text in order to clarify the meaning of the key term first, but Russell translates "ediscere" here as "to learn by heart." On the verb see Charlton Thomas Lewis and Charles Short, *A Latin Dictionary* (Oxford: Clarendon Press, 1993; first published 1879), s.v. "edisco."

[32] [M. Tullius Cicero], *Rhetorica ad Herennium (Ad C. Herennium libri IV De ratione dicendi)*, ed. and trans. Harry Caplan (Cambridge, MA: Harvard University Press, 1981; first published 1954), III.xvi–xxiv (pp. 204–25). Hereafter the *Ad Herennium* will by cited by book and chapter number (and page number in this edition) in the text. On the limited circulation of Quintilian in the Middle Ages see James J. Murphy, "Roman Writing Instruction as Described by Quintilian," 36–76 in *A Short History of Writing Instruction: From Ancient Greece to Contemporary America*, ed. James J. Murphy, 3rd edn. (New York: Routledge, 2012).

strategy, enjoining the student to "rehearse" [frequenta], or read repeatedly, the *Ad Herennium* itself in order to better learn (among other things) such rules for frequent repetition (III.xxiv.40 [pp. 224–5]). The detailed description of schoolroom practice provided in John of Salisbury's *Metalogicon* (1159) shows how the habits of monastic rumination also shaped classrooms in the monasteries: John holds up Bernard of Chartres as an exemplary pedagogue because he "required" his students to recite each day "part of what he had heard on the previous day" [cogebantur exsoluere singuli die sequenti aliquid eorum que precedenti audierant].[33] These practices were clearly widespread outside of the cloisters. A statute for Oxford grammar schools in the fourteenth century directed teachers to give out verses and literary compositions every fortnight so that afterwards pupils could "render them to the teacher by heart" [magistro suo corde tenus reddere].[34]

This insistence on repetition in literacy training was also very much a part of the instruction in the basic reading texts I focused on in previous chapters. As the *Distichs of Cato* put it very simply in the short commands it begins with, "remember what you read" [quae legeris memento] (I.21). In yet another *mise en abyme* of the process, the *Distichs* goes on to enjoin its readers to "remember" to "read these rules often" [haec precepta tibi saepe esse legenda memento] (IV.pro). In the *Liber parabolarum*, the image of the ruminant ox is connected, as a focusing analogy, to the injunction that the student learn by going over what has been read to him again and again:

> An ox chews again the grasses ground down by its teeth,
>   So that crushed so often they might be nourishment.
> Thus if you want to retain the lessons of your teacher,
>   Call to mind often what you received once by ear.
>
> [Dentibus arreptas bos rursus ruminat herbas,
> Ut totiens trite sint alimenta sibi;
> sic, documenta tui si vis retinere magistri,
> sepe recorderis quod semel aure capis.]
>
> (Alan of Lille, *Liber parabolarum*, lines 165–8/p. 159)

---

[33] *Metalogicon of John of Salisbury: A Twelfth-Century Defense of the Verbal and Logical Arts of the Trivium*, trans. Daniel D. McGarry (Philadelphia, PA: Paul Dry Books, 2009), I.24 (p. 68); *Ioannis Saresberiensis Episcopi Carnotensis Metalogicon Libri IIII*, ed. Clemens C. L. Webb (Oxford: Clarendon Press, 1929), I.24 (p. 55).
[34] *Statuta antiqua Universitatis oxoniensis*, ed. Strickland Gibson (Oxford: Clarendon Press, 1931), 171.

In fact, this text understands memorization as the "foundation" [funda-mentum] (610/p. 174) for the movement from literacy to literature:

> ... si quis sublimes tendit ad artes,
> principio partes corde necesse sciat.
>
> [... someone strives toward the sublime arts,
> He must first know his lessons by heart.]

(Alan of Lille, Liber parabolarum,
lines 611–12/p. 174)

The dedicatory epistle that circulated with the *Tobias* contains a maxim that not only prizes reading as a memory procedure but insists that pleasure is its inevitable consequence: "he who has a thing is happy, he who reads it is happier, but he who learns it by heart is happiest" [qui habet felix, qui legit, felicior qui ediscit felicissimus].[35] The last of these phrases could also be translated as "he who re-reads is happiest," since it contains that Latin calque of *ànagignósko* used by Quintilian, the unusual verb *ediscere*. The *Facetus* ("cum [est] nihil utilius") includes a similar lesson at its center in slightly different language: "Inquire, remember, retain, read often things which have been read; thus upright wisdom gives you all the keys" [Quaere, recordare, retine, lege saepe relecta; / sic omnes claves tibi dat sapientia recta] (98/p. 46).

When thinking about learning by heart in a culture as fully shaped by habits of extensive reading as our own, we inevitably default to more recent theories of knowledge and perhaps, most often, to the theory of mind developed by Locke in his *Essay on Human Understanding* (1690). For Locke, as now almost always for us, the mind is a data retrieval system not unlike a library in which items are placed, stored, and then fetched for later use. Our "memory" is a "storehouse" or "repository":

> The mind has a power, in many cases, to revive perceptions which it has once had, with this additional perception annexed to them, that it has had them before... And thus it is, by the assistance of this faculty, that we are to have all those ideas in our understanding, which though we do not actually contemplate, yet we can bring in sight, and make appear again, and be the objects of our thoughts, without the help of those sensible qualities which first imprinted them there.[36]

We have now learned, of course, that such a system rarely runs as smooth as Locke thought it did. Freud, among others, has taught us just how often

---

[35] Matthew of Vendôme, "Epistola Dedicatoria" to *Liber Tobiae Paraphrasis Metrica*, in *Patrologiae Latina*, ed. Migne, 205, cols. 927–31 (col. 929).

[36] John Locke, *An Essay Concerning Human Understanding*, 27th edn. (London: T. Tegg and Son, 1836), II.10.2. Hereafter this essay will be cited from this edition by book, chapter, and section number in the text.

ideas may be firmly "established in the mind" while also being "alienated" from any straightforward processes of retrieval.[37] But even Freud likened the mind to a surface, a blank "writing-pad," on which the "mental apparatus" performing "its perceptual functions" left "permanent traces."[38] Since Locke, we might even say, the mind has simply *been* a "white paper" (I.3.22) with no "innate ideas" (I.4.20), and "no innate principles" (I.2). "All the materials of reason and knowledge" are in this common view derived from "our observation employed either about external sensible objects, or about the internal operations of our minds"—materials that constitute what Locke also calls, in a word, "experience" (II.1.2).

Locke's understandings make it hard for us to take the measure of medieval practices of re-reading, but so too does the extent to which ancient and medieval learning resembled the understanding that Locke is everywhere implicitly correcting, the view attributed to Socrates by Plato that "learning" is always a kind of "recollection" or *anamnesis*.[39] Plato's account is most challenging now where it is most theological, where Socrates argues, for example, that we instantly recognize "the absolute realities" of "beauty and goodness" because "our souls had a previous existence" (76e). Before he reaches these arguments in the *Phaedo* (*c.*399 BC), however, Socrates focuses on simpler acts of perception, the ability to perceive "similarity" when faced with "similar or dissimilar objects," for example, or to judge the "equality" of "stick to stick" or "stone to stone" (74a). In these more specific accounts of learning, Socrates insists that what is innate is less a body of knowledge than certain cognitive capacities—to judge relationships, to categorize, to generalize across a sequence of details—and it is the inherence of these capacities that made it impossible for Plato or Socrates to view the mind as a storehouse waiting to be loaded with data, a writing pad on which an unfolding experience sequentially wrote. In Socrates's model, our perception of external phenomena occurs by means of these innate capacities, in a process he calls *anamnesis*, whereby "perception" actually reminds us of the "knowledge" [*epistemos*] we already possess, and "learning" is always a

---

[37] Sigmund Freud, "The Uncanny," 335–76 in *Art and Literature*, The Penguin Freud Library, vol. 14, trans. James Strachey, ed. Albert Dickson (Harmondsworth: Penguin, 1985), 363.

[38] Sigmund Freud, "A Note on the 'Mystic Writing-Pad,'" 427–34 in *On Metapsychology*, The Penguin Freud Library, vol. 11, trans. James Strachey, ed. Angela Richards (Harmondsworth: Penguin, 1984), 432–3.

[39] Plato, *Phaedo* 40–98 in *The Collected Dialogues*, ed. Edith Hamilton and Huntington Cairns, Bollingen Series 71 (Princeton, NJ: Princeton University Press, 1961), 76a. Hereafter I will cite the *Phaedo* from this translation by "Stephanus" number in the text.

"recollecting" of what we "knew before" (76a). It is such "recollection" that Socrates calls a "sort of experience" (73e). This model of mind resembles Locke's, and even Freud's, where it insists that what we know is compounded of what we perceive of the external world and what we remember. But what Plato insists on that Locke's models of storage and inscription scant or omit is the possibility that what appears at first to be a new perception will always turn out to be a "recovery," that "things which we had not seen for…a long time" will appear *at once* as something we are "noticing" for the first time (73d–e) and something we long knew.

We can use Locke's language here and describe such knowledge as "habitual," lodged so firmly in memory that we recognize it as true without requiring any immediate "proofs" (once we have learned, say, that the "the three angles of a triangle are equal to the two right ones" we never doubt it) (IV.1.8). But when Locke related such processes to pedagogy in *Some Thoughts Concerning Education* (1693), he insisted that this sort of learning was thoughtless, since, for him, whatever has "grown habitual" bypasses cognitive processes and "requires no thought, no reflection."[40] There is medieval warrant for this mechanistic view. Quintilian said that the point of re-reading was to ensure that "the memory of such things stays with us till we are old" [prosequitur haec memoria in senectutem] (I.1, 1: 80–1). But as we have already seen, medieval readers such as Augustine found the process of re-encountering old knowledge as anything but thoughtless. The "comfort" [securitas] Augustine finds in re-encountering the words of Scripture stems from their familiarity, but not only because they are *familiaris*, as he sometimes put it, in the sense of "well-known," but because they are *famliaris* in the sense of "friendly," words that comfort because they have been, and therefore promise to be, faithful companions through all subsequent acts of perception.[41] The term we still use to capture this compounding of habituation, knowing, and pleasure is "recognition," and it is in that use that our attitudes and understanding do still embrace the Platonic model,

---

John Locke, *Some Thoughts Concerning Education* (London: J. and R. Tonson, 1779), §64 (p. 64).

"Perhaps no advice is as common in medieval writing on the subject [of reading], and yet so foreign, when one thinks about it, to the habits of modern scholarship as this notion of making one's own what one reads in someone else's work. 'Efficere tibi illas familiares', Augustine's admonition to Francesco, does not mean 'familiar' in quite the modern sense. *Familiaris* is rather a synonym of *domesticus*, that is, to make something familiar by making it part of your experience," Carruthers, *Book of Memory*, 204–5. Carruthers is citing the *Secretum*, a dialogue in which Petrarch imagines Augustine giving him advice. For the passage she quotes see Francesco Petrarca, *Prose*, ed. G. Martelotti et al. (Milan: Riccardi, 1955), 120–2, 126 and *Secret*, trans. William H. Draper (London: Chatto & Windus, 1911), 97–100.

since "recognition" is really a calque of *anamnesis* (*ana-* "back" + *mimnḗískō*, "call to mind"), both a knowing, and the pleasure that so often accompanies the opportunity to know again.[42] Although we do not see it as the only way to know as Plato did, we do not abjure the process as explicitly as Locke did, and, so, in this word and its meanings, we carry our own recollection of the affect produced by the new encounter with what was well-learned some time ago.

Freud has helped us to see that the feeling that accompanies recognition is not always pleasure, not least as encounters with the "familiar" may be "frightening" insofar as they restore to consciousness what "ought to have remained hidden."[43] It is no accident that Freud relied so heavily in his theories on one of the more unpleasant scenes of recognition in literature, the discovery in Sophocles's *Oedipus* of all the ways that the Delphic prophecy of disaster had come true. Aristotle describes this process in his *Poetics* (*c.*335 BC) with yet another word for "recognize," and therefore a synonym of "anamnesis," (*ana* [again] + *gnorisis* [knowing]).[44] He insists that this *technē* works "best" when the "astounding comes to be through the likely" (1455a16–17), and most of his examples produce horror rather than anything like an Augustinian comfort. These include Philomela's revelation of her rape and mutilation in Sophocles's *Tereus*. But the most famous example Aristotle gives of the technique provides an Augustinian sort of comfort for Odysseus's former nurse and a group of swineherds when, on different occasions after his return to Ithaca, they recognize him by the scar he received from the tusk of a boar in his youth (1454b26–9). These two acts of knowing amalgamate an object of immediate perception (the scar) and a "retrospective narrative" (the "life-story" of Odysseus which includes the boar hunt that the nurse and the swineherds have long known and know well) with an attendant pleasure.[45]

Aristotle focused on recognition in his *Poetics* because he knew—as of course did Freud—just how valuable the affect it produced was to

---

[42] *OED*, s.v. "anamnesis n."

[43] Freud, "The Uncanny," 340 ("familiar" and "frightening") and 364 ("ought to have remained hidden").

[44] "*Anagnorisis* ... just as the name signifies, is a change from ignorance [*agnoia*] to knowledge [*gnosis*]," Aristotle, *On Poetics*, trans. Seth Benardete and Michael Davis (South Bend, IN: St Augustine's Press, 2002), 1452a31–3. Hereafter I will cite the *Poetics* from this translation by "Bekker" and line number in the text. I am here just reversing Cave's clarifying formulation: "The Platonist equivalent of *anagnorisis* is, of course, *anamnesis*," Terence Cave, *Recognitions: A Study in Poetics* (Oxford: Clarendon Press, 1988), 144.

[45] Cave, *Recognitions*, 23. Cave follows Auerbach's "seductive" (5) example in making Odysseus his first example too. For his discussion of the scar see *Recognitions*, 10–24. For his model see Erich Auerbach, *Mimesis: The Representation of Reality in Western Literature*, trans. Willard R. Trask (Princeton, NJ: Princeton University Press, 1953; first published in German, 1946), 3–23.

literature. Just as schoolroom proverbs provided a powerful resource for medieval writers to rediscover their "wisdom"—as I described in the previous chapter—it also left them ever-ripe for the jolt of rediscovery, and, as in the case of the proverbs they knew so well, they could depend on readers to share this knowledge, and therefore expect that any use of, or reference to, well-known schoolroom material might produce that jolt. Augustine's account of his conversion is typical, then, not only in the way it describes the more dramatic acts of recognition, but because it is designed to *produce* that affect in language that is saturated with recollected learning. That is, more often than one might expect in a text so concerned with turning away from pagan error, Augustine uses passages from classical texts such as the *Aeneid* which he tells us he was "forced to remember" [tenere cogebar] in school (1.13 [p. 38]) as so many schoolboys were. He also draws extensively on the language of those scriptures that, like so many schoolboys, he had learned so well, and which ultimately produced the decisive act of recognition in him. In fact, the words he uses to formulate his plea for clearer understanding just prior to his conversion are the words uttered by the "troubled soul" [anima turbata] in Psalm 6: "O Lord, how long? how long, will you be angry forever?" [et tu domine, usquequo? usquequo, domine, irasceris in finem?] (8.12 [p. 462]).[46] The whole of the *Confessions* is a tissue of such recollections, a patchwork exactly like those I described in Chapter 5, an amalgam of Augustine's own words and the words of other texts used exactly as if they were Augustine's too. Such a repurposing of Scripture, like the repurposing of any school text, was bound to be more comforting than astounding since all such knowledge was understood to be inherently helpful, as I also noted in Chapter 5, a "pattern for living" [vivendi norma], a "system for the mind" [mos animi] that ensured its goodness.[47] As a neat mirror image of the school texts that asked students to remember well the very rules enjoining them to remember, the lives of schoolboys were made better— more filled with *securitas*—whenever they discovered the pattern they had been given for living a life in the experience of that life.

Scholars who have looked at the passages from school texts that appear in the mature writings of ancient and medieval writers have tended to understand them in the more mechanical terms of Locke's storehouse. Like Virgil for Augustine, they have been described as "mental furniture," material to be trundled out of a cognitive attic or spare room when

---

[46] "And my soul is troubled exceedingly: but thou, O Lord, how long? Turn to me, O Lord, and deliver my soul" [Et anima mea turbata est valde, et tu Domine usquequo reverte Domine erue animam meam], Psalm 6:4–5.

[47] *Liber cartule*, col. 1312a/p. 63; *Distichs of Cato*, Prologue (unlineated prose).

needed.[48] It is in this same spirit, I think, that borrowings from school texts are usually described as "quotations," even though Langland, Chaucer, and Gower will, as often as not, fail to attribute the borrowed words to a source.[49] The pervasiveness of such patchwork makes it useful and right to notice which old texts make up new ones in the Middle Ages. But it is just as important to notice the new meanings these new texts not only carry with them but make possible. Such knowing was itself a *technē*, and not only for illuminating new contexts and experiences with old learning—and for ornamenting texts with a certain affect—but, also, and perhaps most importantly, for allowing new contexts and circumstances to disclose new meanings in the old, well-known text.

THE POETRY OF EXPERIENCE

As Morton Bloomfield put it, Langland's mind was so "steeped" in Scripture that it was a "real language" to him and he "speaks Bible... as one might speak French or English."[50] As I noted in Chapter 4, schoolroom learning was important enough to Langland for him to cite the Cato of the *Distichs* more than any other authority. These absorptions are particularly marked in the texture of *Piers Plowman* because, unlike other Middle English poets, Langland often absorbs them in the Latin in which he learned them. But he also deployed schoolroom texts in different ways in different versions of his poem—to continue Bloomfield's analogy, he sometimes used the same text to speak very different truths. In such cases, we can see the ideas that Langland *could* have had when writing an earlier version of *Piers*, but did not have until later. The various versions of *Piers Plowman* afford an unusual opportunity, then, to observe, not only what Langland knew by means of a given school text, but the progress of his thinking by means of it.

---

[48] For the phrase "mental furniture" describing Augustine's use of Virgil see Sabine MacCormack, *The Shadows of Poetry: Virgil in the Mind of Augustine* (Berkeley, CA: University of California Press, 1998), p. xviii. For the phrase as a characterization of the role played by "the proverbs of 'Cato'" and later writers' among the learned in the Middle Ages see Jill Mann, "'He Knew Nat Catoun': Medieval School-Texts and Middle English Literature," 41–74 in *The Text in the Community: Essays on Medieval Works, Manuscripts, Authors and Readers*, ed. Jill Mann and Maura Nolan (Notre Dame, IN: University of Notre Dame Press, 2006), 55.

[49] On the particular problems with this terminology when describing *Piers Plowman* see Chapter 4 in the present volume, pp. 148–56.

[50] Morton W. Bloomfield, *Piers Plowman as Fourteenth-Century Apocalypse* (New Brunswick, NJ: Rutgers University Press, 1961), 37.

A relatively simple example of the process can be found in passūs 11 and 13 of the B- and C-texts. The dreamer, Will, has just encountered the figure Ymaginatif for the first time, who has rebuked him for an earlier encounter with Reason. Ymaginatif says Will would have learned more from conversation if he had let Reason speak without interruption. In both B and C Ymaginatif emphasizes this point by quoting a line from Boethius's *Consolatio Philosophiae* about holding one's tongue:

> "Haddestow suffered," he seide, "slepynge tho thow were,
> Thow sholdest have knowen that Clergie kan and conceyved
>   moore thorugh Reson;
> For Reson wolde have reherced thee right as Clergie seide.
> Ac for thyn entremetynge here artow forsake:
> *Philosophus esses, si tacuissses*."

["If you had been patient," he said, "even though you were sleeping, you would have known what Clergy knows and understood more from Reason. For Reason would have told you just as Clergy has said. But because of your interruption you are forsaken here: *You might have been a philosopher, if you had been silent*."]

(B 11.411–14a)[51]

When writing C, however, the citation from Boethius in B reminds Langland of a similar saying about holding one's tongue in the *Distichs of Cato*, and so he adds this line to the passage, which, in this later text, continues as follows:[52]

> Et alibi: Locutum me
>   aliquando penituit, tacuisse nunquam.

[And elsewhere: I have sometimes regretted having spoken but never having kept silent.]

(C 13.223a–b)

Tacuisse ("to have kept silent") functions as the prompt or hook-word drawing the second passage into the B-text, but, along with the verbal homology and the pertinence Langland finds in this passage, there is also clear evidence of an attendant feeling. What was only "philosophy"

---

[51] For these lines in the C-text see William Langland, *Piers Plowman: A New Annotated Edition of the C-text*, ed. Derek Pearsall (Exeter: University of Exeter Press, 2008), 13.221–5a. Hereafter I will cite the C-text from this edition by version, passus, and line number in the text. According to John Alford the quotation is "adapted" from Boethius, *Consolation of Philosophy*, Book 2, prose 7 (*A Guide to the Quotations* [Binghamton, NY: Medieval and Renaissance Texts and Studies, 1992], 78).

[52] Alford sees this as a "paraphrase" of *Distichs of Cato*, I.12b rather than a "quotation" (*Guide to the Quotations*, 78). This is a distich that Chaucer also paraphrases in the last lines of The Manciple's Tale (see Chapter 6 in the present volume, p. 226).

in B—silence makes you a philosopher—becomes the security of knowing how to avoid "regret" in C, a comfort Langland clearly took in recalling this truth but which he also then installed in the C-text by means of this familiar—widely recognizable—line.

A less mechanical but equally simple instance of such recognition can be found in the movement from the A-text to the B-text in passus 10. There, in a wide-ranging discussion on the nature of doing well, Will understands Clergy to have suggested that "kinghed and knighthed and caiseris with erlis" [kingship and knighthood and emperors with earls] (A 219) are "Do well," "Do better" and Do best," but Scripture interrupts him to insist that "Paul" has declared it an "unpossible" that a rich man shall ever enter the into the kingdom of heaven. In A, Langland simply carries on with Will's objection to this view (on the grounds that all the baptized are saved) but, in B, Scripture expands on his views with what amount to two proverbs, one taken from Ecclesiasticus, the next from the *Distichs of Cato*:

> Poul preveth it impossible—riche men have hevene.
> Salamon seith also that silver is worst to lovye:
> *Nichil iniquius quam amare pecuniam*;
> And Caton kenneth us to coveiten it naught but at nede;
> *Dilige denarium set parce dilige formam.*
> And patriarkes and prophetes and poetes bothe
> Writen to wissen us to wilne no richesse.

[Paul proves it impossible (for) rich men to have heaven. Solomon says, also, that silver is the worst thing to love: *nothing is more wicked to love than money*; And Cato teaches us to desire it only when we are in need; *love money but do not love its nature.* And patriarchs and prophets and poets all wrote to teach us not to want riches.]

(B 10.335–9)

Scripture's position does not seem provocative but in both the A- and B-texts it causes a violent reaction in Will ("*Contra*," he shouts), for he hears it as the claim that not everyone can be saved. It is a hard truth, which Scripture also insists upon in both texts, but in B he also softens it by continuing longer in his defense and admitting, at the end of a set of lines absent from A, that while rich men may not claim the right to salvation ("Ther riche men no right may cleyme," B 10.342), they may attain it through "mercy and grace" ("ruthe and grace" B 10.342). The addition of the quotations from Ecclesiasticus and the *Distichs* perform a similar softening function in B prior to this retreat, for what they quietly but firmly announce—to Will and every medieval reader of *Piers Plowman* alike—is that this hard truth is well known. The comfort that comes in

B with the notion that there is grace is anticipated in the comfort inherent in the recognition—again, for Will and every medieval reader of *Piers Plowman* alike—that these truths will not be experienced without having been learned in school, that salvation would only be in question for those who did not heed the warning they had had from the very moment they learned to read.

The strategic—one would have to say "literary"—deployment of such recognition is most clear, however, if we look across a sequence of similar revisions in all three texts of *Piers*. My starting point here is the moment in A when Piers the Plowman has finally appeared and offered to guide Will and a group of other pilgrims to St Truth, but Truth has forestalled the journey by sending a pardon to Piers "for hym and for hise heires for evermoore after" [for him and for his heirs forever after] (B 7.4) There is great rejoicing at this news, but since the language of the pardon seems directed only at "alle libbynge laborers" [all living laborers] (A 8.63; see B 7.60; C 9.58) Langland insists, in the A-text, more or less in his own voice, that only beggars who are truly needy will be pardoned:

> Beggeris & bidderis ben not in þe bulle
> But ȝif þe suggestioun be soþ þat shapiþ hem to begge.
> For he þat beggiþ or bit, but he haue nede,
> He ys fals wiþ þe fend & defraudiþ the nedy,
> And eke giliþ the gyuere ageyns his wille.[53]

[Beggars and alms-seekers are not in this pardon, unless the reason is genuine that causes them to beg. For he that begs or asks, unless he has need, he is as false as the fiend and defrauds the needy, and he tricks the giver against his will.]

This is the same idea that so challenges Will in passus 10 of the A- and B-texts (it also implies that only some will be saved), but, when writing B, Langland encountered the restriction with a prim rigor, insisting on the justness of this view by means of one of the short injunctions at the very beginning of the *Distichs of Cato*, "Cui des videto" [be careful to whom you give] (Pro 17). So in this version of the poem he appends the following lines to the ones I have just quoted:

> For if he wiste he were noght nedy he wolde yyve that another
> That wer moore nedyer than he—so the nedieste sholde be holpe.
> Caton kenneth men thus, and the Clerc of the Stories:
> *Cui des, videto* is Catons techyng.

---

[53] William Langland, *Piers Plowman: The A-Version*, ed. Geoge Kane (London: Athlone Press, 1960), 8.67–71. Hereafter all quotations from the A-text will be taken from this edition and cited by version, passus, and line number in the text.

[For if he knew he (the beggar) were not needy he would give to another who was needier than he—so the neediest would be helped. Cato teaches men thus, and the Clerk of the Stories: *Be careful to whom you give*, this is Cato's teaching.]

(B 7.69–72)[54]

Then, as if this schoolroom phrase were a window onto a great number of parallel texts, Langland demonstrates his resolve in such justice—at this point in the poem—by adding even more authorities in B that insist upon the care necessary in charity:

> And in the Stories he techeth to bistowe thyn almesse:
> *Sit elemosina in manu tua donec studes cui des.*
> Ac Gregory was a good man, and bad us gyven alle
> That asketh for His love that us al leneth:
> *Non eligas cui miserearis, ne forte pretereas illum qui meretur accipere;*
> *quia incertum est pro quo Deo magis placeas.*
> For wite ye neuere who is worthi, ac God woot who hath nede.

[And in the *Historia* (*scholastica*) he teaches you to bestow your alms (thus): *Let your alms remain in your hand until you have been careful to find out to whom you should give.* But Gregory was a good man, and asked us to give to all who ask for love of Him, (on behalf of whom) we all give. *Do not choose whom to take mercy upon, lest by chance you pass over someone who deserves to receive it; for it is not certain for which [act] you may please God more.* For you never know who is worthy—but God knows who has need.]

(B 7.73–5ab)

The second Latin passage here is much the gentlest of all the new material in B (urging almsgiving rather than setting limits on it), but it is capped by the assurance, in Langland's voice, that only God knows who is needy (and so every generous Christian should be very careful because alms can easily go astray). This turns out to be the germ of the thought that Langland expands in and as the revision that becomes the C-text, but that expansion is also a retraction of sorts. For, it is clear that when Langland came again to B—now experiencing it anew, as if he were somehow reading this text for the first time, and encountering its ideas as if they were someone else's thoughts—he saw his earlier satisfactions about justice as sanctimonious, even heartless, and he recoils from them, reading an unbridled generosity back into the pardon's provisions instead. Langland so softens his stance in C in fact, as to almost reverse his views in B,

---

[54] The "Clerk of Stories" is usually assumed to be Peter Comestor (d. 1179), author of the *Historia scholastica*, although the quotation attributed to this "Clerk" here has not been found there. See Alford, *Guide to the Quotations*, 54.

bending the lines which focused there on the way false beggars deprive the "nedieste" of their due, so that they are now a stern injunction *to give*:

> For he þat gyueth for goddes loue wolde nat gyue, his thankes,
> Bote ther he wiste were wel grete nede,
> And most merytorie to men þat he ȝeueth fore.
> Catoun acordeth therwith: *Cui des, videto!*
> Woet no man, as y wene, who is worthy to haue:

[For he that gives for God's love would not give if he had the choice, unless he knew that there was a very great need, and (it would be) most beneficial to those to whom he gives. Cato agrees with this: *Be careful to whom you give!* No man knows, I think, who is worthy to have.]

(C 9.66–70)

Langland retains the line in B that describes God as the only judge of neediness ("For wite ye nevere who is worthi—ac God woot who hath nede" [For you never know who is worthy, but God knows who has need], B 7.76) but removes "God" from the statement. The resulting line no longer means you can never be sure someone is needy (as it did in B) but, rather, that neediness may lie where we least expect to find it—"Woet no man, as y wene, who is worthy to haue" [No man knows, I think, who is worthy to have] (C 9.70)—and, so, care must to be taken to be charitable when in doubt lest the needy be overlooked. To emphasize this view Langland deletes the lines and quotations that had intervened in B between this line and the line from the *Distichs*, so that, in C, tucked up against the injunction to be careful about giving, the line from the *Distichs* endorses that injunction and insists on generosity too: rather than "take *care*" when you give, it now means something like "take care *that* you give!" This meaning is then insisted upon by the hundred lines that are added to C after these, which illustrate the point of the distich by describing, in some of Langland's most vividly realistic poetry, all the claims of the needy that Langland so firmly ignored when writing A and B (these include, among others, the poor without enough to feed their children, the blind and crippled, and the mad):

> Ac þat most neden aren oure neyhebores, and we nyme gode hede,
> As prisones in puttes and pore folk in cotes,
> Charged with childrene and chief lordes rente;
> Þat they with spynnyng may spare, spenen hit on hous-huyre,
> Bothe in mylke and in mele, to make with papelotes
> To aglotye with here gurles that greden aftur fode.

[But those who are most needy are our neighbors, if we take good care, such as prisoners in dungeons and poor folk in hovels, burdened with children and their landlord's rent; what they save by spinning they must pay for housing; also on milk and meal to make porridge to fill the stomachs of their children who cry after food.]

(C 9.71–7)

Because the line from the *Distichs* is a school text it is clear that Langland knew it by heart even when he wrote the A text, but it only became useful to *Piers Plowman*—it only became meaningful to him—once he had altered the meaning of his own text in the direction of what he then perceived to be the meaning of this line. That this meaning should have been reversed when Langland rethinks his own stance in C in no way diminishes the strength of this recovery—of the act of recognition—for in C, just as in B, Langland once more finds in the school text exactly what he wishes to say. Moreover, as the content of the text is turned almost 180 degrees, its affective content remains the same, as one satisfaction yields to another (as an old truth serves an identical turn, even if in a completely different way), as the claims of justice yield to the claims of the needy, a long-held truth is rediscovered in each case. One could say that the line from the *Distichs* triggered each new thought, but it is probably closer to the compositional truth to say that this line was involved in Langland's *thinking*, an injunction that made this text-by-text exploration of what need demands possible. We might also suppose that Langland's views on charity and poverty were altered because of experiences he had between the writing of the B and C texts (even if that experience consisted of no more than his own ruminations). But, because the very meaning Langland gives to the line he learned in school changes in lock step with his thought, it is clear that the line in no way functions like an item stored in the memory to be "quoted" at some suitable moment. In each case, the thinking (and feeling) occurs *by means of* the old learning, a thinking-again (*recognition*) that is above all a new thinking (a re*cognition*).

As I have said, the opportunities literature affords to observe such thought is limited, but a similar sort of experience can be observed in the role played by school texts in Book 7 of John Gower's *Confessio Amantis*. This book largely consists of a disquisition by Genius on "the nature of Philosophie," instructing Amans after "the scole … of Aristotle" (7.3–4) as Aristotle "tauht … Alisaundre" (7.5), with the latter half of the book focusing on the "reule [rule] of Policie" (7.1710) illustrated by a variety of stories of exemplary or flawed rulers. Such teaching draws, almost by definition, on material far from the elementary schoolroom, and yet, in the part of the book devoted to the "ferthe" [fourth] point of "Aristotles lore" (7.3098–9), "Pité" (7.3107), Genius briefly narrates the fable of the mouse and the mountain taken from the elegiac *Romulus*, a collection of beast fables (then as now, often described as "Aesop's Fables") sometimes used in place of the *Fables* of Avianus in literacy training.[55] Just before he tells this story, Genius has warned that a king must not be too merciful lest he seem weak ("if he be doubtous [hesitant] / To slen in cause of rigtwisnesse [justice] / It mai be said no pitousnesse [pity] / Bot it is pusillamité" [7.3524–7]), and this leads him to worry about the dangers of a king seeming too fearful. The fable describes how "in the londes of Archade" (7.3555) people became so afraid of a "wonder dredful noise" [very frightening noise] (7.3556) coming from a hill that they all fled their houses, only to conclude that they were mistaken and what they heard was, in fact, the sound of the hill giving birth to a mouse:[56]

> And ate laste* it was a mous   finally
> The wiche was bore and to norrice*   nursemaid
> Betake*; and tho thei hield hem* nyce*,
>
> entrusted/themselves/foolish
> For thei withoute cause dradde*.   were fearful
>
> (7.3551–5)

The error here lies, of course, not in mistaking a loud noise for a hill in labor but in believing that the "dredful noise" (7.3556) coming from a mountain can be explained by a mouse emerging from a crevice. But the story was obviously useful to Genius (and Gower), not because of its own

---

[55] For the text of the fable (as already noted in Chapter 5 of the present volume, p. 162 n. 9) see "De terra et mure" in *L'Esopus attribuito a Gualtero Anglico*, ed. Paola Busdraghi, vol. 10 (2005) in *Favolisti latini medievali e umanistici*, ed. Ferruccio Bertini (Genoa: Università di Genova, Pubblicazioni del Dipartimento di Archeologia, Filologia Classica e Loro Tradizioni, 1984–2005), 98. As I also note in Chapter 5 the elegiac *Romulus* is widely available in a single-text edition in *The Fables of "Walter of England": edited from Wolfenbüttel, Herzog August Bibliothek, Codex Guelferbytanus 185 Helmstadiensis* ed. Aaron Eugene Wright, (Toronto: Pontifical Institute of Mediaeval Studies 1997), which also includes the commentary that accompanies it in this manuscript. For the fable, in this case called "Mons peperit murem" [The mountain gave birth to a mouse], see that edition, 76–7. Wright notes in his introduction that "in the later Middle Ages" these fables "would come . . . nearly to replace Avianus in the pedagogic canon" (2). For a detailed history of "Aesop's Fables" and their more appropriate designation as elegiac and prose *Romulus* see Jill Mann, *From Aesop to Reynard: Beast Fable in Medieval Britain* (Oxford: Oxford University Press, 2009), 2–14. Gower almost certainly knew this fable from the elegiac *Romulus* rather than its many other forms (Mann observes: "Nearly two hundred manuscripts have been identified to date, and a determined researcher could certainly find more. For any educated person from the thirteenth to the fifteenth century, 'Aesop' would most probably have meant the elegiac *Romulus*" [12]). On the role of "Aesop's Fables" in elementary learning in fourteenth- and fifteenth-century England see Edward Wheatley, *Mastering Aesop: Medieval Education, Chaucer, and his Followers* (Gainesville, FL: University Press of Florida, 2000), esp. 52–96.

[56] Peck gives no source for this fable in his edition, and neither does Macaulay (in *The English Works of John Gower*, ed. G. C. Macaulay, vol. 2, Early English Text Society e.s. 82 [London, 1901]).

conclusion, but because of the conclusions that were habitually drawn from it. According to one surviving gloss, what errors of interpretation in the story teach is the value of misdirection generally:

> Presens appollogus docet nos ne temeamus illos qui multa minantur, sed pocius illos qui tacite insidiantur.

> [This fable teaches us not to fear those who threaten much, but, rather, those who quietly lie in wait.][57]

Genius clearly understood this to be a narrative about the political value of dissimulation. As he says just before he focuses on the need to conceal fearfulness, "a king shal make good visage [expression] / That no man know of his corage [thoughts/feelings]" (7.3545–6). Dissimulation is also connected to fear here by the narrative that precedes this fable which describes how Thameris, Queen of Marsegete, defeated the tyrant Spertachus, king of the Persians when she "feigned / For feere [out of fear] as thogh sche wolde flee" (7.3468–9) and thereby drew Spertachus and 200,000 of his host into an ambush.[58]

Genius is not using this story because it is in some way about "pity," fearfulness, or "kingship," then—on its face, it has nothing to do with *any* of these concepts or issues—but, rather, because it is a tool for thinking through the complicated and subtle relationship between threat and understanding (in the broadest terms, between power and epistemology). This relationship is even more squarely identified by the narrative that follows this story in which Gideon, facing an enormous host with only 300 troops, routs them when he blows his trumpet and that host "loude ascride" [cried loudly] (7.3761):

> This host in the valleie it herde,
> And sih* hou that the hell alyhte*;   how/ hill was lit
> So what of hieringe and of sihte,
> Thei cawhten such a sodein feere*,   became suddenly so afraid
> That non of hem belefte* there.   remained

(7.3768–72)

This part of Genius's long lesson about "policy" turns out to teach, above all, the power inherent in misdirection, in what may be achieved by

---

[57] I quote here from the gloss accompanying the manuscript printed as *The Fables of "Walter of England"* (77).

[58] As Andrew Galloway also observes about this section of Book 7, "pity" for Gower, "always carries some implication of power," "The Literature of 1388 and the Politics of Pity in Gower's *Confessio Amantis*," 67–104 in *The Letter of the Law: Legal Practice and Literary Production in Medieval England*, ed. Emily Steiner and Candace Barrington (Ithaca, NY: Cornell University Press, 2002), 97.

appearing to be strong when you are weak, or weak when you are strong, in either case, dominating those you wished to rule by seeming to be what you are not. This is not advice this fable gives, but it is a thought that can be conceived by its means. It is a clearly schoolroom text that Gower had thought through so carefully that it carried with it for him not just the ideas it contained, but their implications.

The richness of these implications and the extent to which they might shape a Ricardian poet's most ambitious narratives is best illustrated, however, by Gower's other use of a school text in Book 7 of the *Confessio*, the epitome of Matthew of Vendôme's *Tobias* that is the last of this book's narrative examples (7.5313–65). In the *Tobias* both the eponymous character and his father (also named "Tobias") are exemplary insofar as they are "good" [boni] (line 2089/p. 144), and the school text begins with a lengthy account of the elder Tobias's "virtue" [virtus] (line 69/p. 85): he "reproves wrong... and approves right" [reprobat... nefas... probat... fas] (lines 91–2/p. 85); he "distributes his wealth" [partitur opes] (line 73/ p. 85); he "loves justice" [amat... iura] (line 89/p. 85); he "shows compassion" [compatitur] (line 77/p. 84); and he is chaste even in the context of marriage, only agreeing to wed "for the love of offspring" [prolis amore] rather than the "inducement of Venus" [non incentivo Veneris] (line 121/ p. 86). Gower's paraphrase consists of no more than fifty of Book 7's 5,400 lines, but he also introduces it as the "gret ensample," the "conclusion final" that will "make an ende" (7.5307) of the discussion of "Policie" that concludes this book. And rightly so, for the epitome acts as a kind of peroration summing up the "fyf pointz [five points]... of Policie" (7.1706–10) which structure the whole of Genius's teaching throughout this book and also turn out to be precisely those five virtues epitomized by Tobias in the school text. As Gower names them they are "trouthe" [honesty] (7.1724), "largesse" [generosity] (7.1989), "rihtwisnesse" [justice] (7.2707), "pité" [compassion] (7.3707), and "chasteté" [chastity] (7.4240).

The correspondence between the two ethical schemes is inevitably retrospective, and the neat categories—the five distinct virtues—only become visible in the *Tobias* when refracted through the schematic structure Gower gives his own ethics. The characteristic of schoolroom knowledge is once again not only the new thinking it makes possible—what can be understood by its means—but the preposterous structure whereby what was always present in a text is only disclosed by some later use. In this sense, Gower does not use the *Tobias* at the conclusion of this book of the *Confessio* because it identifies the "five points" that most interest him but rather, it is by using this text that he recognizes those five points already, present in the well-known text. A further magnification of this preposterous relationship underscores it in this case because Book 7 has something

of the relationship to the whole of the *Confessio* that the five points of policy
have to the whole of Book 7. As James Simpson has convincingly argued,
this lesson in "policy" must be understood as the culminating moment of
Gower's poem, for it provides the political education necessary to reform
the selfhood that Amans's confession has made the poem's central problem.[59] As a result, Book 7 actually constitutes the "frame" for all of the
Confessio's other eight books, making the structure Gower retrospectively
discovers in the *Tobias*, something like the structure Book 7 is trying to give
the learning provided by the *Confessio Amantis* as a whole. The degree of
this magnification provides still further explanation of why such recognition may be comforting. As these acts of recovery make the *Tobias* the
culmination of all that Gower's poem says, it makes the trajectory of *all* of
this poem's knowing a return to old knowledge, an extended act of
recognition, not unlike Augustine's conversion, whereby the most important things mature perceptions discover turn out to be the first things
learned in school.

SCHOOLROOM LEARNING AS A WAY OF LIFE

Such discoveries and the modes of learning that led to them clearly
remain with us. As Deirdre Lynch has observed, "many of us today know
people .. who re-read Austen each night" or in times of anxiety or trouble.[60]
The impulse to return to the well-known text has had such different cultural
determinants over time that we may well find it hard to notice, let alone
value, the acts of recognition that the most familiar texts still make
possible.[61] The salient change for us received particularly thoughtful
exploration in a moving essay by Carolyn Heilbrun on the relationship
between re-reading and what she most often calls "living," but which she
sometimes also describes as "experience."[62] She begins by describing her
relationship to the books she knew extremely well in much the way that

---

[59] James Simpson, *Sciences and the Self in Medieval Poetry: Alan of Lille's* Anticlaudianus *and John Gower's* Confessio Amantis (Cambridge: Cambridge University Press, 1995), 223.
[60] Deidre Lynch, "On Going Steady with Novels," *The Eighteenth Century* 50 (2009): 210.
[61] As Lynch observes elsewhere, it was the "medicinal value" attributed to "habit" that was at the root of much re-reading in the nineteenth century. See her "Canon's Clockwork: Novels for Everyday Use," 87–110 in *Bookish Histories: Books, Literature, and Commercial Modernity, 1700–1900*, ed. Ina Ferris and Paul Keen (New York, NY: Palgrave Macmillan, 2009), 93.
[62] Carolyn Heilbrun, "From Rereading to Reading," *PMLA* 119 (2004): 211–17. Hereafter I will cite this essay by page number in the text.

Augustine did, and we might imagine Chaucer, Langland, and Gower would have, had they written expressly about it:

> Rereading can...be instigated by the discovery that a book read long ago suddenly appears apposite to one's condition. (211)

The book she sees as apposite to her current experience is *The Ambassadors* because its central character, Lambert Strether, is also "coping with retirement and old age" (211). Re-reading *The Ambassadors* transforms it into a text she can think with rather than only about, a source of the kind of recognition I have been describing, an "opening of the self not to experience alone but to the residue of experience," an amalgam that—as in Augustine, Chaucer, Langland, and Gower—opens onto "the understanding that comes with thought and reassessment" (213).

It is no accident, however, that Heilbrun chooses the word "residue" to characterize the knowledge that returns in this way, for she may also stand in for all of us who have learned to read extensively rather than intensively in her ambivalence about the value of recognition as a mode of knowing. As she notices at the very beginning of her meditation, re-reading is practice that is now only "much recommended to those for whom time is, as Virginia Woolf once put it, flapping around one" (211). And Heilbrun's deepened understanding of the familiar text leads, finally, not to comfort but despondence. She says at the beginning of the essay that she has been struggling since giving up work, and she has returned to *The Ambassadors* for some guidance in how she might still embrace "living" (211) not least because it is little Billham's advice to "live all you can; it's a mistake not to" that she, like many others, understands as the "germ of the novel" (212). For Heilbrun, however, the return to the familiar text leads only to the discovery that "there are no cures for aging despair" (213) and the realization that "repetition of all that we have done before" is, now, only "wearisome" (214). She concludes her attempt to think anew by way of the *Ambassadors* by delineating the definitive cultural change in valuations: "to reread," she simply says, "to return to what we have taught and pondered, seems not to beckon" (215). For Heilbrun "rereading" is finally *opposed* to "living" because the experience of a text is crucially different from the experience external to it.[63]

---

[63] A biographical note accompanying this essay reveals that Carolyn Heilbrun "took her life" between writing it and its publication. The anguish this suggests would differ by orders of magnitude from the anguish Augustine describes prior to his conversion—his sickness and torment (VIII.xi [p. 456])—and yet it cannot be unrelated that re-reading, in both cases, offered itself as a possible comfort and that, in the modern instance, it was most important for Heilbrun to say just how inadequate it was to the task.

Heilbrun begins with re-reading in the old mode but emerges from the process by making clear just how inert such learning can now appear, how much the return can produce, not new knowledge or perception, but a "nostalgia" tinged with "regret" (212). Her account also makes it possible to see what might be at stake in this cultural difference. For Pierre Hadot, the change can be described as a lost relationship between "discourse" and a "way of life."[64] In an argument that shows, first, how "ancient philosophy established . . . an intimate link between philosophical discourse and the form of life" and, second, how scholasticism "theoreticiz[ed]" (254) philosophy so as to make it little more than a "servant of theology" (255), Hadot has made clear exactly how much modern sensibilities have lost of the original practices that constituted what we still call "philosophy." His observations go a long way toward explaining why Plato's notion of *anamnesis* should so accurately describe medieval processes of learning in a way that is also very difficult for us now to notice or value. In insisting (following Whitehead) that, for an ancient philosopher such as Plato, "concepts are always dressed in emotions" (70), Hadot also goes a long way toward explaining why it should be so hard for us to appreciate just how laden with feeling the familiar school text might remain throughout a long life.[65] It would appear, in other words, that a divagation at the very root of all our philosophy makes it difficult for us to see just how Augustine, Chaucer, Langland, and Gower experienced the books they read and knew so well. This is not a loss to our own forms of learning if, like Heilbrun, we believe that repetition really is wearisome. But it is a gap that must be closed, as I have tried to do in these pages, if we are to understand both the extent and nature of the contribution once made by literacy training to literature.

[64] Pierre Hadot, *What is Ancient Philosophy?*, trans. Michael Chase (Cambridge, MA: Harvard University Press, 1995), 55 (but the distinction is fundamental to the whole of Hadot's account). Hereafter I will cite this account by page number in the text.

[65] Hadot is here citing A. Parmentier, *La philosophie de Whitehead et le problème de Dieu* (Paris: Beauchesne, 1968), 222 n. 83.

Bibliography

MANUSCRIPTS

Aberdeen, University Library, MS 123
Aberystwyth, National Library, MS Peniarth 356b
Cambridge, Gonville & Caius College, MS 136
Cambridge, Gonville & Caius College, MS 203/109
Cambridge, Gonville & Caius College, MS 383
Cambridge, Peterhouse College, MS 207
Cambridge, Peterhouse College, MS 215
Cambridge, St John's College, MS 37
Cambridge, St John's College, MS 147
Cambridge, St John's College, MS 163
Cambridge, St John's College, MS F.26
Cambridge, Trinity College, MS O.5.4
Cambridge, Trinity College, MS R.3.56
Cambridge, University Library, MS Ee.4.20
Cambridge, University Library, MS Ii.3.3
Cambridge, University Library, MS Oo.6.110
Cambridge, University Library, MS Additional 2830
Dublin, Trinity College, MS 270
Dublin, Trinity College, MS 509
Durham, Cathedral Chapter Library, MS C.VI.26
Glasgow, University Library, MS U.6.10
Lincoln Cathedral, Chapter Library, MS 88
Lincoln, Cathedral, Chapter Library, MS 132
London, British Library, MS Additional 8151
London, British Library, MS Additional 9066
London, British Library, MS Additional 10090
London, British Library, MS Additional 10093
London, British Library, MS Additional 16380
London, British Library, MS Additional 37075
London, British Library, MS Arundel 394
London, British Library, MS Harley 1002
London, British Library, MS Harley 1587
London, British Library, MS Harley 2251
London, British Library, MS Harley 3362
London, British Library, MS Harley 3490
London, British Library, MS Harley 4967
London, British Library, MS Harley 5751
London, British Library, MS Royal 15.A.VII

London, British Library, MS Royal 15.A.XXXI
London, British Library, MS Royal 17.B.XVII
London, Public Record Office, MS C 47/34/13
Manchester, John Rylands Library, MS Latin 394
Munich, Bayerische Staatsbibliothek, MS clm 4660
New Haven, Yale University, Beineke Library, MS 513
New Haven, Yale University, Beinecke Library, MS Takamiya Deposit 61
New York, Pierpont Morgan Library & Museum, MS M 126
Nottingham, University Library, Mi(ddleton) LM 2
Oxford, Bodleian Library, MS Ashmole 1522
Oxford, Bodleian Library, MS Ashmole 1796
Oxford, Bodleian Library, MS Auctarium F.3.9
Oxford, Bodleian Library, MS Auctarium F.5.6
Oxford, Bodleian Library, MS Bodley 619
Oxford, Bodleian Library, MS Bodley 837
Oxford, Bodleian Library, MS Digby 26
Oxford, Bodleian Library, MS Digby 100
Oxford, Bodleian Library, MS Douce 52
Oxford, Bodleian Library, MS Douce 95
Oxford, Bodleian Library, MS Hatton 58
Oxford, Bodleian Library, MS E Musaeo 54
Oxford, Bodleian Library, MS Rawlinson D 328
Oxford, Bodleian Library, MS Rawlinson G 60
Oxford, Lincoln College, MS Lat. 129
Worcester, Cathedral Library, MS F 61
Worcester, Cathedral Library, MS F 123
Worcester, Cathedral Library, MS F 147
Worcester, Cathedral Library, MS F 154
Worcester Cathedral Library, MS Q.50

OTHER SOURCES

Abelson, Paul, *The Seven Liberal Arts: A Study in Mediaeval Culture*, Columbia
    University Teachers' College Contributions to Education 11, New York, NY:
    Teachers' College Columbia University, 1906.
Accessus ad auctores; Bernard d'Utrecht; Conrad d'Hirsau, ed. R. B. C. Huygens,
    Leiden: E. J. Brill, 1970.
Achilleid, 312–97 in Statius, *Thebaid, Books VIII–XII; Achilleid*, ed.
    D. R. Shackleton Bailey, Cambridge, MA: Harvard University Press, 2003.
Adam of Eynsham, *Magna Vita S. Hugonis Episcopi Lincolniensis*, ed. James
    F. Dimock, London: Longman, Green, Longman, Roberts, and Green, 1864.
Aelred of Rievaulx, *De institutione inclusarum*, 635–82 in Aelred of Rievaulx,
    Opera Omnia, ed. A. Hoste and C. H. Talbot, Corpus Christianorum, Con-
    tinuatio Mediaevalis 1, Turnhout: Brepols, 1971.

Aers, David, "Chaucer's *Tale of Melibee*: Whose Virtues?" 69–81 in *Medieval Literature and Historical Inquiry: Essays in Honour of Derek Pearsall*, ed. David Aers, Cambridge: D. S. Brewer, 2000.

Alexander of Villa-Dei, *Doctrinale*, ed. Theodore Reichling, Berlin: A. Hofmann, 1893.

Alford, John A., "The Grammatical Metaphor: A Survey of Its Use in the Middle Ages," *Speculum* 57 (1982): 728–60.

Alford, John A., "Langland's Learning," *The Yearbook of Langland Studies* 9 (1995): 1–8.

Alford, John A., "The Role of the Quotations in *Piers Plowman*," *Speculum* 52 (1977): 80–99.

John A. Alford, *Piers Plowman*: A Guide to the Quotations. Binghamton, NY: *Medieval and Renaissance Texts and Studies*, 1992.

Althusser, Louis, "A Letter on Art in Reply to André Daspre," 221–7 in *Lenin and Philosophy and Other Essays*, trans. Ben Brewster, London: New Left Books, 1971.

Amassian, Margaret and J. Sadowsky, "Mede and Mercede: A Study of the Grammatical Metaphor in *Piers Plowman*," *Neuphilologische Mitteilungen* 72 (1971): 457–76.

Ancrene Wisse, ed. Robert Hasenfratz, Kalamazoo, MI: Medieval Institute Publications, 2000.

Anstey, Henry, *Munimenta academica: or, Documents Illustrative of Academical Life and its Studies at Oxford*, 2 vols., London: Longmans, Green, Reader, and Dyer, 1868.

Aronowitz, Stanley and Henry A. Giroux, *Postmodern Education: Politics, Culture and Social Criticism*, Minneapolis, MN: University of Minnesota Press, 1991.

Askins, William, "The *Tale of Melibee* and the Crisis at Westminster, November, 1387," *Studies in the Age of Chaucer, Proceedings* 2 (1986): 103–12.

Athenaeus: The Learned Banqueters, 8 vols., Cambridge, MA: Harvard University Press, 2009.

Atkin, Albert, "Peirce on the Index and Indexical Reference," *Transactions of the Charles S. Peirce Society* 41 (2005): 161–88.

Auerbach, Erich, *Mimesis: The Representation of Reality in Western Literature*, trans. Willard R. Trask, Princeton, NJ: Princeton University Press, 1953; first published in German, 1946.

Augustine, *Enarrationes in Psalmos*, ed. E. Dekkers and I. Fraipont, 3 vols., Corpus Christianorum Series Latina 38–40, Turnhout: Brepols, 1956.

Augustine, *Confessions*, ed. and trans. William Watts, 2 vols., Cambridge, MA: Harvard University Press, 1995; first published 1912.

Avesani, Rino, "Il primo ritmo per la morte del grammatico Ambrogio e il cosidetto 'Liber Catonianus,'" *Studi medievali*, ser. 3, 6 (1965): 455–88.

The Babees Book, ed. F. J. Furnivall, London: Chatto & Windus, 1908.

Balbus, Joannes, *Catholicon*, Mainz, 1460.

Baldwin, Anna P., "The Triumph of Patience in Julian of Norwich and Langland," 71–83 in *Langland, the Mystics and the Medieval Religious*

Tradition: Essays in Honour of S. S. Hussey, ed. Helen Phillips, Cambridge: D. S. Brewer, 1990.

Bartholomaeus Anglicus, *De proprietatibus rerum*, Lyons: Pierre Hongre, 1482.

Bateson, Mary, "The Huntingdon Song School and the School of St. Gregory's, Canterbury," *English Historical Review* 72 (1903): 712–13.

Baumgartner, W., "The Wisdom Literature," 210–37 in *The Old Testament and Modern Study: A Generation of Discovery and Research*, ed. H. H. Rowley, Oxford: Clarendon Press, 1951.

Beinecke Library, Medieval and Renaissance Manuscripts <http://brbl-net. library.yale.edu/pre1600ms/docs/pre1600.ms513.htm>, based on *Catalogue of Medieval and Renaissance Manuscripts in the Beinecke Rare Book and Manuscript Library, Yale University*, ed. Barbara Shailor et al., Medieval and Renaissance Texts and Studies 34, 48, 100, 176 (Binghamton, NY: Center for Medieval and Renaissance Studies 1984–).

Bellamy, Elizabeth J. and Artemis Leontis, "A Genealogy of Experience: From Epistemology to Politics," *The Yale Journal of Criticism* 6 (1993): 163–84.

Bennett, J. A. W., *Chaucer at Oxford and at Cambridge*, Oxford: Oxford University Press, 1974.

Bennett, Michael J., "*Sir Gawain and the Green Knight* and the Literary Achievement of the Northwest Midlands: The Historical Background," *Journal of Medieval History* 5 (1979): 63–88.

Berndt, Rolf, "French and English in Thirteenth-Century England: An Investigation into the Linguistic Situation after the Loss of the Duchy of Normandy and Other Continental Dominions," *Sitzungsberichte der Akademie der Wissenschaften der DDR, Gesellschaftswissenschaften* 1G: 129–50.

Biblia Sacra Iuxta Vulgatam Versionem, 5th edn., ed. Roger Gryson, first edited by Robert Weber with B. Fischer, I. Gribomont, H. F. D. Sparks, and W. Thiele, Stuttgart: Deutsche Bibelgesellschaft, 2007; first published 1969.

Bland, Cynthia, "John of Cornwall's Innovations and Their Possible Effects on Chaucer," 213–35 in *The Uses of Manuscripts in Literary Studies: Essays in Memory of Judson Boyce Allen*, ed. Charlotte Cook Morse, Penelope Reed Doob, and Marjorie Curry Woods, Kalamazoo, MI: Western Michigan University, Medieval Institute Publications, 1992.

Bland, Cynthia, "Langland's Use of the Term *Ex Vi Transicionis*," *The Yearbook of Langland Studies* 2 (1988): 125–35.

Bland, Cynthia, *The Teaching of Grammar in Late Medieval England: An Edition, with Commentary, of Oxford, Lincoln College MS Lat. 130*, East Lansing, MI: Colleagues Press, 1991.

Bloomfield, Morton, "Authenticating Realism and the Realism of Chaucer," *Thought* 39 (1964): 335–58.

Bloomfield, Morton, *Piers Plowman as a Fourteenth-Century Apocalypse*, New Brunswick, NJ: Rutgers University Press, 1962.

Bloomfield, Morton, "The Wisdom of the Nun's Priest's Tale," 70–82 in *Chaucerian Problems and Perspectives: Essays Presented to Paul E. Beichner*, ed. Edward

Vasta and Zacharias P. Thundy, Notre Dame, IN: University of Notre Dame Press, 1979.

Boas, M., "De Librorum Catonianorum Historia atque Compositione," *Mnemosyne* n.s. 42 (1914): 2–46.

Boethius Philosophiae Consolationis Libri Quinque, ed. Karl Büchner, Heidelberg: Carl Winter, 1977.

Bourdieu, Pierre, *The Logic of Practice*, Stanford, CA: Stanford University Press, 1990.

Bourdieu, Pierre, *Outline of a Theory of Practice*, trans. Richard Nice, Cambridge: Cambridge University Press, 1977; first published 1972.

Bourdieu, Pierre and Jean Claude Passeron, *Reproduction in Education, Society and Culture*, London: Sage in Association with Theory, Culture & Society, Dept. of Administrative and Social Studies, Teesside Polytechnic, 1990.

Bowden, Betsy, "Ubiquitous Format? What Ubiquitous Format?: Chaucer's *Tale of Melibee* as a Proverb Collection," *Oral Tradition* 17 (2002): 169–207.

Bowers, John M., *The Politics of Pearl: Court Poetry in the Age of Richard II*, Cambridge: D. S. Brewer, 2001.

Bowers, Roger, "The Almonry Schools of the English Monasteries, 1265–1540," 177–222 in *Monasteries and Society in Medieval Britain, Proceedings of the 1994 Harlaxton Symposium*, ed. Benjamin Thompson, Stamford: Paul Watkins, 1999.

Breen, Katherine, *Imagining an English Reading Public, 1150–1400*, Cambridge: Cambridge University Press, 2010.

Bridges, Venetia and Joanna Bellis, "'What Shalt Thou Do When Thou Hast an English to Make into Latin?': The Proverb Collection of Cambridge, St John's College F.26," *Studies in Philology* 112 (2015): 68–92.

Brother Bonaventure [also known as John M. Miner], "The Teaching of Latin in Later Medieval England," *Medieval Studies* 23 (1961): 1–20.

Bruner, Jerome, "Narrative and Paradigmatic Modes of Thought," *Yearbook of the National Society for the Study of Education* 84, Part 2: *Learning and Teaching: The Ways of Knowing* (1985): 97–115.

Brusendorff, Aage, "'He Knew Nat Catoun For His Wit Was Rude,'" 320–39 in *Studies in English Philology: A Miscellany in Honor of Frederick Klaeber*, Minneapolis, MN: University of Minnesota Press, 1929.

Burke, Catherine and Ian Grosvenor, *School*, London: Reaktion Books, 2008.

Burke, Kenneth, "Literature as Equipment for Living," 293–304 in his *The Philosophy of Literary Form: Studies in Symbolic Action*, Louisiana, LA: Louisiana State University Press, 1941.

Burrow, John, *Ricardian Poetry: Chaucer, Gower, Langland and the "Gawain" Poet*, London: Routledge & Kegan Paul, 1971.

Burrow, John, "'The Wolf Shits Wool': *Piers Plowman* C IX 265–265a," *Notes and Queries* n.s. 57 (2010): 168–9.

Bursill-Hall, G. L., "Johannes de Garlandia—Forgotten Grammarian and the Manuscript Tradition," *Historiographia Linguistica* 3 (1976): 155–77.

Burton, Janet, "Priory and Parish: Kirkham and its Parishioners 1496–7," 329–47 in *Monasteries and Society in Medieval Britain, Proceedings of the 1994 Harlaxton Symposium*, ed. Benjamin Thompson, Stamford: Paul Watkins, 1999.

Bushnell, Rebecca W., *A Culture of Teaching: Early Modern Humanism in Theory and Practice*, Ithaca, NY: Cornell University Press, 1996.

Butterfield, Ardis, *The Familiar Enemy: Chaucer, Language and Nation in the Hundred Years War*, Oxford: Oxford University Press, 2009.

Calinescu, Matei, *Rereading*, New Haven, CT: Yale University Press, 1993.

Camargo, Martin, "Chaucer and the Oxford Renaissance of Anglo-Latin Rhetoric," *Studies in the Age of Chaucer* 34 (2012): 173–20.

Camargo, Martin, "The Late-Fourteenth-Century Renaissance of Anglo-Latin Rhetoric," *Philosophy and Rhetoric* 45 (2012): 107–33.

Camargo, Martin and Marjorie Curry Woods, "Writing Instruction in Late Medieval Europe," 114–47 in *A Short History of Writing Instruction: From Ancient Greece to Contemporary America*, ed. James J. Murphy, 3rd edn., New York, NY: Routledge, 2012.

The Cambridge Companion to Chaucer, ed. Jill Mann and Piero Boitani, Cambridge: Cambridge University Press, 1986.

Cannon, Christopher, "The Art of Rereading," *ELH* 80 (2013): 401–25.

Cannon, Christopher, "Class Distinction and the French of England," 48–59 in *A Modern Medievalist: Traditions and Innovations in the Study of Medieval Literature*, ed. Charlotte Brewer and Barry Windeatt, Woodbridge: Boydell & Brewer, 2012.

Cannon, Christopher, *The Grounds of English Literature*, Oxford: Oxford University Press, 2004.

Cannon, Christopher, "The Language Group of the *Canterbury Tales*," 25–40 in *Medieval Latin and Middle English Literature: Essays in Honour of Jill Mann*, ed. Christopher Cannon and Maura Nolan, Cambridge: D. S. Brewer, 2011.

Cannon, Christopher, "Reading Knowledge," *PMLA* 130 (2015): 711–17.

Carlisle, Nicholas, *A Concise Description of the Endowed Grammar Schools in England and Wales*, London: Baldwin, Cradock and Joy, 1818.

Carmina Burana, ed. Alfons Hilka and Otto Schumann, 2 vols., Heidelberg: Carl Winter, 1930–41, vol. 3, ed. Bernard Bischoff, Heidelberg: Carl Winter, 1971.

Carmody, Francis J., *Arabic Astronomical and Astrological Sciences in Latin Translation: A Critical Bibliography*, Berkeley, CA: University of California Press, 1956.

Carruthers, Mary, *The Book of Memory: A Study of Memory in Medieval Culture*, 2nd edn., Cambridge: Cambridge University Press, 2008; first published 1990.

Carruthers, Mary, "Imaginatif, Memoria, and 'The Need for Critical Theory' in *Piers Plowman Studies*," *The Yearbook of Langland Studies* 9 (1995): 103–14.

Catalogue of the Harleian Manuscripts in the British Museum, 3 vols., London: British Museum, 1808.

A Catalogue of the Manuscripts Preserved in the Library of the University of Cambridge, ed. H. R. Luard, 6 vols., Cambridge: Cambridge University Press, 1856–67.

Cave, Terence, *Recognitions: A Study in Poetics*, Oxford: Clarendon Press, 1988.

Chambers, R. W., *On the Continuity of English Prose, EETS* o.s. 191A (1932).

The Chartulary of Cockersand Abbey of the Premonstratensian Order, 3 vols. in 7, ed. William Farrer, Manchester: Chetham Society, 1898–1909.

Chaucer, Geoffrey, *The Canterbury Tales*, ed. Jill Mann, Harmondsworth: Penguin, 2005.

Chaucer, Geoffrey, *The Canterbury Tales: The New Ellesmere Chaucer Monochromatic Facsimile (of Huntington Library MS EL 26 C 9)*, ed. Daniel Woodward and Martin Stevens, San Marino, CA: Huntington Library, 1997.

Chaucer, Geoffrey, *The Complete Works of Geoffrey Chaucer*, ed. W. W. Skeat, 6 vols., Oxford: Clarendon Press, 1899.

Chaucer, Geoffrey, *The Prologue from Chaucer's Canterbury Tales*, ed. Frank Jewett Mather, Boston, MA: Houghton Mifflin, 1899.

Chaucer, Geoffrey, *The Riverside Chaucer*, ed Larry D. Benson, 3rd edn., Boston: Houghton Mifflin, 1987.

Chaucer, Geoffrey, *A Variorum Edition of the Works of Geoffrey Chaucer*, vol. 6: *The Prose Treatises, Part 1: A Treatise on the Astrolabe*, ed. Sigmund Eisner, Norman, OK: University of Oklahoma Press, 2002.

Chaucer Life-Records, ed. Martin M. Crow and Clair C. Olson, Austin, TX: University of Texas Press, 1966.

Chaucer's Poetry: An Anthology for the Modern Reader, ed. Talbot Donaldson, New York, NY: Ronald Press, 1975.

Chaucer: The Critical Heritage, ed. Derek S. Brewer, 2 vols., London: Routledge, 1978.

Chaytor, H. J., *From Script to Print*, Cambridge: Cambridge University Press, 1945.

Cicero, *De Officiis*, ed. and trans. Walter Miller, Cambridge, MA: Harvard University Press, 1997; first published 1913.

[Cicero, M. Tullius], *Rhetorica ad Herennium (Ad C. Herennium libri IV De ratione dicendi)*, ed. and trans. Harry Caplan, Cambridge MA: Harvard University Press, 1981; first published 1954.

Cistercian Statutes, A.D. 1256–7, ed. J. T. Fowler, London: Bradbury, Agnew, 1890.

Clanchy, M. T., *From Memory to Written Record: England, 1066–1307*, Malden, MA: Blackwell, 1993; first published Cambridge, MA: Harvard University Press, 1979.

Clark, Donald Lemen, *Rhetoric in Greco-Roman Education*, New York, NY: Columbia University Press, 1957.

Clogan, Paul, "Literary Genres in a Medieval Textbook," *Medievalia et Humanistica* n.s. 11 (1982): 199–209.

Coffee, Neil, "Active Latin: Quo Tendimus," *Classical World* 105 (2012): 255–69.

Cole, Andrew, *Literature and Heresy in the Age of Chaucer*, Cambridge: Cambridge University Press, 2008.

Cole, Percival R., *A History of Educational Thought*, London: Oxford University Press, 1931; reprinted Westport, CT: Greenwood Press, 1972.

Cooper, Helen, *The Structure of the Canterbury Tales*, London: Duckworth, 1983.

Copeland, Rita, "Horace's *Ars Poetica* in the Medieval Classroom and Beyond," 15–33 in *Answerable Style: The Idea of the Literary in Medieval England*, ed. Frank Grady and Andrew Galloway, Columbus, OH: Ohio State University Press, 2013.

Copeland, Rita, *Rhetoric, Hermeneutics, and Translation in the Middle Ages: Academic Traditions and Vernacular Texts*, Cambridge: Cambridge University Press, 1991.

Copeland, Rita and Ineke Sluiter, *Medieval Grammar and Rhetoric: Language Arts and Literary Theory, AD 300–1475*, Oxford: Oxford University Press, 2009.

Courtenay, William J., *Schools and Scholars in Fourteenth-Century England*, Princeton, NJ: Princeton University Press, 1987.

Covington, Michael A., *Syntactic Theory in the High Middle Ages: Modistic Models of Sentence Structure*, Cambridge: Cambridge University Press, 1984.

The Craft of Numbering, 3–32 in *The Earliest Arithmetics in English*, ed. R. Steele, *EETS* e.s. 118 (1922; reprint 1988).

Crain, Patricia, *The Story of A: The Alphabetization of America from The New England Primer to The Scarlet Letter*, Stanford, CA: Stanford University Press, 2000.

Crampton, Georgia Ronan, "Chaucer's Singular Prayer," *Medium Aevum* 59 (1990): 191–213.

Crane, Susan, "Social Aspects of Bilingualism in the Thirteenth Century," 103–15 in *Thirteenth Century England*, VI, ed. Michael Prestwich, Woodbridge: Boydell & Brewer, 1997.

Curtius, Ernst Robert, *European Literature and the Latin Middle Ages*, Princeton, NJ: Princeton University Press, 1953.

The Cyrurgie of Guy de Chauliac, ed. M. S. Ogden, *EETS* o.s. 265 (1971).

Darnton, Robert, "Toward a History of Reading," *The Wilson Quarterly* 13 (1989): 87–102.

Davies, W. J. Frank, *Teaching Reading in Early England*, London: Pitman House, 1973.

Davis, Natalie Zemon, "Proverbial Wisdom and Popular Errors," 227–67 and 336–46 (notes) in her *Society and Culture in Early Modern France*, Stanford, CA: Stanford University Press, 1975.

Davlin, Mary Clemente, "'Kynde Knowyng' as a Major Theme in *Piers Plowman* B," *Review of English Studies* n.s. 22 (1971): 89–127.

Davlin, Mary Clemente, "'Kynde Knowyng' as a Middle English Equivalent for 'Wisdom' in *Piers Plowman* B," *Medium Aevum* 50 (1981): 5–15.

Dean Cosyn and Wells Cathedral Miscellanea, ed. Aelred Watkin, Somerset Record Society 56 (1941).

Delany, Sheila, *Chaucer's House of Fame: The Poetics of Skeptical Fideism*, Chicago, IL: University of Chicago Press, 1972.

Dempster, Germaine, "A Chapter of the Manuscript History of the *Canterbury Tales*," *PMLA* 63 (1948): 456–84.

Dempster, Germaine, "The Fifteenth-Century Editors of the *Canterbury Tales* and the Problem of Tale Order," *PMLA* 64 (1949): 1123–42.

Descriptive, Analytical and Critical Catalogue of the Manuscripts bequeathed unto the University of Oxford by Elias Ashmole, ed. William Henry Black, Oxford: Oxford University Press, 1845.

Der deutsche Facetus, ed. Carl Schroeder, Berlin: Mayer and Müller, 1911.

Dewey, John, *Experience and Education*, New York, NY: Macmillan, 1938.

Dewey, John, *The School and Society* and *The Child and the Curriculum*, Chicago, IL: University of Chicago Press, 1990; first published 1900 and 1902; rev. edn. 1915.

The DIMEV: An Open-Access, Digital Edition of the Index of Middle English Verse: Based on the Index of Middle English Verse (1943) and its Supplement (1965), ed. Linne R. Mooney, Daniel W. Mosser, Elizabeth Solopova with Deborah Thorpe and David Hill Radcliffe <http://www.dimev.net>, accessed June 12, 2014.

The Distichs of Cato (as *Dicta Catonis*), 585–63 in *Minor Latin Poets*, ed. Duff and Duff.

Dobson, R. B. and John Taylor, *Rymes of Robyn Hood*, Pittsburgh, PA: University of Pittsburgh Press, 1976.

Dolven, Jeff, *Scenes of Instruction in Renaissance Romance*, Chicago, IL: University of Chicago Press, 2007.

Donaldson, E. Talbot, *Piers Plowman: The C-Text and Its Poet*, New Haven, CT: Yale University Press, 1966; first published 1949.

Donatus, *Ars Minor*, 585–612 in Louis Holtz, *Donat et la tradition de l'enseignement grammatical*, Paris: Centre National de la Recherche Scientifique, 1981.

The Early English Versions of the Gesta Romanorum, ed. Sidney J. H. Herrtage, EETS 33 (1879).

The Ecclesiastical History of Ordericus Vitalis, 6 vols., ed. and trans. Marjorie Chibnall, Oxford: Clarendon Press, 1969–78.

Echard, Siân and Claire Fanger, "Introduction," pp. xxv–liv in *Latin Verses in the Confessio Amantis: An Annotated Translation*, trans. Siân Echard and Claire Fanger, East Lansing, MI: Colleagues Press, 1991.

Educational Charters and Documents, 598 to 1909, ed. Arthur F. Leach, Cambridge: Cambridge University Press, 1911.

Egbert of Liège, *The Well-Laden Ship*, ed. and trans. Robert Gary Babcock, Cambridge, MA: Harvard University Press, 2013.

Elliott, Alison Godard, "The *Facetus*: or, The Art of Courtly Living," *Allegorica* 2 (1977): 26–51.

Elliott, Ralph W. V., *Chaucer's English*, London: André Deutsch, 1974.

Englesing, Rolf, "Die Perioden der Lesergeschichte in der Neuzeit," *Archiv für Geschichte des Buchwesens* 10 (1970): 945–1002.

An English Translation of Auctores Octo*: A Medieval Reader*, trans. Ronald E. Pepin, Lewiston, NY: Edwin Mellen Press, 1999.

Enterline, Lynn, *Shakespeare's Schoolroom: Rhetoric, Discipline, Emotion*, Philadelphia, PA: University of Pennsylvania Press, 2012.

The Equatorie of the Planetis, ed. D. J. Price and R. M. Wilson, Cambridge: Cambridge University Press, 1955.

Erasmus, Desiderius, *Adages*, trans. Margaret Mann Phillips, annotated R. A. B Mynors, vol. 31 of *Collected Works of Erasmus*, Toronto: University of Toronto Press, 1974–.

Erasmus, Desiderius, *Adagiorum Chilias Prima*, ed. M. L. van Poll-van de Lisdonk, M. Mann Phillips, and Chr. Robinson, Ordo 2, vol. 1 of Desiderius Erasmus, *Opera Omnia*, Amsterdam: North-Holland, 1969–.

L'Esopus attribuito a Gualtero Anglico, ed. Paola Busdraghi, vol. 10 (2005) of *Favolisti latini medievali e umanistici*, ed. Ferruccio Bertini, Genoa: Università di Genova, Pubblicazioni del Dipartimento di Archeologia, Filologia Classica e Loro Tradizioni, 1984–2005.

Evrard of Béthune, *Graecismus*, ed. Johannes Wrobel, Hildesheim: G. Olm, 1987; first published 1887.

Ewert, A., "The Glasgow Latin–French Glossary," *Medium Aevum* 25 (1956): 154–63.

The Fables of Avianus, 669–749 in *Minor Latin Poets*, ed. Duff and Duff.

The Fables of "Walter of England": edited from Wolfenbüttel, Herzog August Bibliothek, Codex Guelferbytanus 185 Helmstadiensis, ed. Aaron Eugene Wright, Toronto: Pontifical Institute of Mediaeval Studies 1997.

Facetus ("cum [or est] nichil utilius"), in *Der deutsche Facetus*, ed. Schroeder.

Facetus ("moribus et vita"), in Elliott, "The *Facetus*: or, The Art of Courtly Living."

Ferster, Judith, *Fictions of Advice: The Literature and Politics of Counsel in Late Medieval England*, Philadelphia, PA: University of Pennsylvania Press, 1996.

A Fifteenth-Century School Book: from a Manuscript in the British Museum (MS Arundel 249), ed. William Nelson, Oxford: Clarendon Press, 1956.

Formula ["Text Z"], 131–9 in R. M. Thomson, *An Edition of the Middle English Grammatical Texts*, New York, NY: Garland, 1984.

Förster, Max, "Die mittelenglische Sprichwörtersammlung in Douce 52," 40–60 in *Festschrift zum XII. Allgemeinen Deutschen Neuphilologentage in München, Pfingsten 1906*, ed. E. Stollreither, Erlangen: Fr. Junge, 1906.

Foucault, Michel, *Discipline and Punish: The Birth of the Prison*, New York, NY: Vintage Books, 1995.

Fowler, David C., *The Life and Times of John Trevisa, Medieval Scholar*, Seattle, WA: University of Washington Press, 1995.

Freud, Sigmund, "A Note on the 'Mystic Writing-Pad,'" 427–34 in *On Metapsychology*, The Penguin Freud Library, vol. 11, trans. James Strachey, ed. Angela Richards, London: Penguin, 1984.

Freud, Sigmund, "The Uncanny," 335–76 in *Art and Literature*, The Penguin Freud Library, vol. 14, trans. James Strachey, ed. Albert Dickson, London: Penguin, 1985.

Gabriele Zerbi, Gerontocomia: On the Care of the Aged and Maximianus, Elegies on Old Age and Love, trans. L. R. Lind, Philadelphia, PA: American Philosophical Society, 1988.

Galef, David, "Observations on Rereading," 17–33 in *Second Thoughts: A Focus on Rereading*, ed. David Galef, Detroit, MI: Wayne State University Press, 1998.

Galloway, Andrew, "Latin England," 41–95 in *Imagining a Medieval English Nation*, ed. Kathy Lavezzo, Minneapolis, MN: University of Minnesota Press, 2004.

Galloway, Andrew, "The Literature of 1388 and the Politics of Pity in Gower's *Confessio Amantis*," 67–104 in *The Letter of the Law: Legal Practice and Literary Production in Medieval England*, ed. Emily Steiner and Candace Barrington, Ithaca, NY: Cornell University Press, 2002.

Galloway, Andrew, *The Penn Commentary on Piers Plowman*, vol. 1: *C Prologue-Passus 4; B Prologue-Passus 4; A Prologue-Passus 4*, Philadelphia, PA: University of Pennsylvania Press, 2006.

Galloway, Andrew, "*Piers Plowman* and the Schools," *The Yearbook of Langland Studies* 6 (1992): 89–107.

Galloway, Andrew, "The Rhetoric of Riddling in Late-Medieval England: The 'Oxford' Riddles, the *Secretum philosophorum*, and the Riddles in *Piers Plowman*," *Speculum* 70 (1995): 68–105.

Galloway, Andrew, "Two Notes on Langland's Cato: *Piers Plowman* B 1.88–91; 4.20–23," *English Language Notes* 25 (1987–8): 9–12.

Gehl, Paul, *A Moral Art: Grammar, Society and Culture in Trecento Florence*, Ithaca, NY: Cornell University Press, 1993.

Geoffrey of Vinsauf, *Poetria Nova*, 194–262 in *Les Arts Poétiques du XIIe et du XIIIe Siècles*, ed. Edmond Faral, Paris: Champion, 1962.

Gesta Romanorum, ed. Hermann Osterley, Berlin: Wiedermannsche, 1872.

Gieben, Servus, "Robert Grosseteste and Medieval Courtesy Books," *Vivarium* 5 (1967): 47–74.

Gillespie, Vincent, "From the Twelfth Century to c.1450," 145–235 in *The Cambridge History of Literary Criticism*, vol. 2: *The Middle Ages*, ed. Alastair Minnis and Ian Johnson, Cambridge: Cambridge University Press, 2005.

Gower, John, *The Complete Works*, ed. George Campbell Macaulay, vol. 1: *The French Works*, vols. 2–3: *The English Works*, vol. 4: *The Latin Works*, Oxford: Clarendon Press, 1899–1902.

Gower, John, *Confessio Amantis*, ed. Russell A. Peck, 3 vols. Kalamazoo, MI: Medieval Institute Publications, Western Michigan University, 2006–13.

Gower, John, *The Major Latin Works of John Gower: The Voice of One Crying and the Tripartite Chronicle*, trans. Eric W. Stockton, Seattle, WA: University of Washington Press, 1962.

Gower, John, "Mirour de L'Omme," 1–334 in *The Complete Works of John Gower*, vol. 1: *The French Works*, ed. George Campbell Macaulay, Oxford: Clarendon Press, 1899.

Green, R. P. H., "The Genesis of a Medieval Textbook: The Models and Sources of the *Ecloga Theoduli*," *Viator* 13 (1982): 49–106.

Green, R. P. H., *Seven Versions of Carolingian Pastoral*, Reading: University of Reading Press, 1980.

Green, Richard Firth, *Poets and Princepleasers: Literature and the English Court in the Late Middle Ages*, Toronto: University of Toronto Press, 1980.

Guillory, John, *Cultural Capital: The Problem of Literary Canon Formation*, Chicago, IL: University of Chicago Press, 1993.

Gunther, R. T., *Chaucer and the Messahalla on the Astrolabe*, Oxford: Oxford University Press, 1929.

Hadot, Pierre, *What is Ancient Philosophy?*, trans. Michael Chase, Cambridge, MA: Harvard University Press, 1995.

Hahn, Thomas, "Early Middle English," 61–91 in *The Cambridge History of Medieval English Literature*, ed. David Wallace, Cambridge: Cambridge University Press, 1999.

Halmari, Helena and Robert Adams, "On the Grammar and Rhetoric of Language Mixing in *Piers Plowman*," *Neuphilologische Mittelungen* 103 (2002): 73–92.

Halpern, Richard, *The Poetics of Primitive Accumulation: English Renaissance Culture and the Genealogy of Capitalism*, Ithaca, NY: Cornell University Press, 1991.

Hanna, Ralph, "Some Commonplaces of Late Medieval Patience Discussions: An Introduction," 65–87 in *The Triumph of Patience: Medieval and Renaissance Studies*, ed. Gerald J. Schiffhorst, Orlando, FL: University of Florida Press, 1977.

Hanna, Ralph, *William Langland*, Brookfield, VT: Ashgate, 1993.

Hanna, Ralph, "Langland's Ymaginatif: Images and the Limits of Poetry," 81–94 in *Images, Idolatry and Iconoclasm in Late Medieval England: Textuality and the Visual Image*, ed. Jeremy Dimmick, James Simpson, and Nicolette Zeeman, Oxford: Oxford University Press, 2002.

Hanna, Ralph, "Literacy, Schooling, Universities," 172–94 in *The Cambridge Companion to Medieval English Culture*, ed. Andrew Galloway, Cambridge: Cambridge University Press, 2011.

Harvey, S. W., "Chaucer's Debt to Sacrobosco," *Journal of English and Germanic Philology* 34 (1935): 34–8.

Havelock, Eric, *The Literate Revolution in Greece and its Cultural Consequences*, Princeton, NJ: Princeton University Press, 1982.

Hazelton, Richard, "Chaucer and Cato," *Speculum* 35 (1960): 357–80.

Heaton, E. W., *The School Tradition of the Old Testament*, Oxford: Oxford University Press, 1994.

Heilbrun, Carolyn, "From Rereading to Reading," *PMLA* 119 (2004): 211–17.

Heywood, John, "A Dialogue Containing Proverbs," 17–101 in *Works and Miscellaneous Short Poems*, ed. Burton A. Milligan, Illinois Studies in Language and Literature 41, Urbana, IL: University of Illinois Press, 1956.

Heywood, John, "The First Hundred Epigrams," 103–39 in *Works and Miscellaneous Short Poems*, ed. Burton A. Milligan, Illinois Studies in Language and Literature 41, Urbana, IL: University of Illinois Press, 1956.

Heywood, John, *Works and Miscellaneous Short Poems*, ed. Burton A. Milligan, Illinois Studies in Language and Literature 41, Urbana, IL: University of Illinois Press, 1956.

Hirsch, Jr., E. D., *Cultural Literacy: What Every American Needs to Know*, Boston, MA: Houghton Mifflin, 1987.

Historical Poems of the XIVth and XVth Centuries, ed. Rossell Hope Robbins, New York, NY: Columbia University Press, 1959.

Hoggart, Richard, *The Uses of Literacy: Aspects of Working Class Life*, London: Chatto & Windus, 1957.

Holsinger, Bruce, *Music, Body and Desire in Medieval Culture: Hildegard of Bingen to Chaucer*, Stanford, CA: Stanford University Press, 2001.

Holthausen, Ferdinand, "Chaucer und Theodulus," *Anglia* 16 (1894): 264–6.

The Holy Bible, ed. Josiah Forshall and Frederic Madden, 4 vols., Oxford: Oxford University Press, 1850.

The Holy Bible: Douay Version, London: Catholic Truth Society, 1956.

Horace, *Ars poetica*, 442–89 in *Satires, Epistles and Ars poetica*, ed. and trans. H. Fairclough, New York, NY: G. P. Putnam, 1942.

Horobin, Simon, "The Scribe of Bodleian Library MS Bodley 619 and the Circulation of Chaucer's Treatise on the Astrolabe," *Studies in the Age of Chaucer* 31 (2009): 109–24.

Howard, Donald, *Chaucer: His Life, His Works, His World*, New York, NY: Dutton, 1987.

Howard, Donald, *The Idea of the Canterbury Tales*, Berkeley, CA: University of California Press, 1976.

Howell, James, *ΠΑΡΟΙΜΙΟΓΡΑΦΙΑ. Proverbs, or Old sayed sawes & adages in English (or the Saxon Toung), Italian, French and Spanish, whereunto the British for their great Antiquity and weight are added*, J. G., 1659.

Hudson, Anne, *The Premature Reformation: Wycliffite Texts and Lollard History*, Oxford: Oxford University Press, 1988.

Hugh of St Victor, "De Arca Noe Mystica," 146: cols. 681–702 in *Patrologiae cursus completus, series latina*, ed. Migne.

Hunt, R. W., "Oxford Grammar Masters in the Middle Ages," 167–97 in his *The History of Grammar in the Middle Ages: Collected Papers*, ed. G. L. Burshill-Hall, Amsterdam: John Benjamins, 1980.

Hunt, R. W., "Studies on Priscian in the Eleventh and Twelfth Centuries," *Medieval and Renaissance Studies* 1 (1943): 194–231.

Hunt, R. W., *A Summary Catalogue of Western Manuscripts in the Bodleian Library at Oxford*, 7 vols. in 9, Oxford: Clarendon Press, 1895–1953.

Hunt, Tony, *Teaching and Learning Latin in Thirteenth Century England*, 3 vols., Woodbridge: D. S. Brewer, 1991.

Hunt, Tony, "The Vernacular Entries in the 'Glossae Sidionium' (MS Oxford Digby 172)," *Zeitschrift für französische Sprache und Literatur* 89 (1979): 13–50.

Huntsman, Jeffrey F., "Grammar," 58–95 in *The Seven Liberal Arts in the Middle Ages*, ed. David L. Wagner, Bloomington, IN: Indiana University Press, 1983.

Immerwahr, Henry, "Book Rolls on Attic Vases," 17–48 in *Classical, Mediaeval and Renaissance Studies in Honor of Berthold Louis Ullman*, ed. Charles Henderson, Rome: Edizioni di Storia e Letteratura, 1964.

Informacio [Text T], 82–92 in Thomson, *An Edition of the Middle English Grammatical Texts*.

The Instruction for King Meri-ka-re, 155–61 in *Documents from Old Testament Times*, ed. D. Winton Thomas et al., London: T. Nelson, 1958.

Ioannis Saresberiensis Episcopi Carnotensis Metalogicon Libri IIII, ed. Clemens C. L. Webb, Oxford: Clarendon Press, 1929.

Irvine, Martin, "Medieval Grammatical Theory and Chaucer's *House of Fame*," *Speculum* 60 (1985): 850–76.

Irvine, Martin with David Thomson, "*Grammatica* and Literary Theory," 15–41 in *The Cambridge History of Literary Criticism*, vol. 2: *The Middle Ages*, ed. Alastair Minnis and Ian Johnson, Cambridge: Cambridge University Press, 2005.

Isidore of Seville, *Etymologiarum sive originum libri XX*, 2 vols., ed. W. M. Lindsay, Oxford: Clarendon Press, 1911.

Jacob's Well, ed. A. Brandeis, part 1, *EETS* o.s. 115 (1900; reprint 1973).

Jambeck, Thomas J. and Karen K. Jambeck, "Chaucer's *Treatise on the Astrolabe*: A Handbook for the Medieval Child," *Children's Literature* 3 (1974): 117–22.

James, M. R., *A Descriptive Catalogue of the Manuscripts in the Library of Gonville and Caius College*, 2 vols., Cambridge: Cambridge University Press, 1907.

James, M. R., *A Descriptive Catalogue of the Manuscripts of the Library in Peterhouse*, Cambridge: Cambridge University Press, 1899.

James, M. R., *A Descriptive Catalogue of the Manuscripts in the Library of St John's College*, Cambridge: Cambridge University Press, 1913.

James, M. R., *The Western Manuscripts in the Library of Trinity College, Cambridge: A Descriptive Catalogue*, 4 vols., Cambridge: Cambridge University Press, 1900–4.

Jay, Martin, "The Limits of Limit-Experience: Bataille and Foucault," *Constellations* 2 (1995): 155–74.

Jocelin of Brakelond, *Chronica Jocelini de Brakelonda*, London: Camden Society, 1840.

Jocelin of Brakelond, *Chronicle of the Abbey of Bury St Edmunds*, trans. Diana Greenway and Jane Sayers, Oxford: Oxford University Press, 1989.

John of Salisbury, *Metalogicon*, ed. J. B. Hall with K. S. B. Keats-Rohan, Turnhout: Brepols, 1991.

John of Salisbury, *Policraticus*, ed. K. S. B. Keats-Rohan, Corpus Christianorum, Continuatio mediaevalis 118, Turnhout: Brepols, 1993–.

Johnson, Lynn Staley, "Inverse Counsel: Contexts for the Melibee," *Studies in Philology* 87 (1990): 137–55.

Julian of Norwich, *A Revelation of Love*, 61–381 in *The Writings of Julian of Norwich*, ed. Nicholas Watson and Jacqueline Jenkins, University Park, PA: Pennsylvania State University Press, 2006.

Kaske, R. E., "'Ex Vi Transicionis' and Its Passage in 'Piers Plowman,'" *Journal of English and Germanic Philology* 62 (1963): 32–60.

Kaster, Robert A., *Guardians of Language: The Grammarian and Society in Late Antiquity*, Berkeley, CA: University of California Press, 1988.

Kay, Sarah, "Occitan Grammar as a Science of Endings," *New Medieval Literatures* 11 (2009): 39–61.

Kay, Sarah, *Parrots and Nightingales: Troubadour Quotations and the Development of European Poetry*, Philadelphia, PA: University of Pennsylvania Press, 2013.

Kellogg, A. L., "Langland and Two Scriptural Texts," *Traditio* 14 (1958): 385–98.

Kelly, Douglas, "The Scope of the Treatment of Composition in the Twelfth- and Thirteenth-Century Arts of Poetry," *Speculum* 41 (1966): 261–78.

Ker, N. R., *Medieval Manuscripts in British Libraries*, 5 vols., Oxford: Clarendon Press, 1969–2002.

Kibbee, Douglas A., *For To Speke Frenche Trewely: The French Language in England, 1000–1600—Its Status, Description and Instruction*, Amsterdam: John Benjamins, 1991.

Kittredge, G. L., "Chaucer's Discussion of Marriage," *Modern Philology* 9 (1912): 435–67.

Kolb, David A., *Experiential Learning: Experience as the Source of Learning and Development*, Englewood Cliffs, NJ: Prentice-Hall, 1984.

Kunitzsch, Paul, "On the Authenticity of the Treatise on the Composition and Use of the Astrolabe Ascribed to Messahalla," *Archives Internationales d'Histoire des Sciences* 31 (1981): 42–62.

La Capra, Dominick, *History in Transit: Experience, Identity, Critical Theory*, Ithaca, NY: Cornell University Press, 2004.

Laird, Edgar, "Chaucer and Friends: The Audience for the *Treatise on the Astrolabe*," *Chaucer Review* 41 (2007): 439–44.

Laird, Edgar, "A Previously Unnoticed Manuscript of Chaucer's *Treatise on the Astrolabe*," *Chaucer Review* 34 (2000): 410–15.

Les Lamentations de Matheolus et le Liver de Leesce de Jehan le Fèvre, ed. A. G. Van Hamel, 2 vols., Paris, 1893–1905.

Langland, William, *Piers Plowman: The A-Version*, ed. George Kane, London: Athlone Press, 1960.

Langland, William, *Piers Plowman: The B Version*, ed. George Kane and E. Talbot Donaldson, rev. edn., London: Athlone Press; Berkeley and Los Angeles: University of California Press, 1988; first published 1975.

Langland, William, *Piers Plowman: A New Annotated Edition of the C-text*, ed. Derek Pearsall, Exeter: University of Exeter Press, 2008.

Langland, William, *Piers Plowman: A Parallel-Text Edition of the A, B, C, and Z Versions*, vol. 1 (text), ed. A. V. C. Schmidt, London: Longman, 1995.

Langland, William, *The Vision of Piers Plowman: A Complete Edition of the B-text*, ed. A. V. C. Schmidt, 2nd edn., London: J. M. Dent, 1995.

Langland, William, *The Vision of William Concerning Piers the Plowman in Three Parallel Texts*, ed. W. W. Skeat, 2 vols., Oxford: Clarendon Press, 1886.

Latin Verses in the Confessio Amantis: An Annotated Translation, trans. Siân Echard and Claire Fanger, East Lansing, MI: Colleagues Press, 1991.

Law, Vivien, "Grammar" 288–95 in *Medieval Latin: An Introduction and Bibliographical Guide*, ed. F. A. C. Mantello and A. G. Rigg, Washington, DC: The Catholic University of America Press, 1996.

Law, Vivien, *Grammar and Grammarians in the Early Middle Ages*, London: Longman, 1997.

Lawler, Traugott, "Langland Versificator," *The Yearbook of Langland Studies* 25 (2011): 37–76.

Leach, A. F., *Early Yorkshire Schools*, vol. 1: *York, Beverley, Ripon*, Leeds: Yorkshire Archaeological Society, 1899.

Leach, A. F., *A History of Winchester College*, London: Duckworth, 1899.

Leach, A. F., "St Paul's School before Colet," *Archaeologia* 62 (1910): 191–238.

Leach, A. F., "Schools," 244–85 in *The Victoria History of Berkshire*, vol. 2, ed. P. H. Ditchfield and William Page, London: Archibald Constable, 1907.

Leach, A. F., "Schools," 421–92 in *The Victoria History of the County of Lincoln*, vol. 2, ed. William Page, London: Archibald Constable, 1906.

Leach, A. F., "Schools," 201–88 in *The Victoria History of the County of Northampton*, vol. 2, ed. R. M. Serjeantson and W. Ryland D. Adkins, London: Archibald Constable, 1906.

Leach, A. F., "Schools," 179–251 in *The Victoria History of the County of Nottingham*, vol. 2, ed. William Page, London: Archibald Constable, 1910.

Leach, A. F., "Schools," 397–440 in *The Victoria History of the County of Sussex*, vol. 2, ed. William Page, London: Archibald Constable, 1907.

Leach, A. F., *The Schools of Medieval England*, London: Methuen, 1915.

Leach, A. F. and H. J. Chaytor, "Schools," 561–624 in *The Victoria History of the County of Lancaster*, vol. 2, ed. William Farrer and J. Brownbill, London: Archibald Constable, 1908.

Leach, A. F. and E. P. Steele Hutton, "Schools," 301–56 in *The Victoria History of the County of Suffolk*, vol. 2, ed. William Page, London: Archibald Constable, 1907.

Leader, Damien Riehl, "Grammar in Late-Medieval Oxford and Cambridge," *History of Education* 12 (1983): 9–14.

Leclercq, Jean, *The Love of Learning and the Desire for God*, trans. Catherine Misrahi, New York, NY: Fordham University Press, 1961.

Lerer, Seth, "Chaucer's Sons," *University of Toronto Quarterly* 73 (2004): 906–15.

Lewis, Charlton Thomas and Charles Short, *A Latin Dictionary*, Oxford: Clarendon Press, 1993; first published 1879.

Liber cartule (attributed to Bernard of Clairvaux as *Carmen Paraeneticum ad Rainaldum*), vol. 221, cols. 1307–14 in *Patrologiae cursus completus, series latina*, ed. Migne.

Liber parabolarum, ed. Oronzo Limone, Galatina: Congedo, 1993.

Liber penitencialis (identified by its incipit, "Peniteas cito"), 107–28 in *William de Montibus (c.1140–1213: The Schools and the Literature of Pastoral Care)*, ed. Joseph Goering, Toronto: Pontifical Institute of Mediaeval Studies, 1992.

Locke, John, *An Essay Concerning Human Understanding*, 27th edn., London: T. Tegg and Son, 1836.

Locke, John, *Some Thoughts Concerning Education*, London: J. and R. Tonson, 1779.

Lotario dei Segni (Innocent III), *De Miseria Condicionis Humane*, ed. and trans. Robert E. Lewis, Athens, GA: University of Georgia Press, 1978.

Louis, Cameron, "Authority in Middle English Proverb Literature," *Florilegium* 15 (1998): 85–123.

Louis, Cameron, "Proverbs and the Politics of Language," *Proverbium* 17 (2000): 173–93.

Louis, Cameron, "Proverbs, Precepts and Monitory Pieces," 9: 2057–3048 in *A Manual of the Writings in Middle English*, ed. Albert E. Hartung, New Haven, CT: Connecticut Academy of Arts and Sciences, 1967–.

Lucan, *De Bello Civili* (or the *Pharsalia*) in *Lucan*, ed. and trans. J. D. Duff, Cambridge, MA: Harvard University Press, 1962.

Lumiansky, Robert M., *Of Sondry Folk: The Dramatic Principle in* The Canterbury Tales, Austin, TX: University of Texas Press, 1955.

Lutz, Cora E., "A Medieval Textbook," *Yale University Library Gazette* 49 (1974): 212–16.

Lydgate, John, *The Pilgrimage of the Life of Man*, ed. F. J. Furnivall and K. B. Locock, *EETS* e.s. 77, 83, 92 (1899, 1901, 1904).

Lydgate, John, *The Saying of the Nightingale*, 221–34 in *The Minor Poems of John Lydgate*, ed. H. N. MacCracken, vol. 1, *EETS* e.s. 107 (1911; reprint 1961).

Lydgate, John, *The Fall of Princes*, ed. H. Bergen, 4 vols., *EETS* e.s. 121–4 (1924–7).

Lynch, Deidre, "Canon's Clockwork: Novels for Everyday Use," 87–110 in *Bookish Histories: Books, Literature, and Commercial Modernity, 1700–1900*, ed. Ina Ferris and Paul Keen, New York, NY: Palgrave Macmillan, 2009).

Lynch, Deidre, "On Going Steady with Novels," *The Eighteenth Century* 50 (2009): 207–19.

Lyons, John, "Grammar and Meaning," 221–54 in *Grammar and Meaning*, ed. F. R. Palmer, Cambridge: Cambridge University Press, 1995.

Lyons, John, *Introduction to Theoretical Linguistics*, London: Cambridge University Press, 1968.

MacCormack, Sabine, *The Shadows of Poetry: Virgil in the Mind of Augustine*, Berkeley, CA: University of California Press, 1998.

Machan, Tim William, "Language Contact in *Piers Plowman*," *Speculum* 69 (1994): 359–85.

Machan, Tim William, *English in the Middle Ages*, Oxford: Oxford University Press, 2003.

Macray, W. D., R. W. Hunt, and A. G. Watson, *Digby Manuscripts*, 2 parts, Oxford: Bodleian Library, 1999.

Manly, John J., "Chaucer and the Rhetoricians," *Proceedings of the British Academy* 12 (1926): 95–113.

Manly, John J., *Some New Light on Chaucer*, Gloucester, MA: Peter Smith, 1926.

Mann, Jill, *Chaucer and Medieval Estates Satire: The Literature of Social Classes and the* General Prologue *to the* Canterbury Tales, Cambridge: Cambridge University Press, 1973.

Mann, Jill, *From Aesop to Reynard: Beast Fable in Medieval Britain*, Oxford: Oxford University Press, 2009.

Mann, Jill, "'He Knew Nat Catoun': Medieval School-Texts and Middle English Literature," 41–74 in *The Text in the Community: Essays on Medieval Works,*

Manuscripts, Authors and Readers, ed. Jill Mann and Maura Nolan, Notre Dame, IN: University of Notre Dame Press, 2006.

A Manual of the Writings in Middle English, 11 vols., ed. J. B. Severs (vols. 1–2), Albert E. Hartung (vols. 3–10), and Peter G. Beidler (vol. 11), New Haven, CT: Connecticut Academy of Arts and Sciences, 1967–.

Marrou, H. I., *A History of Education in Antiquity*, trans. George Lamb, Madison, WI: University of Wisconsin Press, 1982; first published in English, 1956.

The Master of Game by Edward, Second Duke of York, ed. W. A. Baillie-Grohman and F. Baillie-Grohman, London: Ballantine, 1904.

Matthew of Vendôme, "Epistola Dedicatoria" to *Liber Tobiae Paraphrasis Metrica*, 205: cols. 927–31 in *Patrologiae cursus completus, series latina*, ed. Migne.

Matthew of Vendôme, *Tobias*, 2: 161–255 in Matthei Vindocinensis, *Opera*, 3 vols., ed. Franco Munari, Rome: Edizioni di storia e letteratura, 1977–88.

Maximian, *Elegies*, 319–36 in *Gabriele Zerbi, Gerontocomia: On the Care of the Aged and Maximianus, Elegies on Old Age and Love*, trans. L. R. Lind, Philadelphia, PA: American Philosophical Society, 1988.

Maximian, *The Elegies of Maximianus*, ed. Richard Webster, Princeton, NJ: Princeton University Press, 1900.

McGill, Scott, *Virgil Recomposed: The Mythological and Secular Centos in Antiquity*, Oxford: Oxford University Press, 2005.

McGurl, Mark, *The Program Era: Postwar Fiction and the Rise of Creative Writing*, Cambridge, MA: Harvard University Press, 2009.

Medieval Latin: An Introduction and Bibliographical Guide, ed. F. A. C. Mantello and A. G. Rigg, Washington, DC: The Catholic University of America Press, 1996.

Medieval Literary Theory and Criticism, c. 1100–c.1375: The Commentary Tradition, ed. A. J. Minnis and A. B. Scott, with the assistance of David Wallace, Oxford: Clarendon Press, 1988.

Meech, Sanford B., "A Collection of Proverbs in Rawlinson MS D 328," *Modern Philology* 38 (1940): 113–31.

Meech, Sanford B., "An Early Treatise in English Concerning Latin Grammar," *Essays and Studies in English and Comparative Literature*, University of Michigan Publications, Language and Literature 13 (1935): 81–125.

The Metalogicon of John of Salisbury: A Twelfth-Century Defense of the Verbal and Logical Arts of the Trivium, trans. Daniel D. McGarry, Philadelphia, PA: Paul Dry Books, 2009; first published 1955.

Michael, Ian, *English Grammatical Categories and the Tradition to 1800*, London: Cambridge University Press, 1970.

Middle English Lyrics, ed. Maxwell S. Luria and Richard L. Hoffman, New York, NY: W. W. Norton, 1974.

Middleton, Anne, "Narration and the Invention of Experience: Episodic Form in *Piers Plowman*," 91–122 in *The Wisdom of Poetry: Essays in Early English Literature in Honor of Morton W. Bloomfield*, ed. Larry D. Benson and Siegfried Wenzel, Kalamazoo, MI: Medieval Institute Publications, Western Michigan University, 1982.

Middleton, Anne, "Two Infinites: Grammatical Metaphor in *Piers Plowman*," *ELH* 39 (1972): 169–88.

Millis, Keith K. and Anne King, "Rereading Strategically: The Influences of Comprehension Ability and a Prior Reading on the Memory for Expository Text," *Reading Psychology* 22 (2001): 41–65.

Milner, G. B., "What is A Proverb?," *New Society* 332 (1969): 199–202.

Miner, John M. [also known as Brother Bonaventure], *The Grammar Schools of Medieval England: A. F. Leach in Historiographical Perspective*, Montreal & Kingston: McGill-Queen's University Press, 1990.

Minnis, A. J., *Medieval Theory of Authorship: Scholastic Literary Attitudes in the Later Middle Ages*, London: Scholar Press, 1984.

Minor Latin Poets, ed. J. Wight Duff and Arnold M. Duff, Cambridge, MA: Harvard University Press, 1961; first published 1934.

Mirk, John, *Instructions for Parish Priests*, ed. G. Kristensson, *Lund Studies in English* 49 (1974).

Mooney, Lynne, "Chaucer's Scribe," *Speculum* 81 (2006): 97–138.

Moran, Jo Ann Hoeppner, *The Growth of English Schooling, 1340–1548*, Princeton, NJ: Princeton University Press, 1985.

Morris George R., "A Ryme of Robyn Hode," *Modern Language Review* 43 (1948): 507–8.

Murphy, James J., "Literary Implications of Instruction in the Verbal Arts in Fourteenth-Century England," *Leeds Studies in English* n.s. 1 (1967): 119–35.

Murphy, James J., "Roman Writing Instruction as Described by Quintilian," 36–76 in *A Short History of Writing Instruction: From Ancient Greece to Contemporary America*, ed. James J. Murphy, 3rd edn., New York, NY: Routledge, 2012.

Muscatine, Charles, *Chaucer and the French Tradition: A Study in Style and Meaning*, Berkeley, CA: University of California Press, 1957.

Nabokov, Vladimir, *Lectures on Literature*, ed. Fredson Bowers, New York, NY: Harcourt Brace Jovanovich, 1980.

Nicholls, Jonathan, *The Matter of Courtesy: Medieval Courtesy Books and the Gawain-Poet*, Cambridge: D. S. Brewer, 1985.

North, J. D., *Chaucer's Universe*, Oxford: Clarendon Press, 1988.

"On Contempt for the World," 55–77 in *An English Translation of* Auctores Octo: *A Medieval Reader*, trans. Ronald E. Pepin, Lewiston, NY: Edwin Mellen Press, 1999.

On the Properties of Things: John of Trevisa's Translation of Bartholomaeus Anglicus De Proprietatibus Rerum: A Critical Text, ed. M. C. Seymour, 3 vols., Oxford: Oxford University Press, 1975–88.

Ong, Walter, "Latin Language Study as a Renaissance Puberty Rite," *Studies in Philology* 56 (1959): 103–24.

The Orcherd of Syon, ed. P. Hodgson and G. M. Liegey, *EETS* o.s. 258 (1966).

Orderic Vitalis, *Historia Ecclesiastica*, ed. Marojorie Chibnall, 6 vols., Oxford: Oxford University Press, 1969–80.

Orme, Nicholas, *Education in the West of England, 1066–1548: Cornwall, Devon, Dorset, Gloucestershire, Somerset, Wiltshire*, Exeter: University of Exeter Press, 1976.

Orme, Nicholas, "An English Grammar School, ca. 1450: Latin Exercises from Exeter (Caius College MS 417/447, Folios 16v.–24v)," *Traditio* 50 (1995): 261–94.

Orme, Nicholas, *English School Exercises: 1420–1530*, Toronto: Pontifical Institute of Mediaeval Studies, 2013.

Orme, Nicholas, *From Childhood to Chivalry: The Education of the English Kings and Aristocracy, 1066–1530*, London: Methuen, 1984.

Orme, Nicholas, "A Grammatical Miscellany from Bristol and Wiltshire," 86–111 in his *Education and Society in Medieval and Renaissance England*, London: Hambledon Press, 1989.

Orme, Nicholas, *Medieval Children*, New Haven, CT: Yale University Press, 2001.

Orme, Nicholas, *Medieval Schools: From Roman Britain to Medieval England*, New Haven, CT: Yale University Press, 2006.

Orme, Nicholas, "Schools and Society," 1–21 in his *Education and Society in Medieval and Renaissance England*, London: Hambledon Press, 1989.

Ormrod, W. M., The Use of English: Language, Law, and Political Culture in Fourteenth-Century England," *Speculum* 78 (2003): 750–87.

Orthographia gallica, ed. R. C. Johnston, London: Anglo-Norman Text Society, 1987.

The Oxford Book of Medieval English Verse, ed. Celia and Kenneth Sisam, Oxford: Clarendon Press, 1970.

The Oxford English Dictionary, OED Online, Oxford University Press, November 17, 2014 <http://dictionary.oed.com/>.

Page, Christopher, *The Christian West and its Singers*, New Haven, CT: Yale University Press, 2010.

Pakulski, Jan, "Foundations of a Post-Class Analysis," 152–79 in *Approaches to Class Analysis*, ed. Erik Olin Wright, Cambridge: Cambridge University Press, 2005.

Palomo, Dolores, "What Chaucer Really Did to *Le Livre de Mellibee*," *Philological Quarterly* 53 (1974): 49–55.

Pantin, W. A., "A Medieval Collection of Latin and English Proverbs and Riddles, from the Rylands Latin MS 394," *Bulletin of the John Rylands Library* 14 (1930): 81–113.

Parmentier, A., *La philosophie de Whitehead et le problème de Dieu*, Paris: Beauchesne, 1968.

Parsloe, C. Guy, "Schools," 107–19 in *The Victoria History of Huntingdon*, vol. 2, ed. William Page, Granville Proby, and S. Inskip Ladds, London: Archibald Constable, 1932.

Patience, 195–235 in *The Works of the Gawain Poet: Sir Gawain and the Green Knight, Pearl, Cleanness, Patience*, ed. Putter and Stokes.

Patrologiae cursus completus, series latina, ed. J.-P. Migne, 221 vols., Paris, 1844–64.

Patterson, Lee, *Chaucer and the Subject of History,* Madison, WI: University of Wisconsin Press, 1991.

Patterson, Lee, "The 'Parson's Tale' and the Quitting of the 'Canterbury Tales,'" *Traditio* 34 (1978): 331–80.

Patterson, Lee, "'What Man Artow?': Authorial Self-Definition in *The Tale of Sir Thopas* and *The Tale of Melibee,*" *Studies in the Age of Chaucer* 11 (1989): 117–76.

Payne, Robert O., *The Key of Remembrance: A Study of Chaucer's Poetics,* New Haven, CT: Yale University Press, 1963.

Pearl, 3–81 in *The Works of the Gawain Poet: Sir Gawain and the Green Knight, Pearl, Cleanness, Patience,* ed. Putter and Stokes.

Pearsall, Derek, *The Canterbury Tales,* London: George Allen & Unwin, 1985.

Pearsall, Derek, "Gower's Latin in the *Confessio Amantis,*" 13–25 in *Latin and Vernacular: Studies in Late-Medieval Texts and Manuscripts,* ed. A. J. Minnis, Cambridge: D. S. Brewer, 1989.

Pearsall, Derek, *The Life of Geoffrey Chaucer,* Oxford: Blackwell, 1992.

The Peasants' Revolt of 1381, ed. R. B. Dobson, 2nd edn., London: Macmillan, 1983; first published 1970.

Peirce, Charles, *Collected Papers,* ed. Charles Hartshorne and Paul Weiss, 6 vols., Cambridge, MA: Harvard University Press, 1931–6.

Petrarca, Francesco, *Secret,* trans. William H. Draper, London: Chatto & Windus, 1911.

Petrarca, Francesco, *Prose,* ed. G. Martelotti et al., Milan: Riccardi, 1955.

Phillips, Helen, "Chaucer and Deguileville: The 'ABC' in Context," *Medium Aevum* 62 (1993): 1–19.

Plato, *Phaedo,* 40–98 in *The Collected Dialogues,* ed. Edith Hamilton and Huntington Cairns, Bollingen Series 71, Princeton, NJ: Princeton University Press, 1961.

Plimpton, George, *The Education of Chaucer: Illustrated from the Schoolbooks in Use in His Time,* London: Oxford University Press, 1935.

Polychronicon Ranulphi Higden monachi Cestrensis, vol. 2, ed. Churchill Babington, Rolls Series 41, London: Kraus Reprint, 1964; first published 1869.

Pope, Mildred, "The Tractatus Orthographie of T. H. Parisii Studentis," *Modern Language Review* 5 (1910): 185–92.

Power, Eileen, *Medieval English Nunneries c.1275–1535,* Cambridge: Cambridge University Press, 1922.

Priscian, *Institutiones Grammaticae,* ed. Heinrich Keil, *Grammatici Latini,* vols. 2 and 3, Leipzig: Teubner, 1855–8.

Priscian, *Praeexercitamina,* 551–60 in *Rhetores Latini Minores,* ed Carol Halm, Leipzig: Teubner, 1863.

Proverbs, Sentences, and Proverbial Phrases from English Writings Mainly before 1500, ed. Bartlett Jere Whiting with Helen Wescott Whiting, Cambridge, MA: Harvard University Press, 1968.

Publilius Syrus, 2–111 in *Minor Latin Poets*, ed. Duff and Duff.

Putter, Ad, *Introduction to the Gawain Poet*, London: Longman, 1996.

Quintilian, *The Orator's Education*, ed. and trans. Donald A. Russell, 5 vols., Cambridge: MA: Harvard University Press, 2001.

Rabanus Maurus, *De Clericorum Institutione*, 107: cols. 293–420a in *Patrologiae cursus completus, series latina*, ed. Migne.

Rancière, Jacques, *The Ignorant Schoolmaster: Five Lessons in Intellectual Emancipation*, trans. Kristin Ross, Stanford, CA: Stanford University Press, 1991.

De raptu Proserpinae, 2: 293–377 in *Claudian*, ed. and trans. Maurice Platnauer, 2 vols., London: William Heinemann, 1963.

Rawson, Katherine A. and John Dunlosky, "The Rereading Effect: Metacomprehension Accuracy Improves Across Reading Trials," *Memory and Cognition* 28 (2000): 1004–10.

Reginald of Durham, *Libellus de Vita et Miraculis S. Godrici, Heremitae de Finchale*, London: J. B. Nichols and Sons, 1847.

Reginaldi Monachi Dunelmensis Libellus de Admirandis Beati Cuthberti, London: J. B. Nichols and Sons, 1835.

Les Reports del cases en ley . . . En le temps de . . . Les roys Henry le IV. Et Henry le V. H [Yearbooks 1413–22], London, 1679; reprinted: Abingdon: Professional Books, 1981.

Rewriting Old English in the Twelfth Century, ed. Mary Swan and Elaine Treharne, Cambridge: Cambridge University Press, 2000.

Reynolds, Suzanne, *Medieval Reading: Grammar, Rhetoric and the Classical Text*, Cambridge: Cambridge University Press, 1996.

Rickert, Edith, "Chaucer at School," *Modern Philology* 39 (1932): 257–74.

Rickert, Edith, "Extracts from a Fourteenth-Century Account Book," *Modern Philology* 24 (1926): 111–29 and 249–56.

Rigg, A. G., "Preface," pp. xiii–xxiv in *Latin Verses in the Confessio Amantis: An Annotated Translation*, trans. Siân Echard and Claire Fanger, East Lansing, MI: Colleagues Press, 1991.

Risse, R. G., "The Augustinian Paraphrase of Isaiah 14: 13–14 in *Piers Plowman* and the Commentary on the *Fables* of Avianus," *Philological Quarterly* 45 (1966): 712–17.

The Rites of Durham (1593), ed. J. T. Fowler, Durham: Andrews & Co, 1903.

Robbins, Rossell Hope, "Poems Dealing with Contemporary Conditions," 5: 1385–536 in *A Manual of the Writings in Middle English*, ed. Albert E. Hartung, New Haven, CT: Connecticut Academy of Arts and Sciences, 1967–.

Robson, Catherine, *Heart Beats: Everyday Life and the Memorized Poem*, Princeton, NJ: Princeton University Press, 2012.

Romulus vulgaris, 2: 176–328 in *Les Fabulistes Latins*, ed Léopold Hervieux, 2nd edn., 2 vols., Paris: Firmin-Dido 1893–9.

Rothwell, William A., "The Role of French in Thirteenth-Century England," *Bulletin of the John Rylands University Library of Manchester* 58 (1976): 445–66.

Rothwell, William A., "The Teaching and Learning of French in Later Medieval England," *Zeitschrift für französische Sprache und Literatur* 111 (2001): 1–18.

Rust, Martha Dana, *Imaginary Worlds in Medieval Books: Exploring the Manuscript Matrix*, New York, NY: Palgrave Macmillan, 2007.

S. Editha Sive Chronicon Vilodunense, ed. C. Horstmann, Heilbronn: Henninger, 1883.

Sanford, Eva Matthews, "Classical Authors in the *Libri Manuales*," *Transactions and Proceedings of the American Philological Association* 55 (1924): 190–248.

Scarry, Elaine, *Dreaming by the Book*, New York, NY: Farrar, Straus & Giroux, 1999.

Scase, Wendy, "Latin Composition Lessons, *Piers Plowman*, and the *Piers Plowman* Tradition," 34–53 in *Answerable Style: The Idea of the Literary in Medieval England*, ed. Frank Grady and Andrew Galloway, Columbus, OH: Ohio State University Press, 2013.

Scattergood, V. J., "Chaucer and the French War: *Sir Thompas* and *Melibee*," 287–96 in *Court and Poet: Selected Proceedings of the Third Congress of the International Courtly Literature Society (Liverpool 1980)*, ed. Glyn S. Burgess with A. D. Deyermond, W. H. Jackson, A. D. Mills, and P. T. Ricketts, Liverpool: Francis Cairns, 1981.

Schmidt, A. V. C., "Introduction," pp. xvii–lxxxvi in *The Vision of Piers Plowman: A Complete Edition of the B-text*, ed. A. V. C. Schmidt, 2nd edn., London: J. M. Dent, 1995.

Schweitzer, Edward C., "'Half a laumpe lyne in Latyne' and Patience's Riddle in Piers Plowman," *Journal of English and Germanic Philology* 73 (1974): 313–27.

Scott, Joan W., "The Evidence of Experience," *Critical Inquiry* 17 (1991): 773–97.

Seaborne, Malcolm, *The English School: Its Architecture and Organization*, London: Routledge & Kegan Paul, 1971–7.

Seaman, Jayson and Peter J. Nelsen, "An Overburdened Term: Dewey's Concept of 'Experience' as Curriculum Theory," *Education and Culture* 27 (2011): 5–25.

Secular Lyrics of the XIVth and XVth Centuries, ed. Rossell Hope Robbins, 2nd edn., Oxford: Clarendon Press, 1955.

Seitel, Peter, "Proverbs: A Social Use of Metaphor," *Genre* 2 (1969): 143–61.

Seneca, *On Mercy*, 356–449 in *Moral Essays*, vol. 1, ed. and trans. John W. Basore, Cambridge, MA: Harvard University Press, 1994; first published 1928.

Severs, J. Burke, "The Tale of Melibeus," 560–614 in *Sources and Analogues of Chaucer's Canterbury Tales*, ed. W. F. Bryan and Germaine Dempster, Chicago, IL: University of Chicago Press, 1941.

Seymour, M. C., *A Catalogue of Chaucer Manuscripts*, vol. 1: *Works before the Canterbury Tales*, Brookfield, VT: Ashgate, 1995.

Sharpe, Richard, "Latin in Everyday Life," 315–41 in *Medieval Latin: An Introduction and Bibliographical Guide*, ed. F. A. C. Mantello and A. G. Rigg, Washington, DC: The Catholic University of America Press, 1996.

Shinners, John Raymond and William J. Dohar, *Pastors and the Care of Souls in Medieval England*, Notre Dame, IN: University of Notre Dame Press, 1998.

Short, Ian, "On Bilingualism in Anglo-Norman England," *Romance Philology* 33 (1980): 467–79.

Short, Ian, "*Tam Angli Quam Franci*: Self-Definition in Anglo-Norman England," 153–75 in *Anglo-Norman Studies* 18, Proceedings of the Battle Conference 1995, ed. Christopher Harper-Bill, Woodbridge: Boydell & Brewer, 1996.

Simon, Joan, *Education and Society in Tudor England*, Cambridge: Cambridge University Press, 1966.

Simon, Joan, *The Social Origins of English Education*, London: Routledge & Kegan Paul, 1970.

Simpson, James, "Desire and the Scriptural Text: Will as Reader in *Piers Plowman*," 215–43 in *Criticism and Dissent in the Middle Ages*, ed. Rita Copeland, Cambridge: Cambridge University Press, 1996.

Simpson, James, *Piers Plowman: An Introduction*, 2nd rev. edn., Exeter: University of Exeter Press, 2007.

Simpson, James, *Sciences and the Self in Medieval Poetry: Alan of Lille's Anticlaudianus and John Gower's* Confessio Amantis, Cambridge: Cambridge University Press, 1995.

Sir Gawain and the Green Knight, 239–406 in *The Works of the Gawain Poet: Sir Gawain and the Green Knight, Pearl, Cleanness, Patience*, ed. Putter and Stokes.

Smith, Ben H., *Traditional Imagery of Charity in Piers Plowman*, The Hague: Mouton, 1966.

Södergård, Östen, "Le plus ancien traité grammatical français," *Studia neophilologica* 27 (1955): 192–4.

Sources and Analogues of the Canterbury Tales, ed. Robert M. Correale and Mary Hamel, 2 vols., Cambridge: D. S. Brewer, 2002.

Sources and Analogues of Chaucer's Canterbury Tales, ed. W. F. Bryan and Germaine Dempster, New York, NY: Humanities Press, 1958.

Stans puer ad mensam, 56–62 in Servus Gieben, "Robert Grosseteste and Medieval Courtesy Books," *Vivarium* 5 (1967): 47–74.

Statuta Antiqua Universitatis Oxoniensis, ed. Strickland Gibson, Oxford: Clarendon Press, 1931.

Stevenson, William Henry, "The Introduction of English as the Vehicle of Instruction in English Schools," 421–9 in *An English Miscellany Presented to F. J. Furnivall*, ed. William P. Ker, Arthur S. Napier, and Walter W. Skeat, Oxford: Clarendon Press, 1901.

Stillwell, Gardiner, "The Political Meaning of Chaucer's *Tale of Melibee*," *Speculum* 19 (1944): 433–44.

Stray, Christopher, "Success and Failure: W. H. D. Rouse and Direct-Method Classics Teaching in Edwardian England," *Journal of Classics Teaching* 22 (2011): 5–7.

Sugget, Helen, "The Use of French in England in the Later Middle Ages," *Transactions of the Royal Historical Society* 28 (1946): 61–83.

Tatlock, John S. P., *The Development and Chronology of Chaucer's Works*, Chaucer Society, 2nd series 37, London: Kegan Paul, Trench, Trübner, 1907.

Tertullian, *De praescriptione haereticorum*, Brepols Library of Latin Texts, Turnhout: Brepols, 2010.

Theodulus, *Eclogue*, 26–35 in R. P. H. Green, *Seven Versions of Carolingian Pastoral*, Reading: University of Reading Press, 1980.

Thesaurus proverbiorum medii aevi: Lexikon der Sprichwörter des romanisch-germanischen Mittelalters, ed. Samuel Singer et al., 13 vols., Berlin: Walter de Gruyter, 1995–2002.

Thomason, Sarah Grey and Terence Kaufman, *Language Contact, Creolization, and Genetic Linguistics*, Berkeley, CA: University of California Press, 1988.

Thompson, Sally, *Women Religious: The Founding of English Nunneries After the Conquest*, Oxford: Clarendon Press, 1991.

Thomson, David, *A Descriptive Catalogue of Middle English Grammatical Texts*, New York, NY: Garland, 1979.

Thomson, David, *An Edition of the Middle English Grammatical Texts*, New York, NY: Garland, 1984.

Thomson, David, "A Study of the Middle English Treatises on Grammar," 3 vols., D.Phil. thesis, University of Oxford, 1977.

Thomson, R. M., *A Descriptive Catalogue of the Medieval Manuscripts in Worcester Cathedral Library*, Woodbridge: Boydell & Brewer, 2001.

Thorndike, Lynn, "Elementary and Secondary Education in the Middle Ages," *Speculum* 15 (1940): 400–8.

Thrupp, Sylvia, *The Merchant Class of Medieval London [1300–1500]*, Ann Arbor, MI: University of Michigan Press, 1962; first published 1948.

Thrupp, Sylvia, "The Problem of Replacement-Rates in Late Medieval English Population," *Economic History Review* n.s. 18 (1965): 101–19.

Thurot, Charles, *Extraits de Divers Manuscrits Latins pour Servir a l'Histoire de Doctrines Grammaticales au Moyen-Age*, Frankfurt am Main: Minerva, 1964; first published, Paris, 1869.

Tout, Thomas F., "Literature and Learning in the English Civil Service in the Fourteenth Century," *Speculum* 4 (1929): 365–89.

Travis, Peter, "The Nun's Priest's Tale as Grammar School Primer," *Studies in the Age of Chaucer Proceedings* 1 (1985): 81–91.

Treharne, Elaine, *Living Through Conquest: The Politics of Early English, 1020 to 1220*, Oxford: Oxford University Press, 2012.

Usk, Thomas, *The Testament of Love*, ed. R. A. Shoaf, Kalamazoo, MI: Medieval Institute Publications, 1998.

Van Cleave, Michael, *The Growth of English Education, 1348–1648: A Social and Cultural History*, University Park, PA: Pennsylvania State University Press, 1990.

Venantius Honorius Clemenianus Fortunatus, *Opera Poetica*, ed. Friedrich Leo, Berlin: Weidmann, 1881.

Virgil, *Aeneid*, 261–597 in *Eclogues, Georgics, Aeneid, 1–6*, ed. and trans. H. Ruston Fairclough, rev. G. P. Goold, Cambridge, MA: Harvard University Press, 1999; first published 1916.

Visitations and Memorials of Southwell Minster, ed. A. F. Leach, Camden Society, n.s. 48 (London, 1891).

Wagner, David, "The Seven Liberal Arts and Classical Scholarship," 1–23 in *The Seven Liberal Arts in the Middle Ages*, ed. David L. Wagner, Bloomington, IN: Indiana University Press, 1983.

Wallace, David, *Chaucerian Polity: Absolutist Lineages and Associational Forms in England and Italy*, Stanford, CA: Stanford University Press, 1997.

Walsingham, Thomas, *Historia Anglicana*, ed. Henry Thomas Riley, 2 vols., Rolls Series 28 (London, 1863–4).

Warner, Lawrence, "The Ending, and End, of *Piers Plowman* B: The C-Version Origins of the Final Two Passus," *Medium Aevum* 76 (2007): 225–50.

Warner, Lawrence, *The Lost History of Piers Plowman: The Earliest Transmission of Langland's Work*, Philadelphia, PA: University of Pennsylvania Press, 2011.

Wenzel, Siegfried, "Notes on the Parson's Tale," *Chaucer Review* 16 (1982): 237–56.

Wheatley, Edward, *Mastering Aesop: Medieval Education, Chaucer, and his Followers*, Gainesville, FL: University Press of Florida, 2000.

Wheelock, Frederic M., *Wheelock's Latin*, rev. Ricard A. LaFleur, 6th edn., New York, NY: HarperCollins, 2000.

Whiting, B. J., "The Nature of the Proverb," *Harvard Studies and Notes in Philology and Literature* 14 (1932): 273–307.

Whybray, R. N., *The Composition of the Book of Proverbs*, Sheffield: Sheffield Academic Press, 1994.

Whybray, R. N., *The Book of Proverbs: A Survey of Modern Study*, Leiden: E. J. Brill, 1995.

Wogan-Browne, Jocelyn, *Saints' Lives and Women's Literary Culture c.1150–c.1300*, Oxford: Oxford University Press, 2001.

Wood, Chauncey, *Chaucer in the Country of the Stars: Poetic Uses of Astrological Imagery*, Princeton, NJ: Princeton University Press, 1970.

Woods, Marjorie Curry, *Classroom Commentaries: Teaching the* Poetria Nova *Across Medieval and Renaissance Europe*, Columbus, OH: Ohio State University Press, 2010.

Woods, Marjorie Curry, "Rape and the Pedagogical Rhetoric of Sexual Violence," 36–86 in *Criticism and Dissent in the Middle Ages*, ed. Rita Copeland, Cambridge: Cambridge University Press, 1996.

Woods, Marjorie Curry and Rita Copeland, "Classroom and Confession," 376–406 in *The Cambridge History of Medieval English Literature*, ed. David Wallace, Cambridge: Cambridge University Press, 1999.

Woolley, Reginald Maxwell, *Catalogue of the Manuscripts of Lincoln Cathedral Library*, London: Oxford University Press, 1927.

The Works of the Gawain Poet: Sir Gawain and the Green Knight, Pearl, Cleanness, Patience, ed. Ad Putter and Myra Stokes, London: Penguin Books, 2014.

Wright, Thomas, "Rules of the Free School at Saffron Walden," *Archaeologia* 34 (1852): 37–41.

Yeager, R. F., "'Oure englisshe' and Everyone's Latin: The *Fasciculus Morum* and Gower's *Confessio Amantis*," *South Atlantic Review* 46 (1981): 41–53.

Yeager, R. F., "English, Latin, and the Text as 'Other': The Page as Sign in the Work of John Gower," *Text* 3 (1987): 251–67.

Yeager, R. F., "Did Gower Write Cento?" 113–32 in *John Gower: Recent Readings*, ed. R. F. Yeager, Kalamazoo, MI: Western Michigan University, 1989.

Zeeman, Nicolette, *"Piers Plowman" and the Medieval Discourse of Desire*, Cambridge: Cambridge University Press, 2006.

Zieman, Katherine, *Singing the New Song: Literacy and Liturgy in Late Medieval England*, Philadelphia, PA: University of Pennsylvania Press, 2008.

Ziolkowski, Jan, "Latin Learning and Latin Literature," 229–44 in *The Cambridge History of the Book in Britain*, vol. 2: *1100–1400*, ed. Nigel Morgan and Rodney M. Thomson, Cambridge: Cambridge University Press, 2008.

Index